AN OUTLINE OF INTERNATIONAL PRICE THEORIES

CHI-YUEN WU

The Ludwig von Mises Institute
Auburn, Alabama
2007

First published in 1939

AN OUTLINE OF INTERNATIONAL PRICE THEORIES

By

CHI-YUEN WU

Ph.D. (Econ.)

With an Introduction by

PROFESSOR LIONEL ROBBINS

LONDON
GEORGE ROUTLEDGE & SONS, LTD.
BROADWAY HOUSE: 68-74 CARTER LANE, E.C.

First published 1939

PRINTED IN GREAT BRITAIN BY
STEPHEN AUSTIN AND SONS, LTD., HERTFORD

CONTENTS

CHAPTER III

FROM DAVID HUME TO JOHN STUART MILL: THE
DEVELOPMENT OF THE CLASSICAL THEORIES.

CHAPTER IV

THE CLASSICAL THEORY OF INTERNATIONAL TRADE.

CHAPTER V

POST-CLASSICAL DEVELOPMENT OF THE MONETARY
ASPECTS OF THE THEORY OF INTERNATIONAL PRICE
RELATIONSHIPS : 1848–1918.

CHAPTER VI

DEVELOPMENTS SINCE 1918 : THEORIES OF THE
EXCHANGES UNDER DEPRECIATED CURRENCIES.

CHAPTER VII

CHAPTER VIII

CHAPTER IX

APPENDIX

ACKNOWLEDGMENT

This essay, which has been approved by the University of London for the award of the Degree of Doctor of Philosophy, was prepared by me under the supervision and with the constant help of Professor Lionel Robbins during the years 1935 and 1936. I am indebted to him, firstly, for direction of the large amount of research work which was required, and secondly, for ideas and guidance in the planning and preparation of the essay. He has read through the entire manuscript, and, but for his criticisms and suggestions at every stage of its preparation, it could not have taken its present form. Dr. P. N. Rosenstein-Rodan also gave generously of his time to criticize the first part of the essay. That the essay has many shortcomings is a fact of which I am fully conscious. The responsibility for them, of course, is solely mine.

I owe a debt of gratitude to the Board of Trustees for the Administration of the Sino-British Foundation in Nanking for granting me the scholarship in Economics for 1934–7, because, but for that financial help, my studies in England and the preparation of this essay could not have been undertaken.

Finally, my thanks are due to the authorities of the Library of the British Museum, of the Goldsmiths' Company's Library of Economic Literature, and of the British Library of Political and Economic Science for granting me the use of those institutions.

C. Y. Wu.

LONDON,
1937.

PREFACE

The history of economic thought has a twofold function ; to explain the past and to help us to understand the present. By examining the economic theories of the past we can learn to see the problems of earlier times, as it were, through the eyes of their contemporaries. By comparing them with the theories of the present we can realize better the implications and the limitations of the knowledge of our own day.

There is no branch of economics which more repays this kind of study than the theory of international trade. Modern economics originated in *ad hoc* investigations concerning trade and the exchanges ; the theory of prices and the theory of circulation were first elaborated to explain particular problems of international commerce. Moreover, when attempts began to be made to cast theoretical analysis into a more systematic form, the generalizations which were made to fit what were thought to be the exceptional circumstances of exchange between the non-competing groups called nations, took a form which, in subsequent developments, has proved to be much more fruitful than the general theories to which they were supposed to be a supplement. No one to-day, except the most devout of the Marxians, has much use for the classical theory of value ; the assumptions which give it validity are too specialized. But the classical theories of comparative cost and reciprocal demand have proved to provide principles of explanation of most far reaching generality. Similarly with the theory of money ; it is in the classical discussion of the problems of the regulation of the exchanges, rather than in the more formalistic versions of the quantity theory, that many of the most important propositions of modern monetary theory take their rise.

The treatise which follows is the work of a young Chinese scholar who is at present endeavouring to maintain the traditions of humane culture in the remote fastnesses of Western China into which he and his fellow teachers have been driven by the recent troubles. It was commenced when he was a member of the economics seminar at the London School of Economics. The main sections were

drafted under the shadow of impending catastrophe and
the final version has been corrected amid the distractions
of actual war. Dr. Wu has not attempted to write a comprehensive study of all the literature concerning the subject
with which he deals. His method rather has been selective.
He has attempted, not so much to show the minute origins
and affiliations of the different theories he analyses, as to
take representative specimens of these theories and to
consider their logical relations. In this I think he has
performed a real service. Few, surely, can read his penetrating classifications and commentaries without feeling that
he has added substantially to knowledge, both in his elucida-
tions of particular lines of thought and in his presentation
of the general perspective of development. It is a contribution which merits the respect and the gratitude of all
serious students of these subjects.

LIONEL ROBBINS.

THE LONDON SCHOOL OF ECONOMICS,
    May, 1939.

AN OUTLINE OF INTERNATIONAL
PRICE THEORIES

CHAPTER I

INTRODUCTION

1. In this essay we intend to give a general survey of the historical development of the theory of international price relationships.

The subject of international price relationships is important for two reasons. Firstly, it forms a special problem of the general theory of pricing. By analysing the price relations between nations, one is able to form a clear conception of the price mechanism of non-competing groups and the parts played by space and distance in the theory of pricing. Secondly, the price relations among nations exercise a dominating influence upon the commercial intercourse among nations. A study of the subject brings to light the factors which determine whether a commodity should be imported, exported or omitted from international trade, the factors which decide how the gains from trade are divided among the trading countries and how the average labourer in a trading country is benefited by trade, and finally the factors which govern the rate of exchange and other prices. There are, therefore, sufficient reasons for a specific study of the subject.

2. THE PROBLEMS

What is meant by " international price relationship " ? That term comprehends four distinct problems : (1) the relation between the value of money in one country and the value of money in other countries ; (2) the relation of the price level of one country to the price level in other countries ; (3) the price relations of goods of identical tenchnological composition among trading countries ; and (4) the comparison of prices of factors of production in different countries. Those are the problems which have been discussed by writers on international price relationships, and all of them are covered by this essay.

The meaning of problem (1) can best be demonstrated by an illustration. Suppose the dollar and the pound to be the monies of two countries, A and B respectively. Let N_1, N_2, N_3, ... be the commodities in A, and M_1, M_2, M_3, ... be the commodities in B. Now, if a man has funds in

A's currency deposited in A and funds in B's currency in B, and he wants to buy a certain quantity of M in B, that would cost, say, £100, there arises the question whether he should pay it with dollars and, if so, how many dollars he should pay. If he could pay with either £100 or $500, the value of £1 is the same as the value of $5. When the currencies of the trading countries are based upon a common metal, like gold, the problem becomes more complicated. There is, then, the problem of the metallic content of each money. If the metallic content of £1 is equal to that of $5 and if the cost of transporting gold is zero, the problem becomes whether the value of £1 is the same as the value of $5. If they are the same, we say that the values of the two currencies are equal. If not, we say that the values of them are not equal.

The first problem or the problem of the comparative values of moneys, is fundamentally a problem of the rate of exchange. To say that the value of £1 is equal to the value of $5 is the same thing as to say that the rate of exchange of £1 is $5.

In problem (2) we investigate the relations, if any, between the average price of M_1, M_2, M_3, . . . on the one hand and the average price of N_1, N_2, N_3, . . . on the other hand. The second and the first problems are often confounded with each other and treated as a single problem. In fact, they are two distinct problems. Problem (1) is a problem of the relation between the average price of M_1, M_2, . . . in terms of B's currency and the average price of M_1, M_2, . . . *in terms of A's currency.* Problem (2) is a problem of the relation between the average price of M_1, M_2 . . . in terms of B's currency and the average price of N_1, N_2 . . . in terms of A's currency. The two problems could become one single problem only when N_1, N_2 . . . are both technologically and *economically* the same as M_1, M_2. . . . They cannot be technologically the same, because some goods which are consumed in country A are not consumed in country B and some consumed in the latter are not consumed in the former. Even when they are technologically the same, they cannot be economically the same, because goods which are of identical technological constitution but are not situated in the same place, are not the same commodities from the economic point of view. Rice in China, for example, is not the same commodity as rice in England. For that reason, the general price level in A may be higher or lower than that in B, even when the values of the dollar and the pound are the same.

In addition to the problem of the general price level, there is the problem of sectional price levels. The general price level may be divided into sections in many ways. One division into sections would be (a) the price level of goods which do not enter into international trade, (b) the price level of goods which are exported, and (c) the price level of goods which are imported.

In problem (3) we are concerned mainly with the relation between the price of an article, which enters into international trade, in the exporting country and the price of a similar article (i.e. an article similar from the technical point of view) in the importing country. We also investigate the possible relations between the price of an article, which does not enter into international trade, in one country and the price of a similar article in another trading country.

Problem (4) is the problem of the relations of prices of factors of production in different countries. There is, first of all, the total of the prices paid to all the factors in each country. Since the total of the prices constitutes the aggregate income of the owners of the factors of production in the period under consideration, the problem of the relation of total of the factor prices in different countries is the same as the problem of the comparison of the levels of incomes in different countries. Secondly, we have the problem of the relative positions of the prices of the different factors in different countries. When we come to that question, we shall deal with the reasons why the relation between the price of one factor (say, wage) and that of another factor (say, rent) is not the same in different countries. Finally, there is the problem of the relation between the absolute price of a factor in one country and the absolute price of a technologically similar factor in another country. Under that problem, it is the relation of wages in different countries that requires the most careful consideration.

In distinguishing between those four problems we do not mean that they are unconnected. On the contrary, they are closely related to each other. They may be best viewed as different aspects of the same subject. The first problem, as already indicated, is fundamentally a problem of the rate of exchange. The second, third, and fourth problems involve the comparison of prices in one country with prices in other countries and are insoluble, unless they are attacked together with the problem of the rate of exchange, which makes the comparison of prices possible. The relation between the second and the third problems is still more obvious. It is the average price of individual articles that constitutes the general price level. The third problem is that of the prices of individual articles and is, therefore, closely connected with the second problem, which deals with the general price levels. The relation between the problem of factor prices (i.e. the fourth problem) and the other problems should be emphasized, because the former itself links the different problems together. The problem of factor prices is connected with the problems of product prices (i.e. the second and third problems) in three ways. Firstly, the total price paid to the factors in the preceding period, which is the same thing as the aggregate income of the owners of factors in the preceding period, determines the aggregate expenditure of those owners and, consequently, the total price of all goods in the current period. Secondly, the total price paid for goods in the current period constitutes the total price paid to factors producing those goods. Thirdly, the unit prices of factors of production determine the money costs of production and consequently the prices of goods. There are other connections between those problems, but we need not indicate them at this stage. Let it suffice to say that the four problems are so closely connected that they are simply four aspects of the same subject.

Every one of the problems we are considering raises the fundamental question whether there is always a tendency towards equilibrium or not. If the answer is in the affirmative, the following three questions naturally arise. First, what is the nature of the equilibrium ? Second, how can the equilibrium be disturbed ? Or, to put the question in other words, what are the possible causes of disturbance ? Third, by what mechanism can the disturbance be corrected and the equilibrium be restored ? [1]

[1] It is the practice of some economists to divide economic analysis into three departments, viz., statics, comparative statics, and dynamics. Economic statics deals with the conditions of equilibrium, if they exist at all. By conditions of equilibrium we mean those positions in which the

Theories of money within a closed community are, in a certain sense, the foundation of " international " theories of money. Since our problem is concerned with international prices and international values of moneys, a knowledge of the theories of money in a closed community is essential to the proper understanding of our problem. Up to about the seventies of the nineteenth century, the development of the theories of money in a closed community was closely connected with the progress of theories of international price relationships. Thus, in our description of earlier writers we have to go briefly into their theories of money.

Moreover, our problem being one of the problems of international economics, it is related to the general theory of international trade. The general theory of international trade goes behind monetary demands and monetary supplies and deals with the more fundamental factors governing international price relationships. It constitutes, in fact, the *real* foundation for the theory of international price relationships. We, therefore, devote a part of the present survey to the general theory of international trade.

3. A BIRD'S-EYE VIEW OF THE HISTORY OF THE THEORY
OF INTERNATIONAL PRICE RELATIONSHIPS

In the preceding section we have indicated how the subject of international price relationships might be treated systematically. Unfortunately, it has never been treated upon such lines. The reason is to be found in the fact that theories have been brought forward more as by-products of discussions of practical problems than as results of

price system will remain at rest, once it reaches them, provided that there is no fresh disturbance. That, however, does not imply that conditions of equilibrium must necessarily be reached ultimately by the price system. Comparative statics is concerned with the differences in the conditions of equilibrium in two or more price systems that are due to differences in the given data in the different systems. Economic dynamics deals with the problem, how a change in the fundamental data disturbs the price system and how the disturbances are corrected. It shows us, as Professor Robbins has pointed out, " the actual process of change—-the path followed through time between one equilibrium position and the other." In economic dynamics we have to see whether it is necessary or likely that the original change in data would lead to secondary changes in data. It is mainly because of those secondary changes in data that we have to differentiate between a doctrine of dynamics and one of comparative statics. In the latter we always suppose that when the original data change all other things will remain the same. In dynamics, however, we are not allowed to make the assumption of *ceteris paribus.*

independent studies. Among the practical problems are sudden and violent rises of prices, variations of rates of exchanges, the effects of the making of a large payment to foreign countries, the desire artificially to increase the national stock of the precious metals, and other national objectives.

We may divide the history of the theory of international price relationships broadly into four periods, in accordance with the nature of those practical problems, the discussions of which are responsible for the development of the theory. The four periods are (1) the mercantilistic period, (2) the classical period, (3) the post-classical period, and (4) the post-war period.[1]

In the mercantilistic period (i.e. the period from the beginning of the sixteenth century to about the middle of the eighteenth century), people interested in economic problems paid much attention to the question of the national stock of the money metals. They discussed such problems as why a nation should try to increase its stock of precious metals, how a country which did not produce those metals might increase its stock of them, and by what means the metals obtained might be retained. In discussing those problems they went largely into the subject of international price relationships and produced many suggestive views. Firstly, there was general recognition of the fact that there are definite relations among the rate of exchange, the balance of trade, and international specie movements, although opinions in regard to the nature of the relations differed from each other. In the earlier stage, most persons believed that speculation in the foreign exchange market was the main cause of international movements of specie. Gradually, the view that the balance of trade of a country governed the movement of the money metals gained ground. Next, there arose the formulation of the quantity theory of money,[2]

---

[1] In dividing history into periods, we find it convenient to use certain dates, but the selected dates are only approximately accurate indicators. Nobody can point to a certain date as marking the exact point of time at which a historical stage or period either terminated or began. Nevertheless, we have to draw some lines of demarcation, however inexact they may be.

[2] The term, *quantity theory of money*, is sometimes defined as the theory that, in a given period of time, the product of the total volume of goods bought and sold multiplied by the average price of those goods is equal to the volume of the circulation of the medium of exchange. In such general terms, the theory does not indicate whether an increase in the

which connected the supplies of the money metals with the movements of prices. Thirdly, there was the discussion of the problem of the relations between the prices of a trading country and its balance of trade. Opinion was divided between those who believed that "selling dear and buying cheap" would cause a more favourable balance of trade and those who believed that it would cause a less favourable balance. As time went on, the latter view was more generally accepted by the economists of the time. Fourthly, views on those three points were combined to form different doctrines of international price relationships. One of those doctrines was this : A favourable balance of trade would bring precious metals into the country, an inflow of specie meant an increase in the quantity of money at home, an increase in the volume of money at home would raise the prices of all goods, those changes in prices meant "selling dear and buying cheap", and selling dear and buying cheap would turn the balance of trade against the country. That doctrine is, however, not consistent with the view that a nation should increase its stock of the precious metals. The contradiction involved was noticed at the later stages of the period and attempts were made to escape the difficulty. One group of economists tried to escape from the contradiction by developing the theory that an increase in the volume of money would encourage trade and production, would be accompanied by an increase in the demand for money, and, consequently, would not affect prices and the balance of trade. Another group of economists suggested that, if the government of a country adopted some artificial means to prevent the precious metals imported from influencing prices and trade, the country could continue freely to import those metals.

About the middle of the eighteenth century, the revolt against mercantilism was so strong that this system had to give way to the free trade school. The most important

circulation of money would lead to an increase in the volume of the goods or to a rise in their average price. The causal sequence may run either from the volume of the circulation to the average price of the goods transacted, or from the circulation to the volume of those goods. In the strict sense of the term, however, the quantity theory of money assumes the causal relation to run only from the circulation to the average price. We shall, in this essay, use the term in that strict sense. As to the theory that an increase (or decrease) of money would lead to an increase (or decrease) of the volume of goods and transactions, we shall call it "the doctrine that money stimulates trade and production".

exponents of the doctrines of free trade were the English classical economists. For that reason we call the period (from 1750 to 1848), which succeeded the mercantilistic period, "the classical period." The earlier stages of the period were characterized by the attempt of the economists of the free trade school to show the impossibility of a country continuing indefinitely to increase its stock of precious metals and the advantages of the international division of labour. Those earlier discussions of the advantages of the international division of labour were followed by the formulation of the classical theory of international trade, which not only demonstrated how trading countries were benefited by trade but also gave a real foundation for the theory of international price relationships. The classical economists, furthermore, gave specific answers to each of the four problems which we have stated in the second section.

During the Napoleonic wars, the abnormal conditions brought about by the wars, e.g. the depreciation of the exchanges and the general rise of prices, naturally evoked much attention in the economic world. The problem of depreciated exchanges narrowed down to the question whether it was the excessive issue of currency or the unfavourable balance of payments which was responsible for the situation. There were three different views. Some thought that the state of the balance of payments was the most important, if not the only, cause of the variations of the rate of exchanges. Others insisted that only monetary factors could be a cause of the disturbance of the rate of exchange. The state of the balance of payments, according to them, would not affect the rate of exchange, because the balance of payments had in itself a tendency to adjust itself and consequently did not require any monetary change or change in the rate of exchange to correct it. Finally, there were many economists who believed that the rate of exchange might be disturbed either by monetary changes or by an adverse balance of international payments. All writers who recognized the monetary factor as a cause of disturbance of the rate of exchange had formed definite ideas concerning the relation between monetary changes and the rate of exchange. They believed in the purchasing power parity doctrine. As to the problem of the general rise of prices, opinions were not divided to the same extent on theoretical points. Most, if not all, of the writers on the subject, agreed in principle that an increase in the volume of money and of bank-notes would lead to a general rise in prices. Many of them, moreover, showed how the increased currency could lead to the rise in prices through an expansion in the volume of lending by the banks.

In the post-classical period, i.e. the period from 1848 to 1918, the development of the theory of international price relationships was first stimulated by the gold discoveries of California and Australia in 1848 and 1851. The gold discoveries called attention to the problem of the effects of an increase in the production of gold upon prices both in the gold producing country and in the countries which do not produce gold. In other words, the gold discoveries stimulated the discussion of the problem of domestic and international price adjustments. In the fifties, emphasis was thrown on the effects of the increased supplies of gold on consumers' incomes and expenditures, on the prices of factors and on product prices. In the sixties and seventies, economists paid much attention to the role of the market rate of interest in international price adjustments. In the eighties, the mechanism which connected money and prices through changes in the volume of lendings and in the rate of interest was further investigated by a group of English economists. Finally, in the last decade of the nineteenth century, and the beginning of the twentieth century, many excellent restatements of the theory were produced.

In the period since the Great War, there have been two stages : the stage before 1930 and that of the present decade. In the former stage, two problems aroused much attention. They were the rate of exchange of unstable currencies and the corrective mechanism of disturbances in balances of international payments. At first, the discussions of the problem of the rate of exchange of unstable currencies centred on the problem of the initiating cause of exchange depreciation. The theory had been advanced that the state of foreign trade, international capital movements, and other items in the international balance sheet were the source of exchange depreciation. In opposition to that theory, Professor Cassel advanced his version of the purchasing power parity theory. His version is an incorrect one. Later developments are connected mainly with the correction of the mistakes of Professor Cassel.

The problem of the corrective mechanism of disturbances in the balance of payments was discussed with the reparations problem and the problem of international capital movements. Opinions were divided into two groups. One adhered to the classical doctrine. According to that doctrine, an adverse balance of payments of a country would cause a flow of gold out of the country and the outflow of gold meant an increase in the volume of money in foreign countries and a decrease in the volume of money in the country. Those changes in the volumes of moneys would lead to an increase in the prices of goods produced by foreign countries and a fall in the prices of goods produced at home, and consequently imports would be discouraged and exports encouraged and the balance of payments would return to equilibrium. An alternative doctrine was as follows : An adverse balance of payments of a country meant that the aggregate expenditure of the consumers of that country was greater than their aggregate income. The necessary consequence was for those citizens, whose incomes were less than their expenditures, to contract their expenditures on goods. As soon as the expenditure of every individual again equalled his income, the balance of payments of that country would be in equilibrium. Finally, there was the view that the two doctrines were not contradictory of each other and attempts were made to reconcile them.

In the present decade, the theory of international price relationships has taken a new departure with the publication of the works of Professor Ohlin and others. Their main contribution to the theory of international trade is the extension of the mutual-interdependence theory of pricing to the domain of international economics. They investigate the case of joint production, i.e. production with two or more factors of production, and analyse the positions of the demands and supplies of factors of production in the determination of the course of international trade and international price relationships. They also take into due consideration the role of the cost of conveying goods from one country to another.

4. THE PLAN OF THE FOLLOWING CHAPTERS

The following chapters give a general survey of the

historical development of the theory of international price relationships. The development of the theory, as already indicated, has been more a by-product of the discussions and controversies on practical problems than the result of specific studies. Few authors have treated the subject systematically. Therefore, we shall not make the logical distinction between the different problems in the theory or between the different aspects of a problem, which we have described in the second section, until it is explicitly or implicitly raised by an author, whose theory we are considering. We shall present each doctrine exactly as each author presented it. Sometimes we shall be unable to do so without going into the details of the controversies over problems of currency, foreign exchanges, commercial policy, etc., which gave rise to the particular theory under examination. Even though the method of presentation involves digression from the subject, the method has two distinct advantages. The first is that the reader is helped to form a correct idea of how the theory was evolved, and the second is that the places of the doctrines in applied economics and their bearing upon the problem of policy are indicated.

In the second chapter, we trace the origin and development of the mercantilistic theories and show to what extent the classical theories were indebted to the mercantilistic writings. The third and the fourth chapters are concerned with the development in the classical period. The third chapter is devoted to the formulation and development of the monetary aspects of the classical theories of international price relationships and to the criticisms levelled against them. The real aspects of the problem and many of the important contributions in the classical period are not dealt with in the chapter. They are dealt with in the fourth chapter, in which we describe the classical theory of international trade and show how it is connected with the classical theory of international price relationships. In the fifth chapter we concern ourselves with the post-classical refinements and restatements of the corrective mechanisms, especially in regard to the effects of an increase of money metals or an increase of bank credits on the price structures of the trading nations. The place of the money rate of interest in international price adjustments is also examined. In the sixth, seventh, and eighth chapters we describe contemporary developments, i.e. developments after 1918.

The sixth chapter is concerned with the theories of the exchanges of depreciated currencies ; the seventh chapter with the problem of the corrective mechanism of disturbances in the balance of international payments ; and the eighth chapter with the development in the present decade. In the concluding chapter we give a brief statement of the present position of the theory.

This inquiry, it must be confessed, is neither comprehensive nor exhaustive. In our historical survey we have selected some authors who had advanced doctrines which, in our opinion, fairly represent the trend of thought of the period in which they lived. The fact that we chose them and not others does not mean that they were the only authors who had advanced those views, nor does it mean that their views were the only views in the period in which they lived. As to the scope of the inquiry, it is limited to the more fundamental aspects of the problem. No attempt, for example, has been made to enter into the effects of international commercial policies (tariffs, quotas, etc.) or of imperfect competition upon the price relations between nations. Furthermore, no details are given of the development of the theory of international cyclical movements of prices, because it is so important that it can be examined only in a separate study.

CHAPTER II

THE MERCANTILISTIC THEORIES

I. MERCANTILISM

In order to trace the origin of the theory of international price relationships we are forced to go as far back as the sixteenth century. From about the year 1500 there were many important political and economic changes. The oversea discoveries in the last decades of the fifteenth century had widened the boundaries of international trade and had given rise to a change in its nature and an expansion of its volume. As a result of the opening of new silver mines between 1540 and 1600 in America, Europe was supplied with an abundance of money metals and thus the establishment of a real price economy was facilitated. That change in commerce together with the extension in the use of money accelerated the development of the new spirit of private enterprise and paved the way for the triumph of the moneyed classes. In fact, the time had come for a transition from a number of local economies to a national economy, from feudalism to commercial capitalism, from a state of comparatively little trade to an epoch of extensive international commerce. That change in the economic structure is sometimes called by economic historians the " Commercial Revolution ".

In the world of thought that change in the economic structure found its expression in what is known as " Mercantilism ". But as mercantilism had been developed during a long period of changing economic conditions, it naturally absorbed a great variety of ideas from the epochs through which it had passed. Therefore, mercantilistic theories are by no means a set of rigid doctrines. They may be grouped together as a body of thought simply because they are based on fundamental conceptions, which possess some degree of similarity. First of all, all mercantilists considered the benefit of the State as the end and object of economic activities, and in their view the interests of the

State had always to take precedence to the interests of the individual. The aim of all mercantilistic doctrines is to increase the economic power of the State. Moreover, the interests of the State were, in their eyes, by no means necessarily in harmony with the interests of the individual. Consequently, the mercantilists stood for the regulation of the activities of the individual. According to them, wages, interest, industry, and trade should be regulated so as to benefit the State. Finally, the importance of " treasure " to a State was greatly emphasized. The reasons given in support of their advocacy of the accumulation of the precious metals changed from one time to another, but all mercantilists agreed that a nation must try by all means to increase its " treasure ". In general, they recognized that countries which did not possess gold or silver mines could not increase their stocks of the precious metals except by an annually recurring favourable balance of trade (if peaceful means alone were adopted). Consequently, they gave foreign trade the foremost place among the industries of a nation.

Apart from those conceptions, there was nothing that was held in common by the mercantilists. The subject of international price relationships in particular gave rise to great differences of opinion among them. Originally they had no views of any kind on it. Subsequently, they developed many definite theories.

Mercantilistic thought passed through four stages of development. They are (1) the stage before 1550 or the rudimentary stage ; (2) the stage from 1550 to 1620, which witnessed the formulation of what might be called Malynesian doctrine ; (3) the stage from 1620 to 1680, which was dominated by the doctrines of Thomas Mun ; and (4) the stage from 1680 to 1750, which marks, on the one hand, the highest development of mercantilistism and, on the other hand, the transition from the mercantilistic to the classical school of thought.

The work before the middle of the sixteenth century has only antigarian value. Hence, we start the present survey with the second stage, that is, the period from 1550 to 1620. During that period the development of the theory of international price relationships was associated with two important controversies : that in regard to the price revolution and that in regard to foreign exchanges. We shall describe them separately.

2. THE CONTROVERSY CONCERNING THE PRICE REVOLUTION

In the Middle Ages, the erroneous doctrine that the prince had both the right and the ability to fix the value of money (known sometimes as the *valor-impositus* theory of money) was very popular. In the early decades of the sixteenth century, however, that theory of money was already on the way to its fall, and people generally tended to think of the *valor-intrinsecus* of money and identify the value of a coin with the value of the metal in it. That was a natural reaction to the debasement of coins, which had been common in the sixteenth century and the centuries that preceded it. So, when the great supply of the precious metals from the New to the Old World had by the middle of the century worked out its effects in raising prices, many writers attributed the increase in prices to the debasement of the coins. John Hales and de Malestroit were among the ablest writers who held that view.

About the autumn of 1549, Hales [1] put forth the question, " What should be the cause of this dearth (of all things) ; seinge all thinges are so plentifull ? " After refuting some of the possible causes he said :

> And now I must come to that thinge . . . which I take to be the chiefe cause of all this dearth of thinges, and of the manifest impoverishment of this Realme, and might in breife time be the destruction of the same, yf it be not the [rathere remedyede], that is the basinge or rather corruptinge of oure coine and treasure.[2]

[1] John Hales (?-1571) was connected with a well-known Kentish family He " held an Exchequer post under Henry VIII and Edward VI, sat in Parliament at least twice, bought monastic lands in or near Coventry, and there founded what was probably the first free school in England ". He was known as an agrarian reformer and took an active part in the commission on enclosures in 1548. The committee led by Hales undid much of the work of enclosures and encouraged agrarian resistance. " This brought on his head the anger and successful opposition of the landed gentry and the Earl of Warwick, who accused him of fomenting strife and another peasants' war. When Warwick overthrew Somerset in 1549 Hales had to flee abroad." During his exile he wrote *A Discourse of the Common Weal of this Realm of England*, which was not published until after his death in 1581 by W. S., who claimed to be its author. It is through the work of Miss Lamond that it is attributed to Hales. She had published a new edition of that work of Hales from MSS. (Cambridge, 1893), which is the edition that we have used. The reference is to *Discourse*, Lamond's ed., p. 37.
[2] *Discourse*, Lamond's ed., p. 69.

Since it was the debasement of coins that caused the nominal rise of prices, the real prices of commodities, according to Hales, would have been unchanged, " ffor an ounce of oure silver or golde as much stuffe as ever was gyven for the same." [1] As the value of money was supposed to be stationary, would it not naturally follow that the nation could not gain nor lose from this state of things ? His answer was in the negative. His ground was that different classes of people would be affected differently. The receivers of fixed incomes would lose, and the tenants and others would gain, while the position of the merchant class would be unaffected. Among the former, the King was said to be the heaviest loser, because he did not receive in payment of his revenues such a quantity of gold and silver as before.[2] The other disadvantage of debased coinage was, he said, that by it, " we haue devised a waie for the strangers not onlie to bie our gould and silver for brasse, and not onlie to exhause this Realme of treasure, but also to bie oure cheife commodities in manor for nothinge." [3] So he suggested the remedying of the situation by the restoration of coins " to the old rate and goodness ".[4]

While it is not to be denied that the debasement of coins was one of the causes of the rise of prices, Hales's explanation of the price revolution is incomplete, because, on the one hand, he neglected an important cause of the change in prices and, on the other, he failed to realize that the values of the precious metals were liable to fluctuate. Yet his theory of the disproportionate effects of the rises in prices that are produced by the debasement of coins is on the whole satisfactory. Although he was not the original author of the theory, he deserves to be remembered for his presentation of it.[5]

Hales reflected in his work thought on money and international trade in the sixteenth century. To him money was a different problem to an isolated state and to a state that was a unit in a commercial world. In the former, the problem hardly existed, while in the latter, only gold and silver could be used as money.[6] He gave in detail the

---

[1] *Discourse*, Lamond's ed., p. 101.   [2] Ibid., p. 34.
[3] Ibid., p. 69.   [4] Ibid., p. 105.
[5] For example, St. Thomas Acquinas, Nicholas Oresme, and Molinæus had developed, or at least indicated, a similar theory.
[6] Hales, op. cit., pp. 87, 115 f.

reasons why gold and silver should be used and why they were to be preferred to any other commodity. Briefly, his view rests on the function of money as a store of value.[1] According to him, the precious metals acquired a special position from their durability and their capacity to serve as a store of wealth.[2] The " senows of warre " is another argument that he advanced in favour of the accumulation of the precious metals,[3] for he considered it a great danger " if his grace [the King] should wante treasure to purchase the sayde habylimentes and necessaries for warre, or to fynde soldiers in time of need ".[4] But how could precious metals be acquired ? His answer, which was typical of the economic thought of the time, was by the country selling more to the foreigner than it bought.[5] He fully realized that if buying and selling were not equal, the balance must be paid in specie.[6] He suggested two means of effecting an excess of exports over imports. They are : (a) by protective policies such as the prohibition of the importation of goods that could be manufactured at home and the encouragement

[1] That " theory of the store of value ", as it might be called, has been wrongly credited to Petty by Suviranta (*The Theory of the Balance of Trade*, 1923, pp. 52 f.). That theory is the natural outcome of the financial conditions in the sixteenth century and the greater part of the seventeenth century when gold and silver were alone easily exchangeable values, because foreign investment was practically unknown in those days and goods were not so easily exportable as at later periods.

[2] People having " plentie of things " and wanting to store up the surplus would naturally be willing to exchange these things for " such wares as would lie in lesse Romes, and contineweth longest with out perishinge, and be carried to and fro with lesse charge, and be most currant at all times and at all places ". Gold and silver were " most of that sort " (Hales, op. cit., p. 72). See also p. 73.

[3] *Discourse*, Lamond's ed., pp. 86–7 ; see also p. 113.

[4] Ibid., p. 35.

[5] That is in essence what has been called after Thomas Mun the balance of trade theory. The theory, in fact, had a long process of development. As early as the last quarter of the fourteenth century we find very definite statements of it in English by one of the officers of the Mint in his evidence before Parliament. The statement is as follows : " . . . As to the fact that gold and silver come not to England, whilst that which is in England is carried abroad, . . . if the merchandise exported from England be well and justly governed, the money which is in England will remain, and great plenty of money will come from abroad. It must be ascertained that no more foreign merchandise come within the realm than the value of the merchandise of this country that goes out of the realm." However, the exact term *balance of trade* itself seems to have been coined in 1615 and the term *favourable balance of trade* in as late as 1767. See W. H. Price, " The Origin of the Phrase ' Balance of Trade '," *Quarterly Journ. of Economics*, **xx** (1905), pp. 157–167.

[6] Hales, op. cit., p. 102.

C

of exporting industries [1] ; and (b) by " selling dear and buying good cheap ". [2]

In considering the problem whether the " universal dearth of all things " could have been remedied by a general reduction of rents and other prices, he said that it would be impossible because the foreign merchants would not reduce the prices of their wares accordingly.

They be strangers, and not within obedience of oure soueraigne lord, that dve sell such wares ; as yron, tar, flax and other. Then consider me, if youe cannot compell them, wether yt were expedient for vs to leue strangers to sell theire commodities deare, and we oures good cheape ; yf it weare so, then weare it a great enrichinge of [other Countryes] and impouerishinge of oure owne ; for they should haue much treasure for theires, and haue oure commodities [from vs for a very lyttyl ; except yee coulde devyce to make one price of oure comodytyes] emonst oure selfes, and an other outwarde, which I cannot se howe yt may be.[3]

In other words, he believed, first, that the domestic level of prices could not influence the prices of imported goods, and second, that the precious metals would flow in if the domestic level of prices was higher than the foreign level, because the country could " sell dear and buy cheap ", and selling dear and buying cheap would, according to him, cause a more favourable balance of trade. His description of the connection between high prices and the inflow of the precious metals is clearly erroneous. Normally we should expect selling dear and buying cheap to cause a less favourable balance of trade and, consequently, an outflow of specie. It would, of course, be correct if both the foreign demand for exported goods as a whole and the domestic demand for imported goods were inelastic.[4] But that assumption was neither stated nor implied.

The *Discourse* of Hales exercises an influence upon economic thought only after it had been revised and published by a man, whose identity was concealed under the initials W. S. It was, however, rather the work of a French contemporary, whose arguments were essentially

---

[1] *Discourse*, Lamond's ed., pp. 88, 65.   [2] Ibid., pp. 47, 51 *passim*.
[3] Ibid., p. 40, see also pp. 43 ff., 47 f.
[4] It should be noted that the domestic demand for imported goods could not be permanently inelastic. When the balance of payments of the country turns unfavourable and specie flows out, then, other things being equal, the total income of consumers falls. The fall in consumers' income will sooner or later lead to a reduction in the total value of its imports.

the same as those of Hales, that attracted the most general attention. That work was the *Paradoxes* that Malestroit [1] presented to the French king in 1566. Like Hales, he was mercantilistic, and like Hales he did not recognize the liability of gold and silver to fluctuate in value. He attributed the " dearth " to the debasement of coins. He thus came to the same conclusion as Hales that " for buying of all things we do not give now more gold or silver than we did before " and then argued that the complaint of the " general dearth " of all things " is without cause ".[2] For practically the same reasons as those given by Hales he concluded that the King and other receivers of fixed incomes would lose from the debasement of coins.[3] Unlike Hales, Malestroit said nothing about foreign trade and, as a whole, his work is much inferior to that of Hales.

In opposition to the views of Hales and Malestroit there arose the theory that the general rise of prices had been brought about by the American supplies of the precious metals. Among the writers who put forward the theory, the ablest and the most influential was Jean Bodin.[4] In his *Réponse* to Malestroit (1568) he, first of all, proved that prices did rise during the period under consideration [5]

[1] Seigneur de Malestroit (second half of the sixteenth century) was a " member of the royal council of France and comptroller of the Mint ".

[2] " Lon ne peut dire qu'vne chose soit maintenant plus chere qu'elle n'estroit il y a trois cens ans, sinon que pour l'achepter il faille maintenant bailler plus d'or ou d'argent que l'on n'en bailloit alors. Or, est-il que pour l'achapt de toutes choses, lon ne baille point maintenant plus d'or n'y d'argent que lon en bailloit alors. Doncques puis ledict temps rien n'est enchery en France. Les maxims sont clairs." (*Les Paradoxes sur le faict des Monnyes*, Paris, 1578 ed. used, p. 4). Compare Paul Raveau, *Précédé d'un Étude sur le Pouvoir d'Achat de la Livre*, Paris, 1926.

[3] *Les Paradoxes sur le faict de Monnyes*, Paris, 1578, p. 15.

[4] Other writers, especially Spanish writers, must have more or less noticed the effects of the influx of the American treasure in raising prices. But there can be no doubt that Bodin is entitled to the credit for first giving due emphasis to the importance of the supply of the money metals and that it was from Bodin and not from others that later writers got that explanation of the price revolution. For that reason we feel ourselves justified in choosing Bodin as the representative exponent of that view. See Earl J. Hamilton, *American Treasure and the Price Revolution in Spain*, 1501–1650 (Cambridge, Mass., 1934), pp. 283–306 and Bernard W. Dempsey, " The Historical Emergence of Quantity Theory," *Q.J.E.*, 1935.

[5] Jean Bodin (1530–1596) was born and educated at Angers. He spent his college days in studying law ; became, after his graduation, a lecturer on jurisprudence and later practised law in Paris. Not being very successful at the bar, he entered government service. In 1568 he published his famous *Reponse aux paradoxes de M. de Malestroit touchant l'encherissement de toutes les choses et des monnaies*, which was followed in 1578 by his *Discours sur le rehaussement et diminution des monnaies, pour reponse aux*

and then gave five causes for the rise, of which " the principal and almost the only one is the abundance of gold and silver, which is to-day much greater in the Kingdom [France] than it was four hundred years ago, to go no further back".[1] But where did so much gold and silver come from ? From foreign trade, on the one hand, with Arabia, the Levant, the New World, and other European nations, and, on the other hand, from the exploitation of mines in America.[2] The high profits in France were another cause of the inflow of gold and silver.[3] His essay marked a great advance in both the theory of money and the theory of international price relationships. In his study of the former he showed that the values of the precious metals were themselves subject to change. He was one of the first writers, if not the first,[4] to recognize that truth. He thus blazed the trail for the formulation of the Quantity Theory of Money.[5] In his study of international price relationships he showed very clearly the

paradoxes de sieur de Malestroit. It is, however, as political philosopher that he is chiefly noted. In political theory he was sometimes considered as " one of the most important figures after Aristotle ". His famous work, *Les six livres de la République*, was published in 1576. In it he incorporated the substance of his *Réponse*. The *Réponse* has an English translation in A. E. Monroe's *Early Economic Thought*. The reference is to Monroe's edition, pp. 123–6.

[1] Ibid., p. 127.   [2] Ibid., pp. 128–131.   [3] Ibid., p. 131.

[4] As early as the Saxon coinage controversy around 1530, the opponents of depreciation put forward arguments suggestive of the quantity theory.

[5] By the Quantity Theory of Money we mean the doctrine according to which, to use the words of Wicksell, " the value or purchasing power of money varies in inverse proportion to its quantity, so that an increase or decrease in the quantity of money, other things being equal, will cause a proportionate decrease or increase in its purchasing power in terms of other goods, and thus a corresponding increase or decrease in all commodity prices." One may, of course, use the term, *quantity theory of money* in a broader sense, viz. in the sense that

$$\text{money} \times \text{velocity} = \text{price} \times \text{trade}.$$

The above formula implies not only the proposition that an increase in the volume of money raises prices (i.e. the quantity theory in the sense we use it) but also such propositions as the doctrine that money stimulates trade and the doctrine that changes in the velocity of the circulation of money may lead to changes in prices and/or trade. From the historical point of view, the mercantilists notice both the effects of an increasing circulation on prices and those on trade. Taking their position as a whole, they emphasized more the latter effects than the former. During the nineteenth century, most economists put more emphasis on the effects of money in changing prices than on its effects on the volume of trade and production. It is from them that we have the above or the narrower definition of the " quantity theory of money ". It should, however, be made clear at the outset that the term, quantity theory, may be used in the broader sense.

It should be further noted that we do not assign the credit of first

relationship of foreign trade, the movement of specie, and the domestic price level to each other. He pointed out that by foreign trade gold and silver would be brought into the country and that the inflow of the precious metals would cause a general rise of prices. The causal sequence runs as follows : " Trade—specie flow—internal prices." He did not, however, explain whether the internal price level had any effect on foreign trade or not. It was not until the beginning of the seventeenth century that an Englishman, Malynes, attacked the subject and produced a thesis, which was a curious combination of Bodin's doctrines with those of Hales.

In the general theory of international trade he, like Hales, was mercantilistic. It is interesting, however, to note that in the writings of Bodin as well as Hales, we find that the authors had taken great pains to refute the isolationist argument against foreign trade.[1] That shows that in the middle of the sixteenth century that school of thought, which put foreign trade in the foremost place, had not been fully established. It was only after the controversies of this period that the importance of the precious metals and of foreign trade was generally accepted in economic thought.

Before we take up the exchange controversy, we should perhaps take note of two important contributions to monetary theory during the latter part of the same period. The first was that of an Italian writer, Bernardo Davanzati, in his lecture on money delivered in Florence in 1582. Like writers before him, he discussed such problems as the importance of money and the causal connection between the supply of the precious metals and changes in prices. With regard to the part played by money he considered that money was important because of its position as the " blood of the nation ".[2] In other words, he emphasizes rather the function of money as a circulating medium than its function as a store of value. In connection with the problem of the relation between the supply of money and prices he stated, probably for the first time, the quantity theory of money

formulating the quantity theory of money to either Bodin or any one writer. Bodin was simply one of the earliest writers who had a quantity theory. As early as 1526, Copernicus had noticed that "money loses its value when it has been too much multiplied ".
[1] *Réponse* (Monroe's ed.), pp. 138 ff.
[2] Bernardo Davanzati (1529–1606), *A Discourse upon Coins* (1582). We have used the English translation by John Toland (London, 1696), p. 18.

in the sense of equating the national stock of goods with the stock of money :

> Now all these [earthly things which satisfy men's wants] by the Consents of Nations are worth all the Gold (comprehending also the Silver and Copper) that is wrought in the World. All men then do passionately covert all the Gold, to buy up all things for the Satisfaction of all their Wants and Desires, and so to become happy.[1]

The author's conclusions on the two problems, if combined and logically developed, might imply a new line of approach. He was not, however, quite aware of their full significance, and he failed to go so far.

The other contribution is that of Montchrétien in his *Traicté* which was published in 1615. While accepting Bodin's doctrine that the inflow of a large quantity of the precious metals from the New to the Old World had caused a general rise in prices, he made the important qualification that the rise had not always been in proportion to the increase in the quantity of money.[2]

3. THE FOREIGN EXCHANGES CONTROVERSY

The other question which aroused much interest during this period was foreign exchanges.[3] That was due to two circumstances. They were the confused conditions in currency and finance and the reaction against the growth of financial capitalism. During this period repeated depreciations of currencies in several countries, adverse balances of payments, and manipulations by speculators in foreign exchange had created abnormal conditions in foreign exchange. Countries like England, the currencies of which were depreciated, were naturally greatly interested in the foreign exchanges.[1] Furthermore, the expansion of international trade in the sixteenth century had brought the international financier into existence. That was partly because of the need of capital for the financing of large shipments of goods and partly because of the fact that " dry exchange ", i.e. exchange for the purpose of financing

---

[1] Ibid., p. 15.
[2] Antoyne de Montchrétien, *Traicté de l'économie politique*, 1615, Funck-Brentano ed. (Paris, 1889) used, p. 257.
[3] See Professor R. H. Tawney, *Introduction to a new edition of Thomas Wilson's " Discourse upon Usury "* (London, 1925).
[4] Ibid., p. 60.

trade, was one of the best available means of evading the usury laws. As lending money at rates of interest was not in keeping with the ideas of the time, protests were naturally made against the financing of international trade.

Protests against foreign exchange dealings were based on either or both of the following arguments : (a) the usury argument and (b) what we might call the bullionistic argument. The best specimen of the former is Thomas Wilson's *Discourse* (1572) which we need not consider in this essay. The champions of the bullionistic view held that " unlawful " exchange dealings were injurious to the state, because they caused an outflow of bullion. They all, of course, agreed that foreign trade had to be paid for either in bullion or through the foreign exchanges, and " if the carriage of money from one realme to another is forbidden, it is necessary for the trade of merchants that there should be an exchange ". Exchanges for such a purpose they called real or legitimate exchanges. What they objected to was the so-called dry exchange or " merchandizing exchange ".[1] By means of those " unlawful " exchanges, they contended, bankers and rich merchants were able to make the rates of exchange rise or fall for their own private gain at the expense of the State. By undervaluing the money of a country they were able to procure it cheap and sell it abroad at a profit, and the transaction would mean a loss of gold and silver by the country.[2] Furthermore, such exchange dealings caused not only an international movement of specie but also a rise or fall in the prices of all commodities.[3] The remedies suggested were (a) the authoritative determination of the exchange rates according to the just prices ; (b) the prevention of the lowering of exchange by " pegging " or other means ; (c) the monopolizing of exchange business by the Crown or by persons licensed by it ; and (d) as a necessary corollary of control by the Crown the prohibition

[1] See *Memorandum prepared for the Royal Commission on the Exchanges*, London, 1564, reprinted in *Tudor Economic Documents* (edited by Tawney and Power, London, 1924), vol. iii, pp. 346–359.

[2] Ibid., p. 350.

[3] " The Exchange is the gouernere of prices of all warres enterchangablye vented betweene this Realme and the Low Contreyes, because the greateste quantetye of wares transported ether outeward or inwarde is boughte by money taken vppe by Exchange, and also because, althoughe the wares he boughte with his owne moneye, in sellinge of his hondred poundes worthe of wares he Consydered what gaynes he myght have made by Exchange of so muche moneye, and he maketh the price of his wares accordingly or to some Convenyent overpluse." (Ibid., p. 347.)

of exchange dealings by private individuals. Those measures, together with the then generally accepted doctrine of the prohibition of the export of bullion, it was believed, would have served to purge the foreign exchanges of the existing abuses.[1]

The exchange dealers naturally sought to rebut the charges brought against them.[2] Three important arguments that they advanced in their own defence might be noted. The first was that state intervention in exchange business would prove a very serious hindrance to trade. The second was that, as a result of the decline in trade, the revenues from customs duties would greatly decline. The third and most important argument took the form of an attack upon the theory of foreign exchange of their opponents and the presentation of a theory of their own :

> Towchinge the standarde of the English monye, that you complayne of is kept lowe by reason of the free exchaunge, we can saye nothing but that our exchaunges are made with a mutuall consente betwene merchaunte and merchaunte, and that the abondance of the deliverers or of the takers make the exchange rise or fall.[3]

In spite of those theoretical arguments and of the fact that, in the last quarter of the century, the financial power of the financiers was strong enough to secure the repeal of the usury laws and the rejection of the proposal to nationalize foreign exchange transactions, the bullionistic view of foreign exchange prevailed in the domain of thought as the orthodox view until the end of the second decade of the next century. The bullionistic theory of foreign exchange was, for instance, restated early in the sixteenth century by Thomas Milles.[4]

The net practical result of the foreign exchange controversy was that it had called attention to the importance of the role played by foreign exchange in international trade.[5]

---

[1] See Tawney, op. cit., pp. 138–154.
[2] " Protest against the State Control of Exchange Business," 1576, reprinted in *Tudor Economic Documents*, vol. ii, pp. 169–173.
[3] *Tudor Economic Documents*, p. 172.
[4] See Thomas Milles, *The Cvstomers Replie or Second Apologie* (London, 1604) ; *The Cvstomers Apologie* (London, (1601) 2nd ed., 1609) ; *An out-port-Customers Accompt* (London, 1609) ; and especially *Customers Replie*, pp. 4–5 ; ch. x, pp. 14–32.
[5] Thomas Gresham went even so far as to say : " As the exchainge is the thinge that eatts ought [eats out] all princes, to the wholl destruction of ther common well [weal], if itt be nott substantially looked unto, so

The bullionists had made it clear that the rate of exchange influenced the movement of specie, the state of trade, and the prices of goods. The mere recognition of a relationship among those factors was an important advance in economic thought, although the views that the bullionists held were largely unsound. This controversy deserves, moreover, to be remembered as having led to the formulation of definite proposals for the control of foreign exchange.

4. GERRARD DE MALYNES

The last writer of importance in this period was de Malynes. He refined and restated the bullionistic view of foreign exchange with great ability and combined with it the ideas which sprang from the controversy over the price revolution.[1]

His starting point was the mercantilistic proposition that " the Prince (being as it were the father of the family) ought to keep a certain equality in the trade or traffick betwixt his realms and other countries, not suffering an ouer-ballancing of forreine commodities with his home commodities ".[2] Two causes might contribute to such an overbalance, namely, the export of bullion from the realm and the practice of " selling cheap and buying dear ".[3] It is in connection with the former that he restated the bullionistic view of foreign exchange and it is in connection with the latter that he re-examined the doctrine of John Bodin and his contemporaries.

He attributed the export of bullion from the realm to the

likewise the exchainge is the cheffest [chief] and richest thinge only above all other, to restore your Majestie and your reallme to fine gowld and sillvar . . ." (" Letter to Queen Elizabeth on the Fall of the Exchanges," 1558—quoted from *Tudor Economic Documents*, ii, p. 148). Gresham, it may be noted, has been known for his excellent exposition of the doctrine that bad money drives out good. The doctrine was given the name " Gresham's Law " by H. D. Macleod in 1858. It had, however, been formulated also by other writers.

[1] Gerrard de Malynes (fl. 1586–1641), the son of an English Mint-master, himself became an Assay Master of the Mint and in 1609 was appointed commissioner on Mint affairs. He had wide experience in trade and was frequently employed by Elizabeth and James I as an adviser on commercial questions. His writings, which bear on the present section, are : *A Treatise of the Caker of England's Commonwealth* (London, 1601) and *England's View in Unmasking of two Paradoxes* (by De Malestroit) *with a Replication unto the answer of Jean Bodin* (London, 1603). For his later writings see Sec. 5.

[2] *Treatise of the Caker*, p. 2.   [3] Ibid., p. 3.

manipulation of the foreign exchanges and other abuses.[1] He argued that if the foreign exchanges were not " abused ", that is, if the moneys were valued at par, according to weight and fineness, no bullion would be exported.[2] It followed as a logical corollary that the debasement of coins would not cause the transportation of bullion, so long as the moneys were exchanged " value for value ".[3] It was " the abuse of the exchange for money " that constituted " the very efficient cause of this disease ",[4] for :

[A] If the exchange with vs here be low, so that more will bee giuen for our money being carried in *specie*, then by bill of exchange can be had, then our money is transported.[5]

[B] If the exchange with vs here be high . . . then

[a] euerie man is desirous to make ouer money by exchange, and that money which should be employed vpon the commodities of the realme, is deliuered by exchange to the great hindrance of the vent and aduancement of our home commodities : and yet the forrein commodities not any way therefore sold the better cheap [6] ; [and]

[b] . . . our merchants are inclined to buy forreine commodities, or to barter their commodities for the same, which opportunitie is not only obserued by the Bankers, but also procured.[7]

The remedy he suggested was " that the exchange for all places ought to be kept at a certaintie in price, according to value for value ".[8]

In re-examining the theories regarding the price revolution he criticized both Malestroit and Bodin. He agreed with the former that the alteration of the money itself would cause a general rise in prices,[9] but he considered it merely a nominal rise[10] and rejected even the doctrine of disproportionate rises in the prices of commodities as the result of such a change.[11] The real cause of high prices must be found somewhere else. He accepted the explanation of Bodin[12] and so

---

[1] To him the causal sequence ran as follows : " Foreign exchanges—money—commodities." See also *The Maintenance of Free Trade*, p. 2.

[2] See *Lex Mercatoria*, p. 415 ; *The Maintenance of Free Trade*, pp. 14–15; *The Center of the Circle*, pp. 41 f.

[3] *Caker*, p. 35 ; see also *The Maintenance of Free Trade*, p. 61.

[4] *Caker*, p. 18.   [5] *Caker*, p. 34.

[6] Ibid., pp. 38–9.   [7] Ibid., pp. 42–3.

[8] Ibid., p. 99.   [9] Ibid., p. 10.   [10] Ibid., p. 11.

[11] *England's View*, pp. 55, 60.

[12] " The property of the money . . . is, that plentie of money maketh generally things deare, and scarcitie of money maketh likewise generally

rejected Hales and Malestroit's erroneous view that the values of gold and silver were unchangeable.[1] He was, however, of the opinion " that to shew the alternation of the price of things and the causes thereof, is of small moment, the true ground of the matter . . . must be by making a comparison of the enhauncing of the price of the Commodities of one countrie, with the price of the Commodities of other countries : and thereby to find out, whether things are grown deare with vs in effect ; and whether we pay more proportionably for the forraine Commodities . . . then we do receiuve for the price of our home Commodities ".[2] The examination of that problem was of great importance in his system of thought, because the condition might constitute the alternative cause of an overbalance of trade. The conclusion to which he came, however, was not new. It was simply the second proposition of Hales's doctrine of international price relationships (that is, a country with relatively low prices would sell cheap and buy dear and thereby turn its balance of trade against itself).[3] The value of his contribution lies in the fact that he combined all preceding theories into a comprehensive theory of international price relationships. He started from the bullionistic theory of foreign exchange, went through Bodin's theory of money and prices and reached Hales's doctrine. For instance, he said :

> [Low rates of exchange would cause] our monies to be transported and maketh scarcitie thereof, which abateth the price of our home commodities, and on the contrary aduanceth the price of the forreine commodities beyond the seas, where our money concurring with the monies of other countries causeth plenty, whereby the prices of forrein commodities is aduanced. . . .[4]
> If we sell our Commodities dearer, and buy our victuals

things good cheape. Whereas things particularly are also deare or good cheape, according to plentie or scarcitie of the things themselves, or the vse of them " (*Caker*, p. 10). See also *England's View*, pp. 7 and 9. In discussing the value of " money " Malynes and his contemporaries (e.g. Mun) had used the term " money " in two senses : firstly in the modern sense, and secondly in the sense of money delivered to (or taken from) foreign countries, i.e. bills of exchange. But in the quotation cited the word " money " is unmistakably used in the modern sense.

[1] Professor J. W. Angell has said of Malynes that he was one who considered the value of money as " something absolute and unchanging " (*The Theory of International Prices*, p. 18). That is certainly incorrect.
[2] *England's View*, p. 65.   [3] Ibid., pp. 65 f.
[4] *Caker*, p. 35.

dearer then heretofore ; and that ouer and aboue the price thereof, we must pay farre dearer for the forraine Commodities, then proportionably the price of our Commodities is risen : this causeth vs to be a loser in particular, and bringeth by an ouer-ballancing of forraine Commodities with our Home Commodities, a general losse to the Commonwealth : which to supply, causeth vs to make vp the inequalitie with money, which is the treasure of the realm.[1]

Ouer-ballaunce [of trade] . . . must be made vp and ballanced with the treasure or money of the realme.[2]

If we might be permitted to connect those passages together and express them in the form of causal sequence, we could present a theory of international price relationships which would run as follows :

Low exchange—outflow of specie—relative scarcity of money at home (and plenty of money in foreign countries)—fall of domestic prices (and rise of prices abroad)—" buying dear and selling cheap "—over-balance of trade—outflow of specie.[3]

We cannot help thinking that the above attribution of a relation between " buying dear and selling cheap " and the balance of trade is erroneous, because normally we should expect the former to cause an " under-balance " instead of an " over-balance ". Malynes seemed to have been conscious of that objection, when he said :

To the general obiection, that selling our commodities dearer, would be an interruption to the traffique, we haue already shewed how necessarie our commodities are, and what request thereof is in all places.[4]

That might be interpreted as that he was assuming an inelastic demand for the exported products. He was, however, not consistent on that point.[5] Therefore, it would be too liberal to say with certainty that he was actually making that assumption. Even if that be granted and if

[1] *England's View*, pp. 65-6.   [2] Ibid., p. 70.
[3] Although he recognized that an inflow of specie could produce opposite results, he was of the opinion that a high rate of exchange did not necessarily cause an inflow of specie. He said that " it would be so, were it not for the tolleration of the monies to go currant farre aboue their value beyond the seas " (*Caker*, p. 48). In other words, his theory would apply to countries, the value of whose coins were identical with their metallic contents.
[4] *Caker*, pp. 117–118.
[5] See, for example, ibid., pp. 106 f.

the rate of exchange or the movement of specie itself be considered as a sufficient initial cause of disturbance, Malynes's theory is still subject to another important criticism. That is that he neglected the demand of England for her own imports. It is only if one makes the assumption that both the demand of England for her imports and the demand of other countries for her exports were inelastic that Malynes's theory applies.

For more than a decade after Malynes had published his earlier works, no publication of importance appeared in this field. Then came the second exchange controversy or the " balance of trade controversy ", which opened a new page in the history of mercantilistic thought.

5. THE BALANCE OF TRADE CONTROVERSY

The view of the bullionists in England that unfavourable rates of exchange were the *initial* cause of the outflow of specie had supporters in other European countries. Mark Antony de Santis was one of them.[1] In the early decades of the seventeenth century there emerged, however, a school of thinkers who refuted the views of the bullionists. The new theory has been somewhat inaccurately called the balance-of-trade theory. The first systematic work of this school of thought was Antonio Serra's *Treatise*.[2] The purpose of the treatise was to refute Santis's doctrine that an unfavourable rate of exchange " is the sole cause of the scarcity of money in the Kingdom ", for it " does not permit remittance to be made in cash for the commodities exported from the Kingdom, rather than by exchange ; while remittance for commodities imported is made in cash instead of exchange, because of the profit to be made in each case ".[3] The argument given by Serra is simple and convincing. He said that if anyone obtained funds through the exchanges instead of in bullion, " funds either came into the Kingdom in cash before exchange was resorted to, or must do so

[1] *Discorso intorno alli effett.* . . . (1605). See A. E. Monroe, *Early Economic Thought* (Cambridge, U.S.A., 1927), p. 154. De Santis also stood for an embargo on the exportation of money and for some legal tarif. See Luigi Cossa, *An Introduction to the Study of Political Economy* (London, 1893), p. 180.
[2] *A Brief Treatise on the Causes which can make Gold and Silver Plentiful in Kingdoms where there are no mines* (1613, Naples). We have used the English translation in A. E. Monroe, op. cit., pp. 143–167.
[3] *Ibid.*, p. 154.

later, since otherwise they would be paid into the Kingdom in some way."[1] In other words, the rates of exchange themselves were governed by independent factors and could not be the initial cause of international specie movements. The causes of those movements had, therefore, to be looked for elsewhere. He enumerated the " causes which can make gold and silver plentiful in Kingdoms where there are no mines ". Firstly, there were, according to him, particular factors which could occur only in one country, namely, (a) " a surplus of products grown in a nation in excess of its own need ", and (b) " a superior geographical situation ". Secondly, there were those factors which were common to all countries, including (a) magnitude of industry, (b) quality of population, (c) extent of trading operations, and (d) regulation by the sovereign.[2] Those common and special factors together determined the volume of a country's exports (and imports). It was the excess of exports over imports (or excess of imports over exports) due to the relative advantages or disadvantages of countries and not to the rates of exchange that constituted the initial cause of specie movements.[3] Serra's work, however, attracted very little attention among his contemporaries. It was in the second foreign exchange controversy or the balance of trade controversy, which arose in England in the twenties of the seventeenth century, that mercantilism really reached a new phase and the balance of trade theory exerted a definite influence upon both thought and policy.

The balance of trade controversy[4] differed from the foreign exchange controversy in that the latter was concerned only with foreign exchange, while the former included the consideration of the merits of the East India Trade. The East India Trade had a unique character, because, although India had very valuable muslins and choice spices to sell to the countries of Europe, she imported very few goods from them. European traders had, therefore, to send gold or silver to India in exchange for her goods. To export gold or silver was, however, contrary to the accepted economic doctrines of those days, and it so happened that in the second

---

[1] Ibid., p. 156.   [2] Ibid, pp. 146–153.
[3] It follows that such remedies as the regulation or prohibition of the movement of gold would, according to him, be useless or even harmful. See p. 161.
[4] See P. J. Thomas, *Mercantilism and the East India Trade* (London, 1926), pp. 8–16.

decade of the seventeenth century there was great economic distress in England. Naturally, people in England jumped to the conclusion that the drain of specie to the East was one of the most important causes, and they consequently attacked the East India Company. The ablest advocates of that view were Milles and Malynes. The East India Company had naturally to defend itself, and it found two brilliant champions of its interests in its own ranks.[1] They were Edward Misselden [2] and Thomas Mun,[3] who not only refuted the specific charge that the company was draining the country of treasure but also the theoretical foundations of the arguments of Milles and Malynes, especially their views on foreign exchange.

Misselden and Mun agreed with their opponents that a country should try its best to increase its treasure, but they emphasized the importance of gold rather as a circulating medium than as a store of value.[4] Mun spoke of a favourable

[1] The following are the most important works in connection with that controversy :—
  (a) Malynes, *Lex Mercatoria* (London, 1622).
  (b) Malynes, *The Maintenance of Free Trade* (London, 1622).
  (c) Malynes, *The Center of the Circle of Commerce* (London, 1623).
  In the above writings of Malynes there is nothing new in the theoretical foundation of his arguments. We need not, therefore, concern ourselves with them and may go straight to the examination of the views of the balance-of-trade school.
  (d) Misselden, *Free Trade* (London, 1622).
  (e) Misselden, *The Circle of Commerce* (London, 1623).
  (f) Mun, *A Discourse of Trade from England vnto the East Indies* (London, 2nd ed., 1621), McCullock's reprint used.
  (g) Mun, *England's Treasure by Foreign Trade*, written about 1630 and first published in 1664. We have used the reprint in McCullock, *Early English Tracts in Commerce*, pp. 115–209.
[2] Edward Misselden (fl. 1608–1654), a prominent merchant, was connected with the East India Company at about the time during which he wrote on economic matters. His economic writings were primarily called forth by the appointment of the standing commission on trade in 1622 and were published, as shown in the preceding note, between 1622 and 1623. In October, 1623, he left England, and " the East India Company invited him to act as one of their commissioners at Amsterdam to negotiate a private treaty with the Dutch ". It is believed that during these negotiations he " must have been brought into close relations with " Thomas Mun. Misselden became deputy-governor of the Merchant Adventurers' Company at Delft in 1623. He held that post until 1633.
[3] Thomas Mun (1571–1641) " appears to have been early engaged in mercantile affairs in the Mediterranean, especially in Italy and the Levant ". He was very successful and gained a high reputation among merchants. In July, 1615, he was elected a member of the committee or a director of the East India Company, and " he spent his life in actively promoting its interests ".
[4] See, however, Mun, *England's Treasure*, ch. xviii, especially pp. 189–190.

balance of payments as "affording much wealth and employments to maintain a great number of poor, and to encrease our decaying trade ".[1] Misselden even went so far as to advocate the " raising of money " or inflation.[2]

But how was national treasure to be increased ? Misselden stated his answer in both a positive and a negative form. His positive answer was a favourable balance of trade, which was to him " the centre of the circle ",[3] and free trade in the sense of moderate regulation of imports.[4] His negative answer was an attack upon the bullionistic theory of foreign exchange. Firstly, the *par pro pari* exchange was merely the " natural exchange ", and " if you should so limit or restraine *Exchanges*, that no man should so take or deliuer any money, but according to iust fineness : then the vse of *Exchanges* in all places would bee taken away ".[5] That argument is certainly unsound, for he omitted to take into account the benefit derived by the saving of the costs of transporting bullion. Secondly, in the actual course of exchange, " money is exchanged value for value, according to the *extrinsique* or outward valuation . . . [which] is greater or lesse, according to the circumstances of *time*, and *place*, and *persons*." [6] In that connection he emphasized the part that the bill of exchange played in the financing of international trade.[7] Thirdly, the rates of exchange were not by themselves sufficient to cause a movement of specie. He said :

There is neither *Parity*, nor Purity. For it is not the rate of Exchanges, but the value of monies, here loue, elsewhere high, which cause their Exportation : nor does the Exchanges, but the plenty or scarcity of monies cause their value.[8]

---

[1] Ibid., p. 130 and *passim*. See also Lewes Roberts, *The Treasure of Traffike*, 1641 (E.E.T. reprint), p. 110 ; *England's Great Happiness*, 1677 (E.E.T. reprint), p. 262.

[2] Raising of money would have the advantages, he said, of " plenty of money and quickening of Trade in euery mans hand " (*Free Trade*, p. 106). And " when Trade flourisheth, the King's Revenue is augmented, Lands and Rents improoued, Navigation is encreased, the poor employed " (p. 4).

[3] See *The Circle*, p. 116, and *passim*.

[4] In this respect Misselden's view is not so consistent a balance of trade theorist as Serra and Mun. See *Free Trade*, chs. i and ii.

[5] *The Circle*, p. 97.

[6] *The Circle*, p. 98.   [7] Ibid., p. 100.

[8] *Free Trade*, p. 104. Too much importance should not be attached to that quotation, significant as it might be, because the term " monies " is here rather ambiguously used.

Finally, " it is not the rate of *Exchange*, whether it be higher or lower, that maketh the price of Commodities deare or cheape, as Malynes would here infere ; but it is the plenty or scarcitie of Commodities, their vse or Non-vse, that maketh them rise and fall in price." [1]

The main thesis of the writings of Thomas Mun was practically the same as that of Misselden but it was better stated. Positively, he argued that a favourable balance of trade was the only necessary and entirely sufficient condition of an inflow of specie.[2] He described as many as twelve ways " to encrease the exportation of our commodities, and to decrease our Consumption of foreign wares ".[3] Negatively, he refuted one by one the most important current objections to the East India Trade,[4] and argued against such artificial expedients as the prohibition of the exports of specie,[5] the enhancing of the value of local moneys,[6] or the acceptance of foreign coins at high rates.[7]

To the theory of international price relationships he made valuable contributions. First, he refuted the bullionistic theory of foreign exchange and expressed the opinion that exchanges " are not contracted at the equal value of the moneys, according to their respective weights and fineness . . . because he that delivereth his money doth respect the venture of the debt, and the time of forebearance ".[8] According to him, the rate of exchange could not be considered as the initial cause, and the causal sequence would run as follows :

" Balance of trade—the volume of bills demanded and supplied—the rate of exchange." [9]

That is just the reverse of that advanced by Malynes. Secondly, in opposition to Malynes and others he pointed out that it was " selling cheap ", instead of " selling dear ",

---

[1] *The Circle*, p. 21.
[2] Mun, *England's Treasure*, p. 157. See also pp. 143–6, 186, 208, and *passim*.
[3] Ibid., ch. iii (pp. 127 ff.). It is interesting to note that he had taken into consideration the factor of fishing (p. 130) and that of freight charges (p. 129). That is one of the earliest, if not the earliest, instance of the recognition of the invisible items.
[4] *Discourse of Trade*, pp. 7–41.
[5] *England's Treasure*, chs. 4, 6.
[6] Ibid., ch. 8.   [7] Ibid., ch. 9.
[8] *England's Treasure*, p. 158.
[9] " As plenty or scarcity of money [in exchange] do make the price of the exchange high or low, so the over or under balance of our trade doth effectively cause the plenty or scarcity of money." (Ibid., p. 159.)

which would bring the precious metals home.[1] Therein we find the germ of a new theory of international price relationships, which has sometimes been called the classical theory. The significance of the contribution he thus made to the subject was clearly shown when he combined it with his own doctrines and formed his somewhat complete theory of international price relationships. His views might be indicated by the following quotations :

> Plenty or Scarcity of mony makes all things dear or good cheap ; and this money is either gotten or lost in forraign trade by the over or under ballancing of the same.[2]

> If wee were once poor, and now having gain some store of mony by trade with resolution to keep it still in the Realm ; shall this cause other Nations to spend more of our commodities than formerly they have done, whereby we might say that our trade is Quickned and Enlarged ? no verily, it will produce no such good effect : but rather according to the alteration of times by their true causes wee may expect the contrary ; for all men do consent that plenty of mony in a Kingdom doth make the native commodities dearer, which as it is to the profit of some private men in their revenues, so is it directly against the benefit of the Publique in the quantity of the trade ; for as plenty of mony makes wares dearer, so dear wares decline their use and consumption.[3]

Those ideas might be expressed in terms of causal sequence as follows :

> Favourable balance of trade (—volume of bills—rates of exchange)—inflow of specie—plenty of money—rise of domestic prices—" selling dear and buying cheap "— unfavourable balance of trade.

We may note that that differs from Malynes's theory in two respects : first, the initial cause is the balance of trade ; second, the consequence of " selling dear and buying cheap " is an unfavourable, instead of a favourable, balance of trade.[3] Had he gone a step further, he would have arrived at a theory substantially the same as that advanced by David Hume more than a century later ; but he stopped short and failed to see the contradiction between his theory of international price relationships and his adherence to the policy of increasing national treasure.

---

[1] Ibid., pp. 128, 133.   [2] Ibid., p. 141 (and also *passim*).
[3] Ibid., p. 138.
[4] That is not a question of opinion but simply a question whether the elasticity of demand for imports at home and that for exports abroad are greater or less than unity.

The controversy ended with the complete triumph of the balance of trade school, whose theory was the dominant doctrine up to about 1680. In the intervening period, although a vast number of pamphlets was published, there was no real advance beyond the theory of Mun. Yet we cannot pass over the contributions of three writers, namely, Rice Vaughan, William Petty, and William Potter.

6. VAUGHAN, PETTY, AND POTTER

The *Discourse* of Rice Vaughan,[1] important though it might be in connection with other studies, is of interest to the present study only in two respects. Firstly, he was probably the first English economist who stated the quantity theory of money in the sense of a proportion between money and commodities, for he clearly said : " the price of all things . . . is the Proportion between Money and the things valued by Money." [2] He, moreover, pointed out that the proportion was governed by " Rarity and Abundance ".[3] Secondly, his description of how the " raising of money " would raise the price of all things accordingly is worthy of note. He said :

When the Merchant stranger brings his Commodities, whether he intends to make his return in Moneys or in Commodities, he maketh his own sale by the measure of the Money here, and then examines how much this Money will amount to in the Moneys of his own Country, where he bought his Commodities, and if he find the Money here diminished in intrinsical value, he must then demand so much the higher price, or else he cannot make his Accompt . . . [Therefore] when Money is raised, the price of forein Commodities doth first rise, And the price of forein Commodities being once raised, the price of Domestick Commodities will of necessitie be raised also ; for the price of forein Commodities will make great plenty of them to be imported, and the high price of Money will inforce that they must be returned in domestick Commodities ; By which means domestick Commodities being much sought for, will of necessity be raised in price, and, the price of both these being raised, it follows that the rate of all mans sallaries and hire of Labourers and Endeavorers

[1] Rice Vaughan (fl. 1650), legal writer, son of Henry Vaughan of Machynlleth, Montgomeryshire, barrister of Gray's Inn from 1638, etc. He died in or shortly before 1672. *A Discourse of Coin and Coinage*, which " was written while Charles I, Louis XIII, and Ferdinand II reigned and before certain Dutch and French proclamations were repealed ", was published posthumously in London in 1675.
[2] *Discourse of Coin*, p. 101.　　　[3] Ibid., p. 19 and *passim*.

must rise in Proportion, or else men shall be forced to defer Trade and Endeavours, and then scarcity will encrease the price.[1]

Perhaps it might be added that he anticipated the concept of a due proportion between the national stock of money and the monetary needs of the nation.[2] He was, however, of the opinion that the problem of " too much money " had only philosophical significance and that the sole problem before the business world was the rarity of money.

The first economist who presented a definite and clear doctrine of a due proportion of money was Petty.[3] He said, " There is a certain measure, and due proportion of money requisite to drive the trade of a Nation, more or less then which would prejudice the same." [4] The proportion of money requisite to the trade of any nation was to be " taken from the frequency of commutations, and from the bigness of the payments ". In other words, it depended on the requirements of trade on the one hand and the rapidity of the " revolution and circulation of money " on the other.[5] Suppose in a country, " the Expense being 40 Millions, if the revolutions were in such short Circles, viz. weekly, as happens among poorer artisans and labourers, who receive and pay every *Saturday*, then 40/52 parts of 1 Million of Money would answer those ends : But if the Circles be quarterly, according to our Custom of Paying rent, and gathering Taxes, then 10 Millions were requisite. Wherefore supposing payments in general to be of a mixed Circle between One week and 13, then add 10 Millions to 40/52, the half of the which will be 5½, so as if we have 5½ millions we have enough." [6] That is one of the earliest statements of a doctrine in regard to the velocity of the circulation of money in economic literature.[7] Although it is

---

[1] *Discourse of Coin*, pp. 148–9.
[2] Ibid., pp. 58 f.
[3] *The Economic Writings of Sir William Petty*, ed. by C. H. Hull (Cambridge, 1899). He held to the mercantilistic doctrine that " the great and ultimate effect of Trade is not Wealth at large, but particularly abundance of Silver, Gold and Jewels, which are not perishable, nor so mutable as other Commodities, but are Wealth at all times, and all places". (*Political Arithmetick, ca.* 1676, *Writings*, pp. 259 f.) For an account of the life of Petty (1623–1687) see Hull's edition of his works, pp. xiii–xxxiii.
[4] *A Treatise of Taxes and Contribution*, 1662 (*Writings*, p. 35). See also *Writings*, pp. 113, 446.   [5] Ibid. (*Writings*, p. 36).
[6] *Verbum Sapienti, ca.* 1664 (*Writings*, pp. 112–13).
[7] Two of the other earliest statements were found in the works of G. Montanari and Pierre de Boisguilbert. The contributions of Bois-

undoubtedly an important contribution to the theory of the value of money, Petty did not explicitly[1] or directly connect his discussion of the velocity of circulation with the problem of the value of money. He was primarily interested in the question of the quantity of money required by a nation and found it to be determined by the payments to be made in money and its velocity of circulation. In case there was " too little money ", we must try either to increase it by trade[2] or to economize its use. The best way to economize the use of money was to establish banks, because " where there are Banks . . . there less money is necessary to drive a Trade ".[3] In case there was " too much money ", he would deal with it as follows :

> We may melt down the heaviest, and turn it into the Splendour of Plate, in Vessels or Utensils of Gold and Silver ; or send it out, as a Commodity, where the same is wanting or desired ; or let it out at Interest, where Interest is high.[4]

In other words, hoarding, exportation, and lending abroad are the three remedies recommended.

guilbert will be described in a footnote below. Other contributions of Montanari may be noted here. Firstly, his statement of the quantity theory was as follows :—
" *All human commodities which are in commerce taken together have a value equal to that of gold and silver, and coined copper which may circulate among them in trade.*"
Therein he introduced the concept of money in *circulation* to take the place of the quantity of gold and silver. Secondly he pointed out that while the prices of goods in one isolated country and those in another were unconnected, the opening of commerce approximated the prices of the products of the trading countries to a general level. Before the establishment of communications between one country and the rest of the world, the general price of goods in the former country, like a sea separated from other waters, had its independent level. Prices in the different countries of the commercial world, on the contrary, must be in the same manner as those waters which are in communication and must " level themselves in an equal distance from the center to which they are tending ". See J. St. Lewiński, *Money, Credit and Prices*, London, 1929, pp. 86–7.
[1] Implicitly, Petty's doctrine means the recognition of the relation that
money × velocity = price × trade.
[2] " If the largeness of a public Exhibition should leave less money then is necessary to drive the Nations Trade, then the mischief thereof would be the doing of less work, which is the same thing as lessening the people, or their Art and Industry ; for a hundred pounds passing a hundred hands for Wages, causes a 10000 l. worth of Commodities to be produced, which hands would have been idle and useless, had there not been this continual motive to their employment " (*Writings*, p. 36). He agreed, however, with the view that " to prohibit the Exportation of Money . . . is a thing almost impracticable . . . and vain " (ibid., p. 57).
[3] *A Treatise of Taxes, Writings*, p. 36 ; see also *Writings*, p. 446.
[4] *Quantulumcunque* (1682), *Writings*, p. 446.

The other contribution of Petty was a theory of the foreign exchanges. " As for the natural measures of Exchange," he said, " that in times of Peace, the greatest Exchange can be but the labour of carrying the money *in specie*, but where are hazards [and] emergent uses for money more in one place than another, etc., or opinions of these true or false, the Exchange will be governed by them." [1] Therein we find probably the first clear statement of the so-called " specie-points mechanism ".[2]

The last economist of the period 1620 to 1680 that we have to consider is William Potter,[3] a paper money mercantilist. Like Davanzati, Misselden, and Mun, he emphasized the function of money rather as a circulating medium than as a store of value, and he seemed to be the first writer to favour the policy of increasing the national stock of money on the ground that money stimulates trade and to try to refute the quantity theory of money on the same ground. His starting point was the proposition " that the effect of all Trading, is but the parting with Commodities for such Money, Credit, or valuable Consideration, as procures other Commodities or Necessaries instead thereof ".[4] It followed, according to him, that the larger the volume of " Money, Credit or valuable Consideration ", the more were the commodities parted with in trade. In other words, an increase of money would increase the volume of trade on the one hand [5]

[1] *Treatise* (*Writings*, p. 48).

[2] The meaning of the term " specie-points mechanism " or " gold-points mechanism " can be given in the words of George Clare. " By buying gold in one country or shipping it for sale in another, a certain rate of exchange is yielded, which is called a gold-point—the rate produced by buying at home and selling abroad being the export-point, and that produced by buying abroad and selling at home being the import-point. . . . It is of course obvious that, if the price of London paper rises to the export gold-point, and if the remitter is free to export gold, it is immaterial to him whether he buys a draft or sends gold, but that he would never think of paying more ; on the other hand, if the price falls to the import point . . . the seller of a bill . . . would certainly refuse to take less ; and, provided that the import and export of gold is free, the gold points thus mark the highest level to which an exchange may rise, and the lowest to which it may fall " (*The A.B.C. of the Foreign Exchanges*, 9th ed., London, 1931, pp. 25–6).

[3] William Potter (fl. 1656) was appointed in 1656 registrar of debentures on " the act for the sale of the late king's lands ". He was one of the earliest writers on paper currency. He recommended the issue, by means of a land bank, of bills payable at sight to the bearer, under a guarantee of land mortgages. It was to give an account of his scheme that he published the works mentioned in this essay.

[4] Potter, *The Key of Wealth* (London, 1650), p. 2.

[5] " Let it be supposed, that there is a people amongst whom there is

and quicken it on the other.[1] Quick and large trade would mean prosperity. So he advocated the multiplication of the money of the nation and opposed hoarding in any form. The best way to multiply money and prevent hoarding was to use paper currency, because paper currency would increase trade just as metallic money did and at the same time was " not like to be hoarded up as Money is ".[2]

He was aware of the possible objection from exponents of the quantity theory that " an increase of money would occasion an increase in the prices of Commodities, proportionable to such increase of money and consequently would not occasion any increase in the sale of Commodity ; then not any increase of Trade ". So he attempted to refute the quantity theory.[3] His arguments were, however, on the whole rather confusing and unintelligible. Liberally interpreted, his main argument is that if the volume of money was increased, commodities would be correspondingly increased and the tendency of prices to rise as a sequence to the increase of money would be offset. Nevertheless, he conceded that if the increase in commodities was proportionately less than the increase in money, prices would rise accordingly. For example, he said, " if there be now ten times more money, in the World then formerly, seeing it cannot be conceived, that the whole world is capable of affording, ten times more Commodity then formerly, it must be granted, that an increase of money in the whole World, may occasion an increase in the price of Commodities (though not fully proportionable . . .). "[4]

7. THE FIRST PROTECTIONIST CONTROVERSY

In the last two decades of the seventeenth century, the balance of trade theory began to be questioned, and, as a result, much progress was made in the theory of international trade. The first two steps forward were taken in connection with two controversies, namely the protectionist

now, ten times as much money as formerly . . . then I say the consequence will be, that both trading and riches will encrease amongst them, much more than proportionable to such increase of money " (ibid., p. 6).
[1] " The Advancement of Trade, consisteth chiefly in the great and quick Revolution of Commodity from Sea or Land, through the hands of Tradesmen, to each particular person for his private life. This Revolution of Commodity, is proportionable to the Revolution of Money, or that which goeth for such. Such Revolution of Money is according to the plenty thereof not hoarded up " (The Tradesmen's Jewel, London, 1650, p. 5).   [2] Ibid., p. 7.   [3] See The Key, p. 13.   [4] Ibid., p. 14.

controversy and the controversy between John Locke and Nicholas Barbon.

The protection versus " free trade " controversy [1] at the end of the seventeenth century was connected with the East India trade. In the latter half of that century the imports of Indian textiles into England were increasing, especially in the last two decades. Owing to the high costs of production, the English textile industries could not withstand the competition of the Indian imports. The result was that in the last decade of the century the English woollen and silk industries faced a grave crisis. Those industries were experiencing depression and unemployment, and complaints were made by the weavers and the public in general against the East India trade. The East India Company naturally replied to the attacks that were made on its trade, and the result was the protectionist controversy.

The best spokesmen of the weavers' interests were John Cary [2] and John Pollexfen.[3] Like other mercantilists, they based their contention upon the conception of the state as an economic entity and stood for a definite national economic policy for the benefit of the state, but they differed from the

[1] See P. J. Thomas, *Mercantilism and the East India Trade* (London, 1926), especially chaps. 1 and 4.

[2] John Cary (?–c. 1720) was a prominent Bristol merchant. He was engaged in the West Indian sugar trade and took a political interest in commercial matters. The most important of his economic writings is *An Essay on the State of England in relation to its Trade, its Poor, and its Taxes, for carrying on the Present War against France*, 1695. That essay attracted attention and brought him into correspondence with Locke, who wrote that it " is the best discourse I ever read on that subject ". Its second edition was published in 1719 under the title *An Essay towards regulating the Trade and employing the Poor of this Kingdom ;* and its third edition, after his death, in 1745 as *A Discourse on Trade and other matters relative to it*. The latter editions differ considerably from the first one. In that work is found his plan for providing workhouses for the poor, which through his efforts was brought into operation in Bristol by an Act in 1697. Although his scheme was a financial failure, it was the model for several local experiments in the eighteenth century. His other economic writings include *On the Coin and Credit of England*, 1696, and *A Proposal for paying off the Publick Debts by erecting a Nation Credit*, London, 1719. The former was reprinted along with the second and third editions of his essay on trade. In the latter is found the proposal for a national bank, from which, he claimed in the second edition, " the famous Mr. Laws' drew his scheme."

[3] John Pollexfen (fl. 1697), an English merchant, was born about 1638. He became a member of the committee of trade and plantations in 1675 and was elected a member of the Board of Trade in 1696 (which he held up to 1705). In the following year (1697) he published his *A Discourse of Trade and Coyn*, in which he agitated for the withdrawal of the privileges of the East India Company. When Davenant published his essay in defence of the East India Company Pollexfen produced a reply, entitled *England and East India Inconsistent in their Manufactures* (London, 1697).

balance of trade school in regard to the criterion to be applied in judging the foreign trade of a country. To the latter a country was said to gain or lose according as it had an under or an overbalance of trade. Cary and Pollexfen, on the contrary, judged the benefit of trade rather by the *nature* of the exports and imports than by their quantity and value. In other words, " that Trade is advantageous to the Kingdom . . . which Exports our Product and Manufactures ; which Imports to us such Commodities as may be manufactured here, or to be used in making our manufactures ; which supplies us with such things, without which we cannot carry on our Foreign Trade ; [and] which encourages our Navigation, and increases our Seamen."[1] Judged by those criteria, the East India trade was said to be harmful and not beneficial to England. Nevertheless, they did not abandon the mercantilistic idea of increasing the national stock of money. They differed from their predecessors only in this : they no longer valued foreign trade and the treasure brought by it for their own sakes but for the effects upon home industries and trade. It was, moreover, by raising the question of how the national stock of money could be increased that Pollexfen had contributed something to the theory of international price relationships.

Pollexfen, following Mun, pointed out that cheapness was an essential factor in increasing the sale of home products. He said, " As the goodness of Commodities is absolutely necessary to introduce, incourage, or preserve the Consumption of them, so is the price."[2] How could the prices of commodities in the country be lowered ? The answer was the reduction of the prices of raw materials and the wages of labour. By the prohibition of the exportation of raw materials (for example, wool) which were used for manufactures at home, and the importation of cheap raw materials, the cost of raw materials would be reduced.[3] More important was the labour factor, and it was necessary to increase the supply of labourers and reduce their wages.[4] He disapproved, however, of the suggestion of forcing down interest rates by law. He conceded that low rates of interest and prosperity in trade always came together, but " the increase of Trade is rather the cause of the falling of Interest,

---

[1] Cary, *A Discourse on Trade* (London, 1695), p. 1. See also Pollexfen, *A Discourse of Trade and Coyn* (London, 1697), p. 5.
[2] Pollexfen, *Discourse*, p. 55. [3] Ibid., p. 54. [4] Ibid, p. 55.

than that lowering Interest by Law should occasion the increase of Trade ".[1] Therefore, any attempt to lower the rate of interest by law would be futile.[2] The ablest upholders of the East India Company were Josiah Child [3] and Charles Davenant.[4] They did not deny the obvious fact that the Indian trade was detrimental to certain industries, but they maintained that the fact was not a sufficient condemnation of the East India trade. Nor did they accept Mun's criteria in judging the benefit of trade, namely, the general balance and the exchange rates.[5]

[1] Pollexfen, *Discourse*, p. 62. " Trade governs Interest, and not Interest Trade " (p. 64).

[2] His remarks on paper credit also deserve notice. He said :—
" Notes and Bills may serve as a Cordinal in Cases of Necessity, but as they have not any intrinsick value, they . . . [are] not fit to support the Body Politick longer, then we have Silver or Gold Coins to answer for them " (Preface).
" Such [paper] Credit, as far as it may be necessary to supply the want of *Coyn*, may be very useful, but if it should jostle out the use of *Coyn*, then most dangerous " (p. 67).
" We should . . . not depend too much on Paper Money, least we consume what we have, by forcing it out of the Nation ; *as Paper Money may increase, Silver Money must decrease*, according to the fortuitous Course of Trade " (p. 79).
That view anticipated the main argument of the currency school.

[3] Josiah Child (1630–1699), " the wealthiest Englishman of his time and the most prominent figure in finance and foreign trade," began his career as a merchant's apprentice. He rapidly made his way in business and made a fortune. By the fifties he became Mayor of Portsmouth and was M.P. for Petersfield 1659, Dartmouth 1673–8, and Ludlow 1685–7. He was a director from 1677, deputy-governor from 1684 to 1686 and again from 1688 to 1690, and Governor of the East India Company from 1681 to 1683 and from 1686 to 1688 and " for a rule he ruled over the company absolutely ". The most important of his economic writings was *New Discourse of Trade*, which passed through several stages before it reached its final form. " The first draft was his *Brief Observations concerning Trade and Interest of Money* (London, 1668), followed the same year by *A Short Addition to the Observations concerning Trade*. In 1669–1670 he wrote ten additional chapters and the complete work was issued as *A Discourse about Trade* (London, 1690). In 1693 the same work with little variation, except for an introduction of twenty pages and the name of Child on the title page, appeared as *A New Discourse of Trade*." His other writings include *The Great Honour and Advantage of East India Trade* (London, 1697).

[4] Charles Davenant (1656–1714) was a member of Parliament and an influential Tory politician. He held the office of commissioner of excise from 1683 to 1689. In 1705 he was appointed inspector-general of exports and imports, which office he held until his death. His economic writings are all reprinted in *The Political and Commercial Works of Charles Davenant*, edited by C. Whitworth (London, 1771).

[5] See Child, *A New Discourse of Trade*, London, 1693, pp. 137 ff. ; Davenant, *Works*, i, p. 147. They considered the criterion of a general balance as " doubtful and uncertain ", because they had found that since the exportation of bullion to India had begun to increase, especially towards the close of the century, the usual calculations of the balance of trade had ceased to justify the operations of their company.

In place of those criteria, they tried to establish a new rule for testing whether a trade is beneficial to a state or not :

The best and most certain discovery . . . is to be made from the encrease or diminution of our *Trade* and *Shipping* in general ; for if our *Trade* and *Shipping* diminish, whatever profit particular men may make, the *Nation* undoubtedly loseth. . . . Where-ever Trade is great and continuous so, and grows daily more great and encreaseth in Shipping, and . . . for a succession not of a few years, but of Ages, that Trade must be nationally profitable.[1]

Using that criterion and facts that they had adduced to show that the East India trade had promoted the general prosperity of the nation, they were able to make out a case for the view that the East India trade was beneficial to the country.

Negatively, they tried to show that the proposal to prohibit the wearing of all Indian imported textiles in England would be detrimental to the nation.[2] However, they could not do so without sacrificing some part of their mercantilistic doctrines and approaching the doctrine of free trade. The following quotations perhaps sufficiently reveal their main arguments :

Trade is in its nature free, finds its own channel, and best directeth its own course : and all laws to give it rules and directions, and to limit and circumscribe it, may serve the particular ends of private men, but are seldom advantageous to the public.[3]

For all trades have a mutual dependence one upon the other, and one begets another, and the loss of one frequently loses half the rest.[4]

It should be noted they they were not free traders at heart. They advocated leaving trade free from restraints only in so far as the argument served the purpose of their Company and their views constitute a mere case of special pleading.

As to the question how trade might be promoted, they agreed with Pollexfen that cheapness was essential to the expansion of sales.[5] They also agreed with the latter that a large population was necessary to the enlargement of national wealth and trade, but Child held an opposite view

---

[1] Child, *Discourse*, pp. 148–9.
[2] One of the most important reasons given by Davenant is that since large quantities of the imported Indian textiles were re-exported to the Continent, any limitation imposed by England would divert the trade to the Dutch.   [3] Davenant, *Works*, i, p. 98 ; see also i, p. 429.
[4] Ibid., i, p. 97.   [5] Ibid., i, p. 100 ; Child, *Discourse*, p. 19.

on the questions of wages and interest. As already explained, Pollexfen thought that high wages would spoil trade and low wages would encourage trade. Child was of the opinion that high wages were by no means harmful to trade. On the contrary,

> where-ever Wages are high universally throughout the whole World, it is an infallible evidence of the Riches of that Country; and where-ever Wages for Labour runs low, it is a proof of the Poverty of that place.[1]

On the question of interest his view was also the opposite to that of Pollexfen, for he stood for the lowering of interest by law as a method of promoting trade.[2]

Davenant advanced a theory of a due proportion of money to the monetary needs of the nation similar to that of Petty. He said, " It is not the taking in a great deal of food, but it is good digestion and distribution that nourishes the body and keeps it healthy. The same thing holds in the body politic ; so that gold and silver are often a surfeiting diet to a nation ; and there may be as well too much as too little of this kind of treasure, if it be not turned to proper uses."[3] Later, following the line of reasoning and the methods of Petty, he made an estimate of the quantity of money required.[4]

Before we come to Locke and Barbon, it is perhaps best that we should mention the works of Dudley North.[5] North was perhaps the only thoroughgoing free trader before 1700. One quotation will be sufficient to show his free trade views :—

> The whole World as to Trade, is but as one Nation or People, and therein Nations are as Persons. . . . There can be no Trade improfitable to the Publick ; for if any prove so, men leave it off ; and wherever the Traders thrive, the Publick, of which they are a part, thrives also. To force Men to deal in any prescrib'd manner, may profit such as happen to serve

---

[1] Child, *Discourse*, Preface (p. A 6).
[2] Ibid., p. 159 and *passim*. See also Child, *Brief Observations*.
[3] Davenant, *Works*, i, p. 382.
[4] Ibid., pp. 440 ff.
[5] Dudley North (1641–1690), a leading Tory of his time, made his way in business so early that when twenty-one years of age he was the leading merchant in Constantinople of the Turkey Company. Having made a large fortune, he returned to England in 1680. In 1683 he became one of the commissioners for the customs and carried out important reforms. His chief work is *Discourses of Trade*, published posthumously (London, 1691). We have used the reprint in *Early English Tracts on Commerce*, edited by J. R. McCulloch (London, 1856).

them ; but the Publick gains not, because it is taking from one Subject, to give to another.[1]

North also differed from his contemporaries in attaching less importance to the role of money.[2] He even went so far as to say that " no Man is richer for having his Estate all in Money, Plate, etc. lying by him, but on the contrary, he is for that reason the poorer ". What was important for a man was not money but the things that money bought.[3]

To the theory of international price relationships he also made some contributions. Firstly, together with Petty and Davenant, he was one of the first advocates of the doctrine of a due proportion between money and the monetary needs of a nation. He said :—

> There is required for carrying on the Trade of the Nation, a determinate Sum of Specifick Money, which varies, and is sometimes more, sometimes less, as the Circumstances we are in require. [For example] war time calls for more Money than time of Peace.[4]

> Money is a Merchandise, whereof there may be a glut, as well as a scarcity, and that even to an Inconvenience.[5]

Secondly, he seemed to have held a doctrine of the natural distribution of the precious metals among nations, for he said :—

> In this course of Trade [between Nations] Gold and Silver are in no sort different from other Commodities, but are taken from them who have Plenty, and carried to them who want, or desire them, with as good profit as other Merchandises. So that an active prudent Nation groweth rich, and the sluggish Drones grow poor ; and there cannot be any Policy other than this, which being introduc'd and practis'd, shall avail to increase Trade and Riches.[6]

He did not, however, explain how the precious metals are taken from those who have them in plenty and given to those who are in want of them, although there is the following passage in his essay :—

---

[1] *Discourses of Trade, Early English Tracts*, p. 513 (or Original, p. viii). See also p. 528 (Original, p. 14).

[2] " The Proposition I chiefly aim to prove . . . is, that Gold and Silver, and, out of them, Money are nothing but the Weights and Measures, by which Traffick is more conveniently carried on, then could be done without them : and also a proper Fund for a surplusage of Stock to be deposited in " (*Discourse of Trade*, p. 530 of *E.E.T.*).

[3] Ibid., *E.E.T.*, p. 525 (Original, p. 11).

[4] Ibid., *E.E.T.*, p. 539.

[5] Ibid., *E.E.T.*, p. 513.

[6] Ibid., *E.E.T.*, p. 527.

This ebbing and flowing of Money, supplies and accommodates itself, without any aid of Politicians. For when Money grows scarce, and begins to be hoarded, then forthwith the Mint works, till the occasion be filled up again. And on the other side, when Peace brings out the Hoards, and Money abounds, the Mint not only ceaseth, but the surplus of Money will be presently melted down, either to supply the Home Trade, or for Transportation. Thus the Buckets work alternatively, when Money is scarce, Bullion is coyn'd ; when Bullion is scarce, Money is melted.[1]

But that is not an explanation of " the world distribution of money ". It is essentially a doctrine concerning the automatic adjustment of the monetary and non-monetary uses of the precious metals within a closed community. It amounts to this : If the monetary stock of a community is " abundant ", the value of the precious metals as coins would be less than their value as bullion. Then people would melt down the coins and turn them to non-monetary uses. In other words, " When Money grows up to a greater quantity than Commerce requires, it comes to be of no greater value, than uncoyned silver, and will occasionally be melted down again." [2]   The opposite is true of a relative scarcity of money.

. Finally, North rejected the doctrine that low rates of interest would encourage trade with an argument similar to that of Pollexfen :—

> As plenty makes cheapness in other things, as Coin, Wool, etc., when they came to Market in greater Quantities than there are Buyers to deal for, the Price will fall ; so if there be more Lenders than Borrowers, Interest will also fall ; whereof it is not low Interest makes Trade, but Trade increasing the Stock of the Nation makes Interest low.[3]

8.   John Locke and Nicholas Barbon

In connection with the English recoinage problem in the last decade of the seventeenth century there arose a controversy regarding the raising of the value of silver

---

[1] *Discourse of Trade*, E.E.T., p. 539.
[2] Ibid., *E.E.T.*, p. 531.
[3] Ibid., *E.E.T.*, p. 518. The author of *Considerations on the East-India Trade* (1701) and other upholders of the East India Company had also free trade ideas. But it would be too generous an interpretation to say, as an authority recently did, that they anticipated the doctrine of comparative costs.

crowns between Locke on the one side and Lowndes [1] and Barbon on the other. This controversy is of interest to us, because the former has given us a refined re-statement of many of the then accepted doctrines of money and trade and the latter presented us with one of the earliest systematic criticisms of the same. On the subject of money, Locke,[2] like most of his predecessors, identified money with the money metals and thought that the only difference between money and uncoined silver was that, while money had a public voucher, which testified to its weight and fineness, uncoined silver did not possess one. So money was considered by him as being " perfectly in the same Condition with other Commodities, and subject to all the same Laws of Value ".[3] According to those laws, value was determined by " nothing else but their Quantity in Proportion to their vent ".[4] The term, " vent " of money, is peculiar and therefore deserves special attention :—

> He that will justly estimate the value of any thing, must consider its Quantity, in proportion to its vent, for this alone regulates the Price. . . . But because the desire of Money is constantly, almost everywhere the same, its vent varies very little ; but as its greater scarcity enhances in price, and

[1] See W. Lowndes, *An Essay for the Amendment of the Silver Coins* (London, 1695). Lowndes, being the Secretary of the Treasury, was in the controversy a more important opponent of Locke than Barbon. But from the point of view of the theory of international price relationships the contributions of Barbon were of much more importance. For that reason we shall deal only with the views of Barbon. For the conditions of currency that were responsible for this controversy, see A. E. Feavearyear, *The Pound Sterling* (London, 1931), ch. 6.

[2] John Locke (1632–1704) was the son of John Locke of Pensford in Somersetshire, who took great care in the education of his son. The younger Locke took his B.A. degree at Oxford in 1655 and M.A. in 1658. He later spent some time in studying medicine " not with any design of practicing as a physician, but principally for the benefit of his own constitution, which was but weak ". Yet he was very successful in that line. He was known mainly as a great English philosopher. His famous *Essay on the Human Understanding* was written between 1670 and 1687 and published in 1689. After having served as one of the " commissioners of trade and plantation " and filled other posts, he retired, spending the last fourteen or fifteen years of his life at Oates. He died in the 73rd year of his life. His economic writings are :—

(a) *Some Considerations of the Consequences of the Lowering of Interest and Raising the Value of Money*, 1691 (edition used, London, 1692).

(b) *Further Considerations concerning Raising the Value of Money*, London, 1695 (reprinted in his *Several Papers relating to Money*, London, 1696).

[3] *Some Considerations*, p. 53.   [4] Ibid., p. 53.

increases the scramble, there being nothing else that does easily supply the want of it. The lessening its Quantity, therefore, always increases its Price, and make an equal portion of it exchange for a greater of any other thing.[1]

In other words, the value of money was determined more by the supply of money than by the demand for it or it depended only upon its plenty or scarcity.[2] That is one of the most refined presentations of the quantity theory up to the time. Like Petty, Locke said that a certain proportion of money was necessary to trade,[3] and the reason he gave is the following :—

Every man must have at least so much money, or so timely recruits, as may in hand, or in a short distance of time, satisfy his creditor who supplies him with the necessaries of life, or of his trade. For no-body has any longer these necessary supplies, than he has money, or credit, which is nothing else but an assurance of money, in some short time. So that it is requisite to trade, that there should be so much money, as to keep up the landholder's, labourer's and brokers' credit : and therefore ready money must be constantly exchang'd for wares and labour, or follow within a short time after. This shows the necessity of some proportion of money to trade.[4]

In other words, it is because of the need of the inhabitants of a country for a cash-balance that it has to preserve a certain proportion of money to the value of trade. If the money were " insufficient ", there would be a " decay of trade ".[5] But what is the proportion of money to trade that would be sufficient for a nation ? He said :—

What proportion that is, is hard to determine ; because it depends not barely on the quantity of money, but the quickness of its circulation. The very same shilling may, at one time, pay twenty men in twenty days : at another, rest in the same hands one hundred days together. This makes it impossible exactly to estimate the quantity of money needful in trade ; but to make some probable guess, we are to consider, how much money it is necessary to suppose must rest constantly in each man's hand, as requisite to the carrying on of trade.[6]

---

[1] Ibid., p. 60 ; see also p. 70.
[2] " The *Value of Money* in respect to those [Commodities] depends only on the Plenty or Scarcity of Money in proportion to the Plenty or Scarcity of those things." Ibid., p. 45.
[3] *Some Considerations*, pp. 29, 32.
[4] Ibid., p. 32.   [5] Ibid., pp. 16–17.
[6] Ibid., p. 32. For his calculation of the average cash balance required by each of the several groups of people such as labourers, landlords, tenants, and brokers, see pp. 33 ff.

It is interesting to note the difference between Locke's doctrine of the proportion of money required by a nation and the doctrine of Petty on the same subject Both are of the opinion that the proportion depends on the rapidity of the circulation of money as well as on its quantity. Petty sees money as it is in motion and measures the rapidity of its circulation by the time required by an average unit of money to effect a transaction of trade, while Locke sees money as it is at rest and measures the velocity of its circulation by the amount of it held by the average man in the carrying on of his trade. We must not, however, attach importance to the difference between Locke and Petty, because the two approaches to the question are perfectly reconcilable. Finally, like Petty, Locke did not discuss the problem of the velocity of the circulation, at least directly, in connection with the problem of the value of money, although it cannot be denied that his analysis of the velocity of circulation, like that of Petty, is an important contribution to the theory of the value of money.

He next went a step further and considered the problem of proportion from the standpoint of international trade. He said :—

> In a country that hath open Commerce with the rest of the World, and uses Money made of the same Materials with their Neighbours, any quantity of that Money will not serve to drive any quantity of Trade, but that there must be a certain proportion between *Money* and *Trade*. The reason whereof is this, because to keep your *Trade* going without loss, your Commodities amongst you, must keep an equal, or, at least, near the Price of the same Species of Commodities in the Neighbour Countries, which they cannot do, if your *Money* be far less than in other Countries ; for then, either your Commodities must be sold very cheap, or a great part of your *Trade* must stand still ; there not being Money enough in the Country to pay for them (in their shifting of hands) at that high price which the Plenty, and consequently low value of Money makes them in another Country.[1]

That is nothing but a clarified restatement of the theory advanced by Malynes. What is really new in Locke is

---

[1] *Some Considerations*, pp. 75–6. It follows that money is " not of the same value at the same time, in several parts of the World, but is of most worth in that Country where is the least Money, in proportion to its Trade " (p. 78).

his emphasis on the fact that an insufficient quantity of money depressed trade and had the effect of " drawing away our People . . . who are apt to go where their Pay is best ".[1] As a certain amount of money was necessary to every state, there remained the question as to how a country without mines of gold and silver could increase its stock of the precious metals and in order to answer the question he introduced the main thesis of the balance of trade school that an abundance of money in a country could be ensured only by the balance of trade.[2] Like Mun, he used the balance of trade to explain the foreign exchanges and expressed the view that " it is the present balance of trade on which the exchange immediately and chiefly depends ". But he made two important advances over Mun and his school. Firstly, he saw that international loans would have the same effect upon the exchanges as the commodity balance.[3] Secondly, he gave an exposition of the specie-point mechanism with considerable clearness.[4]

Upon the theoretical foundation outlined above he came to the conclusion that, since money passes only according to its metallic content and since trade was the

---

[1] *Some Considerations*, p. 78. Note that the implicit assumption of this statement is international mobility of labour. Note also that he said nothing about the possibility of " too much " money.

[2] Ibid., pp. 14–15.

[3] Ibid., p. 81.

[4] Although the honour of having given the first descriptions of the specie-point mechanism must be shared by Petty, Locke, and Simon Clement, the description of Clement is the most elaborate of the three. The principal work of Clement is *A Discourse of the General Notions of Money, Trade, and Exchanges* (London, 1695), from which we may quote a few passages to show the essence of his theory of foreign exchanges :—

" People do not currently Receive or Esteem Foreign Coins according to the Value or Computation that Foreigners put upon them ; but according to the Weight that the Silver and Gold will yield, reduced to the Standard of their own Country." (p. 7.)

" The Exchanger also takes such a Consideration from the Remitter, as may not only pay his Charge and Hazard, but also redound to his Profit. Yet this *Praemio*, or Advance on the Exchanges cannot be great, unless upon some extra-ordinary Emergencies. Because People would then rather chuse to send their own Bullion to answer their particular Occasion." (p. 9.)

" [Within the limits set by the specie-point mechanism the rate of exchange] is wholly influenced by the Balance of Trade between Nation and Nation ; and when that falls short, it must be supplied by the sending of Bullion." (p. 17.)

" But whensoever the Demands for Bills to any place is greater, than that these Exchangers can find other Remittances to imburse their Correspondents, they are then necessitated to transport so much in Bullion as will make the Balance." (p. 9.)

only peaceful means ·to obtain the precious metals, to " raise " the value of money was futile. In case its value was " raised ", the consequences would be—

(a) the prices of all things would rise accordingly ;
(b) foreign exchanges would rise to the same extent ; and
(c) the landlords and other receivers of fixed incomes would lose proportionately.

In most respects Barbon's view [1] was antithetical to that of Locke. First of all, he attacked Locke's doctrine on the value of money. Barbon started from a use theory of value,[2] and thought that " nothing can have an Intrinsick value ".[3] The same was true of silver, which was but a commodity and would rise and fall in value as other commodities did. Then he argued that as money was the measure of value and should itself be constant in value, silver, being itself " uncertain in its own Value, can never be a certain Measure of another Value ".[4] Silver was but the material which happened to be used in coining money and must not be identified with money itself.[5] Money,

[1] Nicholas Barbon (1640 ?–1698) was the son of Praisigod Barbone. " He studied medecine at Leyden, received a medical degree at Utrecht in 1661, and was admitted as an honorary fellow of the College of Physicians in 1664. After the great fire of 1666 he established the first insurance office in London and participated actively in rebuilding the city. He was a member of Parliament in 1690 and again in 1695 ; he founded and conducted a land bank in 1695-6." His writings are mainly concerned with the economic events of the period in which he lived. " He defended his scheme of fire insurance ; he advocated building extensions in London ; he discussed the possibilities of land-banking," and he wrote also on money and trade. His contribution to the currency controversy under consideration is A Discourse Concerning Coining the New Money Lighter (London, 1696), and that to the general problem of trade is A Discourse of Trade (London, 1690).
[2] " The Value of all Things, arises from their Use " (Discourse concerning Coining, p. 1). See also ibid, pp. 5, 7, and passim ; Discourse of Trade, pp. 13 ff. It is interesting to note, furthermore, that he clearly pointed out that the " Use of all Wares " depended on scarcity :—
   " Things rare and difficult to be obtained, are General Badges of Honour : From this Use, Pearls, Diamonds, and Precious Stones, have their Value ; Things Rare are proper Ensigns of Honour, because it is Honourable to acquire Things Difficult. The Price of Wares is the Present Value ; And ariseth by Computing the occasions or use for them, with the Quantity to serve that Occasion ; for the Value of things depending on the use of them, the Overplus of Those Wares, which are more than can be used, become worth nothing ; So that Plenty, in respect of the occasion, makes things cheap ; and scarcity dear." (Discourse of Trade, pp. 17 f.)
[3] Discourse concerning Coining, p. 6 ; see also p. 10 and passim.
[4] Ibid., p. 8.   [5] Ibid., p. 13.

on the contrary, " has some Valuation from the authority of the Government where 'tis Coin'd, and not its sole Value from the quantity of Silver in each piece." [1] In other words, by the stamp of the state, a coin might be given value above the value of the silver in it. For instance, he said,

> Mony is a Value made by a Law ; and the Difference of its Value is known by the Stamp, and Size of the Piece. . . . It is not absolutely necessary, Mony should be made of Gold or Silver ; for having its sole Value from the Law, it is not Material upon what Metal the Stamp be set. Mony hath the same value, and performs the same Uses, if it be make of Brass, Copper, Tin or anything else. The Brass Mony of Spain, the Copper Mony of *Sweeden*, and Tin Farthings of *England*, have the same Value in Exchange, according to the Rate they are set at and perform the same Uses, to Cast up the Value of things, as the Gold and Silver Mony does.[2]

The doctrine of Barbon, probably the best statement of the " legal theory of money " in the seventeenth century, is rather inaccurate. It is only if the Government has a monopoly in coining metals into money [3] and limits the quantity of money coined that coins would pass current at higher values than those of their metallic contents. Just as " Plenty and Scarcity, in respect to their occasion, makes things of greater or less Value ", plenty and scarcity determines also the value of money. Barbon, in stressing the importance of the legal stamp on the coin and neglecting the factor of the relative scarcity of money, evolved a proposition, which is misleading, if not erroneous.

His use of the legal theory of money in support of the advocacy of the " raising of the value of money " is certainly erroneous. According to him, the raising of the value of money would cause neither a general rise of prices nor any disproportional effects upon prices. His argument is that " the Mony, having its Value from the Authority of the Government, is always of the same Goodness and Value ".[4] By such a dogmatic proposition he relieved himself of the obligation of considering the factor of the

---

[1] *Discourse concerning Coining*, p. 34.
[2] *Discourse of Trade*, pp. 20–2. He recognized, however, that moneys " change their Value in those Countries, where the Law has no Force, and yield no more than the Price of the Metal that bears the Stamp " (ibid., p. 22). See also *Discourse concerning Coining*, pp. 21–8.
[3] That is that there is no free coinage.
[4] *Discourse concerning Coining*, p. 89.

quantity of money, but his view was, of course, quite mistaken.

He turned next to Locke's argument that, since trade was the only peaceful means of obtaining bullion, to " raise " the value of money was futile. To begin with, he agreed that a nation should preserve its stock of *money*, but he evidently did not hold the view that a nation should also preserve its stock of *gold and silver*. On the contrary, he declared that " gold and silver are but commodities " and were by no means superior to any other kind of commodities.[1] Thus he criticized Locke for having based his opinion " upon this Supposition, That Gold and Silver are the only Riches ".[2] Furthermore, according to Barbon, Locke was mistaken in thinking that a favourable balance of trade brought about an inflow of money. Barbon, moreover, raised two important objections to the balance of trade theory and thus anticipated some of the propositions of a later generation. He denied the actual existence of a balance in the trade of any nation, " for a Nation, as a Nation, never Trades ; 'tis only the Inhabitants and Subjects of each Nation that Trade : And there are no set days or times for making up of a general Accompt." [3] He declared that there was no necessary relationship between the balance of trade (if there was one) and the international flow of money. While he denied that a trade balance could not be settled but by a transfer of money,[4] he held the following opinion :—

> Money is never carried out of any Country where it is Coin'd, except it be to those Countries where the Bullion bears a higher price than what the Money is currant at : Or when the Exchange runs so high to any Country, as it will be more profit to the Merchant to melt down the *money*, and send it over in *Bullion*, than by *Bills of Exchange*. And in both these Cases it may often fall out, that the *money* may be sent over to a Country, and yet no Debt contracted in that Country. And therefore the *Balancing of Accompt*, can't be the reason of drawing the *money* out of a Nation.[5]

In short, it was not the balance of trade, but the difference between the price of bullion abroad and the value of money at home that made money flow from one nation to another.

---

[1] *Discourse concerning Coining*, pp. 40 and 53. See also *Discourse of Trade*, p. 77.
[2] *Discourse concerning Coining*, p. 36.   [3] Ibid., p. 36.
[4] Ibid., pp. 56–9.   [5] Ibid., pp. 56 f.

It followed that the best way to increase " the species of the Mony " and to preserve it " in the Country where 'tis Coin'd " was to raise the value of money at home.[1] Those views were, of course, consistent with his erroneous theory of the value of money.

9. John Law and Others

Apart from the contributions of the participants of the two controversies described in the two preceding sections to the theory of international price relationships, this period, i.e. the period from 1680 to about 1750, is noteworthy also for other important advances in the study of the subject. Those advances arose from two important series of attempts to reconcile some of the conflicting doctrines in the mercantile system of thought. Previous to this period, as already explained, there were two different theories of international price relationships : that of Malynes and that of Mun. The difference between those two writers included a conflict of opinion on the question whether a rise in prices in a country would result in a more or less favourable balance of trade. Both had supporters in a later period. We find, for example, a restatement of Malynes's theory in the writings of Locke. But the view of Mun seemed to be more generally accepted at the time, especially by the leading participants of the protectionist controversy. In the system of thought of Mun, however, there were the contradictory doctrines that a nation should increase its stock of money and that an increase of money would necessarily cause a rise in prices and hence bring about an unfavourable balance of trade. That contradiction could not long remain unnoticed.[2] As early as the year 1650, Potter had made what was probably the first attempt to reconcile the contradiction. Later, Petty, Davenant, and North clearly pointed out that there might be too much as well as too little money in a country. Furthermore, Petty recommended some remedies for an excess of money, while North suggested that the excess would automatically be turned to non-monetary uses. None of them offered, however, a complete reconciliation of the contradictions or advanced a comprehensive alternative theory of

---

[1] *Discourse concerning Coining*, p. 85.
[2] Cf. Angell, *The Theory of International Prices*, p. 211.

international price relationships. Those tasks were left to the authors with whose works we are going to deal in the pages that follow. Those authors might be classified in two groups, those who stood for the doctrine that money stimulates trade or production and those who stood for what we might call the " semi-equilibrium " doctrine. By the former doctrine we mean the doctrine, according to which an increase of the volume of money encourages trade and a decrease of the volume of money depresses trade,[1] thus an increase or a decrease of money is necessarily accompanied by an increase or a decrease in the demand for money, and consequently a change in the volume of money would not affect prices or the balance of trade. In other words, the exponents of that theory tried to escape the difficulty created by Mun's two contradictory doctrines by refusing to accept the second of Mun's doctrines. The second group of authors, on the other hand, accepted both of Mun's conflicting doctrines but insisted that, if the government of a country adopted some artificial means to prevent the precious metals imported from entering into circulation as money and hence from influencing prices and trade, the country could continue freely to import those metals. Thus, unlike the first group of authors, these writers did not try to solve the problem by formulating a new doctrine. On the contrary, they carried Mun's system a step further to its logical conclusion, that if prices and trade are left to adjust themselves, there is a tendency of prices and trade to establish equilibrium, even though they did not desire to leave things alone. That is the reason

---

[1] The doctrine that money stimulates trade was closely connected with the concept of money as a *circulating* medium. Most mercantilists, even Mun and his followers, had the idea that money stimulates trade. But it was in the hands of the writers, with whom we shall deal in the present section, that the idea was not only emphatically developed but also clearly connected with the problems of international trade and international price relationships.

Professor Jacob Viner, in his recent book, has pointed out that " stress on the importance of an abundance of money in circulation if trade was to flourish is already found in very early writers ". He called attention to Thomas More's *Utopia*, which was published in 1516 (Reed's ed., 1929, p. 44). Viner's book, *Studies in the Theory of International Trade* (1937), became available too late to permit me to make use of it extensively. For Viner's description of the doctrine that money stimulates trade and production, see ibid., pp. 36–40.

It should be noted that this essay, which was prepared by me before Professor Viner's book was published, must not be considered in any way as a rival to that excellent work.

why we designate their doctrines as " the semi-equilibrium doctrine ". The whole argument of the first group was based upon the denial of any necessary relationship between the increase of the national stock of money and the rise in prices,[1] while the whole argument of the second group rested upon the denial of a causal relationship between an increase of bullion and an increase of money. The germs of the arguments of the former are found in Potter and of the latter in Petty.

The first advocate of the doctrine that money stimulates trade we are going to consider is John Law,[2] another paper money mercantilist. He recognized that the value of money depended upon its quantity in proportion to the demand for it,[3] but he, nevertheless, advocated an increase of the national stock of money. He saw no contradiction in those

---

[1] As indicated above, Bodin and his followers had a very simple theory of money, viz. that a change in the volume of *Money* would lead to a change in the general *price*. In the hands of Petty, Locke, and others, both the *velocity of the circulation* of money and the volume of *trade* were introduced. Thenceforth, we have the formula :

$$Money \times Its\ Velocity = Price \times Trade.$$

During the period under consideration came the question whether an increase of money would lead to an increase of price or trade. The quantity theorists insisted that money raises prices, while Law and others stood for the doctrine that money stimulates trade.

[2] John Law (1671–1729) a Scotch financier, was the son of James Law, an Edinburgh goldsmith. He was " active in all the controversies arising in England at the time of the creation of the Bank of England in 1694 ", and elaborated many financial and monetary projects. In 1705 he submitted to the Parliament of Scotland a proposal for the establishment of a national bank on the lines indicated in his famous *Money and Trade considered with a proposal for supplying the nation with money*, published in the same year. His scheme was to establish a national bank for the issue of paper currency which would be secured by the value of the nation's land. After the public had gradually become accustomed to this new money, the bank was to extend its activities by engaging in profitable commercial operations in the colonies, in redeeming public debts, etc. The most important precursors of Law were, besides Potter, Hugh Chamberlain, who brought forward a rival scheme to the Bank of England in 1693, John Briscoe, one of the chief promoters of the Land Bank in 1696, and J. Asgill, who in his *Several Assertions Proved* (London, 1696), an essay of little merit, had presented a doctrine somewhat similar to those of Potter and Law. That project of Law's was rejected. He then appealed to various European governments to adopt his plan. In 1716 he finally succeeded in winning the confidence of the French Government. In May of that year he was given the patent to establish a Banque Générale. After he had achieved a brilliant success during four years in the issue of paper money and such supplementary activities as redemption of public debts and the conduct of colonial trade, his system collapsed in consequence of a collapse of the confidence of the public. He died in 1729.

[3] That is based upon his use theory of value : " Goods have a Value from the Uses they are apply'd to ; and their Value is Greater or Lesser,

views. In the presentation of his thesis he started, like Potter, from the proposition that trade depended on money. Expressing himself with great clarity, he said :—

Trade depends on the Money. A greater Quantity employs more People than a lesser quantity. A limited Sum can only set a number of People to Work proportion'd to it, and 'tis with little success Laws are made, for Employing the Poor and Idle in Countries where Money is scarce : Good Laws may bring the Money to the full circulation 'tis capable of, and force it to those Employments that are most profitable to the Country : But no Laws can make it go further, nor can more people be set to Work, without more Money to circulate so as to pay the Wages of a greater number. They may be brought to Work on Credit, and that is not practicable, unless the Credit have a Circulation, so as to supply the Workman with necessaries; If that's suppos'd, then that Credit is Money, and will have the same effects, on Home, and Forreign Trade.[1]

In other words, when money was increased, trade would be promoted and the production of commodities stimulated. " But as Trade and Manufacture increase, the Demand

not so much from their more or less valuable, or necessary Uses ; as from the greater or lesser Quantity of them in proportion to the Demand for them. *Example.* Water is of great use, but of little Value ; Because the Quantity of Water is much greater than the Demand for it. Diamonds are of little use, yet of great Value ; because the Demand for Diamonds is much greater than the Quantity of them." (*Money and Trade Considered*, Glasgow, 1705, p. 3.) He then extended that theory of value to the value of silver : " Silver was Barter'd as it was valued for its Uses as a Mettal, and was given as Money according to its Value in Barter. The additional Use of Money Silver was apply'd to would add to its Value, because as Money it remedied the Disadvantages and Inconveniencies of Barter, and consequently the demand for Silver encreasing, it received an additional Value equal to the greater demand its Use as Money occasioned." (Ibid., p. 10 ; see also p. 72.)

[1] *Money and Trade Considered*, p. 13. Note that the proposition was founded either on the implicit assumption that there was unemployment formerly or that labour was internationally mobile. Thus, in another connection he said : " As Trade depends on Money, so the encrease or decrease of the People depends on Trade. If they have Employment at Home, they are kept at Home : And if the Trade is greater than serves to Employ the People, it brings more from places where they are not Employ'd " (p. 19). Mr. J. M. Keynes, in his recent work *The General Theory of Employment, Interest, and Money*, gives an excellent demonstration of the connection between the quantity of money and the volume of employment. He seems to have thought that his doctrine is a development of what he calls " the element of scientific truth in mercantilist doctrine ". Although we cannot agree with all his interpretations of the mercantilist doctrines, yet we think that his doctrine may be correctly considered as a continuation of the doctrine of Law.

For the mercantilistic argument that a favourable balance of trade would increase the employment of the country see Viner, *Studies*, pp. 51 ff.

for Money will be greater." [1] That increase in demand for money would neutralize its increase in quantity and prevent the price from rising. Particularizing his argument, he said that as the quantity of money increased, " Money being easier borrowed, Merchants would deal for a greater value . . . and [be] able to Sell at less Profit " and " all sorts of Manufacture would be cheaper, because in greater quantity ".[2] Therefore, there would be no rise in prices, and the value of money would not fall. Accordingly, an increase in the national stock of money would not bring about an outflow of specie. On the contrary :—

> If one half of the People are employ'd, and the whole Product and Manufacture consum'd ; More Money, by employing more People, will make an Overplus to Export : If then the Goods imported ballance the Goods exported, a greater Addition to the Money will imploy yet more People, or the same People before employed to more Advantage ; which by making a greater, or more valuable Export, will make a Ballance due. So if the Money lessens, a part of the People then imployed are set idle, or imployed to less advantage ; the Product and Manufacture is less, or less valuable, the Export of Consequence less, and a Ballance due to Forreigners.[3]

So he came to the following conclusion :—

> Most people think scarcity of Money is only the Consequence of a Ballance due ; but 'tis the Cause als well as the Consequence, and the effectual way to bring the Ballance to our side, is to add to the Money.[4]

He conceded that in a country with a metallic standard, an increase of the stock of money beyond the due proportion would produce a rise in prices.[5] But in case a country adopted a paper standard, especially of the form advocated by Law, that is, a paper money issued on the security of the land, " this Paper-Money will not fall in value as Silver-money has fallen, or may fall : Goods or Money fall in

---

[1] *Money and Trade Considered*, p. 117 ; see also pp. 74 ff.
[2] Ibid., p. 75 ; see also p. 20.
[3] *Money and Trade Considered*, pp. 14–15.
[4] Ibid., pp. 115 f. ; see also pp. 59 f., 101.
[5] " If Money were given to a People in greater Quantity than there was a Demand for, Money would fall in its value ; but if only given equal to the Demand, it will not fall in value."—*Money and Trade Considered*, p. 117. See also p. 76.

value, if they increase in Quantity, or if the Demand lessens. But the Commission [that is, the issuer of the notes] giving out what Sums are demanded, and taking back what Sums are offer'd to be return'd ; This Paper-money will keep its value, and there will always be als much Money as there is occasion, or imployment for, and no more."[1] For that reason chiefly he advocated a paper money.

Some of Law's minor contributions may also be noted. He pointed out that an increase in the expenditure of the consumers would turn the balance of trade against the country under consideration and lead to an outflow of specie. Furthermore, he saw clearly that an increase of expenditure on domestic products would ultimately have similar effects on the balance of trade as an increase of expenditure on foreign products. " The too great consumption of the Product and Manufacture of the Country," he said, "may be als hurtful as that of Forreign Goods ; For, if so much is consumed, that the remainder Exported won't pay the Consumption of Forreign Goods, a Ballance will be due, and that Ballance will be sent out in Money or Bullion."[2] Apart from that, he seemed to have made some statements which are very suggestive. In one place he said that silver money " was the same value in one Place that it was in another ; or differ'd little, being easie of carriage."[3] In another place, when he tried to answer the objection that paper money, though current within the issuing country, say, Scotland, would not be accepted abroad at the same value that it had at home, he said, " The Goods of Scotland will always be valued Abroad, equal to Goods of the same kind and goodness ; and that Money tho of Paper, which buys Goods in Scotland, will buy Goods or Money in other places."[4]

About thirty years later, J. F. Melon, a French economist, published his *Essai*[5] in which he embodied many of Law's doctrines. It was, however, in the hands of another Frenchman, Forbonnais,[6] who wrote a little after the middle of

---

[1] *Money and Trade Considered*, p. 89 ; see also p. 102. [2] Ibid., p. 19.
[3] *Money and Trade Considered*, pp. 6 f. [4] Ibid., p. 104.
[5] Jean François Melon, *Essai politique sur le commerce* (Paris ? 1734) ; English translation as *A Political Essay upon Commerce*, translated by David Bindon, Dublin, 1738 ; (nouvelle édition, augmentée de sept chaptres, Paris ?, 1763). Melon was at one time a secretary of John Law.
[6] François Véron de Forbonnais (1722–1800), son of a merchant of Mans, went into trade at the age of 16. By the time that he was about thirty

the eighteenth century that we find the ablest and the most convincing formulation of the doctrine that money stimulates trade. Being a mercantilist, he was opposed to any reduction in the national stock of money and advocated an increase of it, but he recognized that the absolute volume of money was in itself of little significance.[1] What was of great importance was this : whenever a certain amount of money was put into circulation it should not be taken out, for the money that had been issued as a medium of exchange for goods would, after a time, set up for the industrial world its levels of wages and prices. Those wages and prices would soon become conventional. If in the conditions thus established the volume of money were reduced, the inevitable result would be a reduction of production and employment, since a large number of wages would not be susceptible of reduction.[2] Therefore, a decrease in the national stock of money would mean considerable misery and suffering. In contrast, an increase of money—especially a gradual increase [3]—was always beneficial, for it would stimulate work and production. Moreover, an

years of age he had collected so much valuable information on maritime and colonial trade that he began to write on economic subjects. In 1753 he published his *Théorie et pratique du Commerce et de la Marine*, which was soon followed by the *Considerations sur les Finances d'Espagne relativement à celles de France*. His important *Recherches et considérations sur les finances de France depuis 1595 jusqu'a 1721*, printed at Basle, 1758, in 2 vols., " experienced the most distinguished reception both in France and other countries " and made Forbonnais well known in his days. In the next year he was appointed inspector of the depôt of the general financial comptrol. The most important of his economic writings is his *Principes Economiques* (Amsterdam, 1767).

[1] *Principes* (1767). We have used the reprint in the *Collection des Principaus Economists*, ed. by E. Daire and G. de Molinari, Paris, 1843–7, Mélanges, vol. i, pp. 165–240. The reference is to p. 223.

According to Forbonnais, " l'objet du Commerce dans un état est d'entretenir dans l'aisance par le travail le plus grand nombre d'hommes qu'il est possible." (*Elemens du Commerce*, 2nd ed., Leydon, 1754, i, p. 47.) For that reason, he thought that a favourable balance of trade was advantageous to a country, because, for the reasons that we are going to explain, a favourable balance would increase employment.

He also strove for independent nationhood. " La richesse réelle d'un état est le plus grand degré d'independance où il est des autres états pour ses besoins, & le plus grand superflu qu'il a à exporter." (*Elemens*, 2nd ed., i, p. 48.)

Like Cary and Pollexfen, Forbonnais was of the opinion that that trade was advantageous to the state which exported superfluous products, manufactured goods, etc., and which imported raw materials and goods which would be re-exported. (Ibid., i, pp. 52–4.)

[2] *Principes*, p. 224.

[3] Ibid., p. 226.

increase of money would not raise the prices of things. He then presented the proposition that money stimulates production in the following form :—

> When there enters into the circulation of commodities a considerable quantity of silver which was not there before, it is inevitable after a time that the commodities rise in prices. This increase of the profitableness of labour multiplies the working men and the production ; and the new competition offsets, by the diminution in profits as well as by the lowering of interest rates, the rise in prices.[1]

Generally, such an increase in money was due to a favourable balance of trade.[2] If so, " its increase first benefits the commodities which have contributed to its introduction " and then the people who had produced those commodities, that is, those who had engaged in exporting industries, would, as a result of increased profits, increase their consumption and thus give rise to new production.[3] The expansion in production would in turn check the rising tendency of prices.[4]

The increase of the circulation, which was due to a favourable balance of trade, had the beneficial effects, mainly because it was a *gradual* increase. If, however, the increase was not a gradual one and it was due, say, to the discovery of a new mine of silver in the country, the increase in the volume of money would raise prices and not increase employment and production.

The doctrine that money stimulates trade has a measure or truth, but it applies mainly to the transitional period. It would be wrong, however, to think that a large increase of the national stock of money would have no effect upon

---

[1] *Principes*, p. 225.

[2] " Le balance générale du commerce d'une nation, est la différence du montant de ses achats au montant de ses ventes au-dehors. Cette différence doit être nécessairement payée en argent, puis que c'est le seul équivalent qui puisse suppléer au défaut des échanges en nature." (*Elemens*, 2nd ed., ii, p. 310.)
He also explained how the mint or " real " par of exchange was determined (ibid., ii, pp. 74 ff.) and discussed the causes of the deviation of the current rate of the exchanges from the par. Public confidence and alteration of coins apart, the state of the balance of commerce was the main cause. (Ibid., ii, pp. 95 ff.) See also ii, pp. 314 ff.

[3] *Elemens*, 2nd. ed., pp. 151 ff.

[4] See also the work of a later writer, *An Inquiry into the Principles of Political Economy* (2 vols., London, 1767) by James Denham Steuart (1712–1780).

prices. Nor do the authors of the doctrine refute the fact that the mercantilists would defeat their own aim by increasing the national stock of money.[1]

10. CANTILLON AND OTHERS

The principal features of the " semi-equilibrium theory " or " semi-disequilibrium theory " have been described in the preceding section. It resolves itself into four propositions. First, there is the mercantilistic doctrine that a nation should increase its stock of the precious metals by foreign trade. Next, there is the quantity theory of money and the recognition that a rise in prices at home would discourage exportation and encourage importation and thus turn the balance of trade against the country. The third is a corollary of the second proposition, namely a concept of the existence of a due proportion between money and goods. The second and the third propositions, however, are not in harmony with the first, for if we consider an equality between imports and exports as the condition of equilibrium in international trade, the demand for a continuous inflow of the precious metals amounts to a demand

[1] Before we go to the semi-equilibrium theory we may note the contributions of two French economists, viz. Boisguilbert and Montesquieu. Boisguilbert's views of money were not mercantilistic. Firstly he asserted that money was a means and not an end in itself. Secondly unlike Law, Boisguilbert was of the opinion that trade was not stimulated by money but that the circulation of money was stimulated by the movement of trade. He accepted the doctrine that the general price level varies directly with the quantity of money, but he considered the problem of general price level as unimportant. What was important was the quantity of goods exchanged and not the quantity of money or the resultant price level. For it was the volume of transactions which determined the circulation and not the circulation which determined the volume of transactions. When commerce was active the velocity of the circulation of money increased ; when commerce was not active the velocity decreased. Or, as Boisguilbert often put it, money " stops, dislodges, and runs along with consumption ". Where there was very much consumption, " a little silver on account of its frequent appearances, passes for a very large quantity of specie " ; but when consumption was diminishing " silver stops immediately ". In short, it was consumption " that leads the march " of money. Boisguilbert's important works were printed, under the title, *Le détail de la France* (1697, 1707, 2nd edition, 1712, reprinted with a critical note in D. Daire's *Economistes financiers du xviiie siècle*, Paris, 1843). Montesquieu is known as one of the early advocates of the quantity theory of money. (See his *The Spirit of Laws*, published first in French, Geneva, 1748, English edition tr. by Thomas Nugent, new edition by J. V. Prichard, London, 1909. The reference is to the 1909 edition, pp. 54–6.) He also advanced the doctrine that money stimulates trade. (See 1909 ed., p. 56.)

for a continuous disequilibrium. In the second and the third propositions, there is at least the implied recognition of the tendency of money and trade to establish equilibrium. Clearly that view is contradictory of the view embodied in the first proposition. The attempt to reconcile the contradiction brings us to the last proposition, that is that the employment of some artificial means could prevent the theoretically surplus bullion from entering into effective circulation and thus preserve the state of disequilibrium. The first proposition is common to all mercantilists. The second proposition is found partly in Mun and partly in the leading participants in the protectionist controversy. The third and the fourth propositions, as already explained, originate with Petty. But the credit for putting all those elements together and formulating a complete semi-equilibrium theory of international price relationships must be given to three eminent mercantilists—Jacob Vanderlint, Richard Cantillon, and Joseph Harris.[1]

Vanderlint subscribed to the quantity theory of money but in a somewhat different form. He equated the national stock of money not to the volume of commodities but to the number of people inhabiting the country.[2] Moreover, he saw clearly that with the possible exception of a country with silver mines,[3] a country which trades with others could not have a price level permanently higher than that of foreign countries. For example, if we were to open trade with those who could produce everything cheaper than we did, " they would bring us all sorts of Goods so cheap, that our Manufacture would be at an End, till the Money they would by this means get of us rais'd the Prices of their Things so much, and our Want of Money should fall ours to such a Degree, that we could go on with our Manufacture as cheap as they ; and then Trade would stand between that Nation to us, as it dotli between us and other Nations who mutually take Goods of each other." [4] In other words, among trading nations there was a tendency for prices to establish an equilibrium. That being so, was

---

[1] Before them there were only some fragmentary statements of a certain part of this theory. See, for example, John Houghton, *A Collection of Letters* . . . vol. ii (London, 1683), pp. 97–9, 115 ; William Wood, *A Survey of Trade*, pp. 329–373.
[2] Vanderlint, *Money Answers All Things* (London, 1734), p. 3.
[3] Ibid., pp. 52–3.
[4] Ibid., p. 46 and *passim*.

it possible for a nation to increase its stock of the precious metals ? He pointed out that there were two ways out of the dilemma. The first was that the nation could hoard the stocks of the precious metals obtained from trade, for—

> by thus keeping so much of those Metals out of Trade . . . it will give so much greater Employment . . . and prevent our Markets from rising so high, as to hinder the Exportation of our Commodities, or give too great Encouragement to the Importation of foreign Goods.[1]

He accordingly cited with approval the East Indian practice of hoarding silver and argued that it enabled the Indians permanently to maintain a state of low prices and a favourable balance of trade. The second method was to bring more land under cultivation and increase the production of the country so as to create greater abundance and thus check the rise in prices. The mere increase in production would act directly upon prices, while the subsistence thereby afforded to a larger population would act indirectly to the same effect, because the larger population, according to Vanderlint, implied an increase in the demand for money.[2] However, we must distinguish the latter proposition from the proposition that money stimulates trade, for in Vanderlint's theory the increase in the demand for money is produced by an extraneous factor, while in the theory that money stimulates trade the compensation is automatic and incidental.

Vanderlint's view of the functions of banking is very suggestive. He considered that banknotes produced the same effects as metallic money :—

> Banking, so far as one is paid with the Money of another, that is, where more Cash Notes are circulated, than all the Cash the Bankers are really possessed of will immediately answer and make good ; I say, so long as this Credit is maintained, it hath the same Effect, as if there was so much more Cash really circulating and divided amongst the People ; and will be attended with these Consequences, that as the Price of things will hence be rais'd, it must and will make us the Market, to receive the Commodities of every Country whose Prices of Things are cheaper than ours . . . [and hence] turn

---

[1] *Money Answers All Things*, p. 94.
[2] Ibid., p. 6 and *passim*.

the Balance of Trade against us, which will diminish the Cash of the Nation.[1]

If that were so, in order to maintain our stock of money, we must discourage the establishment of institutions of banking.[2] At about the same time (1734), Cantillon completed his famous *Essai*.[3] The practical value of the work and the influence that it exercised upon economic thought were very great. It has sometimes been called " the most important work on economics before the *Wealth of Nations* ". It is of importance in the study of the theory of international price relationships, because we find in it the best formulation of the semi-equilibrium theory.

Before examining his doctrine on international trade it is desirable that we should briefly describe his theory of value and production. He was probably the first economist who drew a sharp distinction between intrinsic value and market value.[4] According to him, the real or intrinsic value of a commodity was " proportionable to the Land and Labour that enters into their production ". It was only the market value of things which " varies with their plenty or scarcity according to the demand ".[5] Silver was no exception. Therefore, he criticized Locke and other English writers for neglecting the real values of commodities and taking account of only their market prices. The quantity theory of money, he argued, applied only to market prices.[6] Even so, in relating the quantity of money to the quantity of commodities three important factors had to be taken into consideration. First, as some commodities in the market could be, or had to be, sold in other markets, the quantity of the commodities was by no means an absolute factor.[7] Secondly, allowance had to be made for the rapidity of the circulation, for " an acceleration or greater rapidity in circulation of money in exchange, is equivalent to an increase of actual money up to a point ".[8] Finally, it was necessary to bear in mind that " the Bankers or

<hr />

[1] *Money Answers All Things*, p. 5.   [2] Ibid., p. 95 n.
[3] Richard Cantillon (1680 ?–1734), *Essai sur la Nature du Commerce en Général*, written about 1734, first published in French in 1775. We have used the edition issued with an English translation by Henry Higgs (London, 1931). Cantillon was a great banker and speculator of his time. For a detailed account of his life, see Higgs's ed. of the *Essai*, pp. 331–389.   [4] *Essai*, Higgs's edition, part i, ch. x.   [5] Ibid., p. 97.
[6] Ibid., p. 117.   [7] Ibid., part ii, ch. i ; see also p. 161.
[8] Ibid., p. 161. See also part ii, ch. iii, and ch. iv. His treatment of rapidity of circulation is the same as that of Petty.

Goldsmiths contribute to accelerate the circulation of money ".[1] The second point is of interest as one of the first *direct* association of the velocity of money with the problem of the value of money. It is true that the concept of the velocity of circulation of money is found in the writings of Potter, Petty, and Locke. But Potter's concept of " revolution of money " is not very clearly stated. The formulations of the concept by Petty and Locke, though excellent, are not directly related to the problem of the value of money.

What was more important, however, was the problem of the actual path through which a change in the volume of money led to changes in the price and income structure, or, to put the same thing in other words, the question " in what way and in what proportion the increase of money raises prices ". His answer to that question is so excellent that we must quote it at some length :—

I consider in general that an increase of actual money causes in a State a corresponding increase of consumption which gradually brings about increased prices. If the increase of actual money comes from Mines of gold and silver in the State the Owner of these Mines, the Adventurers, the Smelters, the Refiners, and all the other workers will increase their expenses in proportion to their gains. They will consume . . . more . . . commodities. They will consequently give employment to several Mechanicks who had not so much to do before and who for the same reason will increase their expenses : all this increase of expense in Meat, Wine, Wool, etc., diminishes of necessity the share of the other inhabitants of the State who do not participate at first in the wealth of the Mines in question. The altercation of the Market, or the demand for Meat, Wine, Wool, etc., being more intense than usual, will not fail to raise their prices. These high prices will determine the Farmers to employ more land to produce them in another year : these same Farmers will profit by this rise of prices and will increase the expenditure of their Families like the others. Those then who will suffer from this dearness and increased consumption will be first of all the Landowners, during the term of their Leases, then their Domestic Servants and all the Workmen or fixed Wage-earners who support their families on their wages. All these must diminish their expenditure in proportion to the new consumption, which will compel a large number of them to emigrate to seek a living elsewhere. The Landowners will dismiss many of them, and the rest will demand an increase

[1] Ibid., p. 301.

of wages to enable them to live as before. It is thus, approximately, that a considerable increase of Money from the Mines increases consumption, and by diminishing the number of inhabitants entails a greater expense among those who remain.[1]

To the relationship between an increase of money and a rise in prices he gave two important qualifications. The first was a proposition of Montchrétien that the rise in prices is not always in proportion to the increase in money.[2] The second was that since the increased expenditure arising out of the increase in money was " directed more or less to certain kinds of products or merchandise according to the idea of those who acquire the money, market prices will rise more for certain things than for others, however abundant the money may be ".[3] He accordingly presented the quantity theory in the following modified form :—

An increase of money circulating in a State always causes there an increase of consumption and a higher standard of expenses. But the dearness caused by this money does not affect equally all the kinds of products and merchandise proportionably to the quantity of money, unless what is added continues in the same circulation as the money before, that is to say unless those who offered in the Market one ounce of silver be the same and only ones who now offer two ounces when the amount of money in circulation is doubled in quantity, and that is hardly ever the case. I conceive that when a large surplus of money is brought into a State the new money gives a new turn to consumption and even a new speed to circulation. But it is not possible to say exactly to what extent.[4]

We may now take up his theory of international price relationships. He pointed out that the quantity of money circulating in a trading country might be increased in one of the following ways : (a) exploitation of mines ; (b) subsidies from foreign powers ; (c) invisible items, such as travellers' expenses, etc. ; (d) a favourable balance of trade ; (e) borrowing ; and (f) violence and arms.[5] He then gave the first detailed explanation of the mechanism by which an increase in money would bring about changes

[1] *Essai*, Higgs's edition, pp. 163–5.
[2] " By doubling the quantity of money in a State the prices of products and merchandise are not always doubled. A River which runs and winds about in its bed will not flow with double the speed when the amount of the water is doubled." *Essai*, p. 177.
[3] *Essai*, Higgs's edition, p. 179.
[4] Ibid., p. 181.   [5] Ibid., pp. 181, 191, 195.

in the balance of trade. In case the increase of the precious metals was due to the first cause, the income of the owners and the labourers connected with the mines would be augmented proportionately. They might either lend the additional income at interest or increase their expenditures. "All this money, whether lent or spent, will enter into circulation and will not fail to raise the prices of products and merchandise in all these channels of circulation which it enters." As market prices rise, "this will naturally induce several people to import many manufactured articles made in foreign countries, where they will be found very cheap " and exportation would, moreover, be checked. The balance of trade would then turn against the country with the silver mines, the new money obtained from the mines would then be drained out of the country, and it would find itself in a state of " poverty and misery ". Spain was cited as a typical example of such a country.[1] The second, third, fifth and sixth, methods of increasing the quantity of money would also prove disastrous. But if the increase of money proceeded from the balance of foreign trade, the situation of the country would be somewhat different, because, for a time at least, " this annual increase of money will enrich a great number of Merchants and Undertakers in the State, and will give employment to numerous Mechanicks and workmen who furnish the commodities sent to foreigner, from whom the money is drawn."[2] Nevertheless, should an increase of money from the balance of trade be considerable, it would not fail to increase consumption, raise the price of everything, to overturn the balance and drain off the money that was in excess.[3]

From the doctrines laid down in the preceding paragraphs, it logically follows that there is an optimum amount for the stock of money circulating in a country and that any sum in excess of it would automatically flow out. Those doctrines include (a) a balance of trade theory that postulates that a favourable balance of trade would cause an inflow of metals, (b) a quantity theory of money that postulates that an inflow of money metals would bring about

[1] *Essai*, Higgs's ed., pp. 163–7.
[2] Ibid., p. 167.
[3] Ibid., p. 169. For the relationship between the rate of interest, on the one hand, and the quantity of money and the balance of trade, on the other, see part ii, ch. ix and x, especially pp. 215, 219.

a rise in prices, and (c) the theory that a rise in prices would turn the balance of trade against the country. For those reasons a country could not continue for long to import bullion upon a very large scale and there was consequently a tendency for prices and trade to establish an equilibrium.[1] He was, however, of the opinion that the leaders of the state should not allow economic factors to take their own course but should intervene to preserve the abundance of money. He gave two arguments in favour of the retention of plenty of money in a state. The first is that a country with plenty of money and a higher level of prices, could, by selling dear and buying cheap, enjoy more advantageous barter terms of trade. For instance, he said :—

> The increase in the quantity of silver circulating in a State gives it great advantages in foreign trade so long as this abundance of money lasts. The State then exchanges a small quantity of produce and labour for a greater.[2]

He considered that condition as being maintainable only during a transitional period. His second argument is that " the revenues of the State where money abounds, are raised more easily and in comparatively much larger amount. This gives the State in case of war or dispute, the means to gain all sorts of advantages over its adversaries with whom money is scarce ".[3]

How, then, is the money obtained to be preserved ? His reply to the question is very clear :—

> When a State expands by trade and the abundance of money raises the price of Land and Labour, the Prince or the Legislator ought to withdraw money from circulation, keep it for emergencies, and try to retard its circulation by every means except compulsion and bad faith, so as to forestall the too great dearness of its articles and prevent the drawbacks of luxury.[4]

---

[1] But when a country, for any reason whatever, has a constant balance due to another country, the prices and the money in circulation cannot be equal in those two countries, and " the inequality is always relative to the balance or debt ". The prices in the receiving country would ultimately be higher to the extent that the paying country would be able to pay its debts in commodities. Therefore the receiving country would be benefited in two ways : first it has a constant income to receive ; and second, owing to its high level of prices, it " will exchange a smaller amount of Land and Labour with the Foreigner for a larger amount so long as these circumstances continue." (*Essai*, Higgs's edition, p. 159.) See pp. 151–9.

[2] *Essai*, p. 235.   [3] Ibid., pp. 189, 235.   [4] Ibid., p. 185.

Furthermore, the circulation of banknotes should be discouraged.[1]

In the main, the views of Harris[2] are similar to those of Cantillon. Like the latter, he declared that " things in general are valued . . . in proportion to the land, labour, and skill that are requisite to produce them ".[3] He, too, subscribed to the quantity theory of money but made some modifications of a minor character.[4] He held that there must be a due proportion of money to the monetary needs of a nation :—

> Where money is grown into great plenty, whatever be the causes of that over-plenty ; labour and all sorts of manufactures will grow dear, too dear for foreign markets : And at the same time that the exportation of home-commodities is decreasing, that of bullion for foreign goods will be increasing ; till at length the tide of the over-plenty of money hath spent its self. . . . Commerce will settle the due proportion of money every-where . . . in respect to the whole wealth and traffic of any country.[5]

He adhered, nevertheless, to the mercantilistic doctrine that a state should preserve its stock of bullion and gave three reasons for that view. The first is that " if the tide of money is a running out ; during this ebb, trade will stagnate, some merchants and shopkeepers will break, some manufacturers will be laid aside, many hands will be unemployed, and murmurs and complaints will be heard among all sorts of people concerned in trade ".[6] The second is the barter terms argument that a nation whose money is decreasing " would be under a great disadvantage, in the purchasing of foreign commodities for ready cash." [7] But those two reasons would not operate long, because the factors are merely of a transitional nature. Therefore,

---

[1] *Essai*, pp. 305, 307, 311, 319.
[2] Joseph Harris (1702–1764) is said " to have been a working black-smith at his native place, but to have removed at an early age to London ". In London he became known as a writer on navigation, trigonometry, optics, and astronomy. He probably held some subordinate post in the Mint before 1748. In that year he was appointed assay master of the Mint. *An Essay upon Money and Coins* was written by him probably about 1750, and was first published in 1757–8 in London.
[3] *Essay* (written *c.* 1750, published London, 1757–8 in two parts). We have used the reprint in McCullock's *A Select Collection of Scarce and Valuable Tracts on Money, etc.*, London, 1856. The reference is to p. 350.
[4] Ibid., pp. 391, 396–8.   [5] Ibid., pp. 406, 407.
[6] Ibid., p. 402.   [7] Ibid., p. 406.

his case rests mostly upon the third reason that the retention would mean " a real increase of wealth ".[1] The way out of the situation created was " to keep that bullion in a dead stock, either by turning it into plate or any other method, so as to prevent its getting into trade as money ". If that was done, " it may continue to go on increasing in more bullion." [2]

II. SUMMARY

The period during which mercantilism was the basis of economic thought witnessed, on the one hand, important speculations upon such problems as money and foreign exchange, a knowledge of which is essential to an understanding of the subject of international price relationships and, on the other hand, the gradual emergence of many important doctrines in the theory of international price relationships. Progress in regard to the latter was in connection with the discussion of such problems as why the national stock of money should be increased, how it might be increased and what would be the effects of its being increased. First in examining the effect of an enormous flow of specie from the New to the Old World, Bodin discovered a causal relation between an increase of the money metals in a country and a rise in its prices. Both Hales and the bullionists made contributions to the subject when they were investigating how the precious metals of a country might be increased or decreased. Hales presented the doctrine that a country with relatively low prices would sell cheap and buy dear and thereby turn the balance of trade against itself. The bullionists rightly recognized the existence of certain relationships between the rates of exchange and the international movement of specie, but they went too far in concluding that the rates of exchange were the *initial* cause of the latter. In the hands of Malynes, the doctrines of Hales, Bodin and the bullionists were combined to form the theory of international price relationships, with which his name is associated. Mun and other members of the balance of trade school also were concerned with the means of increasing the stock of precious metals of a country.

[1] *Essay*, p. 404.
[2] Ibid., p. 404. Harris's work contains one of the best statements of the balance-of-trade theory of foreign exchanges ; see ibid., pt. i, ch. iii.

They were of the opinion that a favourable balance of trade alone would be the true cause of an inflow of specie. Furthermore, Mun pointed out that selling cheap and buying dear would turn the balance of trade of a country in its favour and not against it. Therein lies the germ of the theory of equilibrium in international price relationships. The origin of the equilibrium theory might also be traced in the doctrine of the existence of a due proportion between the national stock of money and the monetary needs of a country. That doctrine was first found in the work of Petty. Both the views of Mun and the doctrine of Petty were repeated by the participants in the Protectionist controversy and were finally combined by Vanderlint, Cantillon, and Harris to form what we call the "semi-equilibrium theory". There was still a third theory, i.e. the theory that money stimulates trade and production, with Potter, Law, and Forbonnais as its advocates. Unlike Malynes, Mun, or Cantillon, the advocates of that doctrine refused to accept the quantity theory of money. They argued that an increase in the volume of money encouraged trade and that an increase in trade would involve an increase in the demand for money and consequently the increase in the volume of money would not affect prices or the balance of trade.

Those are the three dominant mercantilistic doctrines of international price relationships. Each of them in its right place contains an element of truth. The doctrine that money stimulates trade is correct in the short run, especially when it is applied to a country where there is great unemployment of resources. It is erroneous, however, to suppose that a continuous inflow of the money metals could permanently stimulate trade and production to the extent that the consequential increase of the demand for money would be enough to offset entirely the increase in the supply of money. In the long run there is always a casual relationship between money and prices. Furthermore, it might be possible that the very stimulation of trade and production causes the rise in prices and incomes. The Malynesian theory is true only of a country in such exceptional circumstances that both its demand for its imports and the foreign demand for its exports are inelastic. It is only when the elasticity of both those two demands were, to use the terminology of mathematical economics, less than unity that a lowering of the general level of prices would cause an unfavourable and not a favourable balance of trade. The Vanderlint–Cantillon theory is fundamentally sound in principle. Had its advocates been willing to agree to freedom of trade, they would have come to the same conclusion as the classical economists. But as to the policy of artificially keeping the imported specie from going into active circulation, it is questionable to what extent it is correct. Moreover, that policy is no guarantee that there would be no decrease in the stock of the money metals in foreign countries and a consequent fall in their levels of prices, followed by a change of the balance of trade in their favour.

Unlike Mun and his school, Barbon considered the difference between the price of bullion abroad and the value of money at home as the sole cause of the movement of specie from one country to other countries. He objected to the theory of Mun on the ground that the very notion of a balance of trade was obscure, if not fictitious.

The problem of the relative rates of interest and wages of labour had also been raised during the mercantilistic period. Pollexfen thought that high wages would injure trade and low wages maintain a favourable balance of trade. Child, on the other hand, pointed out that high wages were a proof of the prosperity of the country and were by no means harmful to trade.

On the subject of money mercantilistic writers divide themselves into advocates of the " legal theory ", which was so vigorously presented by Barbon, and what might be called " catallactic theorists ", that is, those whose theory of the value of money can be fitted into some theory of the values of commodities. Most of the latter subscribe to the quantity theory of money. The quantity theory, however, usually implies the assumption of *ceteris paribus* or the supposition that things other than prices were not bound to change as a result of the change in the volume of money. The permissibility of making that assumption was questioned by Law and his school, who went so far as to reject entirely the quantity theory. Although Law's doctrine of money must to a large extent be discarded, he must be remembered for having called attention to the importance of the dynamic aspects of the problem of money. The question how an increase of money, consequential on an inflow of specie, would work out its effects upon the price structure of a country was investigated by Cantillon and Forbonnais. The indirect chain of effects connecting money and prices through changes in the interest rates and the volume of borrowing was more or less suggested by Law, who declared that as the quantity of money increased, " Money being easier borrowed, Merchants would deal for a greater Value," etc. But unlike the descriptions of the indirect mechanism by the writers of the nineteenth century, Law was of the opinion that the result of an increase of borrowing was a fall and not a rise in prices.

Considering the mercantilistic writers as a whole, it must be noted that they furnished most of the materials, out of which the classical theory that we are going to deal with in the next chapter was evolved. For example, they provided a quantity theory of money, a doctrine of a due proportion between the national stock of money and the monetary needs of a nation, doctrines of international specie movements, etc. Moreover, the doctrine that " raising the money " would raise the prices of all things accordingly and also force up the rates of foreign exchange to the same extent—a doctrine which has a very close resemblance to the Ricardian theory of foreign exchange—was promulgated by Locke and others. But none of them, with perhaps one possible exception,[1] attacked the real aspects of the problem. They were left to be faced by Ricardo and his school.

[1] That was James D. Steuart. See his *Principles of Political Economy*, London, 1767 (in two volumes).

CHAPTER III

FROM DAVID HUME TO J. S. MILL :
THE DEVELOPMENT OF THE CLASSICAL THEORIES

I. DAVID HUME

While mercantilism was popular in the period described in the preceding chapter, in the latter half of the eighteenth century it gradually came to be considered as a hindrance to economic progress. About the year 1750 many of the mercantilist doctrines were criticized and new systems of thought were advanced in their stead. The most important of the thinkers, who were responsible for the downfall of the mercantilistic system of thought, are David Hume, the French Physiocrats, and Adam Smith. The contribution of Hume lies mainly in his theory of international price relationships, which served the purpose of a refutation of the theoretical foundations of mercantilism. In the writings of the Physiocrats and Adam Smith are reflected the existing economic and social conditions of France and England respectively. They attacked the mercantilists mainly on practical grounds.

Economic conceptions underwent partial change in the hands of Hume. While retaining the mercantilist preconception that the interests of the State and of its subjects were not always in harmony,[1] he brought forward the view that the growth of commerce (both domestic and foreign) was a common interest of both, because it had the effect of " augmenting the power of the State as well as the riches and happiness of the subjects ".[2] On the subject of commerce among nations, he rejected the view that a State could make progress only at the expense of other states and ventured to assert " that the encrease of riches and commerce in any one nation . . . commonly promotes the riches and commerce of all its neighbours ; and that a state can scarcely carry its trade and industry very far,

---

[1] Hume, *Political Discourses*, 1752, reprinted with his other works in *Essays and Treatises on Several Subjects*, 1770 ed. The reference is to *Essays*, vol. ii, pp. 8, 10 (Essay of Commerce).
[2] *Essays*, pp. 15, 16–17.

where all the surrounding states are buried in ignorance, sloth, and barbarism ".[1] He saw the real source of wealth in labour [2] and thought that money was but an instrument of trade.[3] He accepted the view that a state would be at an advantage in wars and negotiations with foreign states if it possessed plenty of money [4] and that in the transitional or intermediate period between the acquisition of money and the rise of prices, " the encreasing quantity of gold and silver is favourable to industry," [5] but he did not attach the same importance to those arguments as the mercantilists.

It was his theory of international price relationships which made him a critic of mercantilism. His theory was based on a rigid quantity theory of money. He considered " a maxim almost self-evident that the prices of everything depend on the proportion between commodities and money ", but he limited the money side to " the money which circulates " and the commodity side to the " commodities which come or may come to market ".[6] He then applied the quantity theory beyond the limits of any one country and formulated what is sometimes known as the classical theory of international price adjustments. The main point of the theory is that there was a *natural* distribution of money among nations and that, if that natural distribution was disturbed, it would be *automatically* corrected mainly by changes in the income and price structures of the trading nations. For instance, he said :—

Suppose four-fifths of all the · money in Britain to be annihilated in one night . . . what would be the consequence ? Must not the price of all labour and commodities sink in proportion. . . ? What nation could then dispute with us in any foreign market, or pretend to navigate or to sell manufactures at the same price, which to us would afford sufficient profit ? In how little time, therefore, must this bring back the money which we have lost, and raise us to the level of all the neighbouring nations ? Where, after we have arrived, we immediately lost the advantage of the cheapness

[1] *Essays*, p. 106 (Essay of the Jealousy of Trade).
[2] Ibid., p. 13 (Essay of Commerce). Both Cantillon and Harris considered Land and Labour as the only two sources of wealth.
[3] Ibid., pp. 43 f., 47 f. (Essay of Money).
[4] Ibid., p. 43.
[5] Ibid., pp. 49, 51, and 60.
[6] Ibid., pp. 54 and 56.

of labour and commodities ; and the farther flowing in of money is stopped by our fulness and repletion.[1]

Thus a country could not continue to maintain an inflow or outflow of specie for a very long time, and the mercantilists would defeat their own end by advocating an increase of the national stock of money. That led him to the conclusion that trade must be mutual and that a country that trades must buy as well as sell.

It should be noted that the mechanism described by him in the passage quoted in the preceding paragraph was not limited to the correction of disturbances originating from the money side. It was applied by Hume also to the adjustment of deficits in the balance of trade that originated on the commodity side.[2] Thus, in justifying the proposition that trade must be mutual, he showed that if the exports and imports of a country were not equal, the mechanism, which corrected disturbances arising from the relative excess of metallic money, would work to bring about an equality in exports and imports. He said that there was " a happy concurrence of causes in human affairs, which check the growth of trade and riches and hinder them from being confined entirely to one people ; as might naturally at first be dreaded from the advantages of an established commerce ". If a state had a favourable balance of trade, it would naturally have its money increased and the prices of its commodities raised so that the poorer states were enabled " to undersel the richer in all foreign markets ".[3] He drew attention, moreover, to another factor, which helps to bring international price relationships into equilibrium :—

> There is another cause, though more limited in its operation, which checks the wrong balance of trade, to every particular nation to which the kingdom trades. When we import more goods than we export, the exchange turns against us, and this becomes a new encouragement to export ; as much as the charge of carriage and insurance of the money which becomes due would amount to. For the exchange can never rise higher than that sum.[4]

[1] *Essays*, pp. 83–4 (Essay of the Balance of Trade).
[2] Professor Angell has wrongly attributed the first attempt to apply this mechanism of the adjustment of disturbance originating on the commodity side to Thornton ; see his *Theory of International Prices*, pp. 45 f.
[3] *Essays*, pp. 44–5 (Essay of Money).
[4] Ibid., p. 85 n. (Essay of the Balance of Trade).

Upon the basis of those considerations, he came to the conclusion that there was a natural distribution of money among trading nations :—

> The same causes, which would correct these exorbitant inequalities . . . must prevent their happening in the common course of nature, and must for ever, in all the neighbouring nations preserve money nearly proportionable to the art and industry of each nation.[1]

We shall designate that doctrine as " Hume's Law " in honour of its ingenious author. It is true that the essential features of the doctrine are found in the writings of the later mercantilists, but it is only in the hands of Hume that the inevitability of a tendency towards equilibrium and the *automatic character* of the working of the correctives take definite form. Furthermore, he was the first economist to point out that the rate of exchange is also a corrective of disturbances.

Hume made another important contribution to the theory of international price relationships, that was his description of the chains of events connecting money and price. His analysis is so excellent that it is worth quoting in full :—

> To account, then, for this phenomenon we must consider that, though the high price of commodities be a necessary consequence of the encrease of gold and silver, yet it follows not immediately upon that encrease ; but some time is required before the money circulates through the whole state, and makes its effect felt on all ranks of people. At first, no alteration is perceived ; by degrees the price rises, first of one commodity, then of another ; till the whole at last reaches a just proportion with the new quantity of specie which is in the kingdom. In my opinion, it is only in this interval or intermediate situation between the acquisition of money and rise of prices, that the enhancing quantity of gold and silver is favourable to industry. . . . When any quantity of money is imported into a nation, it is not at first dispensed into many hands ; but is confined to coffers of a few persons, who immediately seek to employ it to the best advantage. Here are a set of manufacturers or merchants, we shall suppose, who have received returns of gold and silver for goods which they send to Cadiz. They are thereby enabled to employ more workmen than formerly, who never dreamed of demanding higher

[1] *Essays*, pp. 84, 85.

wages, but are glad of employment from such good paymasters. If workmen become scarce, the manufacturer gives higher wages, but at first requires an encrease of labour ; and this is willingly submitted to by the artisan, who can now eat and drink better, to compensate his additional toil and fatigue. He carries his money to market, where he finds everything at the same price as formerly, but returns with greater quantity and of better kinds, for the use of his family. The farmer and gardener, finding that all their commodities are taken off, apply themselves with alacrity to the raising more ; and at the same time can afford to take better and more clothes from their tradesmen, whose price is the same as formerly, and their industry only whetted by so much new gain. . . . There is always an interval before matters be adjusted to their new situation ; and this interval is as pernicious to industry, when gold and silver are diminishing, as it is advantageous when these metals are encreasing.[1]

It will be observed that he (a) called attention to the importance of the *time* element ; (b) put the doctrine that money stimulates trade in its right place, that is, by considering it to be true " only in this interval or intermediate situation " ; and (c) presented an analysis of the mechanism connecting money and prices.

2.   THE PHYSIOCRATS AND ADAM SMITH

Although Hume furnished us with a theory of international price relationships which, to some economists, had " at a single stroke wrecked the balance of trade theory ", yet he established no new school of economic thought to take the place of that of the mercantilists. That task was left to the Physiocrats in France and Adam Smith in England.

The Physiocratic system was the outcome of the economic and financial conditions in France in the first half of the eighteenth century. In those days costly military expeditions abroad, ruinous extravagance, and a corrupt financial administration at home combined to impose upon the French people, especially the farmers, an unbearable burden of taxation. That, together with the fall of the prices of agricultural products, forced the farming populations to live below the standard of subsistence. The sharp contrast between widespread poverty, misery, and starvation on the one hand, and the luxurious life of the nobles on the

---

[1] *Essays*, pp. 49–51.

other, could not fail to evoke criticisms against the existing conditions. The Physiocrats were a group of those critics who thought that the prosperity of agriculture was essential to the opulence of the state. The agrarianism of the Physiocrats can best be shown by their conception of wealth and productiveness. They declared that agriculture alone was productive and that the land alone produced a *produit net* and hence was the only form of true wealth. The mercantilistic dogma that the precious metals were wealth and wealth *par excellence* was entirely rejected by them. Money was defined as merely a kind of *richesse relative ou seconde*. Commerce and industry, to which the mercantilists and the Colbertists had attached great importance, were described as being sterile or non-productive. International trade was considered as at best a *pis aller*.

As the Physiocrats concentrated their attention on agriculture and other internal economic activities, they naturally did not say very much about the problem of international trade. Yet, negatively, we find in the writings of many of them some very severe criticisms of the mercantilistic theory of foreign commerce. The ablest writer on this subject is le Mercier de la Rivière.[1]

He started with a refutation of the mercantilistic conception that the wealth of a nation rested on its foreign trade. He said that " commerce is an exchange of values for equal values " and hence there could be no increase of wealth by foreign trade.[2] Yet foreign trade *might* be beneficial to a country if it lacked within itself a sufficient number of consumers to ensure a *bon prix* for agricultural products and if foreign lands could furnish it with consumers and hence the best possible price for its products. The highest possible price would, in turn, enable it to accelerate the reproduction of the country and maintain its population by agriculture. It was because a country must sell to foreign countries what it could not consume, and buy from them their products which it could not produce, that international trade was both necessary and beneficial.[3] Trade, therefore, must be considered as *une multitude de ventes*

---

[1] Rivière, *L'ordre natural et essential des sociétés politiques*, London and Paris, 1767. See also the works of Quesney (the founder of the school) of Condillac and of Turgot.

[2] *L'ordre*, p. 345.

[3] *L'ordre*, pp. 347–349. Foreign trade would be harmful to a state if it did not procure the best possible price for the cultivators : pp. 349–350.

et d'achat. One could not buy unless one sold, and one could not sell unless one bought. " Every seller must also be a buyer." [1] Hence the ambitions of the mercantilists to obtain a favourable balance of trade, that is to be a seller but not a buyer, was illusory. Moreover, even if a country succeeded in getting a large quantity of money it would not be able to keep it. He said :—

> Well, I will drown the clamour of all your blind and stupid policies. Suppose that I gave you all the money which circulates among the nations with whom you trade. Imagine it all in your possession. What would you do with it ? You must lose so many foreign consumers that you would be ruined by it. . . . A part [of your production] must remain unsold and become superfluous. From that moment your cultivators will not only sell in a less quantity, but also at a lower price, because the result of over-abundance is a diminution of price.[2]

At the same time the excessive dearth of everything at home gave a chance for the inflow of a great quantity of foreign merchandise.[3] That was clearly very near to the theory of Hume. He also held a doctrine of free trade. His reason for freedom of trade was simply the belief that it was only through freedom of commerce that good prices could be secured for agricultural products.[4]

The conditions which were responsible for the anti-mercantilistic views in England were entirely different from those in France. By the time mercantilism was challenged industries in England had been developed to

---

[1] Ibid., pp. 335–340. [2] Ibid., p. 390. [3] Ibid., p. 391.
[4] Isaac de Bacalan was a more thorough-going free-trader. He pointed out that the advantage of international trade consisted in the interchange of commodities and that a surplus balance of money was of no advantage except it was used to exchange for goods. He was of the opinion that free trade was advantageous to a country even though other countries refused to let their trade free. He had also a doctrine of international adjustment very similar to that of Hume. To answer the question what would happen if a country had a favourable balance of trade, he said :—
" Croit-on de bonne foi que cette situation serait durable, et que cet État absorberait peu à tout l'argent qui existe dans le monde ? Non, sans doute. L'augmentation de la quantité d'argent en diminuerait le prix ; le luxe croîtrait et avec lui la consommation des denrées soit nationales, soit étrangères. Il en résulterait donc que cet État transporterait aux autres une moindre quantité de denrées et en retirerait une plus grande quantité. Ainsi il serait obligé à son tour de payer en argent et la circulation se rétablirait."
See his " Paradoxes philosophiques sur la liberté du commerce entre les nations ", MS., 1764, first published in F. Sauvaire-Jourdan, *Isaac de Bacalan et les idees libre-echangistes en France*, Paris, 1903. The reference is to p. 43.

G

such a stage that they were in general superior to those of other countries, did not fear competition from abroad and consequently no longer needed the support of the state. Intervention of the state had become a hindrance instead of a help. Therefore, unlike the Physiocrats, who were more agrarians than free traders, the English school was purely a free-trade school. Adam Smith was its founder. His principal contribution to the theory of international trade was his doctrine of the reciprocal advantages of the international division of labour. It is true that we can find that doctrine in the writings of some liberal mercantilists and of many Physiocrats, but no one before him had demonstrated the soundness of the doctrine with such a wealth of fact and argument or formulated it with so much clarity.[1] In accordance with his doctrine he advocated freedom in international trade, because free trade would ensure the best division of labour among nations.[2] In regard to the theory of international price relationships he merely said :—

> When the quantity of gold and silver imported into any country exceeds the effectual demand, no vigilance of government can prevent their exportation. . . . If, on the contrary, in any particular country their quantity fell short of the effectual demand, so as to raise their price above that of the neighbouring countries, the government would have no occasion to take any pain to import them.[3]

The real implication of that passage is the same as Hume's doctrine, although Smith said nothing about the intermediate mechanism and although the passage might mislead the reader on some points. As Smith was intimately acquainted with the work of Hume and once in his *Lectures* had approvingly presented an abstract of the latter's view,[4]

[1] Adam Smith, *An Inquiry into the Nature and Causes of the Wealth of Nations*, 1776 ; Cannan's edition used. Book iv, chs. 1–3, pp. 413, 453, and *passim*. He also accepted Rivière's argument in favour of foreign trade that " it carries out that surplus part of the produce of their land and labour for which there is no demand among them, and brings back in return for it something else for which there is a demand ". Ibid., p. 413.
[2] See C. Gide and C. Rist, *History of Economic Doctrines*, translated by R. Richards, London, 1915, 1928, pp. 98–9.
[3] *Wealth of Nations*, Cannan's edition, p. 402, book iv, ch. 1. " It is partly owing to the easy transportation of gold and silver from the places where they abound to those where they are wanted, that the price of those metals does not fluctuate continually like that of the greater part of other commodities " (p. 403). See also pp. 188 f., 322.
[4] *Lectures on Justice, Police, Revenue, and Arms delivered in the University of Glasgow*, edited by Edwin Cannan, Oxford, 1896, p. 197.

he could hardly have omitted entirely Hume's doctrine from his celebrated essay.[1] Let us now turn to his doctrines concerning money. Like the Physiocrats, he attacked the mercantilistic preconception that money was wealth *par excellence.* To him money was merely a commodity which served as an instrument to facilitate the circulation of goods and commodities.[2] It was the " great wheel of circulation ", but it formed no part of the net revenue of the nation. " The revenue of the society consists altogether in those goods and not in the wheel which circulates them." Moreover, it required no small expense for its erection and support. Therefore, " the gold and silver money which circulates in any country may very properly be compared to a highway which, while it circulates and carries to market all the grass and corn of the country, produces itself not a single pile of either." If so, in case we could find " a new wheel, which it costs less both to erect and to maintain than the old one ", we must make an improvement of the net revenue of the community. It was on that ground that he considered paper money as a useful institution, for paper money would perform the same work as metallic money and cost very little. According to him, the effect of the introduction of paper money was as follows : When a certain quantity of paper money was issued the total volume of national currency was increased by the same amount. If the original sum of metallic money was just sufficient to answer the " effectual demand " for a circulating medium in the country, its currency would, by the introduction of bank notes, " exceed " the effectual demand of the nation. According to the doctrine laid down above, the excessive part must flow out. As the paper cannot go abroad, gold alone will be exported.[3] With regard to the problem of the value of money his position was not definite. Generally speaking, he was of the opinion that the real value

---

[1] See also *Wealth of Nations*, Cannan's ed., p. 322. For Adam Smith's other ideas, see pp. 39, 71 ff., 99, 351 ff., of the same.

[2] He objected to " the theory of the store of value ", for the durability of a commodity was no reason for accumulating more of it than was wanted. He criticized also the " sinews of war " argument in favour of the accumulation of the precious metals. He said, " It is not always necessary to accumulate gold and silver, in order to enable a country to carry on foreign wars, and to maintain fleets and armies in distant countries. Fleets and armies are maintained, not with gold and silver, but with consumable goods." (See *Wealth o Nations*, Cannan's ed., pp. 405–9.)

[3] Ibid.. book iv. ch. 2.

of gold and silver depended on the quantity of labour embodied in it.[1] That is a labour-cost theory. He said very little, if anything, which constituted a quantity theory of money. One thing is made clear by his writings. That is that the value of a coin was determined by its metallic content, regardless of its nominal designation. He was, however, of the opinion that it was possible to have small occasional fluctuations in the market prices of gold and silver bullion. " But when, under all those occasional fluctuations, the market price either of gold or silver bullion continues for several years together steadily and constantly, either more or less above, or more or less below the mint price : we may be assured that this steady and constant, either superiority or inferiority of prices, is the effect of something in the state of the coin, which, at that time, renders a certain quantity of coin either of more value or of less value than the precise quantity of bullion which it ought to contain. The constancy and steadiness of the effect, supposes a proportionable constancy and steadiness in the cause." [2]

3. THE BANK RESTRICTION CONTROVERSY

More than two decades elapsed after the publication of the *Wealth of Nations* without any important contribution to the theory of international price relationships. Then came the wars between France and England, which started in the spring of 1793. The abnormal financial and monetary conditions caused by those wars, especially the suspension of specie payments by the Bank of England from 1797, naturally evoked much speculation both inside and outside political circles. That led to many important developments in the theory.[3] Among the causes responsible for the suspension of the convertibility of the note issue of the Bank of England were the following—

---

[1] Ibid., p. 34.
[2] *Wealth of Nations*, Cannan's ed., pp. 47–8.
[3] For detailed descriptions of the conditions during the Bank Restriction period see : H. D. Macleod, *The Theory and Practice of Banking*, 5th ed., London, 1892, ch. 9, 10 ; *The Theory of Credit*, 2nd ed., London, 1897, ch. 13 ; A. Andreades, *History of the Bank of England*, English translation, London, 1924, vol. i, part iv ; R. G. Hawtrey, *Currency and Credit*, 3rd ed., London, 1928, ch. 18 ; J. W. Angell, *The Theory of International Prices*, appendix A ; N. J. Silberling, " Financial and Monetary Policy of Great Britain during the Napoleonic Wars," in *Quarterly Journ. of Economics*, 1924 ; and " British Prices and Business Cycles, 1779–1850 " in *Review of Economic Statistics*, 1923.

(a) the continuous heavy remittances of the Government to foreign powers ;

(b) the growing demands of the Government on the Bank for the extension of credit (which the Bank could not resist) ;

(c) the adoption by the Bank of a policy of excessive contraction of its note issue and of the accommodation it afforded merchants as a result of its advances to the Government ;

(d) the general loss of confidence and the increasing demand for guineas, as a result of the general anxiety about the issue of the war and the contraction of credit ; and

(e) the bad harvests.

Those causes combined to depress the exchanges, which reached in May, 1795, the point at which it was profitable to export bullion and thus increase the internal as well as the external drain upon the metallic resources of the Bank of England and thus to bring about the final suspension of specie payments in 1797. So grave and far-reaching an event could not fail to arouse much controversy. People who were unable to obtain credit that they needed from the Bank and those who were opposed to the Bank on general grounds united in attributing the difficulties of the time to the monopoly of the Bank and saw the explanation of the currency crisis in the policy of excessive contraction of credit. The apologists of the Bank, in replying to the criticisms, called attention to the expanding demands of the Government on the Bank for credit and pointed out that its directors were not the real masters of their own policy. They held that the Bank had rendered very valuable services to the progress of the nation and that its monopoly should not be violated.

For the first few years under the Bank Restriction Act everything went on smoothly. The public avowal of the vast majority of bankers and business men of their decision to support the credit of the Bank and the acceptance of the notes of the Bank by the Government in payment of taxes at par reinforced the confidence of the public. The directors acted with great caution and their policy of contracting credit, which had been in operation all through the year 1796, gradually made itself felt. In the years 1797 and 1798, moreover, government remittances abroad were much less than in the preceding years. Those circumstances, together with the unusually good harvests in the years 1797 and 1798 could not fail to produce good monetary conditions. The exchanges soon rose high in favour of England, specie began to flow in and the cash reserve of the Bank continued to increase. By the middle of the year 1799, however, adverse conditions began to set in. The exchanges declined all through the summer of 1799 ; and in May, 1800, gold began to be quoted at a premium in London. Prices, which had been climbing steadily since 1794, rose sharply. All those developments furnished new grounds for an attack upon the Bank. Walter Boyd based his case against the Bank upon those facts. In December, 1801, he sent a letter to Pitt, denouncing the policies of the Bank.[1] He called attention to three facts : First, an increase in the prices of almost all articles of necessity, convenience, and luxury, and indeed of almost every species of exchangeable value " has been gradually taking place during the last two years, and has recently arrived at so great a height " ;[2] second, gold in home markets had a premium of about 9⅛ per cent[3] ; and third, the exchange with Hamburg was about 9 per cent against England.[4] He thought that the existence of those three conditions was a sufficient proof of the existence of a state of depreciation in the currency.[5] That was the first proposition that he wished to prove. It was simply an extension of Smith's principle concerning the debasement of coins to the sphere of paper money. But to what extent that principle was applicable to the conditions in England at the time is very doubtful. As pointed out by Mr. Hawtrey, at that time, both the gold market and the exchange market were in an artificial condition and could not afford an unquestionable measure of depreciation.[6] As to the relationship between money and prices, although the increase of the volume of notes must ceteris paribus cause a rise in prices, a rise in prices is only a possible symptom and not a sufficient proof of the existence of depreciation of paper.[7] The rise in prices might be due to some particular causes such as a bad harvest or to some general causes, such as the relative scarcity of commodities, arising out of the general reduction of production caused by the war and to a general increase of the demand for all

---

[1] Walter Boyd, *A Letter to the Rt. Hon. William Pitt on the Influence of the Stoppage of Issues in Specie* . . . London, 1801.
[2] *A Letter*, p. 60.   [3] Ibid., pp. 25–6.
[4] Ibid., p. 28.   [5] Ibid., pp. 3, 28–9, 50–51.
[6] Hawtrey, op. cit., pp. 332–3.   [7] See Viner, *Studies*, pp. 130–6.

goods.   Boyd argued convincingly that the former was
not possible, because " partial causes never can produce
general effects " and hence a scarcity of grain could not
raise the price of all commodities,[1] but he said nothing
on the latter point. The second proposition that he presented
was that the depreciation of paper money " proceeds chiefly
from the addition to the circulation medium . . . made by
the issue of Banknotes, uncontrolled by the obligation of
paying them, in specie, on demand ".[2]   In other words,
the depreciation was caused by an excessive circulation
of banknotes and an excessive circulation of banknotes
could arise only in the event of the suspension of specie
payments.   He then went on to compare the differences
between the conditions under a convertible paper currency
and those under an inconvertible one.[3]   Two important
differences were pointed out by Boyd.   First, under a
convertible system, should there be a premium on gold or an
unfavourable rate of exchange, so that specie was drained
out, the Bank must, at least for its own sake, try its best to
correct those unfavourable conditions ; but in case the
Bank was no longer required to redeem its notes, it " is not
compelled to any exertions to remedy the evil of an unfavourable exchange, or to restore the equilibrium between coin
and bullion ".[4] Second, in the case of a metallic standard,
if the quantity of money possessed by a nation was excessive,
" that surplus quantity would have soon found its way into
other countries, to seek that employment which it could not
readily have found in this." [5]   But in the case of an inconvertible currency the paper money could not be exported
and, therefore, the full effect of excessive currency must
fall entirely upon the prices at home.[6]   In other words,
in the case of a metallic standard the effect of an excess of
money on prices would be spread all over the world, while
in the case of an inconvertible paper standard, the effect
was limited to a country.   With those differences in mind,
he said that in a country with an inconvertible paper
currency, " circulation is not only carried on by a new wheel,

---

[1] *A Letter*, p. 51.   [2] Ibid., pp. 3, 7.
[3] *A Letter*, p. 4.   Professor Angell, however, says—we think in-
correctly—that Boyd confused convertible with inconvertible conditions. See his *Theory of International Prices*, p. 45.
[4] *A Letter*, p. 33.
[5] Ibid., pp. 8 f.   This is Hume's doctrine.
[6] Ibid., pp. 8–10.

but the wheel is altogether of a different sort of material from those of which such wheels used to be made." That to him meant " a positive degradation of the standard ".[1] The third proposition was that the excess of paper currency could be traced to the Bank of England and that the country banks were entirely innocent. He said: " The circulation of Country Bank-notes must necessarily be proportioned to the sums, in specie or Bank of England notes, requisite to discharge such of them as may be presented for payment ; but the paper of the Bank of England has no such limitation. It is itself now become (what the coin of the country only ought to be) the ultimate element into which the whole paper circulation of the country resolves itself. The Bank of England is the great source of all the circulation of the country ; and, by the increase or diminution of its paper, the increase or diminution of that of every Country-Bank is infallibly regulated."[2]   Finally, we find in his *Letter* a suggestive fragment of theory concerning the beneficial effects of an increase in the quantity of money. That is contained in the following passage :—

> If the increase of prices in the home-market should fortunately not keep pace with the depression of the exchange, all our articles of exportation must feel the effects of the increased demand in the foreign markets, in consequence of the diminished value of British money abroad. . . . Trade may be greatly extended in consequence of the increased demand which the diminished value of British money in foreign countries necessarily tends to create.[3]

That anticipated an important doctrine of the effect of depreciation on the course of foreign trade.

Boyd's work was widely read and succeeded in exerting a great influence upon his contemporaries. His first three propositions were at once accepted by the anti-Restriction group and soon became the orthodox view of the group.

The apologists of the Bank were naturally quick to take up its defence. Immediately after the appearance of Boyd's work Francis Baring published his *Observations* on it.[4] His arguments are rather vague. He conceded that—

[1] Ibid., pp. 64–5.
[2] A Letter, p. 20 ; see also, pp. 22 f.   [3] Ibid., p. 37.
[4] Baring, Observations on the Publication of Walter Boyd.

a considerable portion of Mr. Boyd's Letter contains facts and principles which are indisputable : no intelligent person can doubt but that when paper circulation is pushed much beyond reasonable and proper bounds and that bullion disappears in a comparative degree, the price of all commodities (including provisions) must feel the effects. This is no new discovery. It has been the alphabet or first principle of every financier and merchant for about a century.[1]

What he questioned was the interpretation of the facts. He thought that the increase in the volume of notes was very small and relatively inconsiderable and argued that as banknotes were circulating at par, there could be no depreciation.[2] The Bank of England also found other defenders. Most of them were of the opinion that if currency and credit inflation existed, the country banks were at least as responsible as the Bank of England.

In the following year (1802), there appeared another important work, Thornton's treatise on paper credit.[3] His work is much superior to that of Baring in every respect. Like the latter, however, he accepted " a considerable part " of the principles laid down by Boyd and defended the policy of the Bank mainly on the ground of facts. First of all, he agreed with Boyd that the Bank of England was the controlling element in the country's credit circulation. When the Bank expanded its issues and discounted them it directly increased the reserve of the country banks and hence of their issues of notes. When, however, their issues were expanded independently, the rise in *local* prices and the consequent increase in country purchases in London would cause a great demand for bills on London, reduce the reserves of the country banks and thus force a diminution in the volume of their notes.[4] Moreover, he agreed with Boyd that an increase in inconvertible paper money would lead to a rise in prices of both commodities and bullion and to a fall in the exchanges. He came to a similar conclusion, that is, that it was necessary for the Bank itself to limit its note issues. When he turned to consider the facts of the controversy he differed radically from Boyd. He contended that, in point of fact, since the suspension of

---

[1] Ibid., p. 6.   [2] Ibid., pp. 10, 21-2 *passim*.
[3] Henry Thornton, *An Inquiry into the Nature and Effects of the Paper Credit of Great Britain*, London, 1802.
[4] *An Inquiry*, chs. 7 and 8.

specie payments, the Bank had limited its note issues and had not raised the number of its notes. Hence the Bank's policy was not wrong. The causes of the rise in prices and the fall in the exchanges should, therefore, be looked for elsewhere. Among the causes he mentioned the abnormal conditions of war, the accumulated taxes, the bad harvests in 1799 and 1800 (which had combined to raise the price of all commodities) ; the immense importations of corn and the heavy governmental remittances to foreign countries (which turned the exchanges against England and thus led to a rise in the market price of gold).[1]

Regarding the allegation that the excessive contraction of credit by the Bank was responsible for the conditions of 1797, he took the same line. He agreed in principle that, however effective the deflationary policy might be in rendering the balance of trade favourable, it was a very dangerous weapon, because it would so " distress trade and discourage manufacture as to impair . . . those sources of our returning wealth to which we must chiefly trust for the restoration of our balance of trade and for bringing back the tide of gold into Great Britain ".[2] When he came to explain the cause of Restriction he emphasized the first, fourth, and last causes stated on an earlier page and declared that it was due to the state of alarm that had arisen " at a period in which the stock of gold should have been reduced by the other great cause of its reduction, namely, that of a call having been recently made for gold to discharge an unfavourable balance of trade ". In such circumstances, " the power of any bank, however ample its general provision [of gold] should have been, may easily be supposed to prove insufficient for this double purpose." [3]

But his treatise is much more than a mere defence of the Bank's policy on the basis of facts or a mere refinement of his opponents' doctrines in the domain of theory. His contributions both to the theory of money and that of international trade are important. In connection with the former, he noticed the following points. Firstly, unlike most of his predecessors, he included all negotiable papers in the category of circulating media,[4] and excluded uncoined

---

[1] *An Inquiry*, pp. 217–229.
[2] Ibid., p. 132. See also chs. 4–5.
[3] Ibid., p. 71.
[4] Ibid., p. 40 ; see also chs. 2–3.

metals from the same.[1] Secondly, he called attention to the importance of the rapidity of the circulation of money. " It is on the degree of the rapidity of the circulation of each [money and goods], combined with the consideration of quantity, and not the quantity alone, that the value of the circulating medium of any country depends." [2] His treatment of the velocity of the circulation is, in effect, a combination of Petty's approach and Locke's approach to the question. Velocity of circulation was sometimes viewed by him as a question of the number of times money changes hands in a given period of time and at other times discussed in connection with the " motive for holding it ".[3] Thirdly, he gave an account of how an increase in notes would work out its effect on prices, and that is the most important of all his contributions to the theory of money. He said :—

> Let us suppose, for example, that an encreased number of Bank of England notes to be issued. In that case the traders in the metropolis discover that there is a more than usual facility of obtaining notes at the bank by giving bills for them, and that they may, therefore, rely on finding easy means of performing any pecuniary engagement into which they may enter. Every trader is encouraged by the knowledge of this facility of borrowing, a little to enlarge his speculations ; he is rendered, by the plenty of money, somewhat more ready to buy, and rather less eager to sell. . . . Thus an inclination to buy is created in all quarters, and an indisposition to sell. Now, since the cost of articles depends on the issue of that great conflict between the buyers and sellers . . . it follows, that any circumstance which seems to communicate a greater degree of eagerness to the mind of one party than to that of the other, will have an influence on price.[4]

In that passage are implied two important propositions : (a) that an increase of banknotes would affect prices through

---

[1] " The precious metals, when uncoined (or in the state of bullion), are themselves commodities ; but when converted into money they are to be considered merely as a measure of the value of other articles. They may, indeed, be converted back into commodities ; and it is one recommendation of this use as coin that they are capable of this conversion." (An Inquiry, p. 24.)

[2] Ibid., p. 307.

[3] An Inquiry, passim, especially ch. x. He also pointed out that in a commercial nation, whatever its circulating medium consists of, it was apt to vary in its rates of circulation : an equilibrium state of trade or a high state of mercantile confidence would quicken it ; and a state of distrust and alarm or of disequilibrium in trade would retard it. See pp. 136–7, 47.

[4] Ibid., pp. 195–6.

an increase of borrowing and (*b*) that an increase of the volume of the note circulation would increase the velocity of its circulation.[1] In another place,[2] he elucidated the former proposition and showed how and why an increase of notes would cause an increase of borrowing. He started by explaining the cause governing the willingness of the merchants to borrow :—

> In order to ascertain how far the desire of obtaining loans at the Bank may be expected at any time to be carried, we must enquire into the subject of the quantum of profit likely to be derived from borrowing there under the existing circumstances. This is to be judged of by considering two points : the amount, first, of interest to be paid on the sum borrowed ; and, secondly, of the mercantile or other gain to be obtained by the employment of the borrowed capital. The gain which can be acquired by the means of commerce is commonly the highest which can be had ; and it also regulates, in a great measure, the rate in all other cases. We may, therefore, consider this question as turning principally on a comparison of the rate of interest taken at the bank with the current rate of mercantile profit.[3]

Thus, an extension of note issues by furnishing additional money capital and by lowering the terms of loans would facilitate borrowing and increase the buying-power of the community. Now, " the extraordinary emission of paper causes no immediate difference in the *total* quantity of articles belonging to the kingdom. This is self-evident. But it communicates to the new borrowers at the bank a power of taking to themselves a larger share of the existing goods than they would otherwise have been able to command. If the holders of the new paper thus acquire the power over a larger portion of the existing stock of the kingdom, the possessors of the old paper must have the power over a smaller part. The same paper, therefore, will purchase fewer goods or, in other words, commodities will rise in their nominal value." [4] That rise in prices itself would in turn encourage further borrowing and a further rise in prices :—

---

[1] See Ibid., pp. 264 ff.
[2] The occasion of that statement was his attempt to show that the circulation of the Bank of England might expand beyond all assignable limits, if the Bank's rate of interest would be low enough.
[3] *An Inquiry*, p. 287.   [4] *An Inquiry*, p. 259.

While paper is encreasing, and articles continue rising, mercantile speculations appear more than ordinarily profitable. The trade, for example, who sells his commodity in three months after he purchased it, obtains an extra gain, which is equal to such advance in the general price of things as the new paper has caused during the three months in question : he confounds this gain with the other profits of his commerce ; and is induced, by the apparent success of his undertakings, to pursue them with more than usual spirit. The manufacturer feels the same kind of encouragement to extend his operations ; and the enlarged issue of paper supplies both him and the merchant with the means of carrying their plans into effect.[1]

Those conditions would be perpetuated until the Bank stopped increasing its note issues. " As soon, however, as the circulating medium ceases to encrease, the extra profit is at an end," [2] and the price structure would become stationary after having produced its full effect in raising the prices of goods. " The temptation to borrow . . . will be exactly the same as before ; for the existing paper will then bear only the same proportion to the existing quantity of goods, when sold at the existing prices, which the former paper bore to the former quantity of goods, when sold at the former prices ; the power of purchasing will, therefore, be the same ; the terms of lending and borrowing must be presumed to be the same ; the amount of circulating medium will have altered, and it will have simply caused the same goods to pass for a larger quantity of paper." [3]

That leads us immediately to his attitude towards the doctrine that money stimulates trade. That doctrine was explicitly " admitted to be just ".[4] Furthermore, he said :—

It must be also admitted that, provided we assume an excessive issue of paper to lift up, as it may for a time, the cost of goods though not the price of labour, some augmentation of stock will be the consequence ; for the labourer, according to this supposition, may be forced by his necessity to consume fewer articles, though he may exercise the same industry. But this saving, as well as any additional one which may arise from a similar defalcation of the revenue of the unproductive members of the society, will be attended with a proportionate hardship and injustice.[5]

[1] Ibid., p. 261.   [2] Ibid., pp. 261 f.
[3] *An Inquiry*, p. 290.   [4] Ibid., p. 260.   [5] Ibid., p. 263.

Thereby he anticipated what is now known as the doctrine of " forced saving ", i.e. the doctrine that an increase of money brings about an increase of capital—a doctrine which is so closely connected with the general doctrine that money stimulates trade and production that it may be considered as a part or a particular version of the latter doctrine.[1] He limited, however, the application of the doctrine to the transitional period and gave it its rightful place in the theory of money. He clearly connected the doctrine with his analysis of the mechanism connecting money and prices. He showed that it was because of the very fact that industry was encouraged that the willingness of people to borrow became greater, that the demand both for goods and labour became more intense than before and that consequently the prices of goods and the wages of labour rose higher.[2]

---

[1] Later, the doctrine of forced saving was clearly stated by Jeremy Bentham (1748–1832) in his *Manual of Political Economy*, which was written in 1804 but printed only posthumously in 1843 in his *Works* (edited by John Bowring). Bentham explained how an increase in the volume of the circulating medium might lead to forced frugality or forced saving in the following way :—
" The effect of forced frugality is also produced by the creating of paper money by government, or the suffering of the creation of paper money by individuals. In this case, the effect is produced by a specie of indirect taxation. . . . The effect of every increase of money . . . is to impose an unprofitable *income tax* on the incomes of all fixed incomists. . . . If, on the introduction of the additional money into circulation, it pass in the first instance into hands which employ it in the way of unproductive expenditure, the suffering from this tax remains altogether uncompensated ; if before it come into any hands of that description, it have come into hands by which it has been employed in the shape of capital, the suffering by the income tax is partly reduced and partly compensated. It is reduced by the mass of things vendible produced by means of it : a mass by the amount of which, were it not for the corresponding increase in the mass of money, the value of the mass of money would *pro tanto* have been increased, and the prices of things vendible decreased. It is in a certain degree, though in a very inadequate degree, compensated for by the same means, viz. by the amount of the addition made to the quantity of sensible wealth—of wealth possessing a value in the way of use. Here . . . national wealth is increased at the expense of national comfort and national injustice."
The above passage is quoted from Professor Hayek's article, " A Note on the Development of the Doctrine of Forced Saving," *Q.J.E.*, 1932, pp. 124 f.
[2] *An Inquiry*, p. 261. " It has thus been admitted," he said, " that paper possesses the faculty of enlarging the quantity of commodities by giving life to some new industry. It has, however, been affirmed that an encrease of industry will by no means keep pace with the augmentation of paper " (p. 264). Thereby he implicitly refuted the false doctrine that an increase of money would always increase its demand to the extent that the value of money remained unchanged.

Thus the doctrine that money stimulates trade was reconciled with, or subordinated to, the quantity theory of money.

In the theory of international trade he considered " as a general truth that the commercial exports and imports of a state . . . naturally proportion themselves in some degree to each other ; and that the balance of trade, therefore . . . cannot continue for a very long time to be either highly favourable or highly unfavourable to a country. For that balance must be paid in bullion, or else must constitute a debt. To suppose a very great balance to be paid, year after year in bullion . . . [or] to suppose large and successive balances to be formed into a debt . . . is almost equally incredible ".[1] The reason for the establishment of an equality of imports and of exports was found, partly at least, in the disposition of people to adapt their individual expenditure to their incomes. He accordingly declared that the " equality between private expenditures and private incomes tend ultimately to produce equality between the commercial exports and imports ".[2] Thereby he anticipated one of Wicksell's doctrines of international trade. There must be not only an equality of imports and exports but also an equilibrium in currency conditions among the trading nations. Equilibrium would be established when the quantity of money in a country relative to the quantities in other countries was proportionate to its relative needs in comparison with those of other countries.

Before we take up the problem of disturbance and its correction, it is best, first, to describe his theory of international price relationships, which was based on the doctrine described in the preceding paragraph. He said :—

> Bullion necessarily bears that value, or nearly that value, in each country, in exchange for goods, which it bears in all, allowance being made for the expense of their transmission, inclusive of export and import duties, ordinary profit of the merchant, freight, insurance, and other customary charges. The expense of the transportation of commodities from the several places of their growth or manufacture, an expense which is greater in some cases and small in others, is the measure of the difference subsisting between the bullion prices of the same articles, at the same time, in different parts of the world.[3]

[1] *An Inquiry*, p. 166.   [2] *An Inquiry*, pp. 117–118.   [3] Ibid., p. 299.

The next problem is that of the possible causes of a disturbance and how disturbances are adjusted. Thornton was of the opinion that the initiating cause might originate either on the money side or on the commodity side. If it originated from the former, Hume's Law would operate to restore the equilibrium. He went, however, beyond Hume and extended the latter's doctrine to a depreciated currency :—

> [First] in a country in which *coin alone* circulates, if, through any accident, the quantity should become greater in proportion to the goods which it has to transfer than it is in other countries, the coin becomes cheap as compared with goods, or, in other words, that goods become dear as compared with coin, and that a profit on the exportation of coin arises. This profit, indeed, soon causes the actual exportation of the article which is excessive. . . .
>
> [Secondly] in a country in which *coin and paper* circulate at the same time, of the two taken together should, in like manner become in the same sense of the term, excessive, a similar effect will follow. There will, I mean, be a profit on sending away the coin, and a consequent exportation of it. . . .
>
> [Thirdly] in a country in which *paper alone* circulates, if the quantity be in the same time excessive, supposing the credit of the banks which issued it to be perfect, the paper will fall in value in proportion to the excess, on an exactly similar principle ; or, in other words, that goods will rise ; and . . . a necessity will exist for granting, in the shape of exchange, a bounty on the exportation of them equal to that which would have been afforded in the two former suppositions, assuming the quantity of circulating medium to be excessive in an equal degree in all the three cases.[1]

His doctrine concerning a depreciated currency, as presented here, is substantially what is now known as the " purchasing power parity doctrine ".[2]

---

[1] *An Inquiry*, pp. 276–7.
[2] For the definition of the " purchasing power parity doctrine ", see ch. vi, section 2 of this essay. " In proportion as goods are rendered dear in Great Britain . . . our exports will be diminished . . . [and] our imports also will encrease. . . . [But] those two effects (that of a diminished export and that of an increased import) will follow, provided that we suppose, what is not supposable, namely, that at the time when the price of goods is greatly raised in Great Britain the course of exchange suffers no alteration. For the following reason, I have said that this is not supposable. Under the circumstances which have been described of a diminished export, and an increased import, the balance of trade must unavoidably turn against us ; the consequence of which must be, that the drawers of

The disturbance might be initiated from the commodity side, that is, it might spring from an unfavourable balance of payments. Thornton saw clearly that specie would be exported only if the currency of the country were " redundant ", but he insisted that " it is very possible . . . that the excess of paper, if such it is to be called, is merely an excess above that very low and reduced quantity to which it is necessary (at the time of a very unfavourable balance of trade) that it should be brought down, in order to prevent the existence of an excess of the market price above the mint price of gold. I conceive, therefore, that this excess, if it arises on the occasion of an unfavourable balance of trade, and at a time when there has been no extraordinary emission of notes, may fairly be considered as an excess created by that unfavourable balance, though it is one which a reduction of notes tends to cure ".[1] How is such a disturbance corrected ? In answering that question Thornton advanced a *double* doctrine.[2] One part of his double doctrine was found in the following passage :—

At the time of a very unfavourable balance (produced, for example, through a failure of the harvest), a country has occasion for large supplies of corn from abroad : but either it has not the means of supplying at the instant a sufficient quantity of goods in return, or, which is much the more probable case, and the case which I suppose more applicable to England, the goods which the country having the unfavourable balance is able to furnish as means of cancelling its debt, are not in such demand abroad as to afford the prospect of a tempting or even of a tolerable price. . . . The country, therefore, which has the favourable balance, being, to a certain degree, eager for payment, but not in immediate want of all that supply of goods which would be necessary to pay the balance, prefers gold as part, at least, of the payment ; for gold can always be turned to a more beneficial use than a very great overplus of any other commodity. In order, then, to induce the country having the

bills on Great Britain in foreign countries will become more in number than the persons having occasion to remit bills. This . . . must produce a fall in the price at which the over-abundant bill on England will sell in the foreign market. . . . The fall of our exchange will, therefore, promote exportation and encourage importation. It will, in a high degree, prevent the high prices of goods in Great Britain from producing that unfavourable balance of trade."—*An Inquiry*, pp. 200–1.

[1] *An Inquiry*, p. 130.

[2] Cf. Viner, *Canada's Balance of International Indebtedness*, p. 192 ; Carl Iversen, *International Capital Movements*, pp. 209 ff.

H

favourable balance to take all its payments in goods, and no part of it in gold, it would be requisite not only to prevent goods from being dear, but even to render them excessively cheap. It would be necessary, therefore, that the bank should not only not encrease its paper, but that it should perhaps very greatly diminish it, if it would endeavour to prevent gold from going out in part payment of the unfavourable balance. And if the bank do this . . . [then it may so] exceedingly distress trade and discourage manufacturers as to impair . . . those sources of our returning wealth to which we must chiefly trust for the restoration of our balance of trade, and for bringing back the tide of gold into Great Britain. It is also necessary to notice in this place, that the favourable effect which a limitation of bank paper produces on the exchange is certainly not instantaneous, and may, probably, only be experienced after some considerable interval of time ; it may, therefore, in many cases, be expected that the exchange will rectify itself before the reduction of bank paper can have any operation. . . . For this reason it may be the true policy and duty of the bank to permit, for a time, and to a certain extent, the continuance of that unfavourable exchange, which causes gold to leave the country, and to be drawn out of its own coffers.[1]

The process of adjustment of a disturbance caused by an unfavourable balance of payments, according to the passage quoted above, was as follows—

(a) disturbance caused by an unfavourable balance of payments,
(b) an unfavourable exchange rate,
(c) contraction of the note issue *or* exportation of gold,
(d) changes in the relative prices of the trading nations,
(e) an increase of exports and a decrease of imports, and
(f) a restoration of equilibrium.

The most important point is the fourth one, that is a shift in relative prices. The shift may be brought about either by a contraction of currency or by an export of gold. To Thornton, however, the former had depressing effects and required a certain time to work out those effects, and he, therefore, preferred the latter. The doctrine, which implies a shift in the relative prices as the essential part of the mechanism of adjustment was in effect a restatement of Hume's Law, which is generally known as the " classical theory ". That theory implicitly assumed that the

[1] *An Inquiry*, pp. 161–3.

conditions of international demand in the trading countries
would remain unaffected, in spite of bad harvests or other
causes that might disturb the balance of payments. There
is an " alternative " theory concerning the mechanism of
adjustment, which has sometimes been called the " modern "
theory. Briefly stated, the advocates of that so-called
" modern " theory questioned the validity of the assumption of unchanged demand conditions and argued that a
bad harvest or a transfer of capital itself would alter
the demand condition to such an extent that equilibrium
in the balance of payments would be restored. Thus,
they denied the shift of relative prices as a necessary part
of the mechanism of adjustment. We shall call that theory
" the Wicksellian theory of transfer ", for the following
reason : The theoretical foundation for that theory is to
be found in the doctrine that individuals always adapt
their expenditures to their incomes and that, as a bad
harvest or an export of capital would diminish the income
or income available for expenditure of the people, their
demand curves for all goods would be shifted. That doctrine,
as we shall see, is most clearly expounded by Wicksell.
Therefore, although Wicksell was not the first to advance
that so-called " modern " theory of transfer, we think that
there is sufficient justification for associating it with his
name. The Wicksellian theory of transfer is usually
considered—we think wrongly—as not only irreconcilable
with the classical theory, but also explicitly or implicitly
opposed by Thornton. In reality Thornton very clearly and
and emphatically stated the Wicksellian view :—

There is in the mass of the people, of all countries, a disposition to adapt their individual expenditure to their income.
Importations conducted with a view to the consumption of
the country into which the articles are imported (and such,
perhaps, are the chief importations of a poor country), are
limited by the ability of the individuals of that country to
pay for them out of their income. Importations, with a view
to subsequent exportation, are in like manner limited by the
ability to pay which subsists among the individuals of the
several countries to which the imported goods are afterwards
exported. The income of individuals is the general limit
in all cases. If, therefore, through any unfortunate circumstance, if through war, scarcity, or any other extensive calamity,
the value of the annual income of the inhabitants of a country
is diminished, either new economy on the one hand, or new

exertions of individual industry on the other, fail not, after a certain time, in some measure, to restore the balance. And this equality between private expenditures and private incomes tends ultimately to produce equality between the commercial exports and imports. But though the value of the commercial exports and imports of a country will have this general tendency to proportion themselves to each other, there will not fail occasionally to arise a very great inequality between them. A good or a bad harvest, in particular, will have a considerable influence in producing this temporary difference. . . . The two principles of economy and exertion are always operating in proportion to the occasion for them. But the economy and exertion follow rather than accompany the evil which they have to cure. If the harvest fails and imports are necessary, in order to supply the deficiency, payment for those imports is almost immediately required; but the means of payment are to be supplied more gradually through the limitation of private expenditures, or the encrease of individual industry. Hence a temporary pressure arises at a time of any unfavourable balance. . . .[1]

Thus, he recognized that *in the long run* a disturbance might be adjusted by the following sequence of events :—

(*a*) disturbance,
(*b*) changes in individual incomes,
(*c*) " the limitation of private expenditure, or the encrease of individual industry," that is, to put it in modern terminology, a shift in demand and supply, and
(*d*) the supply of the means of payment and the restoration of equilibrium.

That is substantially the same as the Wicksellian theory. Thornton insisted, however, that that was only the ultimate mechanism of adjustment that took time to work out its effects and that for the correction of the difficulty or of the pressure which arose *immediately* after the disturbance the mechanism described in the classical theory should be relied on.

Thornton's work was reviewed at length by Francis Horner in the *Edinburgh Review*.[2] With respect to the theory Horner made some minor adjustments in the position

---

[1] Ibid., pp. 117–19.
[2] Horner, " An Inquiry into the Nature and Effects of the Paper Credit of Great Britain, by Henry Thornton," *Edinburgh Review*, No. 1, October. 1802.

of Thornton, and in regard to contemporary conditions he took the anti-Bank view first laid down by Boyd.

According to the Restriction Act, the suspension of cash payments should have expired in September, 1802, but, in spite of the conclusion of the Treaty of Amiens early in March and of the declaration of the Bank of its readiness to resume specie payments, Addington, the then Chancellor of the Exchequer, brought in a bill on the 9th April to continue the restriction till the 1st March, 1803. His argument in favour of that measure was contained in the following passage in his speech before Parliament :—

> It cannot be necessary for me to inform the House that the rate of exchange between this country and foreign parts is disadvantageous to ourselves—that the export trade has been for some months at a stand, that while the rate is disadvantageous to us, an augmentation of the circulating cash would create a trade highly injurious to the commerce of this country. For several months past there has been a trade carried on for purchase of guineas with a view to exportation. It is on these grounds that I submit to the House the expediency of continuing the restriction with regard to the cash payments of the Bank.[1]

Addington's statement, whatever might be its merits or demerits, represented the view of the Government and of business circles during the peroid. In February, 1803, for practically the same reason, Addington again asked Parliament for another renewal of restriction. The motion was granted but on this occasion not without some opposition. Charles James Fox was the first to raise an objection in the House of Commons :—

> Perhaps even it might happen that the unfavourable turn of the exchange against this country might be owing to the very restriction on the Bank. . . . In 1772 to 1773, when there was a great quantity of bad money in the country, the course of exchange was then also much against us. . . . As long as our currency continued bad, the exchange was against us ; so is it now, because paper is not much better than bad gold ; or it is attended with the same inconvenience. May it not therefore be expected that as in the former case, when our currency was ameliorated, the course of exchange turned in our favour, so also if the Bank now resumed its cash payments the same favourable circumstances might attend the change ? [2]

[1] Quoted from Macleod, *Banking*, 5th ed., ii, p. 5.   [2] Ibid., ii, p. 6.

That is nothing but rather a poor statement of a part of the first proposition advanced by Boyd two years before. That view was expanded with much skill and clearness by Peter King in the House of Lords on 22nd February.[1] His arguments might be summarized in a single sentence : a rise of the market price of bullion (in terms of paper currency) and a fall of the rate of exchange below the limits of the " real " exchange was the proof and the measure of the depreciation of paper money. Debates on the Restriction problem disappeared with the declaration of war against France on 18th May, 1803.

4. FOSTER AND THE REPORT ON IRISH CURRENCY

Between 1803 and 1810 the problems of currency and trade did not attract much attention. Nevertheless, there appeared no less than three important works in those fields, namely the essays of Foster, Wheatley, and Blake. Foster's work was connected with the problem of the Irish currency. In the last quarter of the year 1797 the exchange in Dublin (on London) began to decline steadily with a corresponding rise in the price of bullion. The exchange reached an extremely bad condition early in 1804. On a motion of Foster, a committee was immediately appointed " to inquire into the cause of the present high rate of exchange between Great Britain and Ireland and the state of the Currency in the latter kingdom ". Foster himself was appointed a member of the committee. It was in connection with his appointment to the committee that he published his famous essay on commercial exchanges.[2]

Foster's general position was similar to that of the anti-Restriction group. He began by making a distinction between the balance of trade, that is " the difference between commercial exports and imports," and the balance of debt, that is " the difference between money to be paid and money to be received ".[3] He pointed out that, while exports might exceed imports, the balance of debt could not be permanently favourable or unfavourable.

[1] See ibid., ii, p. 7. Later he systematized and extended his views and published an essay called *Thoughts on the Restriction of Payments in Specie at the Banks of England and Ireland* (London, 1803). Although there was nothing really new in this book, it was widely read.
[2] John Leslie Foster, *An Essay on the Principles of Commercial Exchanges*, London, 1804.
[3] Ibid., p. 4.

That was the first condition of equilibrium in international trade that he laid down in his essay. There was also another condition, namely that each country should maintain an equalization of the value of the money metals with other nations. For instance, he said :—

The precious metals, like every other commodity, seek a market where they are dear, and retire from one where they are cheap. The trade of the bullion-merchant for ever prevents their value becoming permanently less or greater in any one country than in the rest ; and distributes their quantity to each, in such a proportion to its demand, that their value continues everywhere nearly equal. . . . Their intrinsic value is least in those countries which have the most direct communication with the mines ; in all, it is compound of their value at the mines, and of the expense of their carriage.[1]

Like Thornton, Foster thought that disturbances might arise either from the commodity side or from the monetary side.[2] If disturbances arose from the latter cause, then, under a metallic standard, Hume's law would operate to restore equilibrium. In connection with that point he also gave an analysis of how an increase of the volume of money would raise the prices of commodities. That analysis was made in connection with his attempt to refute the proposition that " the Bank issues cannot be excessive according to the present mode in which they are made ", that is, issued solely on good security so that " the supply follows and does not precede the demand ". Foster presented his argument so excellently that it is worth quoting in full here :—

Without looking farther than the impolitic laws against usury, we may discover the source of a demand on the Bank discounts, which, if complied with, might at length reduce the value of their notes to that of the paper on which they are engraved, and yet without those notes ever being issued except on perfect security. By law the Bank are obliged to discount at 5 per cent: but during war it is almost always possible to make more than 5 per cent of money. If a merchant, under such circumstances, could obtain discounts to the amount of the security he could give, the issues of notes would soon amount to all the security that could be given [if the country is off the gold standard]. . . .[3]

[1] *An Essay*, p. 7 and n.   [2] Ibid., pp. 171 and *passim*.
[3] *An Essay*, p. 113. This and Thornton's statement quoted above are two of the earliest statements of the " indirect " mechanism connecting money and prices, that is, the mechanism with discount rate as the connecting link between money and prices.

Certainly if a country maintained a gold standard, the issues of notes could not continue very long, because the consequential rise of prices would turn the balance of debt against the country, cause gold to flow out of it, and hence serve as a check to further expansion of issues of notes. But no such check existed in the case of a paper standard.

That brings us to the problem of prices and rates of exchange under a paper standard. It should be noted at the outset that Foster understood clearly that an excess of the circulating medium does not necessarily follow a restriction of the operation of the gold standard or the abolition of the gold standard. " The restriction permits excess but does not compel it."[1] When depreciation did exist it is due to one or both of the following causes :—

(a) discredit, and
(b) excess.

In connection with the latter he, like Thornton, advanced a purchasing-power-parity doctrine :—

If the currency of any country become less valuable than formerly, it becomes exchangeable for a less quantity of the currency of any other country, which continues as valuable as formerly.[2]

Although he held the view that no balance of debt could continue permanently against a country, Foster thought that disturbances might arise from the commodity side. He said :—

The balance of debt may be for or against any one country with the whole world, for a limited time : great foreign expenditure, bad harvests, sudden emigrations of the proprietors, may all make the value that must be sent out greater than the value immediately to be received ; the difference in this case must be paid in the precious metals.[3]

The last clause is rather misleading. What Foster really meant was simply that there might be *temporarily* an outflow of specie if the balance of debt, for a short time, turned against the country under consideration, that was Ireland. But he was of the opinion that " an increase of Irish produce must be sent out to recover specie to an

[1] *An Essay*, p. 162.
[2] Ibid., p. 88 ; see also pp. 96, 98, 105, 158 and *passim*.
[3] Ibid., p. 5 ; see also p. 58.

equal amount, as indispensable to the circulation of Ireland ".[1]

As to the Irish exchange, his conclusions were the same as those embodied in the Report of the Select Committee on Irish Currency and Exchange to which we shall now turn. That report was presented in about the middle of 1804.[2] The principles laid down by the report were exactly the same as those of Boyd and King. Its four main conclusions were as follows : first, that the variations of the exchanges could not exceed the expense of transporting and insuring the precious metals from one place to another and that, in case there was an excess of that kind in the exchange rate, it would be a proof of the existence of depreciation ; second, that the price of gold bullion could not long exceed the mint price, unless the currency in which it was paid was depreciated below the value of gold ; third, that there did exist in the case under consideration a state of unfavourable exchange much beyond the export point and a high price of bullion and that those facts constituted a sufficient proof of the existence of the depreciation of the paper ; and, fourth, that the cause of unfavourable exchanges and a high price of bullion was the suspension of specie payments and not the balance of payments, because the latter was said to be favourable, instead of unfavourable.

The minutes of evidence taken by the Committee were published, and from them we learn the views of the directors of the Bank of Ireland, Colville and D'Olier. Three of their arguments might be given here. First, they argued that the sole cause of the unfavourable exchange was the unfavourable balance of payments and that " the mere buying of gold at an advanced price beyond that of the Mint, is the effect, and not the cause, of the exchange, and, therefore, no proof of the depreciation of the paper itself ". In other words, the causal sequence ran from the balance of payments to the exchanges and then to the price of gold and not in the reverse order. Second, they declared that it was inaccurate to speak of " depreciated

---

[1] *An Essay*, p. 23. See also pp. 34 and 35, for another description of the mechanism of transfer.

[2] *Report, Minutes of Evidence, and Appendix from the Committee on the Circulating Paper, the specie, and the Current Coin of Ireland : and also on the Exchange between that part of the U.K. and Great Britain*, May and June, 1804. Reprinted, 1826.

paper money ". The paper had not depreciated, but the price of gold had risen. Third, they were of the opinion that the issues of convertible notes by a bank should be governed by totally different principles from the principles which govern the issues of inconvertible notes. The issue of the former ought to be regulated according to the price of guineas and the rate of exchange, while in the issue of the latter the public demand was the sole criterion.[1]

5. WHEATLEY AND BLAKE

In the first decade of the nineteenth century there appeared some important non-controversial works on the theory of the exchanges, namely the essays of Wheatley [2] and Blake. Wheatley started with an extreme quantity theory of money [3] and applied it unreservedly to paper currency.[4] " The increase of currency by paper," he said, " must cause the same reduction in the value of money, in proportion to the activity of its circulation as an increase of currency by specie. But a reduction in the value of money and an advance in the price of produce, are synonymous terms ; one effect cannot take place without the other ; and if paper depreciate money, it must advance in a similar proportion the prices of articles of subsistence and luxury." [5] He denied in his earlier writings the doctrine that an increase of currency gave a stimulus to industry and argued (rather weakly) that " as the wages of labour are augmented only in proportion to the increase, and purchased no great quantity of produce after the addition than before it, no greater stimulus can in reality exist, and therefore no greater effect is likely to be produced by the deception ".[6] In his later writings, however, he clearly presented the proposition that a hasty reduction of currency would bring about a decay of trade.[7]

He next presented the doctrine that prices tend to have an international " equalization ". Within a nation, nobody

[1] See also Henry Parnell, *Observations upon the State of Currency in Ireland*, Dublin, 1804 ; and Henry Boase, *A Letter . . . in Defence of the Conduct of the Directors of the Banks of England and Ireland*, 1804. Parnell was an anti-Restriction writer, while Boase was a defender of the conduct of the Bank of Ireland.
[2] John Wheatley, *Remarks on Currency and Commerce*, London, 1803 ; subsequently enlarged and revised as *An Essay on the Theory of Money and Principles of Commerce*, vol. i, 1807 ; vol. ii, 1822. [3] *Essay*, i, p. 40 ; *Remarks*, p. 17 and elsewhere. [4] *Remarks*, ch. iv. [5] *Remarks*, p. 180. [6] *Essay*, i, pp. 40 f. ; *Remarks*, pp. 18 f. [7] *Essay*, ii, ch. 6.

"would submit to a material depression in the estimate of his labour or produce in any instance where he could procure a better market ". The same regard for individual interests prevented any particular produce, the cost of conveyance being taken account of, from exchanging at one place for more value than it did at another place either inside or outside the same country. "The facility with which the reciprocal communication of nations is carried on, has a necessary influence on the markets of all and approximates the price of their produce to a general level."[1] That doctrine of *international* equalization of prices was, however, applied only to product prices and not to factor prices. To him the existence of inequality of wages between two countries, say France and England, was not inconsistent with the doctrine of international price equalization. For the inferiority of the wages of labour, say, in France, to the wages of labour in England "only proves that the commonalty of France are compelled to submit to a proportionate inferiority of subsistence, and by no means authorizes the inference, which the variation in the market prices of the two countries might at first view appear to justify, that the same sum measured in one country a greater value than it measured in the other ".[2] What maintained an international equalization of the purchasing power of money, therefore, was the equalization of product prices but not factor prices. If those two propositions were granted, that is, if the product prices were a function of the quantity of money and at the same time the prices of the products were consequently everywhere on a level of equality, it logically followed that the quantity of money each nation could have was limited and that "no one nation can possess a greater relative currency than another ". But how could an equilibrium of international prices be maintained ? He pointed out that "the course of exchange constituted the practical means by which the equivalency is maintained ".[3] Whenever it happened that every country

---

[1] *Essay*, i, pp. 42–6 ; *Remarks*, pp. 22–7, 186. He pointed out that there were some limitations to the realization of a complete equalization. "The difficulties of conveyance must be allowed for." (*Remarks*, p. 24.) "There are two causes that operate in the commercial intercourse of nations, to prevent a complete equalization of prices in the same produce ; the difficulties of intercourse on account of the distance and on account of the restriction of the freedom of trade." (*Remarks*, pp. 26 f.)

[2] *Essay*, i, p. 57.   [3] *Essay*, i, p. 60.

employed such an amount of currency as to establish an international equalization of prices, the exchange between nations " would be invariably at par ".   Otherwise, a relative excess of currency would occasion a premium on a foreign bill and a relative scarcity a discount.   " The course of exchange, therefore, affords an accurate criterion of the relative value of money over the whole world, and constitutes the instrument, by which the interchanges of trade between nation and nation are exclusively estimated." [1] That is what is now known as the purchasing power parity doctrine. He applied it to both metallic and paper standards. Under a metallic or under a convertible paper currency the variations of exchange could not exceed the specie points, because whenever the exchange fell below the specie exporting point, bills " would be purchased by the bullion merchant, and invested in its surplus specie for the profit of exporting it to the state whose proportion of currency was relatively less ".[2]   By that movement of specie equilibrium would soon be restored.   Under an inconvertible paper currency, however, there would be no such limit. He said :—

> When the paper of a country is not convertible into specie at the option of the holder, and a relative excess of currency ensures from its over-issue, as it is not like specie qualified for exportation, nor like paper convertible into specie obnoxious to a forced contraction, the course of exchange has no other means of causing the same sum to express in that country the same value which it expresses in others, than to reduce it to a discount in proportion to its excess.[3]

Although there are many points on which Wheatley comes very near to Hume, the position of the former was different from the latter. It is true that they both stood for an equilibrium theory and that both had a conception of an optimum amount of currency for a country. They also both agreed that there was a tendency towards a balance in a country's international accounts.   They differed,

[1] *Essay*, i, pp. 60–64 ; *Remarks*, pp. 186–7.
[2] *Essay*, i, pp. 65 f., 67 f.
[3] *Essay*, i, p. 69. See also p. 72 and *passim* ; and *Remarks*, pp. 70 ff., 85 ff., 122 f., 207 and *passim*. On the other hand, specie " would bear a premium commensurate with the premium on a foreign bill, and no longer participating in the degraded condition of the paper, would resiliate to its level, and be maintained at the same value with the value of money in other countries." (*Essay*, i, p. 70.) See also *Essay*, i, ch. 4.

however, on the question how equilibrium in a country's accounts, if disturbed, is restored. To Hume, as indicated above, when the balance of payments of a country is not in equilibrium, gold moves from one country to another to settle the debts and the movement of gold means changes in the volumes of currencies and leads to changes in prices. As a result of the changes in prices, the balance of trade is affected and the international accounts will once more be balanced. To Wheatley disturbances arising from the balance of payments automatically adjusted themselves without any effect on the prices of the countries concerned, and equilibrium in international price relationships was consequently not occasioned by the state of the balance of payments. Or, in other words, disequilibrium in international price relationships was occasioned only by monetary factors. Wheatly himself explicitly recognized that his doctrine differed from that of Hume,[1] and tried to defend his own position by attempting to refute the latter's doctrine. First he denied that there was any necessary connection between international balances of payments and international movements of specie. He wrote at length for the purpose of proving the proposition that gold could flow into the country, in spite of an adverse balance of trade and flow out, in spite of a favourable balance. His main argument was simply this : " By a due compression of our currency," whatever might be the international balance of payments, specie would necessarily flow in.[2] That argument is certainly very vague. The question is whether there will be an international movement of gold if a country has to pay a debt or a subsidy to a foreign country while other things remain unchanged. Deflation is one thing and a payment abroad is another. We cannot prove that the latter dynamic factor is ineffective simply because it might be counteracted by the former dynamic factor. More acceptable is another of his arguments, to which he failed to give due emphasis, namely that the balance of payments has in itself a tendency to adjust itself without the help of monetary changes. Of that, he said :—

All commerce with independent states consists in the equal interchange of produce for produce. It is impossible that a

---

[1] *Essay*, i, p. 88.   [2] *Essay*, i, ch. 7–9 and *passim*.

nation could fulfil the relations of commerce, and drive an export trade to the amount of many millions, without importing to a similar extent. The power of buying depends upon the power of selling ; and unless the countries, to whom the produce was exported, were capable of vending an equivalent in return, they would be deficient in means to maintain the intercourse. . . . It may be said, indeed, that according to this principle, the exports and imports should have a reciprocal action on each other, and that the extent of the one should be implicitly governed by the extent of the other ; nor can there be any doubt but that a perfect correspondence would be fully established, did not the payment of a foreign expenditure intervene to obstruct it. . . . If no demand has subsisted in this country from 1793 to 1797 for corn and naval stores, the countries that furnished the supply would have possessed so much less means of expanding our exports, as an inability to sell would, of course, have created an inability to buy.[1]

If we consider that that passage represents the ideas of Wheatley,[2] we can say that what divides Hume from Wheatley is that the former holds to the classical theory of transfer, while the latter holds to what we call the Wicksellian theory of transfer.

Finally, Wheatley made an examination of the relationship between the Bank of England and the country banks. He adopted the view just opposite to that advanced by Boyd, and he attacked the country banks instead of the Bank of England. If the latter had the monopoly of issuing notes, certainly the whole responsibility of inflation rested on it. The country banks had, however, also issued notes. As their paper was also " made to answer the purpose of money, it necessarily depreciates the value of money, exactly in the same proportion as an addition of so much coin ", unless it could be proved that country issues " either led to a corresponding contraction of Banknotes or a corresponding contraction of specie ". Neither of those conditions existed. As a matter of fact, the country bank-notes had increased excessively in times of security and became in times of distress the main source of the difficulties that were being experienced at the time.[3]

Blake's *Observations* exerted a greater contemporary influence than Wheatley's work. Blake began by pointing

[1] *Essay*, i, pp. 236–8.
[2] Wheatley had, in some passages in his *Remarks* (pp. 74 f., 222, etc.) appeared to have accepted the classical theory of transfer.
[3] *Essay*, i, pp. 372 ff. ; *Remarks*, pp. 209 ff.

out that " the price of bills will depend . . . first, on their abundance or scarcity in the market compared with the demand for, them ; and secondly on the value of the currency in which they are to be paid, compared with the value of that with which they are bought ".[1] He called the problems of exchange arising from those two causes respectively as those of " real exchange " and " nominal exchange " and investigated them separately.

He first assumed the coins of all trading nations to be " in a perfect state as to purity and weight " and presented a theory of real exchange. In that case the exchange rate depended on the demand and supply of foreign bills which, in turn, depended on the state of the balance of payments. In the long run, as international accounts had to be balanced, the exchange was inevitably at par. " At any particular period of time, however, it may happen that a nation may have imported to a greater amount than it has exported, and consequently have more payments to be made than to receive." [2] Thus conditions became deviated from the equilibrium, and demand and supply no longer remained equal if the exchange was at par. His description of the mechanism which corrects the disturbance was essentially the same as that of Hume. The only difference was that he laid greater emphasis on the variations of the rate of exchange itself than on the international movement of specie.[3]

He then turned on the problem of nominal exchange, that is, the problem of the effects of monetary changes on the rates of exchange, if other things remained unchanged. His theory was simply a purchasing-power-parity doctrine like that advanced by Thornton and Wheatley.[4]

6. The Bullion Report :   Ricardo and Bosanquet

In 1808 a sharp change occurred in the monetary situation. The price of gold had become so high and the foreign exchange so unfavourable that it was manifest to everyone that the state of the national currency was becoming

[1] William Blake, *Observations on the Principles which regulate the Course of Exchange*, London, 1810. We have used the reprint in *A Select Collection of Scarce and Valuable Tracts . . . on Paper Currency and Banking*, etc., edited by J. R. McCulloch, London, 1857. The reference is to p. 480.
[2] *Observations*, p. 482.
[3] Ibid., pp. 487, 536, 488–9, 492, 497, etc.
[4] *Observations*, pp. 499–531.

critical. . The conditions naturally revived the currency controversy and led to the appointment of the Bullion Committee. The Committee presented its Report in 1810.[1] It embodied the view that the Bank of England was solely responsible for the cause of the trouble and all the principles laid down in the Report of 1804. It was, however, much more radical in its recommendations than the latter. It recommended the adoption of a policy of severe contraction and the abolition of the restriction of specie payments within two years, in spite of war conditions. Its views were strongly opposed by both business circles and the Government. The arguments given by those opponents of the Report were practically the same as those given by the directors of the Bank of Ireland before the Committee of 1804, and we need not, therefore, repeat them here. The recommendations of the Report were finally rejected. It was not until 1819, when the war was over, that the Bank of England began to take steps to resume cash payments.

Among the innumerable participants in this new phase of the Bank Restriction Controversy we need consider only Ricardo and Bosanquet. Ricardo was both an instigator of the anti-Bank view and a supporter of the Bullion Report. His conclusions with respect to the contemporary conditions were essentially the same as those found in the Bullion Report.[2] Like most of the other supporters of the anti-Bank view, he considered money as a commodity and its value as governed by the same law which governed the value of other commodities. " Gold and silver, like other commodities, have an intrinsic value, which is not arbitrary, but is dependent on their scarcity, the quantity of labour bestowed in procuring them, and the value of the capital employed in the mines which produced them."[3] As to the market value of the money metals he seemed to believe it to be governed according to the quantity theory of money.[4] Paper money was considered by him as " a piece

[1] *Report, together with the Minutes of Evidence and Accounts, from the Select Committee on the High Price of Gold Bullion*, 1810.

[2] David Ricardo, *Three Letters on the Price of Gold*, 1809 (ed. by J. H. Hollander, Baltimore, 1903), *passim*; *The High Price of Bullion, a proof of the Depreciation of Bank Notes*, London, 1810, *passim*. The fourth edition of the latter is reprinted with other essays in *Economic Essays by David Ricardo*, edited by E. C. K. Gonner, London, 1923.

[3] *Essays*, p. 3. See also his *Principles of Political Economy*, Gonner's edition, p. 340.

[4] " The value of the circulating medium of every country bears some

of money on which the seignorage is enormous, amounting to all its value ". " Though it has no intrinsic value, yet, by limiting its quantity, its value in exchange is as great as an equal denomination of coin, or of bullion in that coin." [1] But when paper money was not convertible into cash there was always the danger that the issue might be excessive, that is to say, its quantity was no longer limited to that sum which would be employed if the paper money " were to regain its bullion value ".[2] In such a case, specie would have a premium and the exchanges would fall.

Like Thornton and others Ricardo also made efforts to prove that "the circulation can never be over full"; and in doing so he demonstrated how an increase of money would affect prices through changes in the money rates of interest :—

If the Bank were to bring a large additional sum of notes into the market, and offer them on loan, . . . they would for a time affect the rate of interest. The same effects would follow from the discovery of a hidden treasure of gold or silver coin. If the amount were large, the Bank, or the owner of the treasure, might not be able to lend the notes or the money at 4, nor perhaps above 3 per cent ; but having done so, neither the notes, nor the money, would be retained unemployed by the borrowers ; they would be sent into every market, and everywhere raise the price of commodities, till they were absorbed in the general circulation. It is only during the interval of the issues of the Bank, and their effect on prices, that we should be sensible of an abundance of money ; interest would, during that interval, be under its natural level ; but as soon as the additional sum of notes or of money became absorbed in the general circulation, the rate of interest would be high, and new loans would be demanded with as much eagerness as before the additional issues. The circulation can never be over full. If it be one of gold and silver, any increase in its quantity will be spread over the world. If it be one of paper, it will diffuse itself only in the country where it is issued. Its effects on prices will then be only local and proportion to the value of the commodities which it circulates. In some countries this proportion is much greater than in others, and varies, on some occasions, in the same country. It depends upon the rapidity of circulation, upon the degree of confidence and credit existing between traders, and above all, on the judicious operations of banking. . . . No increase or decrease of its quantity, whether consisting of gold, silver, or paper money, can increase or decrease its value above or below this proportion."—*Essays*, p. 34.

[1] See *Principles*, p. 341.   [2] *Essays*, p. 126.

nominal, as a compensation by means of the exchange will be made to foreign purchasers.[1]

That leads us to his theory of international price relationships. Following Hume and others, he said : " The precious metals employed for circulating the commodities of the world . . . have been divided into certain proportions among the different civilized nations of the earth, according to the state of their commerce and wealth, and therefore according to the number and frequency of the payments which they had to perform." [2] " While so divided," he continued, " they preserve everywhere the same value." But what is meant by " the same value " ? Ricardo did not give any cut and dried answer to that question. In order to understand his position fully, we must turn first to his analysis of price relationships. To him the cost of conveyance being taken account of, the prices of " exportable " commodities or " commodities common to both countries " would be internationally equalized.[3] But as all commodities are not " exportable " or " common to both countries ", all prices are not equalized. Accordingly, he said that the " value " of money in terms of many commodities " may differ 5, 10, or even 20 per cent ".[4] It follows that if we measure the value of money in terms of the prices of all commodities taken together it cannot be the same in all countries. In the following passage he clearly showed why the value of money in terms of all commodities could not be internationally equal and how the relative price levels in the trading nations were determined :—

> In the early stages of society, when manufactures have made little progress, and the produce of all countries is nearly similar, consisting of all the bulky and most useful commodities, the value of money in different countries will be chiefly regulated by their distance from the mines which supplied the precious metals ; but as the arts and improvements of society advance, and different nations excel in particular manufactures, although distance may still enter into the calculation, the value of the precious metals will be chiefly

---

[1] *Essays*, p. 35 ; see also *Principles*, pp. 351 f.
[2] *Essays*, p. 3. After the establishment of banks, he pointed out, the increase or decrease of the value of banknotes had the same effects as a similar change in the quantity of metallic money.
[3] *Essays*, pp. 7, 46 and *passim*.   [4] *Principles*, p. 128.

regulated by the superiority of those manufactures. . . .
These I believe to be the only two causes which regulate the
comparative value of money in the different countries of the
world.[1]

In other words the differences in the cost of obtaining
gold for different countries—which are due either to
differences in the expense of conveying goods or to the
qualitative and quantitative differences in the efficiency of
factors of production—determine the differences in the
average prices in different countries. That point was later
taken up by Senior to form the basis of what we shall call
the Seniorian doctrine of international price relationships.
It remains for us to interpret Ricardo's proposition that
money preserves " every where the same value " and to
see how that proposition could be reconciled with the idea
contained in the passage just quoted. In order that the
value of money might be comparable among nations, it
had to be expressed in terms of something, which was
" common " to all countries. The idea of a commodity
" common " to all nations was, however, conceivable only
when we arbitrarily supposed the existence of " exportable
products " as a class distinguished from " non-exportable
products " and assumed that in the case of the former the
expense of conveyance might be ignored. Upon that
assumption, all " exportable products " were commodities
" common " to all nations. They would command, if
trade were free, the same prices in all countries ; or what
was the same thing, the value of money in terms of them
would be everywhere the same. As a " non-exportable
product " in one country and a " non-exportable product "
of an identical constitution in another country were not
commodities " common to both countries ", their prices
would not be the same. In spite of that, as pointed out
by Senior and Mises, the value of money would remain
the same for both countries, because those differences in
the prices of the respective " non-exportable products "
should be explained by differences in the quality of the
commodities offered and demanded but not by the
differences in the value of money itself. Hence there would
be differences in prices though not a difference in the value
of money. It was to explain that divergence of prices that

[1] *Principles*, pp. 124–6.

Ricardo presented what we call the Seniorian doctrine. There is then no contradiction between the Seniorian doctrine and the proposition that the value of money is everywhere the same.

Next we may examine his view on the possible causes of disturbance and on the mechanism of adjustment. Here his view is, in the main, similar to that of Wheatley. He said :—

> The temptation to export money in exchange for goods, or what is termed an unfavourable balance of trade, never arises but from a redundant currency.[1]

In other words, a monetary cause was the only possible cause of disturbance. If such a cause arose to disturb the equilibrium, Hume's law would, according to Ricardo, operate to correct it in the case of a metallic standard. In the case of a paper standard, the purchasing-power-parity doctrine would apply. He denied that equilibrium in international price relationships could be disturbed by changes in the balance of payments. He said :—

> Mr. Thornton has not explained to us why any unwillingness should exist in the foreign country to receive our goods in exchange for their corn ; and it would be necessary for him to show, that if such an unwillingness were to exist, we should agree to indulge it so far as to consent to part with our coin. If we consent to give coin in exchange for goods, it must be from choice, not necessity. We should not import more goods than we export, unless we had a redundancy of currency, which it therefore suits us to make a part of our exports. The exportation of the coin is caused by its cheapness, and is not the effect, but the cause of an unfavourable balance : we should not export it, if we did not send it to a better market, or if we had any commodity which we could export more profitably. . . . If, which is a much stronger case, we agreed to pay a subsidy to a foreign power, money would not be exported whilst there were any goods which could more cheaply discharge the payment.[2]

Ricardo's position here may be summarized in two propositions—

(a) an exportation of gold is always the cause, never the effect, of an unfavourable balance of trade ; and

---

[1] *Essays*, p. 9.   [2] *Essays*, pp. 10–12.

(b) a failure of the harvests, or the grant of a subsidy or a loan to a foreign country, does not create a redundancy of currency, and therefore does not result in the export of gold.

The latter proposition in turn implied that a failure of harvests would immediately and automatically cause a proportionate change in the reciprocal demands of countries for each other's products.   That, as pointed out by Dr. Iverson, pre-supposes " that, consciously or unconsciously, he has based his reasoning upon the idea that a transfer of capital means *eo ipso* a transfer of an equal amount of buying power ", or in other words upon what we call the Wicksellian theory of transfer.   If Ricardo's position is interpreted in that way the only difference between Ricardo and Thornton is that, while to the latter the mechanism of adjustment, as described in the Wicksellian theory, took time to work out its effects, to Ricardo the mechanism was immediately effective.   In fact, the doctrine Ricardo implied in his criticism was the classical theory of transfer as expounded by Hume.

That view was strongly criticized in the *Edinburgh Review* by Malthus.   He, siding with the classical theory, said :—

> The great fault of Mr. Ricardo's performance, is the partial view which he takes of the causes which operate upon the course of Exchange.   Independently of the wearing or the adulteration of the coin, the effects of which are readily intelligible, there are, we conceive, two causes, perfectly distinct in their origin, though nearly similar in their effects, by which the exchange is affected.   The first, and the most ordinary, is the varying demand for different sorts of produce arising from the varying desires and necessities of the nations connected with each other by commerce : The second is a comparative redundancy or deficiency of currency, in whatever way it may be occasioned. . . . [In the first case], the exportation of bullion was the *effect of a balance of trade*, originating in causes which may exist without any relation whatever to redundancy or deficiency of currency.   In other cases, a redundancy or deficiency of currency is the exciting *cause of the balance of trade* and payments, and of the exportation or the importation of bullion. . . . Mr. Ricardo, however, instead of directing his attention to both these causes, confines it to only one of them.   He attributes a favourable or unfavourable exchange *exclusively* to a redundant or deficient currency, and overlooks the varying desires and wants of

different societies, as an original cause of a temporary excess of imports above exports, or exports above imports.[1]

That criticism was immediately answered at length by Ricardo. His argument was essentially the same as before, but he disclosed one of his underlying reasons for rejecting the classical theory of transfer, even as a transitional mechanism, namely that gold would not be exported if it were soon to be re-imported.[2] He conceded, however, that a bad harvest itself might create a redundancy of currency and thus cause an outflow of gold. He said :—

> If the circulating medium of England consisted wholly of the precious metals, and were a fiftieth part of the value of the commodities which it circulated . . . [and if] England, in consequence of a bad harvest, would come under the case mentioned—of a country having been deprived of a part of its commodities, and therefore requiring a diminished amount of circulating medium. The currency, which was before equal to her payments, would now become super-abundant, and relatively cheap, in the proportion of one-fiftieth part of her diminished production ; the exportation of this sum, therefore, would restore the value of her currency to the value of the currencies of other countries.[3]

As pointed out by Professor Viner, that was not the sort of gold movement posited by the advocates of the classical theory. What Ricardo had in mind was that the outflow of gold was a consequence of a change in the proportion of commodities and money and that its purpose was the maintenance unaltered of the original relation between the price levels, whereas the outflow of gold, as described in the classical theory, was the cause of an alteration of the proportion between commodities and money, and hence a change in the price and income structures.

In his private correspondence with Malthus, Ricardo defended his main position, although he admitted that his theory would be applicable only to a society without

---

[1] See T. R. Malthus's unsigned review article entitled " Depreciation of Paper Currency ", in *Edinburgh Review*, February, 1811, pp. 340–372. The reference is to pp. 342–3. In the same article (pp. 363–6) Malthus also presented a doctrine of forced saving similar to that of Bentham. At about the same time Dugald Stewart, in a letter which was not published until 1855, also produced a doctrine of forced saving. See *The Collected Works of Dugald Stewart*, vol. viii, pp. 440–9.

[2] *Essays*, p. 45.

[3] *Essays*, p. 47.

friction and needed some modification when applied to the actual world.[1] He consistently maintained the proposition that gold would not be exported if it would speedily return.[2] He also elucidated the proposition that the varying demand for different sorts of produce could not be the cause but the effect of the state of currency. The demands for particular commodities, he said,

> are in my opinion regulated by the relative state of the currency ; they are not causes but effects. You appear to me not sufficiently to consider the circumstances [which] induce one country to contract a debt to another. [In] all the cases you bring forward you always suppose the debt already contracted, forgetting that I uniformly contend that it is the relative state of the currency which is the motive to contract itself. The corn, I say, will not be bought unless money be relatively redundant ; you answer me by supposing it already bought, and the question to be only concerning the payment.[3]

The same, however, cannot be said of subsidy or similar payments. Ricardo seemed to have found it necessary to concede that a subsidy payment might affect the rate of exchange and internatioanl price relationships. It had that effect, " because a demand for bills arising from such a cause would not be in consequence of the natural commerce of the country. Such a demand would therefore have the effect of forcing the exports of commodities by means of the bounty which the exchange would afford." [4] In connection with his discussion of the payment of subsidy, he recognized that the rate of exchange did play a very important role in the process of adjustment, precisely in the way described by Hume and Foster.[5]

Bosanquet [6] was probably the best critic of the Bullion Report and a strong opponent of Ricardo.[7] He tried to

[1] *Letters of Ricardo to Malthus*, ed. by Boner, pp. 18–19.
[2] Ibid., pp. 19, 1–2, 22 and *passim*.
[3] *Letters of Ricardo to Malthus*, p. 11.
[4] Ibid., p. 15 ; see also pp. 20 f.
[5] Ibid., pp. 18–19.
[6] Bosanquet, *Practical Observations of the Report of the Bullion Committee*, 1810. We have used the 2nd ed. published in London in the same year.
[7] Among the other opponents of the anti-Restriction group we may mention Coutts Trotter, *The Principles of Currency and Exchanges, applied to the Report*, 2nd ed., London, 1810 ; J. C. Herries, *A Review of the Controversy respecting the High Price of Bullion, and the State of our*

refute one by one the main propositions of the anti-Restriction group. With regard to the problem of exchange rates, he said that the proposition that exchange rates could not long vary beyond the specie points unless the currency had been depreciated was true only when the following condition was fulfilled : " The country by which the balance of payment is due shall possess bullion or specie sufficient to liquidate it " and at the same time did not prohibit, or at least effectually prohibit, the export of their currency.[1] But that condition was not fulfilled. Moreover, like other defenders of the Bank, he declared that " the usual cause of variations in the foreign exchanges and price of bullion " was " the fluctuations in the balance of payments, due to or by Great Britain ".[2] As to the problem whether the paper currency of the Bank was issued to excess, he rightly pointed out that the opinion of the Report was founded on the two following propositions.   First the Bank possessed the power of adding to the amount of their notes in circulation beyond the absolute demand for paper, as a circulating medium.   Second the issues of the Bank regulated those of the country banks and were dependent upon and proportionate thereto.[3] He thought that both propositions were untrue.   In his attempt to refute the second proposition, there was very little which was worth notice.[4]   His argument against the first proposition was, however, suggestive. He said :—

Mr. Ricardo has assimilated the Bank of England during the restriction, so far as relates to the effects of its issues, to a gold-mine, the produce of which . . . has the acknowledged effect of depreciating the value of the existing medium, or, in other words, of raising the prices of commodities for which it is usually exchanged. . . . But Mr. Ricardo has not stated, what is essential to the comparison, why it is that the discovery of a gold-mine would produce this effect. It would produce it, because the proprietors would issue it, for whatever services, without any engagement, to give an equal value for it again to the holders, or any wish, or any means, of calling back and

Currency, London, 1811 ; Nicholas Vansittart, Substance of Two Speeches, made . . . in the . . . House of Commons, to which the Report of the Bullion Committee was referred, London, 1811 ; and George Rose, Substance of the Speech delivered in the House of Commons . . . on the Report of the Bullion Committee, London, 1811.

[1] Practical Observations, pp. 16, 21.
[2] Ibid., pp. 44–5 ; see also pp. 128–132.
[3] Practical Observations, p. 149.   [4] Ibid., pp. 73 ff.

annihilating that which they have issued. By degrees, as the issues increase they exceed the wants of circulation; gold produces no benefit to the holder as gold; he cannot eat it, nor clothe himself with it; to render it useful, he must exchange it either for such things as are immediately useful or for such as produce revenue. The demand and consequently the prices of commodities and real properties, measured in gold, increase; and will continue to increase so long as the mine continues to produce. And this effect will equally follow whether . . . the issue be gold from a mine or paper from a government-bank. . . . [But] there is not one point of analogy to the issues of the Bank of England. The principle on which the Bank issues its notes is that of loan. Every note is issued at the requisition of some party, who becomes indebted to the Bank for its amount, and gives security to return this note, or another of equal value, at a fixed and not remote period, paying an interest proportioned to the time allowed. . . . In the case of an excess of bank-paper the remedy is more simple : the surplus . . . would revert to us by a diminished application for discounts and advances on government-securities.[1]

Thereby he anticipated the main argument of the banking school of the Bank Charter Act controversy in the middle of the nineteenth century.

* * * *

The literature of the Bank Restriction controversy had thus pushed the theory of international price relationships another great step forward. The main problem in that controversy was what caused the unfavourable exchange and the high price of bullion. There were three possible explanations : first the excessive issues of bank-notes ; second the unfavourable balance of payments ; and third discredit or the loss of confidence. The last cause had not been advanced as an independent explanation of the situation. The issue was, therefore, limited chiefly to the question whether it is an excessive issue of currency or an unfavourable balance of payments which was responsible for the situation. In connection with the problem of excessive issue as a cause of disturbance there arose two important theoretical questions. First, was there any assignable limit for the circulation of the Bank of England notes ?

[1] Ibid., pp. 51–3. This, though interesting, is a wrong view ; see the criticism in Section 8 below.

Bosanquet, in defence of the Bank, gave a positive answer and argued that if the Bank issued its notes on the principle of loans, they could not be excessive. That view anticipated the so-called Banking Principle which we are going to discuss in a later section. The anti-Bank theorists showed that if the Bank's rate of interest was kept low enough, its circulation could expand beyond all assignable limits. In that connection they presented a valuable analysis of the " indirect " mechanism connecting money and prices (that is, via changes in borrowing). Moreover, if there was an excessive note circulation, what would be the effect of it on prices and the exchanges ? It was in the answering of that question that the purchasing-power-parity doctrine was advanced and Hume's law was re-stated. In connection with the problem of an unfavourable balance of payments as a cause of disturbance in international price relationships, the transfer problem was much discussed. Malthus and others claimed that an unfavourable balance could be a cause of disturbance in the international price relationships and thought that Hume's law would work to restore equilibrium. Foster was of the opinion that while an unfavourable balance might be a cause of disturbance, changes in the rate of exchange would, in most cases, be able to correct it without resort to the international movement of gold. Wheatley and Ricardo denied that an unfavourable balance of payments was a cause of disequilibrium in international price relationships and came near to what we call the Wicksellian theory of transfer. Thornton, though often misinterpreted, was really midway. He had presented, probably for the first time, the Wicksellian theory of transfer in an elaborate and clear-cut form, but he limited it to being an ultimate mechanism of adjustment and thought that during a short period of time the classical theory of transfer was correct.

*   *   *   *

After the resumption of cash payment by the Bank and the return to the gold standard at the old par, there was a long period of deflation. The fall of prices and the economic distress, which ensued, aroused much discussion of the problem whether the resumption of cash payment was responsible for the situation. While Ricardo continued to defend the return to gold at the old par, most economists thought that the return to gold at the old par was a mistake. They emphasized more and more the doctrine that falling prices reduced the volume of trade and retarded production and rising prices stimulated trade and production.[1]

7. Nassau Senior

In the three decades which elapsed between the last phase of the Bank Restriction controversy and the controversy concerning the Bank Charter Act of 1844, there appeared among other works the *Principles* of Ricardo (1817) and the *Lectures* of Senior.[2] With the former the theory of international trade took a new departure because in it was found one of the first formulations of the doctrine of comparative costs. As that doctrine was primarily one concerning the real aspects of the problem, it seems better to examine it in the next chapter where those aspects are fully treated.

The *Lectures* of Senior are mainly concerned with the monetary aspects of the problem. Let us first describe his theory of money under a metallic standard. He began with an attack on the quantity theory of money, because it usually suggested the idea " that the value of money is decided by causes differing from those which decided the value of other commodities ".[3] The value of money, according to him, should follow the general law of value. " The value of the precious metals, as money, must depend ultimately on their value as materials of jewellery and plate ; since, if they were not used as commodities, they could not circulate as money." [4] Furthermore, the causal sequence did not run from quantity to the value of money as supposed by the quantity theory of money, and he

[1] For a fuller description of the post-Restriction discussions see Viner, *Studies in the Theory of International Trade*, pp. 171 ff.
[2] Nassau William Senior, *Three Lectures on the Transmission of the Precious Metals from Country to Country and the Mercantile Theory of Wealth*, London, 1828 ; *Three Lectures on the Value of Money*, delivered before Oxford University, 1829, privately printed, 1840 ; and *Three Lectures on the Cost of obtaining Money and on some Effects of Private and Government Paper Money*, London, 1830. We have used the L.S.E. reprints, London, 1931. His doctrines are reproduced in his *Industrial Efficiency and Social Economy*, published posthumously from original MSS. by S. L. Levy, New York, 1928.
[3] *Value of Money*, pp. 1–8 ; *Social Economy*, ii, pp. 79–81.
[4] *Value of Money*, p. 17.

remarked " that whilst the fertility of the mines is unaltered, every increase of the total amount of silver is *preceded* by an increase of its value, indeed, could not take place, unless so preceded ; and that every diminution of the value of silver is *followed* by a miminution of the whole quantity ".[1]

The general law of the value of money in his analysis was that the value of money would be such that the quantity supplied was equal to the quantity demanded, and it had, in the long run, to equal its cost of production. To begin with, let it be assumed that the production of gold was subject to the law of constant cost. Then the value of gold would become fixed and the quantity of money produced was determined mainly by the demand conditions. In that case, if there were no foreign commerce " the quantity of gold produced would depend partly on the quantity wanted for plate, including under that word all use of gold except as money, and partly on the quantity wanted for money ".[2] The quantity wanted for plate " would, of course, depend on the prevailing fashions of the country ", and called for no further observations. The quantity wanted for money was much more complicated. It was in connection with the explanation of the latter point, that is, the causes determining the quantity of money, which a community should possess, that Senior advanced a clear-cut " cash-balance doctrine " :—

> It is obvious, in the first place, that the whole quantity of money in a community must consist of the aggregate of all the different sums possessed by the different individuals of whom it is constituted. And what this quantity shall be must depend partly on the number of those individuals ; partly on the value in money of the aggregate of their respective incomes ; and partly on the average proportion of the value of his income which each individual habitually keeps by him in money. . . . What proportion of the value of his income each individual shall habitually retain in money . . . may be said to depend, first, on the proportion to his income of his purchases and sales for money ; and secondly, on the rapidity with which they succeed one another.[3]

Thus, while the number of individuals and their money incomes remained the same, the demand for money depended on the proportion in which each individual kept his income

[1] *Value of Money*, p. 55.   [2] Ibid., p. 19.
[3] Ibid., pp. 11 f. See also *Social Economy*, ii, pp. 82 f.

in cash, which in turn depended on the rapidity of its circulation.

In that connection Senior developed the theory first suggested by North that there was a definite relationship between the monetary and the non-monetary uses of the precious metals. He said :—

> Any increase or diminution of the demand for plate occasions an increase or diminution of the demand for silver in the same direction, and a diminution or increase in the demand for money in an inverse direction. An increased demand for money must, in a similar manner, increase the demand for silver and diminish the demand for plate and vice versa.[1]
>
> The demands for plate and money are antagonistic demands, and, in a great measure, neutralize one another : that an increased consumption of plate, by raising the value of silver, occasions less money to be necessary ; and . . . that a diminished demand for plate, by sinking the value of silver, makes more money necessary. . . .[2]

It was the resultant of the two antagonistic uses of the precious metals that constituted the aggregate demand for the precious metals. But of the two Senior considered the non-monetary uses as the more fundamental. " Ultimately and principally [is] the demand for them as commodities ; as the material of plate, gilding, and jewellery ; and through the intervention, and as a consequence of that demand, the demand for them as money." [3]

Although upon the assumption of constant costs in gold production, the quantity of gold produced depended solely upon its demand, demand did not affect the value of gold except for short intervals. He said :—

> I say, except during comparatively short intervals, because though the causes which limit the supply of gold are supposed to be unalterable, those which give it utility, or, in other words, which create the demand for it, might be increased or diminished ; and during the interval between the diminution or increase of the demand, and the increase or diminution of the supply in the market, the value might rise above, or sink below, the cost of production.[4]

Thus, ultimately the value of money was determined by its cost of production. He then removed the assumption of constant costs and demonstrated how the value of money

[1] *The Value of Money*, pp. 46 f. See also pp. 24 f. and *passim*.
[2] Ibid., pp. 53 f.   [3] Ibid., p. 37.
[4] Ibid., p. 23 ; see also pp. 18, 30.

was determined by the cost of production " under the least favourable circumstances ".[1]

In the next place he discussed the problem of the effects of bank credit on prices. He pointed out that by diminishing the use of money in exchange the introduction or expansion of bank credit would cause " a rise in the price of every commodity except plate, and in the wages of all labourers except the gatherers of gold ".[2] He also demonstrated the functioning of the doctrine " that the demands of commerce for loans and discounts at a rate below the usual rate are insatiable ".[3]

One more point should be noted before we go to his theory of international price relationships. The cost of production theory of the value of money, as advanced by Senior, is not irreconcilable with the quantity theory of money. The best way to reconcile the two theories is to use, as Cantillon did, the cost of production theory to explain the intrinsic value of the money metal and to use the quantity theory to explain the market value of the metal. That is the way, as we shall see, in which J. S. Mill tried to reconcile the two theories.

Senior's contributions to the theory of international price relationships were even more valuable. In his doctrine concerning the comparative values of money in different countries he pointed out, like all the other classical economists, that in equilibrium the exchanges would be at par and that the value of money everywhere would be the same. He considered it as " a peculiar and important attribute of the precious metals when used as money : that their value was almost entirely independent of locality ".[4] He was the first economist to give a clear explanation of the meaning of the classical doctrine that the value of money was everywhere the same and to demonstrate that differences in the prices of goods of similar composition in different places were perfectly reconcilable with the assumption of an equality of the value of money. His description of those matters was so excellent that it is worth quoting in full :—

> Because 1,000 sovereigns will purchase 200 acre of land in Wales and not one in London, Mr. [James] Mill considers money estimated in land of greater value in Wales than in London. But 1,000 sovereigns in London will purchase just

---

[1] *The Value of Money*, pp. 32 ff., 57 ff.   [2] *Social Economy*, ii, p. 88.
[3] Ibid., ii, p. 117.   [4] Ibid., ii, p. 55.

as much Welsh land as 1,000 sovereigns in Wales. If there are two purchasers in an auction room at Carmarthen, one of whom has his bag of sovereigns in his hand, and the other Bank of England notes of equal amount (which are only an authority to receive a given amount of sovereigns in London), we shall find that the notes purchase just as much land as the sovereigns. To take another example, 1,000 sovereigns will purchase 1,000 chaldrons of coal in Newcastle, and only 500 in London, but it does not follow that 1,000 sovereigns in Newcastle are of more value, estimated in coal, than 1,000 sovereigns in London. The fact is that a person in Newcastle having 1,000 sovereigns in London will be able to purchase with them just as much Newcastle coal as if he had the sovereigns with him. The only inference from all the facts is that 1,000 sovereigns in London, Wales, or Newcastle, though of precisely equal value themselves, exchange for different quantities of what are in fact different commodities : exchange in a different proportion for coal in Newcastle and for (what is a different commodity) coal in London ; just as they exchange in different proportions for coal and diamonds.[1]

Senior accounted for the uniformity in the value of money as follows :—

This uniform value of money . . . [is] partly without doubt from its portableness. But a bar of gold weighing 20 pounds is as portable as 1,000 sovereigns, and yet such a bar in Liverpool would not exchange in the London market for as much as a similar bar in London. The purchaser would deduct from its price the expense of transport. In the case of the sovereigns he would make no such reduction. The principal cause is that in the case of the sovereigns he does not expect the expense of transport to be incurred. Every day many purchases are made in London by persons whose money is at Liverpool, and in Liverpool by persons whose money is in London. But the payments are not made by a transport of money, but by an exchange of debts, or in commercial language by *bills of exchange*. . . . As long as the debts between London and Liverpool are capable of being adjusted without the transport of money, either by a direct exchange of bills or by an exchange of their respective debts and credits at third places, the exchange between them is said to be at *par*. And equal sums of money in each place are of precisely the same value. . . . The reciprocal value of the moneys of different countries using different coins or, as it is usually termed, the foreign

---

[1] *Social Economy*, pp. 55–6. Professor Mises has independently advanced a similar theory ; see Ch. V, Sec. 7, below. Since Senior's *Social Economy* was not published until 1928, Mises could not have read it when he wrote his *Theory of Money and Credit*.

exchange, is governed by the same principles although their application is more complex.[1]

His opinion of the causes of disturbance and its correction was mainly " classical ". He presented an excellent exposition of Hume's law as a correction of an adverse balance of payments or of an excessive circulation of money.[2] He examined how wages and prices were determined in countries which possessed mines of the precious metals as well as in countries into which the precious metals constantly flowed. In the former, all prices ultimately depended on the cost of producing the precious metals and all the wages of labour on the money wages of the miners. " Though the remuneration paid to the miner is not identical with that received by other producers, yet . . . it affords the scale by which the remuneration of all other producers is calculated." [3] In countries which possessed no mines of the precious metals " the mine . . . is the general market of the world : the miners are those who produce those commodities by the exportation of which the precious metals are obtained, and of the amount of the precious metals, which by a given exertion of labour, and advance of capital, they can obtain, must afford the scale by which the remuneration of all other producers is calculated ".[4] In other words the wages obtained by the labourers of the exporting industries, for whose produce the precious metals were imported, " regulate the wages of all other labourers in the same country." [5] The wages of the labourers in the exporting industries in turn were proportionate to the amount of the precious metals obtained by a certain quantity of labour ; and the amount of the precious metals obtained (or the cost of obtaining money) depended on the efficiency of the labour itself. It followed, therefore, that the more efficient its labour, the higher the level of wages a country had.[6] He declared that this—the relative efficiency of labour— was chiefly responsible for the discrepancies in the wages of

[1] Senior, *Social Economy*, pp. 56–9.
[2] *Transmission of the Precious Metals*, pp. 6–13.
[3] *The Value of Money*, pp. 55–6.
[4] *Cost of Obtaining Money*, pp. 15 f.
[5] Ibid., pp. 12 f.
[6] Ibid., pp. 11–12. " In fact the portableness of the precious metals and the universality of the demand for them rendered the whole commercial world one country, in which bullion is the money and the inhabitants of each nation form a distinct class of labourers. We know that in the small market of every district the remuneration paid to the

labour (in terms of gold or silver) in different countries at the same period.[1] Finally he came to commodity prices in countries which did not mine the precious metals. His conclusion was that the price (that is the value in gold or silver) of all commodities depended upon " the gold and silver which can be obtained by exporting the result of a given quantity of labour, the current rate of profit, and in each case, the amount of the wages which have been paid, and the time for which they have been advanced ".[2] If the cost of obtaining gold was relatively small, the general level of prices would be relatively high. If the difficulty of obtaining it increased, there would be a general fall in prices.[3] That doctrine concerning discrepancies in wages and prices among trading nations we shall designate as the Seniorian doctrine of international price relationships.

8. The Bank Charter Act Controversy

In the decade following the crisis of 1836–7 the long-discussed problem of what was the best form of organization for the Bank of England insistently called for a solution and thus a new controversy arose.[4] Although the controversy was mainly concerned with banking and credit, it had a bearing on the theory of international price relationships, because in discussing the relations of the exchanges to the note issue, credit, and other connected matters, the participants in the controversy went into many departments of the problem of international price relationships. The controversy has been known as the Bank Charter Act controversy. The two opposite parties to the controversy

producer is in proportion to the value produced. And consequently that if one man can by superior diligence or superior skill, or by the assistance of a large capital, or by differing for a longer time his renumeration, or by any advantage, natural or acquired, occasioned a more valuable product, he would receive a higher reward. . . . And for similar reason in the general market of the world an Englishman is better paid than a Frenchman." (p. 14.)

[1] It followed that a high level of wages was the result of high efficiency and by no means unfitted a country for its competition with foreign producers.—*Cost of Obtaining Money*, pp. 26 f.

[2] Ibid., pp. 13–14.

[3] Ibid., p. 21.   Reference should be made to Miss Marian Bowley's *Nassau Senior and Classical Economics*, London, 1937, ch. 6, esp. pp. 221–5.

[4] For a detailed description of the events connected with the controversy, see Macleod, *Banking*, vol. ii, chs. xi–xii. For its bearing on banking policy see Mises, *The Theory of Money and Credit*, English ed., pp. 368 ff., and Wicksell, *Lectures*, English ed., ii, pp. 171–190.

K

have come to be known as the " currency school " and the
" banking school ". The main proposition of the currency
school, or what has also been called " the currency principle ",
was that there is always a danger of an over-issue of banknotes, which therefore should be strictly regulated—so
regulated that the notes might become mere tokens for
metallic money. The Banking School, on the contrary,
denied the possibility of an over-issue of banknotes and
regarded " elasticity " as the essential characteristic of the
note issue. The theoretical foundation of the currency
principle was provided by Thornton and the anti-Bank
writers in the Bank Restriction controversy. However,
the first writer to advance the currency principle as a
banking policy was Thomas Joplin, who is sometimes called
" the inventor of the currency principle ".[1]   As Joplin
dealt primarily with the banking structure, it is best that
we turn at once to Norman, Loyd, and Torrens, the three
most important champions of the currency principle.

Norman started with the classical theory of the value
of money, that is that while the value of money was
ultimately regulated by the costs of production, its market
value depended upon demand and supply.[2]   Then, like the
classical economists, he carried the theory beyond the
frontiers of a single nation and came to the conclusion that
" the whole mass of coin and bullion is distributed according
to the respective wants of the several countries upon the
principle of competition ".[3]   While so distributed, there
would be " general equality of value in the precious metals
over the whole globe ".[4]   Like Senior, he pointed out that
differences in local prices could exist without invalidating
the doctrine that the value of money was internationally
uniform. He said :—

> One, two, twenty, nay, it is possible, though highly im-
> probable, that all the commodities would fall in money price,
> without any appreciation of the currency, that is to say,

---

[1] The most important of Joplin's works is *An Analysis and History of
the Currency Question*, London, 1832. For some of his minor contributions
to the theory of money and international price relationships, see ibid.,
pp. 101 ff., 158 ff., 169, etc.
[2] George W. Norman, *Remarks upon Currency and Banking*, London,
1833, pp. 5, 7.
[3] *Remarks*, p. 6. If it happened at a particular time to be mal-
distributed, Hume's law would operate to establish a natural distribution ;
see pp. 7–10.   [4] Ibid., p. 13.

without the existence of any change affecting the precious metals themselves. If such an event should take place without any derangement in the exchanges, or should continue when, after a derangement, the equilibrium had been restored, we might be sure that the cause was to be sought in some circumstance extrinsic to the currency, unless at the same period a corresponding fall, of an exactly similar amount, could be traced in the money prices of all other countries. Then, indeed, it might be fairly assumed, though not with absolute certainty, that the phenomenon was referable to some alteration of the precious metals themselves.[1]

The key to the question whether the relative values of moneys were equal or not was not the prices of commodities but the rates of exchange. As long as the rate of exchange was at par the value of money at home was equal to that abroad, whatever might be the local prices of commodities. Again, like the classical economists, he pointed out that " an issue of paper money produces precisely the same effect on general prices as would follow from an augmentation in the quantity of the precious metals—it lowers their value ".[2] Hume's law would operate to restore the " general equality of value in the precious metals over the whole globe ". There the exchange rate was also " the sole guide " to the question whether a country's circulation was excessive or not.

That was the theoretical foundation of Norman's opinion on banking policy, which might be summarized in two propositions. First, since the value of the precious metals was ultimately determined by the cost of production and since " there is every reason to believe that during a long course of years, no considerable change has occurred in the cost of producing the precious metals ",[3] he came to the conclusion that " the precious metals afford the best and only safe standard ". Secondly, although a paper currency was more convenient than a metallic currency, it always involved the danger of an over-issue. Therefore he proposed to establish " a single issuing body ", the only business of which " would be to issue notes for gold and gold for notes ", so that the mixed circulation of coin and paper would approach " to what would be the amount of coin in case there was no paper ". Under such a system, he thought, the country would have all the advantages of a

[1] *Remarks*, p. 14.   [2] Ibid., p. 11.
[3] Ibid., p. 4.

pure metallic standard and at the same time retain many of the advantages of a paper currency.[1] The main arguments and conclusions of S. J. Loyd (known in his later years as Lord Overstone) were the same as those of Norman, though they were not systematically stated. He conceived a metallic currency as an ideal currency, because it " will adjust itself ".[2] Under a purely metallic currency, " no danger of total exhaustion of the gold could arise. As a portion of the metallic money was exported, the quantity of that remained being diminished, the value of it would be proportionately increased ; and consequently a limited proportion only of the gold in circulation could be drawn out of the country by any foreign demand." [3] Under a " mixed circulation " of coin and paper, however, there was always the danger of over-issue.[4] Contraction of the currency was generally not cœval with a loss of bullion and the amount of the contraction did not coincide with the extent of the diminution of the bullion. Notes were often issued in place of the metallic money exported and thereby prevented a fall in internal prices and retarded the restoration of equilibrium. " There can then be no certainty that the value of currencies will be thus equalized ; and, consequently, there can be no security that the bullion may not be entirely drained out. . . . Bullion, equal to the amount of the whole circulation may be drained out, if its place be continually supplied by paper issues, and the total amount of the circulation be thus kept diminished." [5] In order to prevent that danger, a mixed circulation of paper and coin should be so regulated that its amount was " equal to what would have been the amount of a metallic circulation ". The best measure of what should be the amount of the currency was " the influx or efflux of bullion ".[6] Torren's [7] view was similar to that held by Norman

---

[1] *Remarks*, pp. 29 f., 57.
[2] S. J. Loyd, *Tracts . . . on Metallic and Paper Currency*, 1837–1857, pp. 341, 343.   [3] Ibid., pp. 244, 250 f.
[4] " I understand by excessive issues, issues which render the amount of the paper-circulation at any moment greater than would be the amount of a metallic circulation." (Ibid., p. 189.)   [5] Ibid., p. 252.
[6] *Tracts*, p. 191 ; see also pp. 202, 380, *passim*.
[7] The principal works of Robert Torrens on this subject was *The Principles and Practical Operation of Sir Robert Peel's Bill of 1844*, 1st ed., 1848 ; 4th ed., 1858. Besides his " currency principle ", Torrens had made some important contributions to the theory of international trade. Firstly (in his *The Economists Refuted*, London, 1808, and particularly in *An Essay on the External Corn Trade*, London, 1st ed., 1815 ; 4th ed.,

and Loyd. He also started from the classical doctrines of the value of money, natural distribution of the precious metals among the trading nations and international price adjustments.[1] Like Norman and Loyd, he insisted on the gravity of the danger of the over-issue of notes in the case of a mixed circulation of coins and convertible paper in the absence of proper control. The danger of an excessive issue would arise from a failure to make the necessary contraction when bullion was lost as well as in the temptation to expand the note issue in such a situation. To him convertibility was no safeguard, for " the effect of convertibility is not to prevent the occurrence of excess and depreciation but, on the contrary, to limit and to check excess and depreciation after they have occurred ".[2] Therefore in order to ensure a timely limitation against the excess it was necessary to rely upon other regulations. The proposal of Torrens was " to cause our mixed circulation of coin and banknotes to expand and contract, as it would have expanded and contracted under similar circumstances, had it consisted exclusively of coin " and to make the banknotes mere tokens of metallic coins.

The Currency School relied, on the whole, chiefly upon the classical doctrine of the natural distribution of the precious metals among trading nations and Hume's law as the theoretical foundation of its banking policy proposals. The term " power of over-issue " was employed by its

1829) he formulated what is now called the doctrine of comparative costs. In the latter work, moreover, he applied the doctrine of comparative costs to the labour market and anticipated the Seniorian explanation of discrepancies of wages (see Edwin R. A. Seligman, *Essays in Economics*, New York, 1925, pp. 74–6). Secondly, in his essay on *The Budget* (London, 1884) he anticipated J. S. Mill's doctrine of international value. Thirdly he participated in the Bank Restriction controversy and in 1812 published *An Essay on Money and Paper Currency*. He concluded that there were three causes of depreciation of the circulating medium, namely " alarm, excessive issues, and an unfavourable course of foreign exchange " (p. 102). In his *Essays on Money*, however, he advanced some views which were not consistent with his currency principle. Fourthly, in his *Essays on Money*, and particularly in his *Comparative Estimate* (London, 1819) he worked out a new concept of an ordered series of commodities, which could be successively called out to meet deficits in the balance of payments (see Angell, op. cit., pp. 62 f.). Finally in his *Essay on the Production of Wealth* (London, 1821) he developed the concept of " lags " in economic relations.

[1] *The Principles of Peel's Bill*, 1st ed., pp. 57 ff. ; 4th ed., chs. ii and iii.

[2] Ibid., 1st ed., p. 106.

members as implying, in the words of Torrens, " that banks of issue may cause a temporary expansion beyond the metallic equilibrium until the level is restored by the expulsion of bullion." [1] Thus the term " excessive issue " was explained in terms of international price relationships. In doing so they failed to give due emphasis to another of their reasons in support of the proposition that convertible paper was liable to over-issue. That was the reason generally brought forward by the anti-Bank group, namely that if the banks kept their interest rates low enough, the demand for their notes would be insatiable. All of them, particularly Loyd, had presented that argument in one form or another,[2] but none of them had given it sufficient emphasis.

Another defect in the arguments of the currency school lay in its definition of money or currency. They held that both coins and central bank notes should be included in the category of " money " but that cheques should not be so included, because cheques did not possess the power of closing transactions. Starting from that position they came to the erroneous conclusion that the volume of cheques could not create a state of " redundancy " in the currency and hence could not have any bearing on the international movement of bullion.[3] That view was certainly incorrect. In reality, banknotes and bank deposits are both fiduciary media and produce essentially similar effects on internal prices and on international price relationships. But, as pointed out by Mises, " the doctrine of the Currency School does not stand or fall on the nature of cheques and deposits. It is enough to correct it on this point,—to take its propositions concerning the issue of notes and apply them also to the opening of deposit accounts. . . . Its mistake on this point is of small significance in comparison with that made by the Banking School. . . . And in any case it does not seem an inexcusable mistake to have made if we take into account the relatively backward development of even the English deposit system at the time when the foundations of the classical theory of banking were being laid and if we further consider the case with which the legal

---

[1] *The Principles of Peel's Bill* (1st ed.), p. 109.
[2] Norman, op. cit., pp. 18–19 ; Loyd, op. cit., pp. 88, 173, 253, 264, 292, *passim* ; and Torrens, op. cit. (1st ed.), pp. 75 f., 107.
[3] Loyd, op. cit., pp. 63, 247, 342 f. ; Torrens, *Principles*, 1st ed., pp. 79 ff. ; 4th ed., ch. i.

differences between payment by note and payment by cheque might give rise to error."[1] The best spokesmen of the opposite view, that is the Banking Principle, were Thomas Tooke and John Fullarton.[2] According to that principle, under a metallic standard, only coins could be classed as money, whether convertible notes were circulating or not. Banknotes and other forms of paper credit, they contended, were essentially the same. It was a mistake to distinguish between them and to say that banknotes had an effect upon prices that was different from the effect produced by deposits and cheques. Only when notes were inconvertible did they become money, for convertibility, they argued, demonetized banknotes, while inconvertibility monetized them.[3]

The next issue which divided the Banking School from the Currency School was the mode of the operation of a pure metallic currency. The members of the former declared that it was necessary to distinguish between the precious metals and money. According to them a great error of the Currency School was that the latter assumed "that the precious metals, gold, and silver, and bullion are synonymous with currency and money, and are convertible terms". Generally the elasticity of a country's bullion reserve in the form of hoards and in the form of commodity made it possible to transmit precious metals from one country to another "to a considerable amount (five or six millions at least), without affecting the amount or value of the currency of the country from or to which the transmissions were made; and without being a cause or a consequence of alternation in general prices".[4] It was not until the increase in the precious metals was extraordinary that the volume

[1] Three other points generally held by the members of the Currency School may be mentioned here. First, they were generally of the opinion that country banks, like the central bank, had the power to make an over-issue of notes, and that their issues should also be regulated. Second, the Currency School stood for centralization of note issues and for the separation of the issuing from the banking departments of the central issuing bank. Third, while they demanded a positive and rigid limit on the note issues of the central bank, they advocated *laisser-faire* for all other banking activities.

[2] Tooke, *History of Prices*, London, vol. i, 1838; vol. ii, 1838; and vol. iii, 1840; vol. iv, 1848; *An Inquiry into the Currency Principle*, 1st ed., 1844; 2nd ed. 1844; *On the Bank Charter Act of 1844*, London, 1856. Fullarton, *On the Regulation of Currencies*, London, 1844.

[3] Tooke, *Inquiry* (2nd ed.) chs. iii–vi; Fullarton, op. cit., ch. ii.

[4] Tooke, ibid., pp. 7, 8, 18, 21, and elsewhere. That is true particularly of England, as she " is also an entrepot for receiving from the mines and

of money would be affected. That point will be further discussed in connection with their criticism of Hume's law. Thirdly, they differed from the currency school, as to the mode of operation of a mixed circulation of coin and convertible notes. To them there were important differences between coins or inconvertible notes (money) and convertible notes both in the volume of issue and in the effects on prices. Of the volume of an issue they said :—

There is this broad and clear distinction between all currencies of value [coins] and currencies of credit [convertible notes], that the quantity of the former is in no degree regulated by the public demand, whereas the quantity of the latter is regulated by nothing else. The gold, which is once melted and converted into coin, can never be returned again into the mine ; there it is, a permanent and irrevocable addition to the stock of money in the world ; the people among whom it is circulated have no voice in directing its destination.[1]

When a government issues paper money, inconvertible and compulsorily current, it is usually in payment for (a) the personal expenditure of the Sovereign or the governing power, (b) Public works and Buildings, (c) Salaries of Civil Servants, (d) Maintenance of Military and Naval Establishments. It is quite clear that paper created and so paid away by the Government not beingereturnable to the issuer, will constitute a fresh source of demand, and must be forced into and permeate all the channels of circulation.[2]

Banknotes, on the contrary, are never issued but on loan, and an equal amount of notes must be returned into the bank whenever the loan becomes due. Banknotes never, therefore, can clog the market by their redundance, nor afford a motive to anyone to pay them away at a reduced value in order to get rid of them. The banker has only to take care that they are lent on sufficient security, and the reflux and the issue will, in the long run, always balance each other.[3]

That doctrine of the impossibility of the over-issue of convertible notes is sometimes called the Principle of Reflux. The way in which that principle chiefly works

distributing the greater portion of the quantity applicable to the consumption of other countries, the bullion trade, totally independently of supplying the currency, must of necessity be very considerable ". (Ibid., pp. 12 f.) See also Fullarton, op. cit., pp. 140 ff.
[1] Fullarton, op. cit., p. 63.   [2] Tooke, Inquiry, pp. 69-70.
[3] Fullarton, op. cit., p. 64. That is substantially Bosanquet's argument ; see also Fullarton, op. cit., ch. v., and Tooke, Inquiry, ch. xi.

is a return of notes to the bank for cancellation of debts. It follows from that principle that, while coins and *fiat* money might be increased to the extent that prices will be affected, banknotes can never be issued in excess or in deficit relative to the " needs " of trade. In the latter case, the rise of prices is not preceded, but followed by an increase in the amount of their circulation. In other words, an increase in the amount of the circulation of notes is the effect, and not the cause of a rise in prices.[1]

To the principle laid down in the preceding paragraph one may raise the objection that the demands of commerce for loans and discounts at a rate below the equilibrium rate are insatiable. That objection, as already pointed out, was a common asset of the anti-Bank group in the Bank Restriction controversy. Tooke, in his *Considerations*, written some two decades previously, had held the same view. To him a new supply of money was bound to have effects on the rate of interest, " since it cannot enter into circulation otherwise than by reducing the rate of interest, other things remaining the same ; as it must inevitably at the time it is issued increase the number of lenders or diminish the number of borrowers. The additional currency, in whatever way it comes into circulation, and whether it is in the form of gold or paper or mere credit, must eventually raise the price of commodities and labour." [2]   When they attempted to explain the banking principle both Tooke and Fullarton were conscious of the contradiction between the banking principle and the classical doctrine of the market rate of interest as a connecting link between money and prices. Fullarton tried to escape the difficulty by limiting the classical doctrine to the case of changes in the volume of legal money. He recognized that an extraordinary influx of gold would work out its effects on prices through changes in the interest rate :—

> The inevitable results [of an influx of bullion and its consequent increase in funds available for productive investment] would be, first, a decline of the market rate of interest ;

[1] Tooke, *Inquiry*, ch. xii (esp. p. 70) ; Fullarton, op. cit., chs. v, vi.

[2] Tooke, *Consideration on the State of the Currency* (London, 1826), pp. 5–29. It should be noted that in his writings before 1840 Tooke was not always consistent with his " banking principle " which he advanced in the forties. Sometimes he went so far in his earlier writings that one may even place him in the currency school. (See T. E. Gregory, *An Introduction to Tooke and Newmarch's A History of Prices*, London, 1928,

next, a rise in the value of land, and of all interest-bearing securities ; and, lastly, a progressive increase in the prices of commodities generally.[1]

Quite illogically, Fullarton insisted that an increase of the note issue did not have a similar result. Tooke, on the contrary, entirely rejected in his *Inquiry* the classical doctrine. He started by pointing out the empirical fact that rising prices very rarely coincide with low or falling rates of interest but much more frequently with rising or high rates. He then drew the conclusion that " a reduced rate of interest has no necessary tendency to raise the prices of commodities. On the contrary, it is a cause of diminished cost of production, and consequently of cheapness ".[2] That view of Tooke's, though plausible, was incorrect. What affected prices, according to the classical doctrine, was not the absolute rate of interest in the market but the deviation of the market rate from the " equilibrium rate ". Whenever the " equilibrium rate " rose or fell, and the market rate did not rise or fall, or did not rise or fall immediately, to a similar extent, there was a deviation of the market rate from the equilibrium rate and prices were affected. The empirical fact, which had been discovered by Tooke, did not, therefore, invalidate the classical doctrine. Tooke was not right, furthermore, in drawing the conclusion, given above, namely that a fall in the rate of interest would, by reducing costs, lower the prices of commodities. As Wicksell rightly pointed out, " the argument is based on the inadmissible, not to say impossible, assumption that wages and rent would at the same time remain constant, whereas in reality a lowering of the rate of interest is equivalent to a raising of the shares of the other factors of production in the product. Indeed, as Ricardo (and more recently Böhm-Bawerk) proved, and as experience has often shown, a rise in wages or rent constitutes *ceteris paribus* just the necessary condition for the profitable employment of more capital in the service of production. A fall in loan rates caused by increased supplies of real capital (increased savings) should thus in itself cause neither a rise nor a fall in the average price level." [3] Tooke also objected

pp. 16, 31 ff., 69–79.) The principle of reflux is practically the same as one of the doctrines advanced by Law and other paper money mercantilists. See Chapter II, Section 9 above.

[1] Fullarton, op. cit., p. 62.   [2] Tooke, *Inquiry*, pp. 81, 123.
[3] Wicksell, *Lectures in Political Economy*, ii, p. 183.

to the doctrine " that a low, and especially a declining, rate of interest operates necessarily as a stimulus to speculation, not only in government stocks and shares both at home and abroad, that is in both British and foreign public and private securities, but also in the markets for produce ". He said :—

There are, doubtless, persons who, upon imperfect information and upon insufficient grounds, or with too sanguine a view of contingencies in their favour, speculate improvidently ; but their *motive* or *inducement* so to speculate is the opinion which, whether well or ill founded, or whether upon their own view or upon the authority or example of other persons, they entertain of the probability of an advance of price. It is not the mere facility of borrowing, or the difference between being able to discount at 3 or at 6 per cent, that supplies the *motive* for purchasing, or even for selling. Few persons of the description here mentioned ever speculate but upon the confident expectation of an advance of price of at least 10 per cent . . . but the utmost difference the rate of discount of 3 per cent and 6 per cent, namely 3 per cent per annum for three months, would on a quarter of wheat [at an average price of about 50s.] amount only to 4½d. per quarter, a difference which, I will venture to say, never induced or deterred a single speculative purchase. But, given the force of the motive, the extent to which it can be acted upon is doubtless affected as regards persons who can buy only on credit, or who must borrow in order to be able to buy, by the greater or less facility of borrowing.[1]

That argument, correct so far as it goes, did not invalidate the classical doctrine. The classical doctrine did not require that a fall in the discount rate should arouse " speculation " in the sense employed by Tooke. What it required was only that the availability of loanable capital at cheaper rates than usual should stimulate those businesses, which were on the point of expanding their activities, and fully maintain those which were about to restrict their activities or to close down altogether. Thus a moderate lowering of the discount rate was sufficient to produce a tendency to increased enterprise, to increased demand for goods and services, and therefore to rising prices.[2]

Closely connected with the question of the rates of discount and prices was a valuable contribution that Tooke

[1] Tooke, *History of Prices*, vol. iii, pp. 153–4. Cf. J. M. Keynes, *A Treatise on Money*, vol. i, pp. 190–6.

[2] See Wicksell, *Lectures*, ii, pp. 185 f.

made. He probably produced the first clear statement of how the bank rate could be used as a means of protecting a country's gold reserve by influencing the rate of foreign lending.[1] Thereby he anticipated Goschen's doctrine, which will be discussed later.

As already explained, the classical doctrine of prices was questioned by Tooke and Fullarton. What was the theory they offered in its stead ? They came near to what is now called " the income theory of prices ". Tooke said :—

> The prices of commodities do not depend upon the quantity of money indicated by the amount of banknotes, nor upon the amount of the whole of the circulating medium ; but . . . it is the quantity of money, constituting the revenues of different orders of the State, under the head of rents, profits, salaries, and wages, destined for current expenditure, that alone forms the limiting principle of the *aggregate of money prices*, the only prices that can properly come under the designation of *general prices*. As the cost of production is the limiting principle of supply, so the *aggregate of money incomes* devoted to expenditure for consumption is the determining and limiting principle of *demand*.[2]

Tooke did not go a step forward to see how the " aggregate of money incomes " might be increased or diminished. Had he done so, he would have discovered that in the long run the aggregate of money incomes was proportional to the quantity of the circulating medium and that an increase of the volume of banknotes due to easier terms of lending meant an expansion of enterprise, an increase of money incomes, and consequently a rise in prices.

Finally, let us examine their criticism of Hume's law. Four propositions can be distinguished. First, based upon their distinction between bullion and money and their doctrine of the elasticity of a country's bullion reserve, they declared that a flow of the precious metals did not necessarily, and generally did not, bring about a contraction of the currency of the country exporting the precious

---

[1] Tooke, *History of Prices*, ii, p. 296 ; iv, pp. 196–202.
[2] Tooke, *Inquiry*, p. 123. See also pp. 67–76. The best exponents of the income theory of the value of money are Freidrich von Wieser, R. G. Hawtrey, and Albert Aftalion. See Wieser, *Social Economics* (English ed., pp. 250–264), Hawtrey, *Currency and Credit* (London, 1919, *passim*), and Aftalion, *Monnaie, prix et change* (Paris, 1927, pp. 157 ff.). We think that the best way to reconcile the quantity theory with the income theory of money is to recognize income as an intermediate mechanism connecting money and prices.

metals or an expansion of the currency of the country, to which the precious metals were exported. Thus the causal relationship between the movement of specie and the changes in the volume of currency was explicitly denied. " Consequently, the doctrine by which it is maintained that every export or import of bullion in a metallic circulation must entail a corresponding diminution of, or addition to, the quantity of money in circulation, and thus cause a fall or rise of general prices, is essentially incorrect and unsound." [1] Second, they pointed out that since the practice of investing capital in foreign securities had become general, the capital required for the liquidation of a foreign debt could be transmitted in the form of investment (as well as in gold) and that that formed a new instrument for the regulation of the exchanges and for the control of the international movements of specie. That point, however, was more important to Tooke than to Fullarton. Third, as to the initial cause of the movements of specie, they were of the opinion that it was governed almost exclusively by the state of the balance of payments.[2] Fourth, a more serious mistake was the extension of Hume's law to the banknote circulation. As convertible notes could never be excessive and could have no effect upon prices, they could not cause any movement of gold or silver. Both the third and the fourth points were obviously erroneous. There was, however, an important element of truth in the first two propositions.[3]

9. THE RESTATEMENT BY J. S. MILL

The equilibrium theory of international price relationships, which was first advanced by Hume and was later modified, refined or attacked by the participants of the Restriction

[1] Tooke, *Inquiry*, p. 121 ; Fullarton, op. cit., p. 122. Cf. Cairnes's criticism of the currency principle ; see Ch. V, Sec. 2, below.
[2] Fullarton, op. cit., pp. 115-120. It should be noted, however, that they also recognized alarm and other psychological factors as important causes of a drain of specie.
[3] Three other points commonly held by the members of the Banking School might be mentioned here. First they were against the separation of the central bank into issuing and banking departments, because " a total separation of the business of issue from that of banking is calculated to produce greater and more abrupt transitions in the rate of interest and in the state of credit." Second, to them what was important was not the regulation of currency but that of credit. Third, even if the regulation of the note issue was necessary, the object of regulating it was not to make them mere substitutes of coins but to maintain the solvency of the issuer and the convertibility of his notes.

and the Bank Act controversies in England, was restated by John Stuart Mill [1] in the form in which it came to be known as the classical theory. The position of Mill was an eclectic one. He wanted to reconcile the antagonistic views of as many of his predecessors and contemporaries as possible and to fuse their conflicting doctrines into an organic whole.

In order clearly to understand his theory of international price relationships, it is necessary to know his theory of money and credit. In those fields also his position was an eclectic one. His definition of money meant that coins and inconvertible notes alone were money. " It seems to be an essential part of the idea of money that it be legal tender." [2] Therefore, convertible notes did not fall into the category of money. On the contrary, notes, like book credits, bills of exchange, and cheques, were but one form of credit. [3]

He next examined how the value of money, that is the purchasing-power of money, was determined and made an excellent attempt to combine the doctrines of the authors of the quantity theory, of Ricardo, and of Senior. Like Ricardo and other classical economists, he pointed out :—

> The value of money, then, conforms permanently and, in the state of freedom, almost immediately, to the value of the metal of which it is made ; with the addition, or not, of the expenses of coinage, according as those expenses are borne by the individual or by the state. [4]

Now, " since gold and silver bullion are commodities," their natural or permanent value, like that of any other commodity, " is in the long run proportional to their cost of production in the most unfavourable existing circumstances, that is at the worst mine which it is necessary to work in order to obtain the required supply." [5] The cost of production doctrine was applied by Mill only to the places in which the precious metals were actually produced. In most countries money, or the material of which it was composed, was a foreign commodity. In the latter case the value of money was subject to the doctrine of international value, and we had to substitute for the cost of its

[1] J. S. Mill, *Essays on Some Unsettled Questions of Political Economy*, London, 1844, 1874 ; *Principles of Political Economy*, London, 1848.
[2] *Principles*, Ashley's ed., p. 539.
[3] Ibid., pp. 514–522.   [4] Ibid., p. 501.
[5] Ibid., p. 502 ; see also pp. 499 ff.

production the cost of obtaining it.[1] The cost of obtaining money was not, however, the same in all countries. As to the causes determining the cost of obtaining money, he combined the doctrine of Ricardo and that of Senior with his own doctrine of international values. His position was summed up in the following passage :—

> The countries whose exportable productions are most in demand abroad, and contain greatest value in smaller bulk, which are nearest to the mines, and which have least demand for foreign productions, are those in which money will be of lowest value or, in other words, in which prices will habitually range the highest. If we are speaking not of the value of money, but of its cost (that is the quantity of the country's labour which must be expended to obtain it) we must add to these four conditions of cheapness a fifth condition, namely " whose productive industry is the most efficient". This last, however, does not at all affect the value of money estimated in commodities : it affects the general abundance and facility with which all things, money and commodities together, can be obtained.[2]

That is the Seniorian doctrine in a modified form. Senior, as it will be recalled, emphasized only the fifth condition mentioned by Mill. Mill went a step further in taking other factors into consideration and giving them due emphasis. In that connection, it should be noted, the term " value of money " referred to the general level of prices and the doctrine advanced concerned the second, and not the first, problem of the theory as defined in our first chapter.

But " the adjustment takes a long time to effect in the case of a commodity [so small in its annual supply], so generally desired [so largely used], and at the same time so durable as the precious metals ".[3] Hence the market or the short-run value of money was more important. There again it followed the general law of value, according to which " the temporary or market value of a thing depends on the demand and supply ". Demand and supply in relation to money needed some explanation : " The supply of money . . . is all the money in *circulation* at the time. The demand for money, again, consists of all the goods offered for sale. . . . We are comparing goods of all sorts

---

[1] *Principles*, Ashley's ed., pp. 505, 607 f., 626 f. For Mill's doctrine of international value, see the detailed description in the next chapter.
[2] Ibid., p. 609.   [3] Ibid., p. 503.

on one side, with money on the other side, as things to be exchanged against each other." [1] He then followed Ricardo and other classical economists in turning the demand-and-supply theory into a quantity theory :—

The value of money, other things being the same, varies inversely as its quantity ; every increase of quantity lowering the value, and every diminution raising it, in a ratio exactly equivalent.[2]

He called attention to the rapidity of the circulation of money and gave it the right place in the quantity theory.[3] He discussed the problem of liquidity preference, i.e. the problem of the willingness to hold money instead of other commodities. He pointed out that if " persons in general . . . liked to possess money more than any other commodity ", there would be a rise in the value of money and a general fall in prices.[4]

On the subject of inconvertible paper money, he said that " an inconvertible paper which is legal tender is universally admitted to be money ". Its value depended on its quantity which was arbitrarily fixed by the issuing authority. If its quantity was increased, all prices would rise and among them the price of gold bullion. The nominal exchange would then fall proportionately.[5]

In regard to the relationships between credit and prices,

[1] *Principles*, Ashley's ed., pp. 490 f.
[2] Ibid., pp. 492–3. See also pp. 542, 539. The form that he gave to the quantity theory was, in general, a very rigid one, because he emphasized that *general* prices varied in *proportion to* the changes in the quantity of money.
[3] Ibid., pp. 494 f. It may be noted that he took pains to explain that Senior's doctrine of the value of money was not, as Senior had thought, inconsistent with the quantity theory.
[4] J. S. Mill, *Essays on Some Unsettled Questions of Political Economy*, 2nd ed., London, 1874, pp. 70–2.
[5] *Principles*, Ashley's ed., pp. 542–555, 634–6. In one of his essays, he also explained how an increase of paper money might lead to forced saving. He said: "If the paper is inconvertible, and instead of displacing specie depreciates the currency, the banker by issuing it levies a tax on every person who has money in his hands or due to him. He thus appropriates to himself a portion of the capital of other people and a portion of their revenue. The capital might have been intended to be lent, or it might have been intended to be employed by the owner : such part of it as was intended to be employed by the owner now changes its destination, and is lent. The revenue was either intended to be accumulated, in which case it had already become capital, or it was intended to be spent : in this last case revenue is converted into capital : and thus, strange as it may appear, the depreciation of the currency, when effected in this way, operates to a certain extent as a forced accumulation." (*Essays*, p. 118.)

Mill, like Tooke and Fullarton, declared that after the introduction of credit, credit occupied in the determination of *market* prices a more important position than currency.[1] Credit economized the use of money and was itself a purchasing-power like money.[2] The grant of facility for the multiplication of credit transactions might, however, lead to one form of credit having a greater effect on prices than others. For instance, banknotes as well as cheques were more powerful instruments in raising prices than bills.[3] It did not follow, however, that although credit had the power of raising prices it would be freely created for that purpose. Nor was it true that one form of credit would be more used than another, because it could be more used. " When the state of trade holds out no particular temptation to make large purchases on credit, dealers will use only a small portion of the credit power." [4] " The inclination of the mercantile public to increase their demand for commodities by making use of all or much of their credit as a purchasing-power depends on their expectation of profit." [5] It was only when the circumstances of the markets and the state of the mercantile mind were such as to make the dealers willing to use their credit that credit was actually extended. There he implied that the initial cause of an increase in prices was on the demand side and not on the supply side of credit. That leads us immediately to his opinion on the banking and the currency principles. Like Tooke and Fullarton, Mill pointed out that the difference between banknotes and other forms of credit was only a difference in degree and not in kind. He also agreed with them in their doctrine of the impossibility of the banks increasing the circulation of banknotes " except as a consequence of, or in proportion to, an increase of the business to be done ", and of the impossibility of convertible

---

[1] " It is hardly necessary to say that the permanent value of money—the natural and average prices of commodities—are not in question here. These are determined by the cost of producing or of obtaining the precious metals." (*Principles*, Ashley's ed., p. 523.)

[2] " In a state of commerce in which much credit is habitually given general prices at any moment depend much more upon the state of credit than upon the quantity of money. For credit, though it is not productive power, is purchasing-power ; creates just as much demand for the goods, and tends quite as much to raise their price, as if he made an equal amount of purchases with ready money." (*Principles*, Ashley's ed., p. 514.)

[3] Ibid., pp. 529–541.

[4] Ibid., p. 531.

[5] Ibid., pp. 525 f.

L

banknotes raising prices—so far as those doctrines were applied to a quiescent state, that was one " in which there was nothing tending to engender in any considerable portion of the mercantile public a desire to extend their operations ", or, in an expectant or speculative state, so far as " it is confined to transactions between dealers ".[1] But he thought (a) " that this can no longer be affirmed when speculation has proceeded so far as to reach to producer ", and in that case, the " employment of banknotes must have been powerfully operative on prices at the time when notes of one and two pounds' value were permitted by law "[2]; and (b) that the increase of banknotes in the duration between the ascending period of speculation and the revulsion necessarily " tends to prolong the duration of the specula-tion . . . enables the speculative prices to be kept up for some time after they would otherwise have collapsed ; and therefore prolongs and increases the drain of the precious metals for exportation, which is the leading feature of this stage in the progress of a commercial crisis : the continuance of which drain at last endangering the power of the banks to fulfil their engagement of paying their notes on demand, they are compelled to contract their credit more suddenly and severely than would have been necessary if they had been prevented from propping up speculation by increased advances, after the time when the recoil had become inevitable ".[3] Unlike Tooke and Fullarton, Mill recognized, once at least, that the project of the currency school did have the advantages of preventing the retardation of the recoil and the ultimate aggravation of its severity.[4] He, nevertheless, opposed the Bank Charter Act of 1844, because he thought that those advantages were " purchased by still greater disadvantages ".[5]

His attempt to reconcile the banking principle with the currency principle apparently did not prove a successful one. We entirely agree with him that the actual volume of credit demanded depends largely upon the expectation of profit. Is it not true, however, that the central bank can, by diminishing the market rate of interest and exciting expectation of profit, increase the quantity of credit

---

[1] *Principles*, Ashley's ed., pp. 653–5.
[2] Ibid., pp. 655–6. [3] Ibid., p. 656.
[4] Ibid., pp. 657 ff. Cf., however, his *Essays*, 2nd ed., pp. 68, 110.
[5] Mill, *Principles*, Ashley's ed., pp. 662 ff.

demanded and thus expand its issue of notes excessively ? Mill himself, in another connection, explicitly recognized the classical doctrine that the bank could throw additional notes into the circulation if it lowered the market rate of interest.[1] The classical doctrine being accepted, was Mill consistent in partially accepting the banking principle ?

Having presented his doctrine of money and credit, we can now turn to his doctrine of international price relationships. His theory was " an equilibrium theory ". The equilibrium was established when the precious metals " distribute themselves in such proportions among the different countries of the world, as to allow the very same exchanges to go on, and at the same values, as would be the case under a system of barter ", and when the exchange rate was at par.[2] The exchange rate was at par when imports and exports balanced. In regard to the problem of the comparison of general levels of prices in different countries his doctrine was, as already indicated, the Seniorian doctrine in a modified form. He said : " The currencies of all countries had come to a level ; by which I do not mean . . . money became of the same value everywhere, but . . . the differences were only those . . . which corresponded to permanent differences in the cost of obtaining it."

As to the mechanism which corrects disequilibrium he, like other classical theorists, stood by Hume's law. On that question, too, his attitude was an eclectic one. He embodied in his views many of the arguments of the critics of the doctrine and made many refinements of his own. We shall now describe what his position was separately with respect to each of the following four sets of relationships which must be included in any version of Hume's law :—

(a) Initial causes of disturbance—flow of specie ;
(b) Flow of specie—volume of currency ;
(c) Volume of currency—prices of commodities ;
(d) Prices of commodities—rate of exchange (and the restoration of equilibrium).

First, as to the initial causes of specie flow, he gave us four alternatives : (i) alternations in the state of money

---

[1] *Principles*, Ashley's ed., pp. 646–7.
[2] Ibid., pp. 625, 629.

and credit ; (ii) alternations in the state of trade ; (iii) international payments of a non-commercial character ; and (iv) the state of the money market.[1] Mill had thus held a view which was much wider than either the doctrine of Wheatley and Ricardo or the doctrine of Bosanquet, Tooke, and Fullarton. His view was also more comprehensive than the view of Hume and Thornton, for he gave a fourth possible cause. Of that cause, he said :—

It frequently happens that money, to a considerable amount, is brought into the country, is there actually invested as capital, and again flows out, without having ever once acted upon the markets of commodities, but only upon the market of securities, or, as it is commonly though improperly called, the money market. Let us return to the case already put for illustration, that of a foreigner landing in the country with a treasure . . . . He might very probably prefer to invest his fortune at interest, which we shall suppose him to do in the most obvious way, by becoming a competitor for a portion of the stock, exchequer bills, railway debentures, mercantile bills, mortgages, etc., which are at all times in the hands of the public. By doing this he would raise the prices of those different securities, or in other words would lower the rate of interest ; and since this would disturb the relation previously existing between the rate of interest on capital in the country itself, and that in foreign countries, it would probably induce those who had floating capital seeking employment, to send it abroad for foreign investment rather than buy securities at home at the advanced price. As much money might thus go out as had previously come in, while the prices of commodities would have shown no trace of its temporary presence. This is a case highly deserving of attention : and it is a fact now beginning to be recognized, that *the passage of the precious metals from country to country is determined much more than was formerly supposed by the state of the loan market in different countries, and much less by the state of prices.*[2]

So much for the disturbance arising from the fourth cause. Let us turn now to disturbance arising from the first cause. His view was similar to that of Hume, Thornton, and others. Under a metallic standard Hume's law would operate to restore equilibrium and under an inconvertible paper standard the purchasing power parity doctrine was correct.

[1] *Principles*, Ashley's ed., (i) pp. 629–636 ; (ii) pp. 619–625 ; (iii) pp. 627 f. ; and (iv) pp. 496–7.
[2] Ibid., pp. 496–7, italics mine.

Disturbance might be due to an adverse balance of payments (the second and the third causes). In regard to such a disturbance he agreed with Hume and Malthus and differed from Ricardo.[1] He also recognized that there could be temporary causes of disturbance which did not cause any movement of specie. In that case Mill, like Hume, considered the exchange itself as a sufficient corrective.[2]

Would the gold or silver exported for the purpose mentioned be drawn from the circulation of the country exporting it ? If the exportation of gold was due to the state of the currency, the answer would be in the affirmative. If it was due to the second or the third causes, the answer depended upon circumstances. In case the variations were not permanent, Mill thought that Tooke and Fullarton were right in giving a negative answer. " The gold or silver exported for the purposes in question . . . would be drawn from hoards, which under a metallic currency always exist to a very large amount ; in uncivilized countries, in the hands of all those who could afford it ; in civilized countries, chiefly in the form of bankers' reserves." [3] It was when the variations were permanent that the volume of circulation would be eventually affected. If the initial cause was the fourth one, the movement of specie would not necessarily, or even probably, bring about a change in the volume of circulation.[4]

In case the volume of currency was affected, would the prices of commodities be affected accordingly ? Mill's position implied adherence to the most rigid form of the quantity theory.[5] How could a change in prices restore equilibrium ? Like other classical writers, he declared that the change in prices would work out its effects through a change in the state of trade or the balance of payments.

10   SUMMARY

This chapter covers mainly the period of the Industrial Revolution in England from about 1770 to about the middle of the nineteenth century. The spirit of that period might be summarized in two words, " Free trade." One of the

[1] *Principles*, Ashley's ed., pp. 627–8.   [2] Ibid., pp. 617 f.
[3] Ibid., p. 665 ; see also pp. 620, 634.   [4] Ibid., pp. 496–7.
[5] He also tried (pp. 630–631) to show how, in case the initial cause was due to an alteration in the state of the currency the production of gold and silver and the permanent value of money would ultimately feel the effects and be adjusted accordingly.

most important theoretical foundations for free trade was found in the classical theory of international price relationships. It was only natural, therefore, that from the standpoint of the theory of international price relationships, the period was chiefly notable for the rise and the development of the classical equilibrium theory.

The classical economists had given a solution for each of the four problems posed by the theory of international price relationships. In solving the problem of the relation between the value of money in one country and the values of money in other countries, they started with a doctrine of the natural distribution of money, as a result of which the precious metals were distributed in certain proportions among the different trading nations according to the respective needs of the nations. " While so divided they preserved everywhere the same value." That doctrine of the international equality of the value of money was first advanced by Foster, Ricardo, and others, and very ably expounded by Senior and Norman. It was also shown that when the international equality of the value of money was established, rates of exchange were at par. The views of the classical economists on the problem of the relation of the price level of one country to the price levels in other countries are embodied in the Seniorian doctrine. That doctrine was first found in Ricardo. It was very ably stated by Senior and vigoriously expounded by Mill, who modified it. As to the problem of the price relations of goods of identical technological composition among trading countries, the classical economists demonstrated that there was a tendency of the prices of all traded goods to reach international equalization. That proposition was most ably explained by Thornton, who was, however, surpassed by Wheatley. Finally, Senior gave the classical explanation of the differences in wages in different countries.

The contribution of the classical economists was not limited to the static aspects of the subject. They also discussed how equilibrium might be disturbed and restored. All of them agreed that disturbance might be caused by the currency. If that happened under an international metallic standard, Hume's law would operate to restore equilibrium. If it happened under an inconvertible paper standard, prices and exchanges would be adjusted according to the purchasing power parity doctrine. Hume's law was first advanced by Hume, la Rivière, and others. In its most general form, the causal sequence according to that law runs as follows :—

Initial disturbance of equilibrium—flow of specie—changes in the volume of circulation—changes in prices—restoration of equilibrium.

The most important set of relations is that between the volume of the circulation and the changes in prices. According to the classical theory, an increase of the former necessarily brings about a rise in the latter. Hume brilliantly demonstrated how an increase of money would work out its effects on prices through purchases and gave one of the best descriptions of what is known as the " direct " mechanism connecting money and prices. In that connection, Thornton made two other important contributions. First, he called attention to the importance of the velocity of circulation in the problem of money and prices and gave an ingenious account of its effects. Moreover, in his hands the doctrine that money stimulates trade was reconciled with, and subordinated to, the quantity theory of money. Hume's law had its critics. Tooke and Fullarton, for example, pointed out that it was not so " automatic " as it was supposed to be. That criticism was accepted by Mill and incorporated by him in the classical theory.

Hume's law was applicable only to the case of an international metallic standard. When the countries under consideration were under an inconvertible paper standard, the classical economists had a more general doctrine, namely, the purchasing power parity doctrine. Among the ablest exponents of that doctrine were Boyd, Thornton, Wheatley, Foster, Blake, and Ricardo.

The question whether the expansion or contraction of bank credits (notes and cheques) would be an initial cause of disturbance was also raised during the period under review. The banking school gave a negative and, we think, an erroneous answer. The currency school successfully refuted the doctrine of the banking school but made an illogical distinction between cheques and notes and contended that cheques could not be considered as an initial cause of disturbance.

The economists of the classical school all agreed that in a state of equilibrium a country's accounts of international indebtedness must be balanced. They differed on the question how an adverse balance of payments was to be adjusted and whether disequilibrium in the international balance of payments might be an initial cause of disturbance of the equilibrium in international price relationships. Hume, Malthus, and Mill were of the opinion that Hume's law was also applicable to this case and that equilibrium was restored by changes in the price and income structures of the trading nations. That view was known as " the classical " view. In opposition to the classical view, Wheatley and Ricardo advanced what we call the Wicksellian doctrine that disequilibrium in the balance of payments always adjusted itself and produced no changes in international price relations. Thornton stood midway : he accepted the Wicksellian doctrine as valid in the long run but sided with Malthus and others when temporary effects were considered.

For many classical economists the rate of exchange itself was a sufficient corrective mechanism for a disturbance of a temporary character. Hume, Foster, Blake, and Mill were the ablest writers who expounded that view.

Both Tooke and Mill gave expositions of how the bank rate could be used as a means of protecting a country's gold reserve by its effect upon the rate of interest on foreign loans. They thus anticipated a doctrine of Goschen.

In this and the preceding chapters we have dealt exclusively with the monetary aspects of the theory of international price relationships. The appearance of the *Principles* of Ricardo, however, drew attention to the real aspects of the problem and in the next chapter we deal with the latter aspects of the problem.

CHAPTER IV

THE CLASSICAL THEORY OF INTERNATIONAL TRADE

1. THE ARGUMENT FOR A SEPARATE THEORY FOR INTERNATIONAL TRADE

In the two preceding chapters we have described the development of the doctrines concerning the monetary aspect of the problem of international price relationships up to the middle of the nineteenth century. But these doctrines hardly deal with an important element, viz. the real aspect of the problem. It was only in the hands of Ricardo and his followers that the element began to receive adequate treatment, and there appeared for the first time a systematic theory of international trade. The theory, which was soon known as the classical theory, dominated the field until recent years.[1]

The following are three of the problems discussed by the classical economists : Firstly, what are the grounds for a separate theory of international trade ? Secondly, what determines the international movement of commodities ? In other words, what commodities should a country import and what should it export ? Thirdly, what are the laws governing the barter terms of trade ? We shall describe the answers of the classical economists to the three problems and show how their doctrines of international trade were used as a foundation for their theory of international price relationships.

Ricardo was perhaps the first classical economist to advocate for a separate theory of international trade, as distinguished from the theory of intra-national trade. He definitely said that exchange within one country and exchange between two or more countries were not governed by the same conditions,[2] because labour and capital were

---

[1] It does not mean, however, that the classical theory long remained unchallenged. Criticisms had been made against it. In the present chapter we shall deal with some of the criticisms.

[2] David Ricardo, *Principles*, Gonner's ed., p. 113.

immobile between nations while they were free to move within one nation.[1]

That point, unimportant it may appear, has been the subject of much criticism. First there has been the criticism that the difference between international and intra-national trade is only a difference in degree and not a difference in kind.[2] On the one hand there are many obstacles to the free mobility of labour and capital within a nation; on the other hand, as economic relations between nations become closer and closer, factors of production, especially capital, tend to be more and more cosmopolitan. Based upon those facts, some critics argue that both internationally and intra-nationally labour and capital are not perfectly mobile[3]; while others contend that mobility of labour and capital is true of both international and domestic trades.[4]

To those criticisms a later expounder of the classical theory, J. E. Cairnes, answered: " It is by no means necessary to the truth of the doctrine, as it has been laid

[1] *Principles*, Gonner's ed., pp. 114 f. Cf. J. S. Mill, *Principles*, Ashley's ed., p. 575 ; C. F. Bastable, *The Theory of International Trade* (London, 1893), 4th ed., 1903, pp. 1–13.

[2] The criticism of H. D. Macleod may be noted. He said that if exchange between " places near each other " were governed by one rule and exchange between distant places or foreign countries by another, there was the difficulty in drawing the line of demarcation between " places near each other " and distant places. " Now," he said, " let us suppose that the commodities are produced in places which are at a gradually and continuously increasing distance from each other. When do the places cease to be *near* each other, and when do they become *distant* from each other ? . . . This mode of argument is . . . a breach of the Law of Continuity." (*The Principles of Economic Philosophy*, vol. i, 2nd ed., London, 1872, p. 356.)

[3] That is the criticism of T. E. C. Leslie. " The distinction which Mr. Mill has drawn between international trade and home trade, in respect of the transferability of labour and capital and the equalization of wages and profit, if it had once some foundation when trade at home was simpler and better known, and when foreign countries were almost wholly unknown, cannot now be sustained. Not that the doctrine of the equality of profits and of the determination of comparative prices by comparative cost of production is now applicable to both, but that it is applicable to neither. It was a step in the right direction to recognize its inapplicability to the exchanges between different countries, but the further step is now required of abandoning it altogether. In both home trade and international trade the migration of labour and capital has some effect on wages and profits, and the comparative cost of producing different commodities some effect on their comparative value and price ; but in both cases the effect is uncertain, irregular, and incalculable." (*Essays in Political Economy*, 2nd ed., Dublin, 1878, pp. 232–3.)

[4] For example, J. A. Hobson, *International Trade* (London, 1904), p. 56.

down, for example, by Ricardo and Mill, that there should be an absolute impossibility of moving labour and capital from country to country. What the doctrine requires is not this, but such a degree of difficulty in effecting their transference as shall interfere substantially and generally—that is to say, over the whole range of the commodities exchanged—with the action of industrial competition." [1]

Granting that the answer of Cairnes is acceptable, the classical economists have still to face another criticism : that the argument used by Cairnes is applicable rather to inter-regional trade than to international trade. The difficulty of the free mobility of labour and capital and the obstacles preventing an equalization of wages and profits exist usually between different regions but not necessarily between neighbouring nations that are very close together. Hence, it would be more accurate to say that the classical economists have advanced a theory of inter-regional trade rather than a theory of inter-national trade.

That criticism, we think, is unimportant. The classical economists never claimed that their definition of " nation " coincided with the political or the generally accepted definition of " nation ".[2] They only claimed that their theory was applicable to trade between " non-competing groups ", i.e. groups between which labour and capital did not move freely. Whether the immobility of labour and capital applies to nations or to regions is unimportant if we remember that the classical theory is a theory of trade between non-competing groups.[3]

2.   THE DOCTRINE OF COMPARATIVE COSTS

The next question is what determines the movement of commodities between nations or, what is more correctly, non-competing groups. The answer of the classical economists to the question is found in the doctrine of comparative costs. According to the doctrine, to use the words of Ricardo, " under a system of perfectly free commerce, each country

---

[1] Cairnes, *Some Leading Principles of Political Economy Newly Expounded,* London, 1874, 1888, p. 303.
[2] In order to prevent misunderstanding, Bastable had suggested the term " inter-regional trade " to take the place of " international trade " (see Bastable, op. cit., 12 n.). Mill also used the term " distant places " (Mill, op. cit., p. 575).
[3] See Cairnes, op. cit., *passim* ; Bastable, op. cit., ch. i.

naturally devotes its capital and labour to such employments as are most beneficial to each." [1] By an employment " most beneficial " to a country is meant that in which it enjoys the greatest advantage or that in which it has the least disadvantage compared with other countries. In order to find out what is the commodity in regard to which a country has the greatest comparative advantage, we have to compare the costs of production. Suppose that in countries A and B the efficiencies of labour in the production of commodities M and N were such that—

in A, 1 unit of labour produces $20M$ or $15N$,
in B, 1 unit of labour produces $16M$ or $8N$.

To compare the costs of production of the two commodities in the two countries,[2] we have :—

Commodity M, A : B :: 10 : 8
Commodity N, A : B :: 10 : 5¼.

As a result of the comparison, we can see that A has a greater comparative advantage in the production of N than M, while B has a less comparative disadvantage in the production of M than N. It will, therefore, be profitable for A to specialize in the production of N and B in that of M for that would lead to increased total production.

[1] Ricardo, op. cit., p. 114.   Cf. Mill, op. cit., pp. 576–8. Essentially that is an extension of the doctrine of the division of labour between particular persons. Cf. the following quotation which shows the Ricardian doctrine of the division of labour :—

" Two men can both make shoes and hats, and one is superior to the other in both employments ; but in making hats he can only exceed his competitors by one-fifth, or 20 per cent, and in making shoes he can exceed him by one-third, or 33⅓ per cent. Will it not be for the interest of both that the superior man should employ himself exclusively in making shoes, and the inferior man in making hats ? "

It does not follow, however, that the division of labour among persons and that among countries are entirely the same. As pointed out by Haberler, there are two important differences. " (a) The former often consists in different persons performing different processes in the production of a common product, as in a factory, so that their individual products are not exchanged against one another. The division of labour between occupations corresponds much more closely to the international division of labour, since the products of the farmer, baker, tailor, and so on, are exchanged against one another. (b) The other, and more important, distinction is that specialization by persons increases the capacity of each to perform the task on which he specializes ; practice makes perfect. We do not think of this circumstance, or at any rate not primarily, when we speak of the advantage of division of labour between countries." (Gottfried von Haberler, The Theory of International Trade, English ed., p. 130.)

[2] Cairnes once said, " When it is said that international trade depends on a difference in the comparative . . . cost of producing commodities, the costs compared, it must be carefully noted, are the costs in each

What, according to the classical theory, makes the difference between international and domestic trades ? The difference lies in the fact that in certain conditions, from which domestic trade cannot arise, trade between nations might be possible. If A and B in the illustration are two adjacent places within the same country, all labourers will migrate from B to A and have both commodities produced at A. Consequently there would be no trade between A and B. According to the classical theory, therefore, a comparative difference in costs is a sufficient condition for the existence of international trade [1] ; while within a nation the existence of trade between two places requires an absolute difference in costs.[2]

country of the commodities which are the subjects of exchange, not the different costs of the same commodity in the exchanging countries." (*Some Leading Principles*, p. 312.) That is incorrect. As Viner has recently pointed out, " It is not cost at all which are directly to be compared, but *ratios between costs*, and it is unessential whether the cost ratios which are compared are the ratios between the costs of producing different commodities within the same countries or the ratios between the costs of producing the same commodities in different countries." See Viner, *Studies in the Theory of International Trade*, 1937, pp. 438-9.

[1] " The one condition, therefore at once essential to, and also sufficient for, the existence of international trade, is a difference in the comparative, as contra-distinguished from the absolute, cost of producing the commodities exchanged " (Cairnes, op. cit., p. 310). That assertion, as pointed out by Bastable, " is only true if all retarding elements—all those hindrances which arise from cost of carriage and custom duties—are neglected, and if the inquiry is confined to two countries " (Bastable, op. cit., pp. 15-16).

[2] There are three kinds of differences in costs : (*a*) comparative differences, (*b*) absolute difference, and (*c*) equal difference. In the supposed case given above, we have a comparative difference in costs. The following is an example of absolute differences in costs :—

Country A, 1 unit of labour can produce 20*M* or 15*N*
,, B, ,, ,, ,, 16*M* or 18*N*
Under that condition it is possible to have both international and domestic trade—A will specialize in producing *M* and B in *N*. The following is an example of equal differences in costs from which neither foreign nor domestic trade can arise :—

Country A, 1 unit of labour can produce 20*M* or 15*N*
,, B, 1 ,, ,, ,, 16*M* or 12*N*
(See Taussig, *International Trade*, pp. 3-33.) Those cases can also be expressed algebraically. Let m_a denote the number of *M* that one unit of labour produces in *A* ; m_b that in B. Let n_a denote the number of *N* a unit of labour produces in A ; and n_b that in B. Then there is an

absolute difference in costs if $\frac{m_a}{m_b} > 1 > \frac{n_a}{n_b}$, or $\frac{m_a}{m_b} < 1 < \frac{n_a}{n_b}$. There is a com-

parative difference in costs if $1 < \frac{m_a}{m_b} < \frac{n_a}{n_b}$, or, $\frac{m_a}{m_b} > \frac{n_a}{n_b} > 1$. There is

an equal difference in costs if $\frac{m_a}{m_b} = \frac{n_a}{n_b}$

That is the doctrine of comparative costs as advanced by Ricardo and his disciples. There has been much debate on the question as to who was the first to discover the law of comparative costs. The credit has been assigned to Torrens by E. Lesser and E. R. A. Seligman.[1] Torrens advanced the doctrine when he was discussing the influence of a free external trade in corn upon the agriculture of a country. He refuted the doctrine that if corn could be grown as cheaply in England as, say, in Poland, it would be raised in England. That doctrine, he said,

> however obvious and natural it may at first sight appear, might, on a closer examination, be found entirely erroneous. If England should have acquired such a degree of skill in manufactures that, with any given portion of her capital, she could prepare a quantity of cloth, for which the Polish cultivator would give a greater quantity of corn than she could, with the same portion of capital, raise from her own soil, then tracts of her territory, though they should be equal, nay, even though they should be superior, to the lands in Poland, will be neglected; and a part of her supply of corn will be imported from that country. For though the capital employed in cultivating at home might bring an excess of profit over the capital employed in cultivating abroad, yet, under the supposition, the capital which should be employed in manufacturing would obtain *a still greater excess of profit*; and this greater excess of profit would determine the direction of our industry.[2]

Professor Hollander, however, insisted on the view that Ricardo was the first expounder of the doctrine of comparative costs.[3]   We think that the correct view is that of Professor Viner. He says :—

> There can be no reasonable doubt that Ricardo is entitled to the credit for first giving due emphasis to the doctrine, and that it was from Ricardo and not from Torrens that later economists learned the doctrine. . . . The fact remains, however, that the first published statement of the doctrine was by Torrens and not by Ricardo.[4]

[1] See E. R. A. Seligman, *Essays in Economics*, New York, 1925, pp. 74–6.
[2] See Robert Torrens, *An Essay on the External Corn Trade*, London, 1815, pp. 264–5, italics mine.
[3] J. H. Hollander, *David Ricardo, A Centenary Estimate*, Baltimore, 1911, pp. 94 ff.
[4] J. Viner, " The Doctrine of Comparative Costs," *Weltwirtschaftliches Archiv.*, October, 1932, p. 362.   Professor Arnold Plant called attention to an anonymous author's tract, *A Letter on the True Principles of Advantageous Exportation*, which was published in London, in 1818.   In that tract is found a statement of the doctrine of comparative costs with the help of algebraic symbols. See *Economics*, 1933, pp. 40 ff.

We may now return to the doctrine of comparative costs itself. We have already indicated that, according to the doctrine, if each country produces the commodity in the production of which it enjoys a comparative advantage, the total production would be increased. Suppose, to return to our illustration, that the two countries have each 10,000 units of labour and that before the opening of trade A employs 40 per cent of its labour in the production of M and 60 per cent in that of N, while B employs half of its labour in each production. Then before they specialize their total production is :—

A's production :   80,000M. 90,000N.
B's production :   80,000M. 40,000N.
Total production : 160,000M. 130,000N.

After trade begins and A specializes in the production of N and B in M, the total production becomes 160,000M (produced by B) and 150,000N (produced by A). Is it not clear that they together gain 20,000N ?

Critics like Vilfredo Pareto pointed out that that way of calculating gross gain did not always give a correct result. In case the original distribution of labour and capital in production was different, the result would also be different. Suppose countries A and B each employ, before they begin to specialize, 50 per cent of their labour force in the production of each of the two commodities ; their original total production would be 180,000M and 115,000N. After they specialize, they together produce 35,000 units more of commodity N but 20,000 less of commodity M. We must assume that the loss of 20,000M can be compensated by the gain of 35,000N in order that we can say that by specialization they will produce more. If the loss of M cannot be compensated by the gain of N, the conclusion arrived at by the classical economist becomes incorrect.[1] But normally one should expect the former case to be true. Should the gain of 35,000N fail to become a compensation for the loss of 20,000M, there is no reason to suppose that A should devote, after the opening of trade, all its labour force to the production of N. Normally A would devote 90 per cent of its resources to produce N

[1] " Nous ne savons pas si, en tenant compte du gout des individus, il y a, ou il n'y a pas, compensation. S'il y a compensation la proposition de Ricardo est vrai ; s'il n'y a pas compensation, la proposition est fausse " (Pareto, *Manuel D'Economie Politique*, traduit sur l'edition Italienne par A. Bonnet, Paris, 1909 ; 1927, p. 508).

and 10 per cent to produce M. If so the total production after the division of labour becomes 180,000M and 135,000N—a net gain of 20,000N.[1]

Mill was wrong, however, when he said that upon the assumption of a zero cost of carriage and a constant cost of production, every commodity would, if trade were free, be either regularly imported or regularly exported and a country would make nothing for itself which it did not also make for other countries.[2] Should Mill's dictum be correct, A must devote, after the opening of trade, all its labour to produce N and consequently Pareto is right in his criticism.[3]

3. THE SAME SUBJECT CONTINUED

Although we have assumed that there are only two commodities, the doctrine of comparative costs is applicable to the case of any number of commodities. The doctrine may then be restated as follows : Country A enjoys a comparative advantage over country B in all its export commodities relatively to all its import commodities.[4] Let us arrange the various goods in the order of the comparative advantage of B over A so that :—

$$\frac{m_a}{m_b} < \frac{n_a}{n_b} < \frac{o_a}{o_b} < \frac{p_a}{p_b} < \ldots < \frac{q_a}{q_b}$$

in which m_a, n_a, o_a, p_a . . . q_a denotes the number of units of commodities M, N, O, P . . . Q that one unit of labour produced in A, and m_b, n_b, o_b . . . the same in B. After the opening of trade, A will produce those goods which are on the right-hand side and B those on the left-hand side.

We cannot, however, draw the dividing line between the category of goods produced by A and that by B, if we only judge from the cost conditions. Hence when the

[1] Cf. Preeto, ibid., p. 513.
[2] J. S. Mill, *Principles*, Ashley's ed., p. 598.
[3] Cf. Frank D. Graham, "The Theory of International Values Re-examined," *Q.J.E.*, 1923 ; A. F. Burns, "A Note on Comparative Costs," *Q.J.E.*, 1928. Reference may also be made to the answers for the classical school by Viner ("Comparative Costs : A Rejoinder," *Q.J.E.*, 1928 ; *Studies in the Theory of International Trade*, pp. 449 ff.) and Haberler (" The Theory of Comparative Cost once more," *Q.J.E.*, 1929).
[4] Cf. Haberler, *The Theory of International Trade*, German ed., 1933 ; English ed. tr. by A. Stonier and F. Benham, London, 1936. The reference is to the English edition, p. 136.

number of commodities is numerous, although " the nature of the problem would not have greatly changed . . . its wording would ", to use the words of Marshall, " have been more complex." In order to overcome the difficulty Marshall suggested that we might measure all the exportable goods of a country in terms of a common unit or " bale ", which was defined as embodying a constant quantity of labour and capital of the country. Thus the exports of A may be expressed in terms of representative bales or units of A's goods or in terms of units of a representative commodity N, each unit being equivalent to the produce of a given quantity of labour and capital. The real cost of each unit is constant, but the individual goods that compose the unit may change. In that way the case of more than two commodities may be treated as easily as the case of two commodities.[1]

Recently the doctrine of comparative costs has been restated in terms of opportunity costs. The work has been excellently done by Professor Haberler. In order to do it he first makes a digression on the connection between the labour theory and the general theory.[2] His argument amounts to this : If there is only one factor of production, viz. homogeneous labour, the Labour Theory is correct. In that case, suppose a unit of labour can produce in country A (at constant cost) $20M$ or $15N$. Then, according to the Labour Theory, if A is a closed community, the exchange-ratio between M and N would be $4M/3N$, which is equal to the labour-cost-ratio. If money is introduced, the price ratio between the two commodities will be 3 to 4, the reciprocal of $4M/3N$. It may also be expressed in terms of opportunity cost. Instead of saying that the cost of $20M$ is one unit of labour, one now says that the cost of $20M$ is $15N$ or the cost of $15N$ is $20M$. The ratio $20M/15N$ (or, more generally, m_a/n_a) becomes now a substitution-ratio, i.e. the number of units of one commodity which must be forgone in order that one unit of the other commodity may be produced. The price ratio or the exchange ratio between the two commodities will be determined by the substitution ratio. As soon as we reach that point, " we have no further need of the Labour Theory of Value.

---

[1] Marshall, *Money, Credit, and Commerce*, London, 1932, pp. 157, 161 ff., 330 ff., and *passim*.

[2] Haberler, *The Theory of International Trade*, English. ed., pp. 126, 175 ff.

We can derive the conditions of substitution between the two commodities and express them in the form of a substitution-curve, when many different factors of production are available just as well as when there is only homogeneous labour. However many factors there may be, the relative prices of the two commodities will be determined (given the demand) by their opportunity costs." [1] The assumption of increasing costs does not invalidate the conclusion. The only difference is that the substitution-curve is no longer a straight line (and is concave towards the origin). Similarly, the existence of specific factors of production only makes the substitution-curve to take a different form and does not alter the main proposition, namely that " the exchange-ratio between two commodities will equal their (indirect) substitution-rates or opportunity-cost (in terms of one another) ".[2]

It follows, he says " that, if the exchange-ratios between commodities are equal to their substitution-ratios, the doctrine of comparative advantage is perfectly valid even if we discard all the simplifying assumptions of the Labour Theory of Value." He then continues :—

In order to show this, we should have to set out, instead of a series of absolute labour-costs, a series of relative prices or exchange-ratios, using any one commodity as a *numeraire* with which to measure prices. This series would equally represent the substitution-ratios, since these are the same as the exchange-ratios. Each country would specialize in those branches of production in which it had a comparative advantage or, in other words, would produce those goods whose opportunity costs were relatively lowest.[3]

To illustrate the argument, let us return to our hypothetical case. The opportunity cost of one unit of N is $1\frac{1}{3}$ units of M in A and 2 units of M in B. Obviously A will export N to B. Similarly, the opportunity cost of M in terms of N is smaller in B than in A and A will import M from B.[4]

[1] Haberler, op. cit., p. 177.
[2] The case of varying costs has been discussed by Bastable and other classical economists. According to Bastable, if we replace the assumption of constant cost by that of varying costs, the consequence is " that the limits set by cost of production which, up to the present, we have regarded as fixed becomes moveable " (Bastable, op. cit., p. 29).
[3] Haberler, op. cit., p. 182.
[4] See A. Lerner, " The Diagrammatical Representation of Cost Conditions in International Trade," *Economica*, 1932. In that article, Mr. Lerner shows how the substitution curve (or, what is the same thing,

4. The Doctrine of Reciprocal Demands

Although Ricardo had demonstrated how nations may gain by trade, he had not shown how the gain by trade is divided among the trading countries, that is to say how the exact ratio of interchange between the trading goods is determined. The ratios of interchange or, what is the same thing, the barter terms of trade, depend not only on the cost conditions, but also on demand conditions. To fill in the gap, a doctrine which makes clear the part played by international demands in the determination of barter terms of trade was advanced by a group of English economists, viz. Longfield, Torrens, Pennington, and Stuart Mill.

The doctrine was advanced partly in connection with the correction of an error committed by James Mill and partly in connection with a controversy concerning the problem of retaliation. James Mill, in the first edition of his *Elements*,[1] committed the error of attributing all the gain to each of the trading countries. In other words, he considered, to use our illustration, the barter terms of trade to be either the ratio $10M : 7\frac{1}{2}N$, or the ratio $10M : 5N$. James Mill's treatment was criticized by his friends and his son at some time between 1825 and 1826,[2] and consequently James Mill removed the error from the third edition of the *Elements*, where he stated that " the result of competition would be to divide the advantage equally " between the two trading countries.[3] The correction that James Mill made is itself a mistake, and he did not succeed in contributing towards the solution of the problem of the determination of the exact ratio of the barter terms of trade. In order to fill up the deficiency, Stuart Mill wrote in 1829–1830 his famous essay on the laws of interchange between nations.[4] In that essay Stuart Mill advanced the doctrine that " when

the opportunity curve or the production-indifference curve) of one country may be added to that of the other country to form the composite substitution curve for the two countries and how the point where the composite substitution curve is touched, without being cut, by a consumption-indifference curve is the equilibrium point.

[1] James Mill, *Elements of Political Economy*, London, 1821, p. 86.
[2] J. S. Mill, *Autobiography*, London, 1873, pp. 120–122.
[3] James Mill, *Elements of Political Economy*, 3rd ed., London, 1826, p. 122.
[4] J. S. Mill, " Of the Laws of Interchange between Nations ; and the Distribution of the Gains of Commerce among the Countries of the Commercial World," written 1829–1830, reprinted as Essay I of his *Essays on Some Unsettled Questions of Political Economy*, London, 1844 ; 2nd ed., London, 1874.

two countries trade together in two commodities, the exchangeable value of these commodities relatively to each other will adjust itself to the inclinations and circumstances of the consumers on both sides, in such manner that the quantities required by each country, of the article which it imports from its neighbour, shall be exactly sufficient to pay for one another ". His essay was not published until 1844, and Pennington had in 1840 made a correction of James Mill's error, without knowing that it had already been removed in the third edition of the *Elements*. Pennington showed, to use again our illustration, that the barter term of trade would fluctuate between $0.5N$ per M and $0.75N$ per M " according to the temporary variation of demand and supply ".[1]

But Pennington was not the first one to formulate the doctrine that the barter terms of trade were determined by the conditions of international demands (and supplies). Five years before Pennington wrote, Longfield, for instance, had presented the proposition that a decrease or an increase in the demand of a country for its imports would turn the barter terms of trade more or less favourable to it, although he did not connect the proposition with the doctrine of comparative costs.[2]

The doctrine had also been advanced in connection with a controversy concerning the problem of retaliation in tariff policy that arose in England in the forties. Torrens was the leading advocate, and Senior the leading opponent of the policy of retaliation. It is unnecessary to describe the controversy in this general survey. Suffice it to say that the two economists differed in opinion about the theory of international value, upon which their answers to the problem of tariff policy depended. Torrens's theory of international value is this :—

The terms of international exchanges are determined, not by cost of production, but by the principle of demand and supply.[3]

He demonstrated how, due to the mobility of labour and

[1] James Pennington, *A Letter to Kirkman Finlay, Esq., on the importation of Foreign Corn, and the value of the Precious Metals in Different Countries*, London, 1840, pp. 36, 40 f.
[2] Saml. Mountifort Longfield, *Three Lectures on Commerce and One on Absenteeism*, Dublin, 1835, pp. 81, 101, 109.
[3] R. Torrens, *The Budget : A Series of Letters on Financial, Commercial, and Colonial Policy*, London, 1841-3, p. 334 ; or *Postscript to a Letter to . . . Peel*, London, 1843, p. 6.

capital within a country, "the cost of production adjusts the relation of demand to supply and, consequently, becomes the ultimate regulator of exchangeable value," and how, owing to the immobility of labour and capital between countries, the cost of production was no longer the ultimate regulator of international value and "the terms of international exchange are regulated by the reciprocal relations of demand and supply", or, more briefly, by "reciprocal demands ".[1] Therefrom the doctrine has been known as the doctrine of reciprocal demands. Senior, on the contrary, insisted that the cost of production was the regulator of international value. He said :—

> Cost of production . . . is the real regulator, not only of domestic, but of international commerce. Everything which can be produced at will, is subject to two different costs of production ; the one the *minimum*, below which price cannot permanently fall, the other *maximum*, beyond which price cannot permanently rise. The first, which may be called the cost of production to the producer, or seller, consists of the sum of the sacrifices which must be made, or, in other words, the sum of the wages and profits which must be paid or retained by the producer, in order to enable or induce him to continue to produce ;—including, of course, the wages of his own labour, and the profit of his own capital. The second, which may be called the cost of production to the consumer, or purchaser, consists of the sum of the sacrifices which must be made by the consumer, if, instead of purchasing, he produce for himself. The amount of the interval between these two extreme is one of the measures of the advantages derived from the division of labour. . . . So far as the price of a commodity is not affected by any natural or artificial monopoly, it coincides with the cost of production to the producer. . . . That this is true with respect to domestic commerce, is obvious ; it appears to us obvious, that it is equally true with respect to international commerce. The English spinner sells his yarns to the French importer at precisely the price which he charges to his English customer. The French weaver sells his silks to the English importer at precisely the price which he charges to his French customer. In many cases, neither the one nor the other knows for what market he is producing, or to whom he is selling. He produces the quantity for which he expects to get a remunerating price.[2]

[1] R. Torrens, *The Budget, passim* ; *Letters on Commercial Policy*, London, 1833 ; *A Letter to N. W. Senior*, London, 1843 ; and Hansard's *Parliamentary Debates*, 3rd series, xiv (1832), pp. 18–19.

[2] N. W. Senior, " Free Trade and Retaliation," the *Edinburgh Review*,

Senior is right in pointing out, first, that when the price of an international commodity is expressed in terms of money it should be equal to the money cost of production and, second, that when costs are expressed in terms of real costs the price of a commodity cannot be higher than the cost to the consumer or lower than the cost to the producer. But Senior is wrong when he thinks that the price of an international commodity coincides with the cost to the producer. As Torrens had pointed out in his reply,[1] international value is not a matter of free competition, since labour and capital are not free to move from one country to another.

Torrens's discussion aroused the interest of Stuart Mill, who was then led to publish the essay written in 1829–1830. Mill restated his doctrine in his *Principles*. It was, as pointed out by Viner, from Mill's *Principles* and not from other works that later economists took over the doctrine.[2] For that reason we shall concentrate on Mill's version of the doctrine.

Mill's doctrine of international value may be summarized in four propositions.[3]

(1) The value of an imported article is not determined by the cost of production but by its cost of acquisition or, in other words, "the cost of production of the thing which is exported to pay for it." That, sometimes spoken of as the first law of international values, is, as pointed out by Hobson, "not a law at all," because :—

> To say that "the value" of an imported article means the cost of production of the thing exported to pay for it merely affirms that the value of the foreign article is equal to (or signifies) the article exported as its equivalent. What we desire to know is, "What determines the *quantum* of the export goods we pay with ? "[4]

It is to answer that question that Mill presented the other three parts of his doctrine.

(2) What determines the quantity of the exported article which is necessary to pay for a unit of the imported article ? What determines the barter terms of trade ?

July, 1843, p. 37. Compare Marian Bowley, *Nassau Senior and Classical Economics*, pp. 225 ff.
[1] Torrens, *A Letter to Senior, passim*.
[2] Viner, op. cit., p. 365.
[3] The first two parts may be deduced from the work of Ricardo. See Mill, *Principles*, Ashley's ed., pp. 582–606.
[4] J. A. Hobson, *International Trade*, p. 58.

Mill said that "the limits, within which the variation is confined, are the ratio between their costs of production in the one country, and the ratio between their costs of production in the other ".[1] In our illustration, the two limits are $10M : 7\frac{1}{2}N$ (i.e. the ratio between the costs of production of M and N in country A) and $10M : 5N$ (i.e. the ratio in country B). The barter terms of trade cannot go beyond those two limits. Thus, in order to import one unit of M from B, A will not pay more than $0.75N$ and also must not pay less than $0.5N$, for if A be required to pay more than $0.75N$, it will pay it better to produce M itself. For the same reason, B will be unwilling to sell M for a price less than $0.5N$.

(3) Within those two limits how is the barter term ultimately determined ? To answer that question Mill presented his so-called "Law of Equation of International Demands ", which may be given in his own words :—

> The produce of a country exchanges for the produce of other countries, at such values as are required in order that the whole of her exports may exactly pay for the whole of her imports.[2]

If A, in our illustration, exports $6,000N$ to exchange for $10,000M$, the barter terms of trade will be $10M : 6N$.

---

[1] Mill, op. cit., p. 587. To that proposition, Cournot raised an objection. He asked if country A was absolutely incapable of producing M (or country B was not able to produce N) what would be the limits within which the variation of the barter terms of trade was confined ? Bastable tried to answer for the classical school in the following way : " The answer to this very plausible objection is to be found in the express statement of an element which is implicitly contained in Mill's theory, viz. the limit set to exchange by the comparative utility of the commodities . . . So long as the comparative costs of production were closer than the comparative utilities there was no necessity for dwelling on this latter condition . . . When, however, this power of producing at home the commodity required is withdrawn, the limit set by utility comes into operation, and it would furnish the really ultimate and complete limiting condition in cases of absolute monopoly on both sides." (Op. cit., pp. 37–8.)

[2] Mill, op. cit., p. 592. " This law of International Values is but an extension of the more general law of Value, which we can call the Equation of Supply and Demand . . . All trade, either between nations or individuals, is an interchange of commodities, in which the things that they respectively have to sell constitute also their means of purchase : the supply brought by the one constitutes his demand for what is brought by the other. So that supply and demand are but another expression for reciprocal demand : and to say that value will adjust itself so as to equalize demand with supply, is in fact to say that it will adjust itself so as to equalize the demand on one side with the demand on the other." (pp. 592–3.)

Consequently, the equilibrium of trade would be established in the following way :—

A sends 6,000N to B at 10N : 16·66M, total 10,000M.
B sends 10,000M to A at 10M : 6N, total 10,000M.

This part of his doctrine, however, still does not answer the question, because the law of equation of international demands is, as pointed out by J. L. Shadwell,[1] simply a re-statement of the problem in a different way. To say that international value is determined at a point at which international balances of payments are balanced is the same thing as to say that it is determined at the point at which it is determined. What we want to know is why A exports 6,000N and not another amount to pay for 10,000M. It was in the fourth part of his doctrine that Mill really gave an answer to the question.

(4) Mill's answer to the question, what are the forces in operation that produce the equation mentioned in the third part of his doctrine, is found in the following passage :—

> The values at which a country exchanges its produce with foreign countries depend on . . . the amount and extensibility of their demand for its commodities, compared with its demand for theirs. . . . The more the foreign demand for

---

[1] The following is Shadwell's criticism of Mill's doctrine : "In the case which Mill was considering, it was assumed that the two countries concerned had no transactions with one another except those of simple exchange, and as in such a case the exports and imports must be equal, the law which he enunciated amounts to statements that the ratio of exchange is such that the exports pay for the imports. But the fact that the exports pay for the imports implied that the two exchange for one another, and to say that the ratio is that in which the two exchange, is to say that the ratio determines itself." (*A System of Political Economy*, London, 1877, p. 406.)

He next suggested an alternative doctrine of international value. "The principle, however, which governs the case, is the same as that which applies to the products of different classes of labourers within the same country. An article which a farm labourer has produced in a day does not exchange for one which a watchmaker has spent an equal time in producing, because the latter is a more skilful operation, and the remuneration of labour depends upon its efficiency as well as on the irksomeness. In the same way, a country in which labour is highly efficient is able to procure commodities from other countries whose labour is less efficient on more favourable terms than the producing countries themselves . . . To the question what determines the value of a foreign commodity, it may be answered that it depends on three things, the cost of production, the difference between the efficiency of labour in the two countries, and the cost of carriage." (Ibid., p. 405.) It may be noted that with the exception of his objection to Mill's doctrine of international values, he accepted the main conclusion of the classical economists.

its commodities exceeds its demand for foreign commodities, . . .
. . . the more favourable to it will be the terms of interchange.[1]
What is meant by the " amount and extensibility " of
demand ? He did not give a definite answer. But in one
connection at least he came very near to what is known,
after Alfred Marshall, as " the elasticity of demand ".[2]

Professor Graham has passed a criticism on the classical
doctrine of international values. He says that the classical
economists had tacitly assumed that the two countries
were of the same size and the two commodities of the same
importance. It was only upon that assumption that the
classical economists could come to the conclusion that
normally one should expect the barter terms of trade
to be well within the two limits set by the conditions of costs.
Otherwise the barter terms of trade would be very near
to one of its two possible limits.[3]   Graham's argument is
essentially correct. If a country is so small in size or if a
country produces a commodity so important to the trading
countries that it can specialize exclusively in the production
of that commodity (while other countries cannot do so),
the terms of trade will be exclusively in its favour.[4]

Like the doctrine of comparative costs, the classical
doctrine of reciprocal demands is applicable also to the
case of more than two commodities. There are, however,
two necessary modifications. First, by the doctrine that the
exports of each country must exactly pay for its imports
is meant " now the aggregate exports and imports and
not those of particular commodities taking singly ".[5]   In
other words it is a necessary condition of equilibrium that
the credit side and the debit side of the balance of payments
are equal. Arrange the commodities M, N, O, P, Q . . .
in such an order as that described above. That condition
will help us to determine the exact position of the line

[1] Mill, op. cit., p. 603.
[2] Mill, ibid., p. 594. The answer was immediately criticized by Thornton,
who pointed out that sometimes several different rates of international
value might all fulfil the condition given by Mill. Mill tried, in the third
edition of his *Principles* (1852), to escape the difficulty but without
success. Thornton's case, however, is simply one of an exceptional case
of demand conditions.
[3] Frank D. Graham, "The Theory of International Values Re-examined,"
Q.J.E., 1923 ; " The Theory of International Values," *Q.J.E.*, 1932.
Similar argument was advanced in 1897 by J. S. Nicholson, in his *Principles
of Political Economy*, vol. ii, pp. 301 ff.
[4] See Bastable, op. cit., p. 43.
[5] Mill, op. cit., p. 590.

dividing the commodities which country A imports from those which it exports—whether between M and N or between N and O, and so on. Second, " the introduction of several commodities on each side will produce a steady effect."[1] For if there is a great number of actual and potential export-goods and import-goods it will require only a slight alteration in the terms of trade to bring many goods into the category of exports or to take many goods out of the category of imports. Hence the terms of trade will be more stable when the number of commodities exported and imported is large.[2]

We may conclude with a word about the classical theory of value. The classical economists based their theory of international trade upon the Labour Theory of Value. Authorities are still divided on the question whether and to what extent the deductions obtained with the aid of the Labour Theory of Value do or do not depend upon the validity of that theory of value. Since that question is related more to the pure theory of international trade than to the theory of monetary international trade, we do not propose to examine it in the present survey.[3]

5. MARSHALL'S RESTATEMENT OF THE THEORY OF INTERNATIONAL VALUE

Although Mill presented a comprehensive theory of international value, he did not succeed in getting rid of all obscurities and difficulties. The apparatus employed by him is inadequate. In order to fill in the gap Alfred Marshall devised an ingenious geometrical apparatus which is now known as the Marshall curves.[4]

Marshall began by making the following five assumptions. First, there were two countries carrying on trade with

[1] Bastable, op. cit., p. 36.
[2] Cf. Graham, " The Theory of International Values," *Q.J.E.*, 1932, pp. 583 ff. ; Haberler, op. cit., pp. 149 f. Similarly, to introduce a greater number of trading countries than two, one should expect it to produce a steady effect; see Cairnes, op. cit., p. 352.
[3] See, however, Edward S. Mason, " The Doctrine of Comparative Cost " (*Q.J.E.*, 1929) ; B. Ohlin, *International and Inter-regional Trade*, Appendix III ; Haberler, *The Theory of International Trade*, chaps. x and xii ; Taussig, *International Trade*, pp. 43–75 ; and J. Viner, " The Doctrine of Comparative Costs " (*Weltwirtschaftliches Archiv.*, vol. 36, Oct., 1932).
[4] Alfred Marshall, *The Pure Theory of International Trade*, printed for private circulation in 1879. We have used the L.S.E. reprint, London, 1930. 1935.

each other but only with each other. Second, the pure theory of domestic values had provided the means of measuring the value in any one country (say A) of all the various articles exported by it in terms of any one of them (say N). Similarly, a representative article (say M) might be chosen for the other country (say B). Third, the two countries " are not under any obligation to make foreign payments excepting those arising from trade, so that in equilibrium the exports of each country exchange for her imports ". Fourth, the processes of production were not completed until the commodities are delivered to the importing nations. In other words, each country bore the expense of delivering her exports to the other's frontier ; and their values were reckoned on that basis. The supposition enables us to avoid all discussion of the costs of transport. Fifth, every merchant was supposed to do an all-round trade, and to bring back the goods which were obtained in return for his exports, so that he did not need to draw any bill against his exports. Thus the problem of the foreign exchanges does not arise.

Marshall then presented his mathematical apparatus. In order to explain it clearly we better begin with a numerical illustration. Let us suppose that trade is opened between country A and country B, with N and M as their respective representative export goods. Let us construct A's supply schedule and B's demand schedule for commodity N.[1]

A's Supply Schedule for Commodity N

(1) Price of N in terms of M. M	(2) Quantity of N supplied. N	(3) $(1) \times (2)$ M
0·10	10,000	1,000
0·20	20,000	4,000
0·30	30,000	9,000
0·35	40,000	14,000
0·40	50,000	20,000
0·46	60,000	27,600
0·55	70,000	38,500
0·68	80,000	54,400
0·78	90,000	70,200
0·83	100,000	83,000
0·86	110,000	94,600
0·885	120,000	106,200

[1] Those two schedules are adopted from the table appearing in Marshall's *Money, Credit, and Commerce*, p. 162. We have used countries A and B to take the places respectively of countries E and G and commodities N and M to take the places respectively of commodities E and G.

B's Demand Schedule for Commodity N

(4) Price of N in Terms of M. M.	(5) Quantity of N demanded. N.	(6) (4) × (5) M.
2·30	10,000	23,000
1·75	20,000	35,000
1·43	30,000	42,900
1·22	40,000	48,800
1·08	50,000	54,000
0·95	60,000	57,000
0·86	70,000	60,200
0·825	80,000	66,000
0·78	90,000	70,200
0·76	100,000	76,000
0·745	110,000	81,950
0·7375	120,000	88,500

Of those two schedules, we may note the following two points. Firstly, column (2) is numerically the same as column (5). Secondly, we can easily change the first schedule to a demand schedule of A for commodity M. If we divide one by the numbers in column (1) so that the barter terms of trade are expressed in terms of N per unit of M, column (3) becomes a column representing the quantities of M demanded, and column (2) becomes a column representing the total quantity of N for which A is willing to part with the respective quantity of M demanded. By the same way, B's demand schedule for commodity N may be transformed into B's supply schedule for M. Therefore, we may call the first schedule, A's " demand-for-M-and-supply-of-N schedule " and the second schedule B's " demand-for-N-and-supply-of-M schedule ", or, more briefly, A's and B's " trading schedules ".

Those schedules may be represented graphically. Let distances measured along a fixed straight line Ox (Fig. 1) represent the number of units of N and distances measured along a straight line Oy at right angles to Ox represent the number of units of M. Let a curve OA (which may be called A's curve) be drawn to represent the terms on which A is willing to trade. Thus, if P be a point moving along it and PN be drawn always perpendicular to Ox, then ON represents successively the numbers in column (2), NP (or OM) will represent the corresponding numbers in column (3). Similarly, let B's curve, OB, be drawn to represent the terms on which B is willing to trade. Thus if Q be a point moving along it and Qn be drawn always perpendicular to Ox, then On represents successively the numbers in column (5), and nQ (or Om) will represent the corresponding numbers in column (6). The pair of curves obtained are Marshall's curves.

In order to explain clearly the characteristics of those curves and to consider the problems of international demands and of equilibrium by the aid of this apparatus we need first to express these two curves analytically.

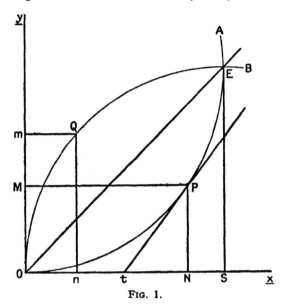

FIG. 1.

Let p be the price of M in terms of N and, then $1/p$ represents the variables in columns (1) and (4). Let D_{am} and D_{bn} denote A's demand for M and B's demand for N respectively. Then D_{am}, $p\,D_{am}$, D_{bn}, and $1/p\ D_{bn}$ represent respectively the successive numbers in columns (3), (2), (5), and (6). We can express the pair of Marshall's curves by :—

$$F[(D_{am}),\ (pD_{am})] = 0 \ \text{(A's curve)}$$
$$f[(1/p\ D_{bn}),\ (D_{bn})] = 0 \ \text{(B's curve)}$$

We may proceed now to some of the geometrical features of the two curves. Firstly, they are symmetrical in the sense that both the ordinates and abscissae are homogeneous quantities each representing totals. Every statement as to the shape which it is possible for A's curve to assume has corresponding to it a similar statement as to the shape which it is possible for B's curve to assume; but wherever x-axis occurs in the former statement, y-axis will occur in the latter and vice versa. Secondly, the curves must start from the origin, because when $D_{am} = 0$, $p \, D_{am} = 0$. Thirdly, since

$$p = \frac{p D_{am}}{D_{am}} = \frac{MP}{OM} = \frac{ON}{OM},$$

the price of M in terms of N is represented by the tangent of the angle POM. Fourthly, the elasticity of demand for A's curve is measured geometrically by[1] :—

$$\frac{\text{Price}}{\text{Price} - \text{Marginal Revenue}} = \frac{\dfrac{ON}{OM}}{\dfrac{ON}{OM} - \dfrac{tN}{OM}} = \frac{ON}{ON - tN} = \frac{ON}{Ot}$$

Fifthly, the curve OA cannot be cut more than once by a horizontal line in any case and the curve OB cannot be cut more than once by a vertical line. In other words, for a given value of D_{am}, there could not be two values of $p \, D_{am}$. For if it did, it would imply, say, that 4,000M are just capable of being sold for the expenses of producing 20,000N as sold for the expenses of producing 40,000N. That is clearly impossible.

If the demand conditions are normal, there are five more characteristics. (a) Every increase in D_{am} (or NP) is accompanied by an increase in $1/p$ (or OM/ON). (b) It follows that if P be any point on OA, every point on that portion of OA which is between O and P must lie below the straight line OP and every point on the remaining portion of OA must lie above the straight line OP. Therefore OA cannot cut twice any straight line through the origin. (c) It can be proved directly from the last point that the portion of OA which is adjacent to O lies below that portion of OB which is adjacent to O. (d) The curve OA cannot cut the same vertical line more than once. (e) The curves OA and OB cannot cut each other in more than one point (besides O).

Finally he came to the problem of equilibrium. He said that " every point in which the two curves cut one another

[1] See A. P. Lerner, " The Diagrammatical Representation of Elasticity of Demand," *The Review of Economic Studies*, 1933.   See also Marshall, *Money, Credit, and Commerce*, pp. 337-8 n.

corresponds to an equilibrium of the trade ". When the demand conditions are normal, there is only one equilibrium point.

The *Theory* was only privately printed and his analysis was not made public until two decades later (1889) in a book by Pantaleoni.[1] In 1889 also appeared a book by Auspitz and Lieben,[2] in which a similar mathematical apparatus, i.e. curves of import demand and export supply in the total form, was independently worked out. But the Auspitz-Lieben curves are not entirely the same as Marshall's curves, because in the former, total *money* value or cost was consistently adopted as ordinate while in the latter the units of commodities had been used. Later, in 1894, Edgeworth made, in his series of articles on " The Theory of International Trade ",[3] a brilliant application of the Marshallian graphics to a variety of problems and gave an algebraic description of equilibrium. Those works, important as they are in certain problems of international trade, are not directly connected with the problem of international price relationships and may hence be passed over.

6. Cost of Transport as a Factor in International Trade

In our description of the classical theory we have hitherto ignored the cost of carriage. When the cost of carriage is introduced there are, according to the classical economists,[4] three important effects. The first effect is that the international movement of goods will depend not only upon the comparative costs of production but also upon the cost of transport. The condition, $\frac{m_a}{m_b} < \frac{n_a}{n_b}$ is no longer sufficient for the establishment of trade between A and B in the way described in the preceding sections. It requires two more

[1] Maffeo Panteleoni, *Pure Economics*, first published in Italian, Florence, 1889 ; English trans. by T. Boston Bruce, London, 1898. The reference is to pp. 197–209.
[2] Rudolf Auspitz and Richard Lieben, *Recherches sur la théorie du prix*, first published in German, Leipzig, 1889 ; French translation by L. Suret, Paris, 1914. See especially French trans., pp. 267–280.
[3] First appeared in the *Economic Journal*, 1894 ; revised and reprinted in his *Papers relating to Political Economy*, vol. ii, pp. 3–60.
[4] See Mill, op. cit., pp. 584–590; Bastable, op. cit., pp. 34 f.; Marshall, op. cit., pp. 326 ff.; Viner, op. cit., pp. 373–7 ; Haberler, op. cit., pp. 141 f.

conditions, viz. $\dfrac{m_a}{m'_b} < \dfrac{n_a}{n_b}$ and $\dfrac{m_a}{m_b} < \dfrac{n'_a}{n_b}$, in which m'_b denotes the number of units of M which just requires a unit of B's labour both to produce and to deliver it to A and n'_a that of N which just requires a unit of A's labour both to produce it and to carry it to B. If $1M$ be the cost of carrying m_b of M from B to A and $1N$ that of carrying n_a of N from A to B, then $m'_b = m_b - 1M$ and $n'_a = n_a - 1N$. The second effect is that on international value. Before we introduce costs of carriage, the ratio of interchange between commodities M and N is the same in both countries and its two possible limits are common to both countries, namely $10M = 7\frac{1}{2}N$ and $10M = 5N$. As soon as we introduce carrying costs, then for every ratio of interchange between M and N in A there is a corresponding, but different, ratio in B. Similarly, the two limits for the ratio of interchange are not the same in the two countries though there is a definite relation between those limits in the two countries. The limits for A are now $10M = 7\frac{1}{2}N$ and $10M = 5\frac{5}{14}N$, while those for B, $10M = 7\frac{1}{32}N$ and $10M = 5N$. For either A or B the limits are narrower. That is natural because the existence of carrying costs means a lessening of the gain by foreign trade. As to the final determination of international value, it would still " depend on the play of international demand ". The third effect of the introduction of transport costs is that it gives rise to goods of domestic trade, i.e. goods which are neither exported nor imported. Any article, the transport cost of which is so great that when we introduce money and have all costs expressed in terms of money, the transport cost exceeds the difference between the costs of production of A and B, will fall within the category of domestic goods. There is, however, no fixed line of demarcation between domestic goods and international trade goods. Any change in the conditions of international demands may shift an article from one category to another.

Henry Sidgwick [1] was the most distinguished economist who, before the war, had dealt with the cost of transport as a factor in international trade. He went so far as to attempt to advance a theory of international trade exclusively on the ground of the existence of transport costs. He declared that the importance of the element of

[1] Henry Sidgwick, *The Principles of Political Economy*, London, 1883 ; 3rd ed., edited by J. N. Keynes, 1901.

distance, instead of immobility of labour and capital, was the real ground for a separate study of international trade.[1] There are, according to him, five cases in which commodities may be produced at a considerable distance from their consumers (i.e. in a foreign country) and still be produced remuneratively : (a) commodities like metals and products of special quality which are generally demanded but " cannot be produced at all except in certain localities situated at a considerable distance from important sections of their consumers " ; (b) commodities including many important products of agriculture which, though could be generally produced in many places, can be most economically produced only at " certain places which offer special natural advantages for their production " ; (c) commodities which " can be most economically produced for distant markets not on account of any special advantages afforded by the place in which they are made, but because the cost of carriage is outweighed by the economic gain through co-operation and division of labour, obtained by the concentration of a manufacture—or of several connected manufacturers—in one locality ", that is by the economic gain of large scale production ; (d) food, fuel, and certain other commodities required in large quantity for the ordinary consumption by the large, closely packed masses in modern industrial towns ; and (e) the case of comparative differences in costs which can be a cause of foreign trade only in " so far as physical or social obstacles render the mobility of labour temporarily or permanently imperfect ".[2] He then turned to the problem of international values and declared that " the peculiarity of the theoretical determination of the values of the products of such trade depends primarily not on the imperfect mobility of labour, but on the cost of carriage ". The following passage exactly summarizes his doctrine of international values :—

In explaining the determination of international values—or rather of the values of wares interchanged between distant places—we have to take into account not merely the expense of conveying wares into the foreign country, but also the expense of bringing home their value in some form or other. If we take this double cost of carriage into account we shall find that the " cost of production including carriage " has an

[1] *The Principles of Political Economy*, pp. 209, 222 f.
[2] Ibid., pp. 210–212.

N

important relation to the determination of the price of the products of foreign trade, as giving the limits between which the competitive price tends to vary according to the varying conditions of demand for foreign products in each country.[1] In other words, " the home cost of production together with double cost of carriage gives us a *maximum* value, and home cost of production without cost of carriage a *minimum* value." Within those two limits, " the division of double cost of carriage between the two countries will depend upon the degree in which the demand in either country for the foreign wares of the other is more easily extensible than the corresponding demand on the other side . . . The more this is the case, the larger will be the share of the double cost of carriage that will tend to be added to the imports of the country in question."[2] That doctrine is useful as a supplement to the classical theory but cannot be considered, as Sidgwick claimed, to be an independent theory.

7. THE CLASSICAL THEORY OF INTERNATIONAL TRADE AS THE FOUNDATION OF THE CLASSICAL THEORY OF INTERNATIONAL PRICE RELATIONSHIPS

Having described the classical theory of international trade, we may now see how it has been used as the foundation of the classical theory of international price relationships. As soon as we come to the problem of international price relationships, we are introducing the element of money. According to the classical doctrine, indirect exchange with money as the medium of exchange obeys the same laws as direct exchange without money, and all trade is ultimately barter. That proposition is based upon two doctrines, namely, first, the so-called doctrine of the natural distribution of precious metals among commercial nations and, second, Hume's law. According to the former, " gold and silver having been chosen for the general medium of circulation, they are, by the competition of commerce, distributed in such proportions amongst the different countries of the world, as to accommodate themselves to the natural traffic which would take place if no such metals existed and the trade between countries were purely a trade

[1] p. 214.   [2] pp. 218, 219.

of barter." [1]   If for any reason trade by means of money fails to conform with trade by barter, Hume's law would work so that the accommodation of the former to the latter will ultimately be produced. If it happens that the price level in A is higher or lower than what would make trade conform with barter, gold will flow into or out of A, and the price level of A will rise or fall until the equilibrium point is reached.

The classical theory of international trade does not help us to have any better understanding of the classical theory of the comparative values of money among nations than that presented in the previous chapter. But the theory of trade, as given in the preceding sections, is the basis upon which the classical theory of the relations of the wage-levels of the trading nations is built. We shall now turn to the connections between the two theories.

As the doctrine of comparative costs shows us the direction of the movement of the two commodities between the two countries and the two limits within which the barter terms of trade may vary, it also helps us to set the two limits of possible variations of the relative levels of wages. Let us turn to the hypothetical case. The cost data gives us the following ratios :—

Commodity M, A : B : : 10 : 8.
Commodity N, A : B : : 10 : 5$\frac{1}{3}$.

From those ratios we can see that the average wage of B cannot be higher than 80 per cent of that of A and not be lower than 53$\frac{1}{3}$ per cent. Let us suppose that the wage per unit of labour in A is £5 or 100s. Then in country A :—

The money-cost or price per unit of M is 5s. 0d.
The money-cost or price per unit of N is 6s. 8d.

If B's wage is 80s. (i.e. 80 per cent of that of A), then :—

The price per unit of M is 5s. 0d.
The money cost per unit of N is 10s. 0d.

If B's wage is 53s. 4d. (i.e. 53$\frac{1}{3}$ per cent of that of A), then :—

The price per unit of M is 3s. 4d.
The money cost per unit of N is 6s. 8d.

It is obvious that only within those two limits A can export

[1] Ricardo, op. cit., 117. Cf. Mill, op. cit., pp. 619–628.

N to B and at the same time B can export M to A. If B's wage is more than 80 per cent of that of A, then it pays for B to import both M and N from A. The balance of payments of B becomes unfavourable and Hume's law would work to bring down B's wage-level within the upper limit. Similarly B's wage cannot fall below the lower limit.

It may be noted that when B's wage-level reaches its upper limit, the barter terms of trade are at the limit which is exclusively in B's favour, i.e. $10M : 7\frac{1}{2}N$. When B's wage level reaches its lower limit the barter terms of trade are $10M : 5N$, exclusively in A's favour.

That can also be expressed algebraically. In the hypothetical case, the cost ratios are such that $\dfrac{m_a}{m_b} < \dfrac{n_a}{n_b}$. The ratio $m_a : m_b$ represents the upper limit of the wage of B relative to A and also the lower limit of the wage of A relative to B. Similarly $n_a : n_b$ represents the lower limit of B's relative wage-level and the upper limit of A's. Let W_a denote the money wage (per unit of labour) in A and W_b that in B. Let R denote the rate of exchange, i.e. the number of units of A's currency which exchange for one unit of B's currency. Then $\dfrac{W_a}{W_b \times R}$ cannot be smaller than $\dfrac{m_a}{m_b}$ and also cannot be greater than $\dfrac{n_a}{n_b}$. If there are more than two commodities, whose cost-data are such that

$$\frac{m_a}{m_b} < \frac{n_a}{n_b} < \frac{o_a}{o_b} < \frac{p_a}{p_b} < \ldots < \frac{q_a}{q_b}.$$

the wage ratio, $\dfrac{W_a}{W_b \times R}$, has $\dfrac{m_a}{m_b}$ and $\dfrac{q_a}{q_b}$ as its two limits: it cannot be smaller than the former nor greater than the latter.

It is clear, therefore, that the relative efficiency of labours in the trading countries influences the relations of the wage or income levels between countries in two ways. First it shows us whether A will have a higher wage-level than B, or A will have a lower one, or A will have either. In the case $\dfrac{m_a}{m_b} < \dfrac{n_a}{n_b}$, (a) if both $m_b < m_a$ and $n_b < n_a$, the wage-level in A will be higher than that of B ; (b) if both $m_b > m_a$

and $n_b > n_a$, the wage-level in A will be lower than that of B ; (c) if $m_b > m_a$ but $n_b < n_a$, then the wage-level in A may be either higher or lower than that of B. Second it sets the limits (viz : $\frac{m_a}{m_b}$ and $\frac{n_a}{n_b}$) beyond which the average wage or income level of a trading country (relative to that of the other country) cannot move. That doctrine is, in effect, a part of what we call the Seniorian doctrine of international discrepancies in wages.[1]

The cost-data alone, however, do not determine the exact point of equilibrium and hence do not establish the actual relation between the wage-level of A and that of B. The exact position is determined by the demand-and-supply conditions.

Generally speaking, within the limits set by the cost-data, the wage-level of a country is high (relative to the other country) when the barter terms of trade are in the former's favour. Thus like the barter terms of trade, the relative wages of trading countries are a problem which the classical doctrine of reciprocal demands helps to solve. We may lay down in accordance with that classical doctrine the following three general propositions : (i) When the capacity of a country as a market and as a producer is greater than that of the other country, the barter terms of trade tend to be favourable to the latter and the level of wages tends to be high in the latter. (ii) The more the relative importance of N in comparison with M, the lower the wage-level of B relative to A. (iii) Other things being equal, the less elastic the demand of a country (say A) for the export article (M) of the other country (B), or the more elastic the latter's demand for the former's export (N), the higher will be the relative wage-level of the former (A) in comparison with that of the latter (B). Those three propositions amount to Mill's modifications of the Seniorian doctrine.

One more word may be said of the relation between the ratio of the wage-level of A to that of B and the barter terms of trade. Under the simplifying assumptions of two countries producing altogether two goods which are both subject to the law of constant costs, the wage ratio and the barter term of trade will always move together. Let us express the barter term of trade in terms of a number of

[1] Cf. Taussig, op. cit., pp. 7–42 ; Haberler, op. cit., pp. 133 f., 136 ff.

units of M per unit of N. Then we have the following equation :—

$$\text{Barter terms of trade} = \frac{W_a}{n_a} \div \frac{W_b \times R}{m_b} = \frac{W_a}{W_b \times R} \times \frac{m_b}{n_a}.$$

Under the assumption of constant cost, $\frac{m_b}{n_a}$ becomes a constant ; the relation between the barter terms of trade and the wage ratio is a clear linear relation. If production is subject to varying costs, the relation, though still definite, is more complex.

It is useful, therefore, to distinguish between the concept of barter terms of trade, which may also be called commodity terms of trade, and the concept of " factorial terms of trade ". The factorial terms of trade of a country may be defined as the number of units of factors of production of the other country which produces the quantity of products that will exchange for the output of one unit of the factors of production of the country under consideration. In the case that we are examining, i.e. the case of only one factor of production (viz. homogeneous labour), the factorial terms of trade become the number of units of B's labour which produces that quantity of M which will exchange for the output of one unit of A's labour. If the commodity term of trade is $\frac{Q_m}{Q_n}$, Q_m and Q_n being the quantity of M and N respectively, the factorial term of trade is :—

$$\frac{\dfrac{Q_m}{m_b}}{\dfrac{Q_n}{n_a}} \text{ or } \frac{Q_m}{Q_n} \times \frac{n_a}{m_b}$$

or, according to the equation given in the preceding paragraph, $\frac{W_b}{(W_b \, R)}$, i.e., the wage ratio.[1]

When there are more than two commodities that enter into international trade, it is no longer convenient or even possible to express the commodity term of trade in terms of physical units of the trading commodities. In that case it

[1] Marshall, as already indicated, suggested to measure value in international trade in terms of " representative bales, that is bales each of which represents uniform aggregate investments of her labour (of various qualities) and of her capital ". When Marshall's method is used, the term of trade obtained is the factorial term.

is common to measure the commodity term by the ratio between the index of export prices and the index of import prices. But the relation between the commodity term of trade and the factorial term of trade remains the same.[1]

The preceding paragraphs deal only with the relations of the levels of factor prices among the trading nations. Nothing has been said about the international relationships of product prices. That is natural because we have hitherto assumed a zero cost of carriage. Abstracting cost of carriage, the prices of all goods must be equal in both countries and very little is necessary to be said about it. The introduction of cost of carriage makes the case different. The chief difference will then be that M and N will no longer exchange for each other at precisely the same rate in both countries. M will be dearer in A by the cost of carrying it from B to A, and N will be cheaper in A by the expense of transporting it from A to B. Suppose the cost of carrying m_b of M from B to A be $1M$ in the sense that in order to deliver $15M$ at A, B has to pay the transportation company $16M$. Suppose, in the same sense, the cost of carrying n_a of N from A to B be $1N$. Then the price of $15N$ in A should be the same as $14N$ in B and that of $15M$ in A, the same as $16M$ in B. Let the indices of the import price level and the export price level in B be both equal to 100. Then in comparison with B, A's index for import prices (M) should be $106\frac{2}{3}$ and that for export prices (N) $93\frac{1}{3}$. Algebraically :—

$$P_{an} = P_{bn} \times \frac{n'_a}{n_a}$$

$$\text{and } P_{am} = P_{bm} \times \frac{m_b}{m'_b}$$

in which P_{am} and P_{an} denote the prices respectively of M and N in country A and P_{bm} and P_{bn} those in B. It is obvious

[1] For discussions of the problems of commodity and factorial terms of trade, see J. Viner, " International Trade : Theory," *Encyclopædia of Social Sciences*, and Roland Wilson, *Capital Imports and the Terms of Trade* (Melbourne, 1931), pp. 49 ff. Professor Taussig suggested the concept of " gross barter term of trade ", as distinguished from the concept of " net barter term of trade ". Taussig suggested that concept when he discussed the problem of invisible or non-commodity items. The term gross barter term of trade " regards the whole volume of goods, both imports and exports ", while the term net barter term " regards those goods only when paid for goods ". See Taussig, *International Trade*, New York, 1928, p. 113. Recently, Professor Viner suggested other concepts of terms of trade ; see his *Studies in the Theory of International Trade*, pp. 558–564.

from the equations that if the cost of carrying N from A to B is increased, other things being equal, P_{an} and hence the general price level in A will be lower in comparison with B. Similarly if cost of carrying M from B to A is increased, other things being equal, P_{am} and hence the general price level in A will be relatively higher. It is partly in that sense that the classical economists come to the conclusion that cost of carriage plays an important role in the determination of relative prices between trading countries.

The wage relations between A and B are also affected by the introduction of transport cost. The limiting ratios will now be $\frac{m_a}{m'_b}$ and $\frac{n'_a}{n_b}$, that is to say $\frac{W_a}{W_b \times R}$ cannot be smaller than $\frac{m_a}{m'_b}$ and also cannot be greater than $\frac{n'_a}{n_b}$. Let the costs of carriage be the same as those supposed in the preceding paragraphs (i.e. $1M$ and $1N$). Suppose the wage per unit of labour to be fixed in A, say at 100*s*. Then in country A :—

> The money-cost per unit of M is 5*s*. 0*d*.
> The price per unit of N is 6*s*. 8*d*.

If B's wage is 75*s*. (i.e. 75 per cent of that of A), then :—

> The price per unit of M at B is 4*s*. $8\frac{1}{4}d$.
> The cost of carrying a unit of M to A is $3\frac{3}{4}d$.
> The price per unit of M at A is 5*s*. 0*d*.
> The money-cost per unit of N at B is 9*s*. $4\frac{1}{2}d$.

If B's wage is 57*s*. $1\frac{5}{7}d$. (i.e. $57\frac{1}{7}$ per cent of that of A), then :—

> The price per unit of M at B is 3*s*. $6\frac{5}{7}d$.
> The money-cost per unit of N at B is 7*s*. $1\frac{6}{7}d$.
> The cost of carrying $1N$ from A to B is $5\frac{6}{7}d$.

Obviously, B's wage cannot be higher than 75 per cent nor lower than $57\frac{1}{7}$ per cent of that of A.

CHAPTER V

POST-CLASSICAL DEVELOPMENT OF THE MONE-TARY ASPECTS OF THE THEORY OF INTER-NATIONAL PRICE RELATIONSHIPS: 1848–1918

1. The Controversy concerning the Gold Discoveries of 1848–1851

About the middle of the nineteenth century the economic structure all over the world was affected by a series of events among which were the new discoveries of gold in California (1848) and in Australia (1851). The opening up of fresh sources of gold in those countries opened a new chapter in the world's monetary history, because it made an international gold standard possible and, moreover, stimulated theoretical speculations. The participants in the controversy that ensued and the economists whose writings are examined in the latter part of this chapter greatly forwarded the study of the monetary aspects of the theory of international price relationships.

Among the problems raised in the controversy were the following five: (a) To what extent were prices increased by the new gold supplies? (b) How did the increase of the quantity of the precious metals work out its effect upon prices (the problem of diffusion)? (c) What would be the future of prices? (d) What were the effects, if any, of the increase of the quantity of money on interest rates? (e) Whether the rise in prices brought about by the new gold was really beneficial? It was in connection with those problems, especially (b) and (d), that the actual mechanisms involved in both domestic and international price adjustments were discussed.

Business men were generally of the opinion that the increased production of gold would not cause any rise in the prices of commodities and that it would lower the rate of interest. Therefore, its effects would be mainly beneficial Objections were soon raised to that view by many economists, among whom we may mention Austin, Stirling, and Chevalier. The theoretical foundation of Austin's

185

argument was the quantity theory in its most extreme form, but he contributed nothing which was really new.[1] Like Austin, Stirling[2] also tried to prove that, owing to the discovery of new gold mines, gold had actually depreciated. His arguments, however, did not rest on the quantity theory but on the Seniorian theory of money (that the natural value of money was determined by the cost of procuring gold).[3] He suggested that, as the cost of production of gold was reduced, the value of gold was bound to fall. As to the effects of the discovery of gold on the rate of interest, he made a concession to the view of the business world. Instead of holding the mechanical view, which denied any relationship between the changes in the volume of the circulating medium and those in the rates of interest, he argued as follows :—

Interest, as is clearly shown by Adam Smith, depends not on the numerical amount of money in circulation, but on the general rate of profits and the amount of capital in the market seeking investment. No doubt *during the progress* of the great change which we have seen now on the eve of witnessing, an impetus will be given to trade in all its departments ; and while the influx of gold continues, the amount of capital for investment will be increased, and the rate of profits, in consequence, temporarily depressed. More remittances, in the first instance, will be made in gold, and fewer in produce. The reserves of the banks will be increased, *loanable* capita, (so to speak) will for a time be more than usually abundant, and interest will fall. But this effect will be transient. The additional capital will no longer be kept floating but will be sent abroad, or get absorbed in the various departments of domestic production.[4]

The problem was more elaborately worked out by Chevalier.[5]

[1] William Austin, *On the Imminent Depreciation of Gold*, London, 1853. See especially pp. 5 ff.
[2] Patrick James Stirling, *The Australian and Californian Gold Discoveries, and their Probable Consequences*, London, 1853.
[3] Ibid., pp. 59–92, 203–210. He explicitly rejected the quantity theory, but in reality, as pointed out above, the Seniorian theory of money is not irreconcilable with the quantity theory.
[4] *Gold Discoveries*, p. 50.
[5] Michel Chevalier, *De la baisse probable de l'or des conséquences commerciales et sociales* . . . (Paris, 1859), English translation under the title, *On the Probable Fall in the Value of Gold*, translated by Richard Cobden, published the same year in London and Manchester. In his *Cours d'économie politique* (Paris, 1841–1850), he presented a part of the classical theory of international price relationships and made a combination of Say's *loi des débouchés* with Hume's law.

After a careful examination of the conditions of the demand and supply of gold he came to the following conclusion :—

In no direction can a new outlet be seen sufficiently large to absorb the extraordinary production of gold which we are now witnessing, so as to prevent a fall in its value. There is but one way of disposing of these masses of gold, it is by coining them and forcing them into the current of circulation into countries which are already sufficiently provided with a gold currency. This current will absorb them, for it is, so to speak, insatiable ; it receives and carries off all that is thrown into it ; but the process of absorption and assimilation is on one condition, namely that gold diminishes in value, so that in those transactions where heretofore ten pieces of gold had for example sufficed, eleven, twelve, fifteen, or even more, will be henceforth required. In a word, if gold is to enter into circulation in indefinite quantities, it is by being subjected to the rigorous law of *a continually increasing depreciation*.[1]

Adopting a different line of approach, Newmarch [2] put himself in opposition to Austin, Stirling, and Chevalier and gave a theoretical foundation for the view prevailing in the business world. According to him increased gold production, though having the tendency to raise prices, had the effect, through its influence on trade, of calling into operation so many tendencies of a contrary nature that the depreciation of its value would proceed with such slowness that it would have no practical significance. Moreover, the increase in prices would not be proportionate to the increase in the quantity of gold, even though the period was long enough to let the increase of gold work out its effects upon prices. He criticized strongly the mechanical version of the quantity theory of money :—

It is not true that the effect of even a largely increased quantity of metallic money in raising prices is a hasty process ; nor is it true, that according to the facts of the last three hundred and sixty years, a doubling of the quantity of metallic money has led either hastily or ultimately to a doubling of prices ; nor, further, is it true, that the circumstances connected with the diffusion of the larger quantity of metallic money are

---

[1] *On the Probable Fall*, pp. 99–100. The italics are ours. He also noted that as the leading bi-metallic country, " France seems temporarily as a parachute to retard the fall of gold " (ibid., pp. 60–63).
[2] William Newmarch, *A History of Prices*, vol. vi, London, 1857. Newmarch and Tooke were the joint authors of *History of Prices*. Undoubtedly, Newmarch was much influenced by Tooke.

so purely collateral that they may be left out of view. On the contrary ... by the process of the Diffusion there are brought into operation causes which go very far to invalidate the *a priori* inferences adopted on abstract grounds.[1]

He gave a detailed analysis of the order and the extent of the changes produced by the discoveries of gold. (i) The first and immediate effect of the discoveries was a quadrupling of the wages of all miners. As the remuneration paid to the miners regulated the wages of all other labourers in the same country, the wages of all kinds of labour in the gold-producing countries was also quadrupled. (ii) The expenditure of the labourers correspondingly increased, and the increased expenditure raised the prices of those things which were consumed by them. The extent of the rise of the prices of those things varied during a short period of time. The rise was regulated by the extent to which supplies could be increased. There was an over-supply and consequently an exceedingly low range of prices of imported articles (as supplies could be easily increased), while articles of colonial production remained relatively scarce and consequently dear in price. (iii) Ultimately, by an order of progression, beginning with the lowest class of labourers and ascending to the richest capitalists, larger incomes were provided for all the classes in the gold-producing countries. (iv) In the process of internal diffusion many important economic changes occurred, and of particular note among them the rapid and large " accumulation of real wealth and real resources ". (v) The general increase of income and of expenditure in the gold-producing countries could not fail to increase the demand for foreign goods. The effects of the discoveries of gold extended to the places which supplied goods to the gold-producing countries. It had " extended to the districts which supplied the raw materials

---

[1] *A History of Prices*, vol. vi, p. 195. " In the Inquiry in Appendix II relatively to Influx of the Precious Metals from America in the sixteenth and seventeenth centuries, it has been shown ... that during the eighty years from 1492 to 1570, the increase of General Prices were exceedingly partial and insignificant ... that the rise of prices which did take place in consequence of the American Supplies, was not accomplished in a shorter space of time than the seventy years between 1570 and 1640 ; and that at the end of those seventy years, the increase of prices was only 200 per cent, while it is beyond doubt that the Stock of the Precious Metals in Europe and America had been augmented since 1492 in the proportion of 600 per cent " (pp. 195-6).

of those articles; and, pursuing the same order of progression, the area of the increased demand for Commodities—or, what is a better term, the area within which increased Incomes are expanded—is necessarily wider in each succeeding month ". (vi) Consequently the gold " within those countries to which the Gold has been sent in exchange for commodities has produced the same effects ", namely stimulation of industry, accumulation of capital, and increase of real wealth.[1]

It was mainly owing to the facts in the fourth and the last propositions that " the range of Prices, neither in Victoria [that is, the gold-producing country] nor in other mercantile countries has been raised in any proportion corresponding to the quantity of New Gold raised and distributed ".[2] As the distribution of the new gold was accomplished only by an increased employment of labour for the production of an increased quantity and number of commodities, " the increase of transactions and exchanges arising out of this extended production has *ipso facto* rendered necessary a large amount of Gold as a Circulating Medium "; and hence the rising tendency of Prices had been checked. That was substantially the doctrine that money stimulates trade, which was first advanced by Potter, Law, and others. In connection with that doctrine the following passage is worth quoting :—

A similitude employed by Adam Smith will assist us in this difficulty. He compares the function of Money to the function of a Highway. . . . To increase, therefore, the Stock of Money is almost the same thing as to impart to production the impulse which would be communicated by the conversion of a common Turnpike into a Railway. . . . And to increase the Stock of Money year by year, is very much the same thing as to construct, year by year, a new and additional Network of Railways. But if these illustrations have any force it follows that, during some period, longer of shorter, an addition to the Quantity of money is the same thing as an addition to the Fixed Capital of the country ; and exerts on production an influence of the same beneficial kind as the provision of imposed harbours, roads, or manufactures.[3]

Although that might be true only of transitional periods, yet a considerable interval " must elapse before additions

---

[1] *A History of Prices*, vol. vi, pp. 230–6, 804–812, 224–9, 188–193.
[2] Ibid., p. 813.   [3] Ibid., pp. 215–16.

to the quantity of Money can be neutralized by corresponding additions to the range of Prices ".[1]

In connection with the fifth proposition he dealt with the problem of the distribution of the new gold throughout the world. His doctrine was simply the Seniorian doctrine as modified by J. S. Mill. " The New Gold has been distributed throughout the commercial world, in the first instance, in proportion to the skill and resources of each country in the production of Exportable Goods in demand in the Gold Regions ; and in the next instance, in proportion to the skill and resources of each country in the production of Exportable Goods, not only in demand in the Gold Regions, but in demand in any other region to which any part of the New Supplies of Gold may have been carried." [2]

Finally he examined the extent of the connection between the new gold and the rate of interest.[3] He found that, as the new gold flowed into England it naturally increased the cash reserve of the Bank of England, because the latter was " the safest and most convenient place of deposit ". The natural and inevitable result of the large addition to the Reserve " was to reduce the rate of discount and the market rate of interest ".[4] " The most immediate consequence of the extreme reduction of the Rate of Interest was to lessen the cost of producing commodities, and to increase the profits of all persons requiring the accommodation of advance for short or long period." That led to an extension of trade and enterprise. The extension of trade and enterprise itself, however, soon raised the requirements for capital beyond the supply and thereby forced the successive raisings of the rate of discount, in spite of the continuous inflow of specie during the period. Still the continuous inflow of specie (even in the latter stage) could not fail to have beneficial effects, because it had in a great measure enabled England to pass through " perils. and calamities " for many years " without encountering any

---

[1] *A History of Prices*, p. 217.
[2] Ibid., p. 210.   [3] Ibid, pp. 200–203.
[4] " It is not necessary in this place to point out the absurdity of any doctrine which connects the rate of interest with the mere amount of the Circulating Medium. The rate of discount in 1852 fell to 1½ per cent, not because the eight millions of New Gold had been added to the Circulation of this country ; but because the eight millions had been added to the Reserve of Capital seeking employment " (p. 201).

consequences more disastrous than a rise in the Rate of Interest and Discount ". That analysis was excellent so far as it went,[1] but he did not say anything, at least explicitly, of the possibility of the influence of variations in discount rate on prices.[2]

2. THE SAME SUBJECT CONTINUED

Newmarch's *History* was immediately followed by the works of two eminent economists, Levasseur and Cairnes. Levasseur [3] found, first of all, that the increase of the quantity of the precious metals had caused a rise in the prices of all commodities, but that the rise was not uniform for all products. Generally speaking, the prices of natural products, the quantities of which could not be rapidly increased in response to an increased demand, would rise most, while the prices of goods, the supplies of which could be rapidly increased (that was, manufactured goods) would rise least. For example, at the end of the decade following the discoveries of gold in California, the estimated increase of the prices of the natural products of France (which was due to the increase in the supply of gold) was about 42 per cent, while that of the prices of manufactured goods was only about 8 per cent.[4] Moreover the increase in the supply of gold had the effect of encouraging trade and industry.[5] He also examined the influence of the supply of gold on the rate of interest. Like many other economists, he pointed out that in the long run the rate of interest was determined, on the one hand, by the abundance or scarcity of capital, and on the other by the rate of profit. In short-term relations, however, the increase of gold did have an effect on the discount rate :—

In reality, the instant that the metals begin to reach the market in great quantity, they constitute a floating capital which cannot immediately be employed. The holders of money

[1] The power to influence the discount rate and stimulate industry by an increase in volume, according to him, was true only of gold and of paper money. Bank notes and other forms of credit were not admitted to have the same influence.

[2] Like Newmarch, McCullock doubted the existence of any depreciation, and thought that if there were any depreciation, it must be both temporary in degree and partial in extent.

[3] L. Levasseur, *La question de l'or: les mines de Californie et d'Australie* (Paris, 1858).

[4] *La Question de l'or*, pp. 174–197, 252 f., 344.

[5] Ibid., pp. 161 ff.

then offer it cheaply, and interest falls. But the reaction does not delay to come : the borrowers increase ; the money finds an employment ; the production expands ; and, once the movement started, the demand would be sufficient for the consumption of all the precious metals that the mines continue to supply ; the old level is re-established, and sometimes even surpassed, because the ardour of speculation has augmented the demand more rapidly than the labour has increased the capital.[1]

Like Newmarch, however, he did not connect the discount rate with the problem of price changes. Finally, we may note his restatement of the quantity theory of money. He declared that the value of money was determined by demand and supply, meaning by supply "the quantity of metal actually disposable, multiplied by the rapidity of circulation ", and by demand "the total sum of merchandise and services actually for sale, multiplied by the rapidity of their circulation and subtracted (from) the total quantity bought by means of credit ".[2] Let T denote the total sum of services and merchandise, C the rapidity of general circulation, Cr credit in all forms, M the quantity of the precious metals, R that part of the precious metals which are fixed in quantity or reserved, C' the rapidity of the circulation particular to the money metals. Then [3]

[1] *La question d l'or*, p. 171. " Il est impossible de ne pas reconnaître en présence de ce fait que l'accroissement de la quantité d'or n'a sur le taux de l'intérêt aucune influence sérieuse, que la baisse qu'il produit est un accident plutôt qu'une loi économique, qu'elle est de très-courte durée et qu'elle est souvent suivi d'une réaction beaucoup plus importante " (p. 173).

[2] Ibid., pp. 343–4.

[3] Ibid., p. 150. Levasseur's equation is not, however, the first algebraic statement of the so-called " equation of exchange ". Four years before the publication of his work (1854), Guillaume Roscher had, in his *Principles of Political Economy*, section 123, given the equation $u = ms$, where u denotes the sum of payments made during a given period of time ; m the quantity of money in a state ; and s the rapidity of circulation of a unit of money. (English translation by J. J. Lalor, vol. i, p. 369, n. 6.) Later, in 1856, Francis Bowen, after having approvingly quoted the quantity theory, as stated by J. S. Mill, restated Mill's doctrine algebraically by

$$gs = mr$$

where g denotes the quantity of goods on sale ; s the number of times the goods are resold ; m the quantity of money in circulation ; and r the number of purchases effected by each piece of money or the rapidity of its circulation (*The Principles of Political Economy*, London, 1856, pp. 307–8).

Both those statements have the defect of not giving explicitly any place to the term P (a price level) and are hence definitely inferior to the equation of Levasseur.

The value of the money metals

$$= \frac{TC}{(M - R) \ C' + Cr}$$

That is very similar to the formula given some fifty years later by Professor Irving Fisher. Fisher's equation,[1]

$$PT = MV + M'V'$$

may be written as—

the value of money $= \frac{1}{P} = \frac{T}{MV + M'V'}$

While $M'V'$ and V in Fisher's equation have respectively the same meanings as Cr and C' in Levasseur's equation, the only difference is that we have M instead of $M - R$ and T instead of TC in Fisher's equation.

In many respects the opinions of Cairnes[2] were similar to those of Levasseur. That was true especially of the first of Levasseur's propositions, namely that the increase of the quantity of the precious metals had caused a rise in the prices of all commodities, but that that rise was not

---

[1] Irving Fisher, *The Purchasing Power of Money*, New York, 1911. The reference is to the 1922 ed., p. 48. In that equation, M denotes the average amount of money in circulation in a given community during a given year; V the velocity of the circulation of money which is, by definition, equal to the year's expenditure on goods in the community divided by M; M', the total bank deposits subject to transfer by cheques; V' the average velocity of circulation of the deposit currency; P the average price; and T the volume of transaction.

The "equation of exchange", including the term P, may be said to have originated with Levasseur. It was later found in Léon Walras, *Eléments d'économie politique pure* (Lausanne, 1st ed., 1874, p. 180), in Simon Newcomb, *Principles of Political Economy* (New York, 1885, p. 346), in A. T. Hadley, *Economics* (New York, 1896, pp. 196-7), and in E. W. Kemmerer, *Money and Credit Instruments in their Relation to General Prices* (New York, 1906, 2nd ed., 1909, pp. 11 ff.). It was from Newcomb that Fisher got the idea. Their formulæ may be given in the notation of Fisher as follows :—

(a) Levasseur	. .	$MV + M'V' = PGv$
(b) Walras .	. .	$MV + M'V' = PGv$
(c) Newcomb	. .	$MV = PT$
(d) Hadley .	. .	$MV = PT$
(e) Kemmerer	. .	$MV + M'V' = PT$

In those equations G is the total number of commodities exchanged and v the average velocity of circulation of goods.

[2] J. E. Cairnes, "The Course of Depreciation" (1858), "The Australian Episode" (1859), "International Results" (1860), and other essays concerning the gold question. All are reprinted in his *Essays in Political Economy*, London, 1873.

uniform for all products. The theory of money upon which Levasseur had based his conclusion was not, however, exactly the same as that of Cairnes. The latter's view was more of the Seniorian character, while the former's view inclined more towards the quantity theory.[1] The general position of Cairnes concerning changes in prices was precisely laid down in the following passage :—

> When an advance in the price of any of the great staples of industry becomes definitive (and monopoly apart), there are two, and only two, adequate explanations of the fact : either the cost of producing the article (understanding by cost, not the money outlay, but the real difficulties of production) has increased ; or the cost of producing or obtaining money has diminished. A change in supply and demand will indeed produce temporary effects upon prices, but apart from the conditions just stated it is incapable of permanently altering them.[2]

He then traced, step by step, the consequences of the new discoveries of gold on prices and thereby produced one of the best analyses of the " direct " chain of effects that connect money and prices. According to him, " the process by which an increased production of gold operates in depreciating the value of the metal and raising general prices appears to be twofold ; it acts, first, *directly* through the medium of an enlarged money demand and, secondly, *indirectly* through a contraction of supply." [3] With respect to articles which were exclusively consumed by the productive classes and hence were directly affected by the new money, the sequence of events was as follows : By the discovery of gold, a common labourer was enabled to obtain a quadruple rate of wages. That in turn caused an increase of expenditure and consequently an increase in money demand. That was followed by a temporary rise in prices, in advance of the general movement, and increased production. How long that temporary rise in price would last depended on the nature of the articles themselves. " That portion which consists of finished manufactures, though their price may in the first instance be rapidly increased, cannot continue long in advance of the general movement owing to the facilities available for rapidly advancing the supply ;

---

[1] The difference is, of course, a difference of emphasis only.
[2] *Essays*, p. 7. [3] Ibid., p. 57.

whereas, should the production, from over-estimation of the increasing requirements, be once carried to excess, their prices, in consequence of the difficulty of contracting supply, may be kept for some considerable time below the normal level. . . . Such raw products as fall within the consumption of the classes indicated, not being susceptible of the same rapid expansion as manufactures, may continue for some time in advance of the general movement, and among raw products, the effects would be more marked in those derived from the animal than in those derived from the vegetable kingdom." After that adjustment of prices and the restoration of equilibrium, there would remain a net permanent rise in prices. Articles which did not come directly within the range of the new demand felt the effects of the discovery of gold differently. The producers of those articles first found that as wages in other branches of industry had been raised they could not continue to pay their workmen at the old rate. When they paid them according to the current rate of wages, their profits fell and a curtailment of production became inevitable. The curtailment of production in turn raised the sale prices of their products. " An increased supply of money thus tends, by one mode of these operations, to raise prices in advance of wages and thus to stimulate production ; by another, to raise wage in advance of prices, and thus to check it ; in both, however, to raise wages, and thus ultimately to render necessary, in order to maintenance of profits, a general and permanent elevation of prices." [1] He then presented the same proposition as Levasseur that the rise in prices was not uniform for all products. Briefly stated the position of commodities in the upward trend of prices depended upon three things : first the direction of the new expenditure ; second the facility for extending the supply which in turn depended upon (a) the extent to which machinery was employed in production, and (b) the degree to which the process of production was independent of natural agencies ; and third the facility with which supply could be contracted. Manufactured products, the supply of which was easiest to extend, but most difficult to contract, would have a rise in price quickly corrected by the increased production ; and consequently the rise of price was not significant. The

[1] *Essays*, pp. 59–60, 64–5.

opposite was true of raw products, especially the raw animal products.[1]

The discovery of gold had another effect on the economic conditions of the gold-producing countries, that was by changing their status in foreign trade :—

> The essence of the gold discoveries, regarded economically, consisted . . . in the reduction in the cost of raising gold, which was thereby effected—a reduction which, not being shared by other countries, involved a change in the comparative costs of Australian and foreign productions. The consequence of this change has been a corresponding change in the character of her foreign trade, brought about . . . through an action on money wages. Thus Australia, instead of raising her own corn, as under ordinary circumstances she would do, imports the greater portion of it.[2]

The next problem of importance was how and to what extent the new gold would make its effects felt on the price structures of foreign nations. Generally speaking, as " the supply of gold required, in order to render possible a fall in its value over so large an area of transactions, was immense, money raised throughout the world at large did not, and could not, advance with the same rapidity with which they advanced in the gold countries ".[3] The advance, moreover, would be different with different nations. It " will proceed most rapidly in the productions of England and the United States ; after these, at no great interval, in the productions of the continent of Europe ; while the commodities the last to feel the effects of the new money, and which will advance most slowly under its influence, are the productions of India and China ".[4] That was due to three reasons. First, the diffusion of the new gold throughout the world was not uniform over the

[1] *Essays*, pp. 60–64.
[2] Ibid., p. 37. See also his *Leading Principles*, p. 315.
[3] Ibid., p. 26. As a result of this there would be a divergence of local prices in the gold-producing countries from the general level of the commercial world. He pointed out that that was beneficial to them. " Prices throughout the world have not risen in the same degree as the cost of gold has been reduced ; and consequently upon this portion of their dealings Australia and California are gainers—gainers directly in proportion to the reduced cost of their gold, modified by the rise, so far as it has taken place, in foreign prices. A given exertion of labour enables them to command, not only more gold, but more of every other thing which foreign countries can supply " (p. 39).
[4] *Essays*, p. 73.

various countries. It first flowed to the principal markets of England and the United States, and only comparatively small portions went directly to the markets of Asia. Secondly, the currencies receiving the new supplies did not have uniform susceptibility. England, for example, required a less quantity of gold than India to raise her prices to the level of the gold-producing nations, because in England the credit element prevailed and the currency was highly elastic and expansible, while in India the metallic proportion of the currency was much greater. Thirdly, the correctives upon which either country depended for restoring the equilibrium of its price level with the price levels of other countries were not the same. Generally speaking, there were two kinds of correctives. First the most powerful corrective was that " which is supplied by the competition of different nations, producers of the same commodities, in neutral markets ". Second, the less effective corrective was that " which exists in the reciprocal demand of the different commercial countries for each other's production ". While England and other European states could use both of the correctives, the Asiatic states could use only the latter one.[1]

Nevertheless, given time, the advance of prices would produce from commodity to commodity and from country to country and ultimately bring about an equal change in all commodities. Thus, he said :—

> Now I am quite prepared to admit that an increase of money tends ultimately, where the conditions of production and demand remain in other respects the same, to affect the prices of all commodities and services in an equal degree ; but before this result is attained a period of time, longer or shorter, according to the amount of the augmentation and the general circumstances of commerce, must elapse. In the present instance . . . some thirty or forty years.[2]

Before we examine the contribution of Jevons, we may make a digression on Cairnes's important criticism of the currency principle or the principle involved in the Bank Charter Act of 1844, which was made ten years after the Act had been passed. The Currency School relied, as indicated above, upon Hume's law as a part of the theoretical foundation of its banking policy proposals. Hume's law

[1] Ibid., pp. 65–73.
[2] Ibid., p. 56.

was opposed by Tooke and Fullarton, who pointed out that changes in the volume of bullion did not necessarily lead to changes in the volume of circulation. Cairnes accepted that proposition. Moreover, he went a step further in refuting the doctrine that gold, in the event of a foreign drain, " can never come back, unless a contraction of the currency really takes place." Cairnes admitted that " the efflux and influx of gold are in all cases ultimately governed by the relation between our exports and imports " and that by lowering prices at home, which would act as an inducement to exports and a check to imports, a contraction of circulation might bring back the gold. His objection to the doctrine is this, " Though true as far as it goes, it is incomplete." [1] For the state of prices in the trading countries was not the only circumstance affecting importation and exportation. He said :—

> The quantity of foreign goods . . . which we import from foreign countries, does not depend solely upon the prices at which these commodities are to be purchased ; it depends quite as much on the means at the disposal of people in this country for procurement of such articles. . . . If any circumstance should occur to render industry less profitable, or to diminish the general wealth of the country, the means at the disposal of the community for the purchase of foreign commodities would be curtailed. Without supposing any alteration in prices, therefore, the demand for such commodities would decline and consequently the amount of our imports would fall off. And conversely if the opposite conditions should occur, if the wealth of the country were to increase, we should each on an average have more to spend ; a portion of this increased wealth, without necessarily supposing any fall in prices abroad, would go in extra demand for foreign commodities ; and our imports would consequently increase. It thus seems plain that any circumstance which has the effect of enriching or impoverishing the country, must operate in augmenting or diminishing the amount of goods which we import from abroad ; and what takes place here will of course take place equally in foreign countries. It follows, therefore, that the relation between our exports and imports and, by consequence, the influx and efflux of gold, depends not only on the state of prices here and abroad, but also on the means of purchase which are at the command, respectively, of home and foreign consumers. It is quite conceivable therefore

[1] J. E. Cairnes, *An Examination into the Principles of Currency involved in the Bank Charter Acts of 1884*, Dublin, 1854, pp. 33, 36.

without supposing any alteration in the prices of commodities, and consequently without the necessity of any contraction of the circulation—it is quite conceivable, that the relation between our exports and imports may be altered and, consequently, the exchanges adjusted, simply in consequence of a change having taken place in the comparative wealth of this and other countries. Now such a change takes place . . . when the harvest fails at home, or when the staple of any of our manufactures is deficient, or when large military expenditure is to be supported abroad ; in short, when any of the ordinary causes occur which require this country to export gold. The transference of so much gold from this country to foreign countries . . . alters the disposable wealth comparatively of this and other countries ; their means of expenditure is proportionally altered, and consequently their demand for each other's goods. There is thus, in the circumstances attending a transmission of gold from this country, a provision made for its return, quite independently of the state of prices or of the circulation.[1]

The doctrine contained in the passage quoted above is similar to Thornton's doctrine of transfer. Like Thornton, moreover, Cairnes was of the opinion that a contraction of the circulation, though a possible means of adjusting the balance of international payments, was a dangerous weapon to use. For a contraction of the circulation would greatly discourage home production, retard or prevent " the fabrication of those manufactures which constitute our only means of purchasing ", back the gold, and consequently defeat the very object of the contraction.[2]

Not quite consistent with the proposition that a contraction of the circulation would discourage trade and production is his interesting attempt, in his *Essays*, to refute the doctrine that money stimulates trade and production. According to that doctrine, Cairnes said,

each addition to the circulating medium, forming the basis of a corresponding increase of the demand, gives a corresponding impetus to production ; every increase of money thus calls into existence an equivalent augmentation in the quantity of things to be circulated ; and the proportion between the two not being ultimately disturbed, prices, it may be presumed, will return to their original level. The least reflection, however, will show that this doctrine has been suggested by a very superficial view of the phenomena. For—not to press the

[1] *An Examination*, pp. 34–6.   [2] Ibid., pp. 37–8.

obvious *reductio ad absurdum* to which this argument is liable—how is this extension of production to be carried out ? In the last resort it is only possible through a more extended employment of labour. But when once all the hands in a community are employed, the effect of a further competition for labour can only be to raise wages ; and wages once being generally raised, it is plain (supposing all other things to remain the same) that profit can only be maintained by a corresponding elevation of prices.   When, therefore, the influence of the new money has once reached wages, it is evident that there will be no motive to continue production to that point which would bring prices to their former level, and that consequently an elevation of price must, at this stage of the proceedings, be permanently established.[1]

Note the conditioning clause, " when once all the hands in a community are employed." It is only upon the assumption that an increase in employment would lead to an increase in wages that his criticism could really stand.   He also criticized a corollary of the main thesis of the doctrine that money stimulates trade, that the new gold would cause an increase in real wealth.   He declared that, while the gold-producing countries would gain because of the lag of the world level of prices behind their local prices, the world as a whole had made no change in its wealth.   " The gain of Australia and California from their goldfields is confined to that portion of their trade which they carry on with foreign countries. . . . The operation of the new gold will be confined to causing a new distribution of real wealth in the world without affecting its aggregate amount ;   and consequently the gain of the gold countries must be reaped at the expense of other nations." [2]

A few years later Jevons made an attempt to ascertain the fall in the value of gold.[3]   After a careful comparison of the prices of thirty-nine chief and seventy-nine minor articles, he found that prices had risen between 1845–50 and 1860–62 by at least 10½ per cent or gold fell in value by 9½ per cent.   The value of his contribution, however, lay not so much in his conclusions as in his method of

[1] *Essays*, pp. 58–9.
[2] Ibid., pp. 43–4.
[3] W. S. Jevons, *A Serious Fall in the Value of Gold Ascertained,* London, 1863.   We have used the reprint in his *Investigations in Currency and Finance,* London, 1884.   In his *Money and the Mechanism of Exchange* he also discussed many aspects of the theory of money, but without great originality.   See Greidandus, *The Value of Money,* pp. 49–51.

approach—he had, for example, suggested the use of geometrical means to obtain an average change of prices and had shown how a permanent fluctuation of prices might be discriminated from a temporary one. As to the theory of money and trade itself, only two points made by him are worth mentioning here. First he pointed out that even in countries where the credit element prevailed gold still served as the basis of the price structure. " While the elasticity of credit may certainly, as it seems, give prices a more free flight, the inflation of credit must be checked by the well-defined boundary of available capital, which consists at the last resort in the reserve of notes, equivalent to gold, in the Bank of England. *Prices temporarily may rise or fall independently of the quantity of gold in the country ; ultimately they must be governed by this quantity.* Credit gives a certain latitude without rendering prices finally independent of gold." [1] Secondly, he declared that the depreciation of the value of gold would be regressive.[2] " If a be the quantity of gold in the world at any time, and b the quantity added in each succeeding year, then at the end of n years, the value of gold is reduced as 1 to $\dfrac{a}{a + nb}$, which is always growing less as n increases, but at a constantly less rate. Thus the fall during the nth year is as 1 to $\dfrac{a + (n - 1)\, b}{a + nb}$ which as n increases constantly approaches unity." [3]

In the following years (1864–65) the problem was taken up by Leslie.[4] He advanced three important propositions. First of all he came, like Newmarch, to the conclusion that the rise in prices due to the new gold was " temporary in degree and partial in character ".[5] Secondly, he emphasized the fact that the effects of the new gold on prices was not uniform. His arguments, being very suggestive, are worth quoting in full :—

The additional money has been unequally distributed by the balance of trade to different countries, and very unequally shared by different classes in the countries receiving it ;

---

[1] *Investigations*, pp. 31–2.
[2] That is just the opposite of Chevalier's view.
[3] *Investigations*, p. 65.
[4] Thomas Edward Cliffe Leslie, *Essays in Political Economy*, 2nd. ed., 1888. [5] *Essays*, p. 307.

again it has been spent by the classes receiving it, not upon all commodities alike, but unequally, and the supply of something upon which there has been an additional expenditure has increased very much more than that of others. Moreover, a low range of prices is raised more by a given addition to money than a high one, which is one of the reasons why the change has been the greatest in places once remarkable for their cheapness. And from what has been said it is plain that a change in comparative incomes and prices would have been caused by the new gold alone, since it would increase the incomes and expenditures only of the classes, beginning with the miners, to whose hands it successively came.[1]

The fact is, that the scale of relative incomes, and of relative prices, in different places, and with respect to different commodities, has been so altered that the old level of profits in different employments and the old rates of expenditure in different situations, have been permanently disturbed, and new elements must be imported into all calculations respecting the best markets to buy and sell in, the cost of living in different localities, the outgoings and returns in different trades, and the rate of interest which different investments will yield.[2]

Thirdly he called attention for the first time to the fundamental difference between the price revolution of the sixteenth century and the price changes of the nineteenth century. During the sixteenth century the commercial centres of the world were most sensitive to the new supplies of the precious metals, while the remote parts of every country or the remote countries of the world were very little affected by the event. In the nineteenth century the monetary movements of the sixteenth century had been inverted, and the rise of prices had been much greater in the remoter parts of a country than in its capital and greater in the Asiatic countries than in the European countries.[3]

.   .   .   .   .   .

The literature of the gold discoveries controversy had thus forwarded the study of the monetary aspects of the theory of international price relationships. On the one hand, the quantity theory had been criticized, modified, and restated. On the other hand, the doctrine that money stimulates trade or production had been restated by Newmarch, and it had been criticized by Cairnes. The

---

[1] *Essays*, p. 303.   [2] Ibid., p. 301.
[3] Ibid., pp. 274–298.

mechanical doctrine that prices of all commodities would be everywhere uniformly affected by a change in the volume of money had been questioned by Levasseur, Cairnes, and particularly Leslie. The analysis of the " direct " chain of effects that connect money and prices and the problems of diffusion which were first presented in the writings of Forbonnais, Cantillon, Hume, and Senior, were well developed by both Newmarch and Cairnes. The connection between the volume of gold and the money rate of interest was made clear by Stirling, Newmarch, and Levasseur. None of them, however, had said anything about the connection between the current rate of interest and prices. Hence, a complete analysis of the " indirect " chain of effects connecting money and prices was left to later writers. Finally, the institutional approach of Leslie was both suggestive and interesting.

3. GOSCHEN, BAGEHOT, AND LAUGHLIN

During the period discussed in Chapter III, as we have shown, some attempts were made to describe the function of bank rate in the international movement of specie and in international price adjustments. In the latter half of the nineteenth century many excellent works on the subject were published and there was marked progress made in understanding the operation of bank rate.

First of all there was that body of thought which regarded bank rate as a regulator of the international movement of specie, that is by influencing the rate of foreign lending. That body of thought had developed over a long period of time. As early as the sixteenth century Jean Bodin had noticed a connection between interest rates and the international movement of specie. When the controversy concerning the justification or unjustification of the lowering of the rate of interest by law occurred in England in the latter half of the seventeenth century, the opponents of the policy of the lowering of interest by law clearly pointed out that " the Lowering of Interest . . . shall either make the Foreigner call home his money, or your own People backward to lend ".[1] In the first half of the nineteenth

---

[1] John Locke, *Some Considerations of the Consequences of the Lowering of Interest, etc.*, 1692 ed., p. 43.

century Took, Mill, and others [1] clearly recognized the function of bank rate in regulating specie movements. But it was Goschen who first produced a systematic exposition of the effects of bank rate.[2]

In his classic treatise on the foreign exchanges [3] Goschen declared that the primary cause which determined the fluctuations in the exchange rates was the balance of international indebtedness.[4] That, however, would cause a variation only within the limits of the specie points.[5] Sometimes the exchanges did rise or fall much beyond the specie points, and in those cases it was necessary to try to discover the other factors. He found that the state of credit in the money market played an important role. For instance, a stringent money market in the country where the bill was drawn could act " materially upon the exchanges, inducing sellers [of bills] to force sales, and creating a reluctance on the part of purchasers to buy unless absolutely compelled to remit ".[6] As regards bills with a certain time to run [7] it was necessary to take into consideration, in addition to the state of credit, other determining elements, especially the relative rates of interest in the two countries. He said: " In the rate of exchange for all bills other than bills at sight, there is no element of value so constant and so effective as the rate of interest in the country on which the bill is drawn." [8] Finally fluctuations in the rate of exchange might

[1] See T. H. Milner, *On the Regulation of Floating Capital and Freedom of Currency*, London, 1848.

[2] At the time when Goschen wrote, the importance of the bank rate in controlling the exchanges and international specie movements had been recognized by both men of action and men of thought. See, for example, Macleod, *The Theory and Practice of Banking* (1856) 5th ed., (1892), vol. ii, p. 365. Goschen was merely the first to describe the mechanism systematically.

[3] George J. Goschen, *The Theory of the Foreign Exchanges*, London, 1861 ; we have used the ninth edition, London, 1876.

[4] Ibid., pp. 3–8, 11–22, 42–6. "The balance of indebtedness, in its widest sense, is most fundamental, entering in a greater or less degree into almost every case in which Foreign Exchanges are concerned," p. 122.

[5] Ibid., pp. 47–8.   [6] Ibid., pp. 48–52.

[7] For recent works on the problem of forward exchange see the Bibliography appended to P. C. Einzig. *Theory of Forward Exchanges* (London, 1937).

[8] Goschen, *The Theory of the Foreign Exchanges*, p. 55. " It must be borne in mind that it is the price of short bills, not those which have some time to run, which determines the course of bullion shipments. Most of the primary elements of value affect long and short bills equally ; but the rate of interest and the question of credit exercise an additional influence upon the former, and so modify the fluctuations in their price as to render them unreliable as indications of the currents of gold " (pp. 88 f.).

be caused by a fourth factor, namely differences in currency.[1]

He analysed the relations between the balance of international payments and the relative rate of interest in the trading nations and concluded that both of them were determining elements of fluctuations in rates of exchange. He found that :—

> These two influences will be generally found to be operating simultaneously in opposite directions. Money will be dear and scarce in the country which owes much to foreign creditors, and plentiful in that which has exported much ; and high interest will be attracting money to that quarter whence specie is flowing out in payment of foreign debts. The adverse balance of trade will, as far as its power extends, render the bills on the country which is most in debt difficult of sale, and tend to compel it to export specie ; whereas the high rate of interest, which is generally contemporaneous with a drain or the prospect of a drain, of specie, will revive a demand for bills on this same country, and enhance their value in other quarters ; for there will be a general desire to procure the means of remitting capital to that market where it commands the highest value.[2]

That leads us immediately to correctives of the foreign exchanges. He pointed out that " when the exchanges are manifestly against any country, and it is perceived that a balance of indebtedness is the cause, the equilibrium can be restored only in two ways : the one being the increase of exports and the diminution of imports ; the other an advance in the rate of interest ".[3] When the initial cause (that was an adverse balance of indebtedness) was a permanent one, the disequilibrium in trade could be only corrected by the former expedient. He did not say anything, however, as to how exports might be increased or how imports might be decreased. When the derangement was but temporary the latter expedient was the most effective :—

> Where a considerable efflux of specie is taking place, the rate of interest will rise in the natural course of things. The abstraction caused by the bullion shipments will of itself tend to raise that rate ; and banking establishments will in their own interests (which will be identical with the interests of the public) accelerate this result as far as lies in their power.[4]

---

[1] *The Theory of the Foreign Exchanges*, pp. 58–83. [2] Ibid., p. 127.
[3] Ibid., p. 128. [4] Ibid., p. 132.

When the English rate of interest advances, there will be a general desire on the Continent to take advantage of this circumstance, and to remit capital to England for temporary advantageous investment ; but how is the transmission to England to be effected ? Of course in bills, so long as they can be procured ; and consequently those who are holders of bills on England, and are willing to sell them, find themselves in possession of an article which is suddenly in great demand, and are thus enabled to make a higher price. Competition raises this price, till remittances by means of bills become almost as expensive as a shipment of bullion itself . . . and as the supply of bills tends to become insufficient, gold is actually sent. This is the technical explanation of the rapid rise of the price of bills on any country as soon as any advance in the general rate of interest obtainable there takes place.[1]

Almost every advance in the Bank rate of discount is followed by a turn of the exchanges in favour of England ; and, vice versa, as soon as the rate of interest is lowered, the exchange becomes less favourable.[2]

That was the first systematic statement of " the mechanism connecting the bank rate and the international movement of specie " as a corrective of disturbances in the equilibrium of the exchanges and trade.

That doctrine of Goschen was immediately accepted and pushed a step ahead by two Continental economists, whose contributions we shall examine in the next section. It was further developed in the seventies by Bagehot [3] ; and early in the present century by Laughlin.

Laughlin's primary concern was the problem of the value of money. He started with a criticism of the quantity theory of money.[4] He argued that as gold or silver was a commodity its value was determined, on the one hand, by the expenses of its production and, on the other hand, by the condition of demand for it as money and as plate. His analysis came on many points very near to that of Senior.[5] He extended his analysis to the problem of international price relationships and of international specie movements. He denied that Hume's law was a corrective of disturbances in equilibrium. He seemed to have recognized that an

---

[1] The Theory of the Foreign Exchanges, pp. 146 f. See also pp. 129 ff., 138 ff.   [2] Ibid., p. 134.
[3] W. Bagehot, Lombard Street, chaps. 5–7. See especially Withers's ed. 1915, pp. 109 ff., 187 f.
[4] J. Laurence Laughlin, The Principles of Money, London, 1903. The reference is to pp. 312–334.   [5] Ibid., pp. 335–365.

adverse balance of international payments might bring about an international movement of specie, for he definitely said that " the movement of gold follows . . . the events which determine the course of international trade ".[1] But to him the inflow or outflow of specie could never, in turn, cause the trade balance to change so as to bring about a restoration of equilibrium. Firstly he denied the connection between the movement of specie and internal prices, as described in Hume's law.[2] That was inherent in his refusal to accept the quantity theory. Secondly, he did not see the possibility that a level of prices within a country could be, even in a transitional period, different from that abroad. He said :—

The action of international markets, with telegraphic quotations from every part of the world, precludes the supposition that gold prices could in general remain on a higher level in one country than another (cost of carriage apart) even for a brief time, because, in order to gain the profit, merchants would seize the opportunity to send goods to the markets where prices were high.[3]

That does not appeal to us as a sufficient argument against a possibility of a connection between price levels and the flow of gold. On the contrary, it amounts to saying that differences in prices, if they do exist at all, will be adjusted quickly by the movement of goods. That was exactly what the classical theorists maintained.

After having attempted to refute the classical theory he presented a theory of his own. According to that theory the interest rate was a much more important factor than the trade balance, and the international movement of capital in the form of securities was much more important than the movement of gold. He said :—

The reason why balances in favour of a country may not be paid in gold is due to the possibility of investing those balances at a higher rate of interest in a foreign country than can be obtained at home. The relative rates of interest have an influence even wider than that upon the movement of balances.

---

[1] *The Principles of Money*, p. 388, see also p. 377.
[2] " It does not at all follow that the importation of the money metal, which is used as the standard of prices in the importing country . . . will pass into use as a medium of exchange and, by being offered against goods, will raise the general prices ; and yet, according to the usual statement of the quantity theory, this is the only way in which the imported specie can affect prices." Ibid., p. 371.
[3] Ibid., pp. 369 f., see also pp. 380 f.

It is the rate of interest upon sound international securities as well as the rate in the loan market, which determines whether credit due, for instance, to the United States shall be left abroad or brought home in the form of goods or specie. The general accounting in foreign trade must include the operations of loans, and the movement of capital for investment from one country to another. Indeed, the rate of interest is behind the movement of securities mentioned above. The purchase of securities is, of course, one form of investing capital. Therefore, in determining the causes affecting prices and the movement of gold in international trade, it must be kept in mind that the relative rates of interest in the trading countries will influence the passage of loanable capital to and fro, thereby acting as a factor in adjusting merchandise credits and debits, and seriously affecting the transmission of gold. Instead of gold being the originating cause of new exports and imports, as once generally held, it is the very last thing to move ; and even then merchandise balances may be entirely reversed by changes in the rates of interest in New York or foreign centres, which may cause capital to flow from the creditor to the debtor country. The recognition of the force exerted by the rate of interest on the movement of loanable capital gives the final *coup de grâce* to the old theory, which based its change of general price upon the international movement of specie. The order of events is quite the other way : relative prices cause exports and imports of goods; and the shipment of gold is not necessarily made even to cover balances of merchandise. If gold moves, it goes not merely because of the account in goods and securities, but of the investment of international capital.[1]

That is very similar to the analysis of Goschen. Laughlin did not recognize, however, any connection between the money rate of interest and prices. He rejected the proposition that an influx of gold, in the modern banking system, would affect prices through raising bank reserves and expanding the purchasing-power, which was offered for goods. He argued " that, in legitimate banking, loans are made because of satisfactory collateral or actual transfers of goods, and not merely because reserves are high. To be sure, if reserves rise, rate of interest will fall and new loans are possible ; but merely because a bank can loan, it does not follow that it does loan. . . . The imported gold first passes into the banks, and only as much as is needed for legitimate business is retained. Having a value in and for

[1] *The Principles of Money*, pp. 382-3.

itself it can be disposed of as easily as any other form of property ".[1] That argument tacitly assumed that the demand for loans was absolutely inelastic ; while in truth the assumption had never been found to be true, at least in modern conditions.

4. DE LAVELEYE AND JUGLAR

Goschen's doctrine of the interest rate as a regulator of international movements of specie was immediately accepted and carried a step further by Laveleye and Juglar. Laveleye's chief concern was the explanation of business cycles and crises.[2] According to him cyclical movements were a phenomenon peculiar to the credit economy and dependent largely upon the state of credit. Countries with a big superstructure of credit, based upon a small volume of gold or silver, were most susceptible of economic perturbations.[3] In those countries crises were always the result of a contraction of the media of exchange, money, and credit [4]; and the contraction of the media of exchange was usually produced by a derangement in the balance of trade.[5] The causal sequence leading to a crisis was as follows :—

Unfavourable balance of trade—unfavourable exchange—outflow of gold—rise of the discount rate—contraction of credit media—the crisis.

The rise in the discount rate itself had a remedying effect, for " to raise the rate of interest meant that one prepares to pay a higher rent for the use of cash. It follows that the disposable money in places where it is relatively plentiful and where it is cheaply hired will rush toward the market where people consent to pay dear for it. This is the inevitable consequence of the law of demand and supply ".[6] In other words, the very rise in the interest rate, which was consequent on the drain of specie, would encourage foreigners to transfer their loanable money to the centre which was losing specie.

---

[1] *The Principles of Money*, p. 387.
[2] Emile de Laveleye, *Le Marché monetaire et ses crises depuis cinquante ans* (Paris, 1865) ; *Les Elements de L'Economie Politique* (Paris, 1882, English translation under the title of *The Elements of Political Economy*, by Alfred W. Polland, N.Y., 1884 ; in pages 224–5 there is a precise summary of his theory of business cycles).
[3] *Le Marché Monétaire*, p. 128.
[4] Ibid., pt. ii, chap. 3, esp. p. 117.
[5] Ibid., pt. ii, chap. 4.
[6] Ibid., pp. 168–9.

P

The remedying effect would also be felt through another channel, that was through commodity prices and security prices. He pointed out :—

The certain, undisputed effect of a rise in interest is to depress the prices of commodities and of all securities. It is so because a great number of persons always want credit for maintaining their operations and when credit is contracted they must liquidate and must sell their goods or securities in order to meet their operations. Since commodities and securities fall in prices, it is inevitable that the capitalists of countries where money is still abundant will give some orders of purchase. In order to pay for their purchases, they have to make remittances, and then cash returns to the country where the rise of interest has led to a fall in price [equilibrium would thus be restored].[1]

Thereby he, on the one hand, connected Goschen's doctrine of the interest rate as a regulator of the movement of specie with Hume's law and, on the other hand, connected the cyclical analysis with the theory of international price relationships.

Laveleye also made an important contribution in connection with the problem of how an increase in the volume of the money metals (subsequent to the gold discoveries of Australia and California) worked out its effects on prices. He recognized clearly both the direct mechanism and the indirect mechanism. He said :—

[1. *Direct Mechanism*] : The enormous quantities of gold have been distributed over the world. A part of that gold has penetrated into the circulation in the form of purchases of products, raising prices without having any effect on the rate of interest.

[2. *Indirect Mechanism*] : But another part, a much greater one, has passed first into the hands of moneylenders, banks, bankers, and capitalists, who, in seeking for a profitable employment, offer it in the money market, thus contributing to the depression of the interest rate.

This will be the immediate effect. By a second, more remote effect, that new quantity of money will tend to raise prices.[2]

That was true, however, only when other things were equal. The increase of money or the lowering of the rate of interest itself stimulated the spirit of enterprise and multiplied the

[1] *Le Marché Monétaire*, pp. 174–5.
[2] Ibid., pp. 143–4.

volume of production and trade. That in turn offset the tendency towards an increase of prices. " The [increased] money will encourage industry," he said, " as long as it does not exceed the need of circulation, for the abundance of money facilitates the exchanges and loans . . . and lowers interest without raising prices ; beyond that limit, it raises prices without lowering interest."[1]

His theory of international price relationships might also be presented in the following way : A country's trading relations with other countries could be in equilibrium when its imports exactly balance its exports. The infallible indication of the existence or the non-existence of an equilibrium was the state of the exchanges.[2] In case there was an adverse balance of trade, the exchanges would turn unfavourable, gold would flow out, and a crisis would result ; but that would soon be corrected mainly by the mechanism connecting interest rate and specie movement and to a certain extent also by Hume's law.

At about the same time Juglar [3] presented a similar theory. Like Laveleye, he drew heavily upon Goschen and connected the money market mechanism with the international movement of the precious metals, on the one hand, and business cycles on the other. Since much of his doctrine was identical with that of Laveleye, it need not detain us long. We need only note two points. First he called attention to the fact that ever since 1800 there had been perfect regularity in the increase and decrease of the stocks of metallic reserves of England and France. That rhythmic variation of the stock of specie coincided with the cyclical movement of prices. During the upward trend of the cyclical movement prices rose and specie flowed out. The drain would continue as long as the high level of prices persisted : neither a rise of the rate of discount nor the lowering of the reserve could stop the drain. Then followed the crisis when all the factors would combine to bring down prices. The fall in prices in turn led to a rapid reflux of specie. Thus the international movement of specie was clearly connected with the business cycle.[4] Second, he accepted the doctrine that an increase of the quantity of money, by stimulating enterprise and

---

[1] *Le Marché Monétaire*, p. 141 n. [2] Ibid., p. 167.
[3] Clement Juglar, *Du change et de la liberté d'emission* (Paris, 1868). See also his *Des crises commerciales et de leur retour périodique*, Paris, 1862.
[4] *Du Change*, pp. 172 f., 468 f.

production, increased the demand for money so that the tendency of prices to rise (due to the increase in the supply of money) was checked.[1]

5. SIDGWICK, GIFFEN, AND MARSHALL

The indirect mechanism which connects money and prices by means of changes in bank reserves and in discount rates is usually associated with the name of Alfred Marshall. The importance of the interest rate in the relations between money and prices had, however, been noticed long before his time. As early as the year 1705, Law gave that factor a place in his doctrine of money. He pointed out that, as the quantity of money increased, money would be more easily borrowed and merchants would deal in larger sums of money. Law, however, came to the conclusion that as the market rate of interest fell, merchants would be able to sell at less profit and all sorts of manufacture would be cheaper. That proposition was, by implication, based upon the inadmissible assumption that the prices of other factors of production remained unchanged as the rate of interest changed. Later very clear statements of the indirect mechanism were found in the writings of Thornton, Ricardo, and other classical economists. In France the mechanism was excellently described by Laveleye, who had gone a step further in associating it with the mechanism connecting the interest rates and international movements of specie. In the eighties that view had, in one form or another, been very commonly, though rather vaguely, held by people in the business world. The contributions of Marshall and his contemporaries lay rather in scientifically presenting the mechanism and in giving due importance to it.

The first writer of the eighties to give a systematic description of the indirect mechanism was Henry Sidgwick.[2] In his discussion of the value of money, he pointed out that " the term, ' value of money ' was used in two ways : in economic structures it usually means the purchasing-power of money or its exchange value measured in commodities other than money ; in practical discussions about the

[1] Ibid., pp. 25–37. Their statements of the doctrines that money stimulates trade and production are two of the best statements of the period under consideration.

[2] Henry Sidgwick, *The Principles of Political Economy*, London, 1883 ; we have used the third ed.. 1901.

' money market ' it denotes the rate of interest paid for the temporary use of money ".[1] He was of the opinion that there existed a definite connection between those two meanings. He said :—

> It should be observed that those who confound the two meanings of " value of money " are not wrong in supposing that the value of the use of money [discount rate] tends to be lowered by an unusual influx of metallic money or bullion, and raised by an efflux ; they are only wrong in overlooking the transitoriness of these effects. An increased supply of gold, not accompanied by a corresponding increase in the work that coin has to do (or a rise in the demand for gold otherwise caused), tends ultimately to lower the purchasing-power of money relatively to commodities generally ; but, in the first stage of the process that leads to this result, the increment of coin . . . must pass through the hands of bankers, and so increase the amount of the medium of exchange that they have to lend. Hence the price paid for the use of money will tend to fall, and this fall will tend to cause increased borrowing, and consequent extended use of the medium of exchange ; and then through the resulting rise in prices generally the greater part of the new coin or bank-notes will gradually pass into circulation. Thus, the fall in the purchasing power of money, consequent on an influx of gold, will nominally establish itself through an antecedent and connected fall in the value of the use of money.[2]

That is clearly a very able statement of the indirect mechanism connecting money and prices.

Three years later, Giffen [3] not only presented a more elaborate statement of the indirect mechanism but also made an attempt to verify it statistically. He found that there was always an intimate connection between the annual supply of gold, on the one hand, and both the rate of interest and the prices of commodities on the other. That connection might be carried out either by a direct mechanism or an indirect one.[4] In a simple industrial system (that was one without paper circulation and without an extended credit system) the increase of the annual supply of gold would be *immediately* distributed and *directly* connected with

---

[1] *Principles*, p. 240.
[2] Ibid., p. 255. The converse is true of a decrease in the national stock of money.
[3] Robert Giffen, *Essays in Finance*, second series, London, 1886; 3rd ed. used, 1890.   [4] Ibid., p. 37.

prices. "The rate for loans is also directly affected, cash being relatively a very important item of circulating capital.[1] There could hardly arise any problem of indirect mechanism which was peculiar to credit economy. In the latter, however, the indirect mechanism played a dominating part in connecting the volume of money and the rates of discount as well as the level of prices. Cash no longer affected prices directly nor did they continue to constitute a significant item of circulating capital.[2] It still exerted tremendous influence on both discount rates and prices because of its dual capacity as bankers' reserves and as small change. As bank reserve it set a limit to a banker's liabilities ; in other words, to his loans and investments which were the condition of his ability to receive deposits. In that way it gave a limit to the bank's expansion and affected its rates of discount. An increase of cash, by acting on the bank's reserve, would lower the discount rate, while a diminution of the quantity of money would raise it.[3] The rise or fall of the discount rate in turn caused a variation in prices. The fall of the money rate of interest would encourage borrowing. As " borrowers borrow in order to purchase or to avoid selling ", an increase of borrowing tended to raise prices. The opposite was true of a rise in the money rate of interest.[4] As small change, cash also set a limit to the variation in prices. " A certain level for wages and prices implies the use by a community at a given time of a corresponding amount per head of notes and cash of different kinds. If wages and prices rise from that level more notes and cash, ' other things being equal,' are required. . . . Prices and wages cause a demand for cash as small change, and are necessarily limited by the amount of cash available."[5] Those two uses of money, moreover, were interconnected. On the one hand, it was through the use of cash as small change that an increased reserve (due to an increase of the quantity of cash) could pass the increased money into ordinary circulation. He said :—

An increase of lending [consequent on an increased reserve] tends to raise prices. . . . The rise of prices adds to the nominal

---

[1] *Essays in Finance*, ii, pp. 40, 82.
[2] Ibid., pp. 82–3.   [3] Ibid., pp. 44 f., 47, 83 ff.
[4] Ibid., ii, p. 49.
[5] Ibid., p. 46. " The requirements of cash on the latter account [i.e. as small change] appear to be larger than those in connection with the reserve " (p. 83).

capital, and particularly to the nominal capital represented by the loans and deposits of banks. Wages in turn rise, and with their rise . . . requirements for small change are increased, and the banking reserve trenches upon.[1]

On the other hand, a reserve would be " more efficient if there are large amounts of coin circulating to be drawn upon ".[2] Finally, he seemed to have suggested that by the very rise in prices, which was consequent on an increased reserve, the process of expansion would be *automatically* checked. A rise in prices, as explained above, drained cash from the bank into circulation, reduced the bank reserves and thus turned the price in an opposite direction. He declared :—

> The rate of discount and the level of general prices . . . are connected at some points. A change in the level of prices affects the money market. A rise tends to make " money " in demand and to raise discount rates ; a fall to make " money " abundant and to lower rates. At the same time a change in the discount rates acts on prices. A rise tends to lower prices ; a fall to raise them. Prices in turn react on discount rates. There is incessant action and reaction.[3]

In his memoranda and evidence before the Gold and Silver Commission of 1887-8, Alfred Marshall[4] gave an excellent account of the indirect mechanism. He recognized, first of all, the quantity theory that " *other things being equal* prices rise or fall proportionately to every increase or diminution in the metal or metals which are used as the standard of value ". But the conditioning clause " other things being equal " was of overwhelming importance, for other things might not remain the same. The methods of doing business might undergo some alteration ; the cost of producing the money metals might be increased or diminished ; and account had also to be taken of the volume of things on sale, " the average number of times each of these things changes hands during the year," the use of token coins as well as the velocity of the circulation of money.[5] If all those elements were unchanged, prices would rise in proportion to the volume of the money metals.

---

[1] *Essays in Finance*, ii, p. 49.
[2] Ibid., p. 83.
[3] Ibid., pp. 38–9.
[4] Both his memoranda and his oral evidence are reprinted in *Official Papers by Alfred Marshall*, edited by J. M. Keynes, London, 1926.
[5] Ibid., pp. 21–2, 34–35, 39–40.

By what mechanism, however, would an increase of gold in, say, England work out its effects on prices ?   His answer was given in the following passages :—

It would act at once upon Lombard Street, and make people inclined to lend more ; it would swell deposits and bank credits, and so enable people to increase their speculation with borrowed capital ; it would, therefore, increase the demand for commodities and so raise prices.[1]

If there was more gold in circulation than people wanted to do that part of their business which they prefer to do with currency, they would simply send it to the banks.   From the banks it would go into the reserve ; from the reserve it would go back on to the general market, inflating credit, increasing speculation, enabling people to borrow who could not borrow before, raising prices.   When prices had once been raised, say 10 per cent all round, then supposing there to be no dose of arsenic with the incantation, and the habits of business to be exactly the same as before ; then people would require 10 per cent more cash in their pockets than they did before.[2]

In the first of the two passages quoted above Marshall gave a statement of the indirect mechanism in its simplest form, while in the second passage he also took into consideration the quantity of currency people keep in their purses.   Although it might be doubtful whether that was exactly the same as Giffen's cash for small change, the two were really very similar, and both doctrines must be given a place in the historical development of the cash balance approach of the quantity theory.[3]

[1] *Official Papers by Alfred Marshall*, p. 38. See also pp. 49, 142 and *passim*.
[2] Ibid., pp. 40–41 ; see also p. 45.
[3] In the same year in which Giffen published his *Essays*, Léon Walras presented an algebraic formulation of the cash balance doctrine. (Walras, *Théorie de la monnaie*, Lausanne, 1886, p. 41.) His equation is very similar to Mr. Keynes'equation, $n = pk$. See A. W. Marget, " Léon Walras and the Cash-Balance Approach to the Problem of the Value of Money," *J.P.E.*, 1931. Reference should also be made to the second and later editions of the *Eléments of* Walras.   The cash balance doctrine was later fully elaborated by Knut Wicksell, Mises, Cannan, and the Cambridge economists. See Wicksell, *Interest and Prices* (1898), Lectures, ii (1906) ; Mises, *The Theory of Money and Credit* (1912).   For Cannan's contribution, see T. E. Gregory, " Professor Cannan and Contemporary Monetary Theory," in *London Essays in Economics*, pp. 29–65 (esp. p. 37) ; Edwin Cannan, *An Economist's Protest*, p. 387, and *Money : its Connection with Rising and Falling Prices* (1918).   The most important algebraic formulations of the doctrine are those of Professor Pigou and Mr. Keynes. See Pigou, " The Exchange Value of Legal Tender Money," *Q.J.E.*, 1917, reprinted in his *Essays in Applied Economics* ; and Keynes, *A Tract on Monetary Reform* (London, 1923), p. 77, Mr. Keynes' equation is :

$$n = p(k + rk')$$

In his later work on money and trade,[1] Marshall restated his cash balance doctrine as follows :—

> In every state of society there is some fraction of their income which people find it worth while to keep in the form of currency ; it may be a fifth, or a tenth, or a twentieth. A large command of resources in the form of currency renders their business easy and smooth, and puts them at an advantage in bargaining ; but, on the other hand, it locks up in a barren form resources that might yield an income of gratification if invested, say, in extra furniture ; or a money income if invested in extra machinery or cattle. . . . Whatever the state of society, there is a certain volume of their resources which people of different classes, taken one with another, care to keep in the form of currency ; and, if everything else remains the same, then there is this direct relation between the volume of currency and the level of prices, that, if one is increased by ten per cent, the other also will be increased by ten per cent. Of course, the less the proportion of their resources which people care to keep in the form of currency, the lower will be the aggregate value of the currency, that is, the higher will prices be with a given volume of currency.[2]
>
> A country's . . . stock of gold at any time tends to be equal to the amount, which (at that value) equals the purchasing power that the people care to keep in the form of gold either in their own custody or in their banks ; together with the amount that the industrial arts of the country will absorb at that value.[3]

Two other points should be noticed in connection with the indirect mechanism. They were that not all increases of the central bank reserves will act on prices and that not all low rates of interest will stimulate enterprise and raise prices. Whether an increase in the reserve would

in which *n* denotes the total quantity of cash ; *k* the number of consumption units (which are defined as units " made up of a collection of specified quantities of . . . the public's standard articles of consumption or other object of expenditure ") which the public required in cash ; *k'* the number of consumption units which the public required in bank credits ; *r* the proportion of the banks' cash reserves to their deposits ; and *p* the price of a consumption unit. In case no bank money is used, *k'* becomes zero and the equation may be written as $n = pk$. Reference should also be made to Gustav Cassel's *Theory of Social Economy* and D. H. Robertson's *Money*. In those two works we find how the cash balance approach may be reconciled with the approach of Lavasseur and Fisher.

[1] Marshall, *Money, Credit, and Commerce*, London, 1923.
[2] Ibid., p. 45.
[3] Ibid., p. 39.

make the indirect mechanism operate or not depends on the nature of the banking system. Thus he said :—

I do not think that prices are affected by any accumulation of reserves, such as the Bank of France, for instance, may hold.[1]

When a bank has more gold than it really wants as the basis of its currency which, of course, the Bank of France is supposed often to have had, that gold is to all intents and purposes hoarded. If gold comes out of the hoards of a country it does not act on prices at all . . . It would only act on prices . . . if it came out of coin or bullion which was acting as the basis of currency, or if it affected credit.[2]

As to the problem whether a low rate of interest would give activity to trade and bring about a permanent rise in prices, he considered the initial cause of the fall of interest as the determining factor. If the fall in the rate of discount was produced by an abundance of loanable capital in the market due either to an increase of saving or to an over-crowding of the field for investment, it could not have that effect ; but if it arose from an increase of the money metal it would cause a rise in prices. The difference between those two cases was excellently described in the following passage :—

The mean rate of discount is governed by the mean rate of interest for long loans ; that again is determined by the extent and the richness of the field for the investment of capital on the one hand, and on the other by the amount of capital seeking investment. The amount of capital has been increasing so fast that, in spite of a great widening of the field of investment, it has forced down the rate of discount. The fall in the rate of discount so caused failed to stimulate speculation, because it was itself caused by the difficulty of finding good openings for speculative investment ; this difficulty being in part due to the fear that prices would go on falling. Equilibrium is found at that rate of interest for long loans (and the corresponding rate of discount for short loans) which equates supply and demand. But next, this equilibrium being established, we set ourselves to inquire what will be the result of a new disturbance, viz. the influx of a good deal of bullion into the City. This does not increase the amount of capital in the strictest sense of the word ; it does not increase the amount of building materials, machinery, etc., but it does

[1] *Official Papers*, p. 38.
[2] Ibid., p. 124.

increase the amount of command over capital, which is in the hands of those whose business it is to lend to speculative enterprise. Having this extra supply, lenders lower still more the rate which they charge for loans and they keep on lowering it till a point is reached at which the command will carry off the larger supply. When this has been done there is more capital in the hands of speculative investors, who come on the markets for goods as buyers and so raise prices. Further, it must be remembered that the influx of bullion would have caused people meanwhile to expect a rise of prices and, therefore, to be more inclined to borrow for speculative investments. Thus it might not be necessary to lower the rate of discount very much. The increased demand would meet the increased supply half-way and, after a time, might outrun it, causing a rise in the rate of discount. But as this rise would be merely an incident in a series of changes which put more command over capital in the hands of speculative investors, it would go with an increased demand for goods and a continued rise of prices. This then is my account of the way in which this extra supply of the precious metals would bring prices up.[1]

In an earlier work, Marshall had shown how an increase in the demand for goods would lead to a further increase in the demand for goods, and how a rise in prices to a further rise in prices. When the demand for goods was increasing, he said,

producers . . . expect to sell at a profit, and are willing to pay good prices for the prompt delivery of what they want. Employers compete with one another for labour ; wages rise ; and the employed in spending their wages increase the demand for all kinds of commodities. New public and private Companies are started to take advantage of the promising openings which show themselves among the general activity. Thus the desire to buy and the willingness to pay increased prices grow together ; Credit is jubilant, and readily accepts paper promises to pay. Prices, wages, and profits go on rising : there is a general rise in the incomes of those engaged in trade : they spend freely, increase the demand for goods, and raise prices still higher. Many speculators seeing the rise, and thinking it will continue, buy goods with the expectation of selling them at a profit. At such a time a man, who has only a few hundred pounds, can often borrow from bankers and others the means of buying many thousand pounds worth of goods ; and every one who thus enters into the market as a buyer

[1] *Official Papers*, pp. 51-2.

adds to the upward tendency of prices, whether he buys with his own or with borrowed money.[1]

The movement would go on for some time. Then, for one reason or another, the lenders of money capital would find it necessary or desirable to contract their loans. But the demand for loans would continue to increase. The rate of interest would consequently be raised very high, distrust would begin and the movement of prices would turn downward :—

> Distrust increases, those who have lent become eager to secure themselves ; and refuse to renew their loans on easy or even on any terms. Some speculators have to sell goods in order to pay their debts ; and by so doing they check the rise of prices. This check makes all other speculators anxious, and many rush in to sell. . . . When a large speculator fails, his failure generally causes that of others who have lent their credit to him ; and their failure again that of others. . . . As credit by growing makes itself grow, so when distrust has taken the place of confidence, failure and panic breed panic and failure. The commercial storm leaves its path strewn with ruin. When it is over there is a calm, but a dull heavy calm.[2]

Marshall also enriched the theory of international price relationships by restating the classical doctrine with regard to the international comparison of the values of moneys. He first considered a case of trade between two countries, A and B, both with a gold currency. Then " trade tends so to adjust the supplies of gold relatively to the demands for gold in the two countries as to bring gold prices at the sea boards of the two countries to equality, allowance being made for carriage ". Any deviation from the equilibrium would bring Hume's law into operation to restore the equality in the values of moneys in the two countries.[3] He next considered the case that B had a paper standard, say roubles, instead of a gold standard. In that case, equilibrium would be established when the gold price of B's paper currency was fixed just at the ratio which gold prices in A bear to the paper-rouble prices in B. If prices were higher in A than in B, there would be a temporary bounty on exportation from B to A and a check to

---

[1] Alfred Marshall and Mary Paley Marshall, *The Economics of Industry*, London, 1879, p. 152.
[2] Ibid., p. 153.
[3] *Official Papers*, pp. 170, 191.

importation. Then the volume of bills offered and those demanded would change, and ultimately equilibrium would be restored.[1] He finally came to the case in which B had a silver currency, say the rupee. " This case differs from the preceding only in consequence of the fact that silver is, and the rouble is not, an exportable commodity." When equilibrium is established, the nature of the equilibrium would be the same in both cases. Trade tended so to adjust the supplies of gold and silver in the two countries relatively to demands as to bring gold prices in A to bear to silver prices in B (after allowing for carriage) a ratio equal to the gold price of silver. However, when the equilibrium was disturbed, whereas adjustment in the second case would take place almost simultaneously with the disturbance, it would be liable to be delayed in the third case. The reason was this. In the former case bills (on the foreign country) that each country held were useful to it only in buying foreign goods. Therefore, when disturbance occurred, it would act at once on imports and exports. In the latter case, on the contrary, foreign bills were useful also in the purchase of the money metals and adjustment might act indirectly through a change in the volume of money.[2]

6. KNUT WICKSELL

The theory of bank rate as a regulator both of the international movements of gold and of commodity prices was expounded with singular clarity by Wicksell.[3] He stood for the quantity theory of money and pointed out that the most important problem in the theory of money was how an increase of the quantity of money worked out its effects on prices. He showed that in modern times an increase or a decrease of the quantity of money caused the money rate of interest to deviate from the " real rate of interest " and consequently brought about a rise or a fall in prices. In a modern economy, especially when the

[1] *Official Papers*, pp. 172 f., 191 f.
[2] Ibid., pp. 175–8, 192–3.
[3] Knut Wicksell, *Interest and Prices*, first published in German, Jena 1898, English translation by R. F. Kahn, with an introduction by Professor B. Ohlin, London, 1936 ; " The Influence of the Rate of Interest on Prices," *E.J.*, 1907 ; *Lectures on Political Economy*, first published in Swedish, 1906. English translation by E. Classen, edited with an Introduction by Professor L. Robbins, London, 1934–5.

organization of credit was highly developed, credit had a similar or a more far-reaching influence on prices than metallic money—at least during short periods of time.[1] He said :—

> If, other things remaining the same, the leading banks of the world were to lower their rates of interest, say 1 per cent below its ordinary level and keep it so for some years, then the prices of all commodities would rise and rise and rise without any limit whatever ; on the contrary, if the leading banks were to *raise* their rate of interest, say 1 per cent above its normal level and keep it so for some years, then all prices would *fall* and fall and fall without any limit except zero.[2]

That was the main thesis of his theory of price levels. That thesis, in its pure form, applied only to cases when the two following assumptions were fulfilled : first that other things remained the same, and second that all the leading banks of the world simultaneously raised or lowered their loan rates. " A single bank, of course, has no such power whatever ; indeed, it cannot put its rates, whether much higher or lower than prescribed by the state of the market ; if it did, it would in the former case lose all profitable business ; in the latter case its speedy insolvency would be the inevitable consequence. Not even all the banks of a single country united would do it in the long run ; a too high or a too low rate would influence its balance of trade and thereby turn an influx or a reflux of gold in the well-known way, so as to force the banks to apply their rates to the state of the universal money market."[3] In other words, the factor of international payments set a limit to the possibility of deviation of the loan rate from the natural rate. Thereby he recognized the importance of the money rate of interest as a regulator of the international movement of specie.[4] There was another limitation, namely the requirements for small change. As prices rose business required

---

[1] *Interest and Prices*, ch. 7–9.
[2] " The Influence of the Rate of Interest on Prices ": " I believe that the thesis here propounded, if proved to be true, will turn out to be the corner-stone of the mechanics of prices, or rather one of its corner-stones, the influence of the supply of precious metals and of the demand for commodities from the gold-producing countries being the other " (pp. 213 f.).
[3] " The Influence of the Rate of Interest on Prices," p. 217.
[4] *Interest and Prices*, pp. 112 ff., 163.

greater cash holdings, bank loans increased without corresponding deposits, bank reserves and often bullion reserves began to fall, and the banks were compelled to raise their rates.[1] It was necesssary to keep in mind, however, that " the influence of credit or the rate of interest is only one of the factors acting on prices ; the other is the volume of metallic money itself, especially in our times the supply of gold, and so long as the gold itself remains the standard of value, this factor evidently will take the lead in the long run ".[2]

Having described his statement of the indirect mechanism connecting money and prices, we may now turn to the problem whether an increase in the volume of circulation would lead to increased production and forced saving. Wicksell was of the opinion that if production was increased at all, the increase must be very limited. He said :—

> It is impossible to endorse the widespread view that under suitable conditions a country's output can be expanded almost indefinitely by " arousing the spirit of enterprise " and the like. This fallacious view is derived by concentrating attention on one single branch of production, provided perhaps with an excess of fixed capital (buildings, machines, etc). In such a single branch of production it would be possible to increase output immediately, but only at *the expense of the other branches of production* from which labour and liquid capital have to be drawn. The impossibility under normal conditions of a *general* expansion of production is, I think, demonstrated by the figures of unemployment at different periods, recently collected in various countries. The average number of unoccupied workers is relatively small, about 1 per cent. A *general* expansion of production would thus be possible only as a result of longer hours—which are neither desirable nor feasible over any length of time—or as a result of further technical progress.[3]

An increase in the volume of circulation would, however, cause forced saving. He said :—

> Different in nature is the benefit conferred by a fall in the rate of interest on those enterprises which employ " more capital ", i.e. in which the period of investment is longer than elsewhere. An expansion takes place in their activities, but on the other hand those enterprises which employ less

---

[1] *Lectures*, vol. ii, p. 206, and *passim*.
[2] " The Influence of the Rate of Interest," p. 218.
[3] *Interest and Prices*, English tr., p. 143.

capital are forced to *contract* as a consequence of the resulting rise in wages, in prices of raw materials, etc.[1]

The *real saving* which is necessary for the period of investment to be increased is in fact *enforced*—at exactly the right moment—on consumers as a whole ; for a smaller quantity than usual of consumption goods is available for . . . consumption.[2]

In his *Lectures*[3] he made a noteworthy modification or, rather, a shift in emphasis, in his analysis of the mechanism connecting money and prices. That change involved the assignment of a less important role to the bank rate of interest than that given in his *Interest and Prices*. He said :—

I had formerly, in close accordance with the opinion of the classical school, imagined that this influence is mainly exercised chiefly through the intervention of the rate of interest ; gold production in excess of needs ought in the first place to cause an increase in the gold stocks of banks and thereby a reduction of their interest rates, which in its turn should cause a rise in prices. . . . After further reflection I have, however, come to the conclusion that the main emphasis ought rather to be placed on *the demand for commodities* from the gold-producing countries ; if this demand is not offset by an equally large *supply of goods* from other countries—in other words, by a need for new gold—it must necessarily lead to a rise in prices, and this *immediately* ; thus the money rate of interest is perhaps not at all affected or possibly affected even in the opposite direction.[4]

Gold flows into the country from abroad to some extent directly in payment for goods. In such a case it should immediately give rise to an increase in commodity prices, and this increase may even precede the arrival of the gold, so that in relation to the continually rising price level there may be

---

[1] *Interest and Prices*, pp. 143–4.

[2] Ibid., p. 155. About twenty years before Wicksell published his *Interest and Prices*, Walras had given a very clear statement of the doctrine of forced saving. See Léon Walras, *Théorie mathématique du billet de banque*, 1879, reprinted in his *Etudes d'économie politique appliqué* ; Lausanne and Paris, 1898. It was probably from Walras that Wicksell got the doctrine. Wicksell's doctrine of forced saving has been accepted and developed by modern writers (such as Mises, Pigou, Robertson, Keynes, Hayek. . .). See Professor Hayek's *Prices and Production*, London, 1931, 2nd ed., 1935.

[3] *Vorlesungen über Nationalökonomie*, 1901–6.

[4] Ibid., preface. Quoted from Ohlin's introduction to the English translation of Wicksell's *Interest and Prices* (p. xv).

no excess of gold and consequently no reason for lowering the rate of interest.[1]

A rise in prices may be conceived as due to increased demand even before the cases of gold have been received in payment for exported goods, perhaps even long before, since even the preparations for gold mining require large amounts of labour and capital, i.e. of goods which will only be paid for in the future by the newly mined gold, and the capital perhaps may only be partly created by actual savings (and thus by a diminished demand for goods) the rest being brought into being by claims on bank credit. Meanwhile a rise in prices becomes possible and may perhaps be caused in the first instance by a freer use of credit, and interest rates will have a tendency to rise rather than to fall. The increasing gold stocks would then act as a kind of buttress to the price movement, preventing it from falling back, as it would otherwise sooner or later have to do in consequence of the contraction of credit, i.e. as a prop introduced *later* for a rise in prices which has already started, rather than as its prime cause. . . . We might explain the heavy fall in the value of money, which is usually the consequence of successive issues of *paper money* in very much the same way.[2]

In other words he emphasized the " direct " but not the " indirect " mechanism. That did not mean that he no longer held that the rate of interest of money could be a connecting link between money and prices. On the contrary, he still recognized that " to some extent also the new gold enters the country and finds its way to the banks as ' capital ', i.e. the owner of the gold has not purchased goods for the amount and has no immediate intention of doing so, but wishes to lend the money out at interest. If we now assume, as we may, that large quantities of this gold are deposited in the banks by domestic and foreign capitalists, then the banks, in order to put it—or an equal amount of notes—in circulation must inevitably lower their loan rate, and in accordance with our argument we may further assume that they will succeed in their object, i.e. all commodity prices will rise and business will thus require more media of exchange. As soon as that happens there will be an end to the relative excess of money, the banks will again raise their rates to the normal, i.e. to

[1] *Lectures*, English translation, ii, pp. 197 f.
[2] Ibid., pp. 164–6.

correspond with the real rate, and at that rate the prices already raised will be maintained ".[1]

His view on the problem of price relationships of goods of identical technological composition among trading nations was similar to that generally held, namely that " the price of the same commodity cannot vary in two different countries by much more than the import duty and the freight ".[2] Using that doctrine as a basis he went into the problem of comparative prices of factors of production in different countries. He declared that wages between one country and another would not generally be equalized. He said :—

> Both real and money wages for the same kind of work are, in fact, different in different countries. . . . If despite this we were to endeavour to enforce equal money wages everywhere it would not make commodity prices more variable and could not be realized without customs duties, for it is absurd that one and the same commodity should have different prices on both sides of a duty free frontier.[3]

As to the problem of the rate of interest of money, he clearly pointed out that banks in every single country were forced to relate their rates to the state of the universal money market.[4]

What would be the international price relationship when we considered the price structure as a whole ? Wicksell adhered in the main to the classical doctrine as described in our third chapter, but made important modifications. He accepted the doctrine of Ricardo and Senior that the relative price levels of different countries depended partly on their distance from the mines which supplied the precious metals. Like Ricardo, Wicksell declared that that factor would be important only " if the conditions of production in all the countries were identical (or uniformly different), so that they all had to compete for the precious metals by means of the same products ". In the world of reality, however, that factor was unimportant :—

> It can easily happen that the general level of prices is higher in a country which imports the standard of value, for instance gold, than in a country where it is produced ; provided that gold does not constitute the sole or the main export of the

[1] *Lectures*, English translation, ii, p. 198.
[2] Ibid., p. 158.
[3] Ibid., p. 131 ; see also pages 157/8.
[4] " The Influence of the Rate of Interest," p. 217.

latter country. It can already be seen that the relative price levels of different countries cannot be related to their relative distances from the sources of the precious metal. . . . It is, however, broadly true that if two countries exhibit no particular distinguishing features and if their distances from the sources of the precious metal are fairly equal, then prices in these two countries will be at the same general level : they have to deliver up the same amount of goods in order to obtain a given quantity of gold.[1]

Wicksell refused to accept the doctrine that differences in the level of prices in different trading countries depended on their differences in the efficiency of labour. Wicksell said :—

The latter factor, as Mill points out, accounts for differences in real wages (which, as a matter of fact, were at that time abnormally low in England) but not differences in prices. If prices moved with money wages, real wages would be no higher in civilized countries than in uncivilized countries : what then would be the advantage to the worker of his greater efficiency ? [2]

Nor did Wicksell accept uncritically Mill's doctrine, namely that prices would tend to stand highest " in the countries for whose exports there is the greatest foreign demand, and which have themsleves the least demand for foreign commodities ". Wicksell made the following comment :—

This view may be correct when it is a question purely of the *direction* of the deviation of prices and not of its *magnitude*. For no matter how eagerly the products of one country may be demanded by another country—the two countries may be separated by a political frontier or they may consist of two neighbouring parts—*no* appreciable difference of prices can persist when there is a free interchange of goods. In finding an answer to the above question, it is important to differentiate between these two factors (the direction of the deviation on the one hand and its magnitude on the other) ; for they take their origin in different, though partly interconnected, causes. . . . We can now see what it is that determines the *direction* of the deviation of general price levels. It does not depend on the fact that one country is superior to other countries in *all* branches of production, but rather on the fact that its superiority is confined to a *small number* of branches of production, while the other countries either possess no advantages whatever or possess advantages only

---

[1] *Interest and Prices*, p. 161.
[2] Ibid., p. 159.

in respect of commodities of which the value is small compared with the necessary costs of transport. On the other hand, the *magnitude* of the deviation is determined by the general level of costs of transport. It therefore depends in particular on the distance between the two countries, on the height of the tariff walls, etc.[1]

In other words, the state of comparative advantages and the intensity of the reciprocal demands determine the direction of the international deviation of prices, and the costs of conveyance determined the magnitude of the deviation.

In equilibrium the price relationships between countries must also maintain a balance in the international accounts for each of the trading nations. He said :—

> The price equilibrium in our and other markets pre-supposes, in the main, that imports and exports balance, and that can never happen so long as one part of our exports is paid for in gold beyond the normal requirements of turnover.[2]

To him trade, by its nature, always tended towards equilibrium. " *Vis-à-vis* the goods imported from abroad there is always alternatively a *consumer* who, in order to obtain possession of the goods, offers an equivalent value, i.e. goods of the same exchange value saleable directly or indirectly to the foreign country." [3] Hence the aggregate sales and the aggregate purchases must be equal.

The principle laid down in the preceding paragraph is the foundation of the theory of transfer which we associate with the name of Wicksell. The main proposition of the theory is that, because of the endeavour of people to maintain a balance of their incomes and expenditures, the balance of payments, if disturbed, would correct itself automatically. Wicksell said :—

> Since people as a rule endeavour to improve or at any rate to maintain, their economic position, a surplus of debts or of claims outstanding can really only be conceived on one of the following assumptions. A public calamity or an adverse crisis may occur as a result of which the goods saleable abroad are available in smaller quantities or at lower prices than usual, or else the customary imports rise in price considerably . . . or finally, consumption goods such as grain, usually produced

[1] *Interest and Prices*, pp. 159–161.
[2] *Lectures*, ii, p. 163.
[3] Ibid., p. 96.

within the country, must be imported to a larger extent than usual owing to a bad harvest or other circumstances. . . . In consequence of persistent drought, for example, the production of milk [at home] is less than usual, the dairies reduce their output of butter, and the farmers therefore receive less money with which to buy coffee [i.e. an imported article] ; or the price of timber falls, and with it the wages of the timber workmen who are forced to consume less of the agricultural products of other parts of the country than usual and possibly obtain them at a lower price, or with the same result to the farmers : reduce capacity to buy their usual articles of consumption, including coffee. . . . It may indeed happen that the demand for foreign goods, such as grain, is so great during a famine year that a restriction in the use of other imported goods cannot fully make up the difference. In such a contingency, of course, individuals must obtain credit for consumption purposes, which in this case has the same effect as if they had consumed their own capital. . . . But even a credit for purposes of consumption will in the nature of things be of short duration. The worsening of the individual's business position must be remedied, and is remedied, partly by diminished consumption and partly also, no doubt, by greater intensity of work in the immediate future, the more so if the State or other great corporations are able to employ their foreign credits for the future benefit of industry, whilst at the same time assisting in the correction of the increased requirements of consumption and the balance of payments. Our purpose here is merely to point out the fact which is often forgotten that an unfavourable balance of trade or payments undoubtedly *corrects itself automatically* in most cases by the steps taken by individual consumers and producers and this, too, without any serious disturbance of the price or credit structure or, indeed, any influence on the currency other than, at most, a temporary shipment of a part of the gold reserves.[1]

In an article, published later (1918), Wicksell further elucidated his theory of transfer.[2] He contrasted two hypothetical cases : first the case of two countries, which were divided only by a " land-boundary " or, more correctly, which were so close to each other that the costs of transportation might be disregarded entirely ; and, second, the case of two countries which were separated by the ocean or,

[1] *Lectures*, ii, pp. 97–8.
[2] " International Freights and Prices," *Quarterly Journal of Economics*, 1918.

more correctly, between which the costs of transportation were so considerable that they could not be ignored. In the former case, since costs of transport were assumed to be equal to zero, all commodities would be international commodities and prices between two countries must be equalized. He said :—

> If these countries were both living under a specie regime there could not possible exist different prices of the same commodity on both sides of the frontier ; and if we suppose, which, of course, is not exactly true, that the level of prices in the frontier of each country is materially the same as in the boundary districts, there could be no difference of prices at all between them.[1]

How, then, would a disturbance in the international balance of payments due to a movement of capital from one country to another be adjusted in the first case ? To put the question in another way : How could the imports of the borrowing country be stimulated and its exports discouraged so that the loan could be paid by goods ? Wicksell was of the opinion that the stimulus to increased imports and decreased exports in the borrowing country " is not to be found in a difference of prices in the two countries, which would be theoretically impossible and practically confined in very narrow limits ; the increased *demand* for commodities in one country, the diminished demand in the other, would in the main be sufficient to call forth the changes alluded to ". It was Wicksell's view that the consequent shifts in the demand curves of the borrowing and lending countries would succeed in making the necessary adjustments, whether the increased buying power in the borrowing country was directed, in the first instance, towards imported goods or towards the home-produced commodities. If the borrowing countries used the money borrowed to buy home-produced commodities, the amount of its commodities available for exports would diminish and its exports would be reduced accordingly. If it used the increased buying-power to buy imported commodities, its imports increased obviously. The result was the same, that was, its imports would exceed its exports to the extent that the loan was transferred by means of goods. Like Ricardo, he admitted

[1] " International Freights and Prices," *Quarterly Journal of Economics,* p. 405.

that as the borrowing country had a larger quantity of merchandise it would " require " a greater amount of gold to circulate it and that a certain quantity of gold would very likely pass automatically from the lending to the borrowing country in the initial stage of a capital movement of long duration. That movement of gold was different from that posited by the classical doctrine, for it did not serve to increase prices in the borrowing country but merely to maintain them at their original level.

A new factor entered into the consideration of the second case, that of two countries separated by the ocean. That factor was the cost of conveyance. Because of the existence of that factor there would hardly be the same price for any commodity in the two countries. The introduction of the factor of freight charges and the consequent difference in all prices complicated the problem of transfer not only by their mere existence but also by the fact that they might be changed as a result of the international movement of capital. To illustrate the latter point he supposed two countries (America and England), the transportation costs between which were such that, in the initial stage, they were of equal amount in both directions. In such a case the average level of prices in both countries would be about the same. If a disturbance arose from the contraction of a loan by America in England, America would have an excess of imports over exports and freight costs and price relations would be affected as follows :—

The increased number of ships going from England to America with full load, and bound to go back in ballast or with insufficient cargo, must needs increase the transport charges on goods going one way and diminish the cost of sending goods the other way . . . the difference of prices in the two countries shown by the goods carried from England to America will be greater than before, whereas the goods going the opposite way will show a smaller difference of prices than before. Both the imported and the exported commodities, therefore, will have a tendency to rise in America and to fall in England. . . . Consequently the general level of prices will have been raised in America and lowered in England.[1]

In the case described gold was likely to flow, at the beginning of the borrowing period, from England to America,

[1] " International Freights and Prices," *Quarterly Journal of Economics,* p. 407.

but " this influx would be the effect, not the cause, of the rise of American prices ".[1]

There were, according to Wicksell, two other causes of disturbance of the equilibrium in international price relationships. The first cause was abnormal conditions in the money market. His analysis of that cause has been described above. Briefly stated, if the loan rate at home was relatively low, " money, bullion, will necessarily begin to flow out of the country and . . . it will not return of itself, for there exists no direct reason for the public to restrict its consumption." The direct influence of the banks on the money market was necessary in order to restore equilibrium.[2] Secondly, trade might be temporarily unbalanced because of the gold movements which are due to changes in demand and supply for the money metal. There was a natural distribution of gold, and it would automatically stop after the adjustments had been made.[3]

From what has been said it is clear that Wicksell did not assign an important place to the mechanism of specie flow in the restoration of equilibrium. On the contrary, he attached decreasing importance to gold flows.[4] He summed up his criticism of Hume's doctrine of international price adjustments in the following words :—

> In my view the abstract truth of this thesis cannot be denied, but its practical importance, especially under modern commercial conditions, is not so great. A fall of the commodity price level in one country is not in itself desirable unless the level was previously abnormally high, which may possibly, though not necessarily, be the case with an unfavourable balance of trade. It is not impossible that as a result of a heavy fall in our export prices, total money receipts, in spite of larger sales, might be less than before and therefore counterbalance these effects.[5]

7. Later Restatements of the Classical Doctrines

In the present century the classical doctrines of international price relationships have been very ably restated by two very eminent economists, namely Professor Mises

[1] See Iversen, op. cit., pp. 245 f.
[2] *Lectures*, ii, pp. 98–102. See also pp. 110–111.
[3] Ibid., pp. 109, 120.
[4] Ibid., pp. 120 f.
[5] Ibid., pp. 109 f.

and Professor Taussig. The classical doctrine of the international comparison of the values of moneys is expounded with great clarity by Mises.[1] Like Ricardo, Mises declares that the money metal is distributed among different trading countries " according to the extent and intensity of the demand of each for money ".[2] While so divided it maintains, upon the assumption of free trade, the same value in all countries. In order to understand the proposition of the international equality of the values of moneys, we should first know the relation between space and the concept of commodity. Of that he says : " Things that are of perfectly identical technological composition must yet be regarded as specimens of different kinds of goods if they are not in the same place and in the same state of readiness for consumption or further production. . . . It is hardly possible to ignore the fact that drinking-water in the desert and drinking-water in a well-watered mountain district, despite their chemical and physical similarity and their equal thirst-quenching properties, have nevertheless a totally different significance for the satisfaction of human wants."[3] He suggests that " two economic goods, which are of similar constitution in all other respects, are not to be regarded as members of the same species if they are not both ready for consumption at the same place ".[4] In the case of money, however, he thinks it " permissible in certain circumstances to ignore the factor of position in space. For the utility of money, in contrast to that of other economic goods, is to a certain extent free from the limitations of geographical distance. Cheques and clearing systems, and similar institutions, have a tendency to make the use of money more or less independent of the difficulties and costs of transport ".[5] A similar abstraction of differences in the geographical situation would not, however, be admissible in the treatment of other economic goods. Approaching the problem in that way, he gets the following so-called " law for the exchange-ratio between money and other economic goods " :—

Every economic good, that is ready for consumption (in the sense in which that phrase is usually understood

---

[1] Ludwig von Mises, *The Theory of Money and Credit*, first published in German, 1912, English edition tr. by H. E. Batson, edited with an introduction by Professor Lionel Robbins, London, 1934.
[2] Ibid., p. 249.   [3] Ibid., p. 81.
[4] Ibid., p. 170.   [5] Ibid, pp. 170-1.

in commerce and technology), has a subjective use-value *qua* consumption good at the place where it is, and *qua* production good at those places to which it may be brought for consumption. These valuations originate independently of each other ; but, for the determination of the exchange-ratio between money and commodities, both are equally important. The money-price of any commodity in any place, under the assumption of completely un-restricted exchange and disregarding the differences arising from the time taken in transit, must be the same as the price at any other place, augmented or diminished by the money-cost of transport.[1]

Then he comes to the conclusion that the value of money is the same everywhere.[2]

Mises also states that doctrine in the form of a theory of the foreign exchanges :—

For the exchange-ratio between two or more kinds of money, . . . it is the exchange-ratio between individual economic goods and the individual kinds of money that is decisive. The different kinds of money are exchanged in a ratio corresponding to the exchange-ratios existing between each of them and the other economic goods. If 1 kg. of gold is exchanged for *m* kg. of a particular sort of commodity, and 1 kg. of silver for $\frac{m}{15\frac{1}{2}}$ kg. of the same sort of commodity, then the exchange-ratio between gold and silver will be established at $1 : 15\frac{1}{2}$.[3]

He criticizes the allegation of differences in the value of money in different countries. To him those who believe in national differences in the value of money have left out of account the positional factor in the nature of economic goods ; otherwise they should have understood that the alleged differences are explicable by differences in the quality of the commodities offered and demanded.[4] In effect, " the exchange-ratio subsisting between commodities and money is everywhere the same. But men and their wants are not everywhere the same, and neither are commodities." [5]

On the causes disturbing the international equality of the values of moneys or the equilibrium rate of the foreign exchanges, he stands for the doctrine that monetary trouble is the only source of disturbance. " Rates of exchange vary

---

[1] *The Theory of Money*, p. 171.   [2] Ibid., p. 176.
[3] Ibid., p. 181.   [4] Ibid., pp. 173, 176.
[5] Ibid., p. 178.

because the quantity of money varies and the prices of commodities vary." [1] Like Ricardo, he denies the possibility of a trade-origin of disturbance :—

> International movements of money are not consequences of the state of trade . . . they constitute not the effect, but the cause, of a favourable or unfavourable trade-balance.[2]

To him the balance of payments theory must be totally rejected. He argues: "The balance-of-payments theory forgets that the volume of foreign trade is completely dependent upon prices; that neither exportation nor importation can occur if there are no differences in prices to make trade profitable." [3] He also criticizes the Malynesian argument. He says: "However strong the desire of the Austrians for foreign bread, meat, coal or sugar may be, they can only get these things if they are able to pay for them. If they wish to import more they must export more shares, bonds, and securities of various kinds. . . . And the balance of payments would be brought into equilibrium, either by the export of securities and the like, or by an increased export of dispensable goods." [4]

The most important twentieth-century exponent of the classical theory of international trade and of the classical theory of international price relationships is Professor Taussig. He adopts the doctrine of comparative costs as advanced by Ricardo and calls attention to the fact that in reality "international trade rests largely on absolute differences " in costs.[5] He restates Mill's law of reciprocal demands with the following refinement :—

> Something must be added to this. It is not merely the character of the American demand for German goods that has to be considered. Regard must be had also to the demand schedules of the Americans for their own products, of the Germans for theirs. When German linen falls in price, the Americans, while tempted to buy more linen, must consider the fact that in order to do so they must dispense with some wheat which they have been consuming.[6]

He then follows the examples of Senior and Mill in extending

---

[1] *The Theory of Money*, p. 250.   [2] Ibid., p. 180 ; see also pp. 184–5.
[3] Ibid., p. 250.   [4] Ibid., p. 251.
[5] F. W. Taussig, *Principles of Economics*, 3rd ed., New York, 1921, pp. 479 ; see also pp. 488 f. For his restatement of the theory of comparative costs, see his *International Trade*, New York, 1927, pp. 3–33, and for his verification of it, see *International Trade*, pp. 161–195.
[6] *International Trade*, p. 32.

the above doctrines to the analysis of international price relationships and the international comparison of wages and gives a penetrating restatement of the Seniorian doctrine, as modified by Mill. Professor Taussig starts from the supposition that all goods come within the range of international trade. He finds that in that case " the purchasing power of money in terms of goods will be the same in the two countries . . . while money wages vary ".[1] The proposition that prices are the same in the trading countries needs no comment since it is based on the assumption that all goods enter into international trade. But the question as to what determines the range of money wages in a given country needs some elucidation. According to Professor Taussig :

> Those countries have high money wages whose labour is efficient in producing exported commodities, and whose exported commodities command a good price in the world's markets.[2]
> Money wages . . . are high in a country which has advantageous terms of international trade, which carries on trade with other countries in such a way as to secure large gains from the trade—favourable barter terms of trade. The main factors on which these gains depend have been sufficiently indicated : an outstanding comparative advantage, and the play of demand in the terms of trade.[3]

If we remove the assumption that all goods enter into international trade, money wages of the exporting industries would still depend directly on the intensity of foreign demand and on the relative effectiveness of labour, but the proposition that the prices of all goods are equal in two countries no longer holds good. " We must distinguish between the *international* and the *domestic* goods : those, on the one hand, which are the objects of import and export trade and are the same in price throughout the international field ; and those, on the other hand, which are not imported or exported at all, and do not necessarily have the same price in one country as in another." [4] With respect to domestic goods, Professor Taussig says :—

[1] *International Trade*, p. 34.
[2] " Wages and Prices in International Trade," *Quarterly Journal of Economics*, 1906, p. 510.
[3] *International Trade*, p. 36.
[4] Ibid., p. 35. J. E. Cairnes seems to be the first to have emphasized the differentiation between international and domestic goods.

Prices of domestic goods obey laws of their own. Some of them may be higher in price than abroad, some may be lower ; and the general level of domestic prices may therefore be higher or lower. So far as the effectiveness of labour in producing domestic goods is great (great, that is, in comparison with that of labour applied in other countries to the same goods) they will tend to be lower in price. Conversely, they will tend to be higher if the effectiveness of labour in producing them is small.[1]

Thus, money prices both of goods and of labour will be different in different countries. Moreover, within a country, the absolute value of domestic prices does not necessarily go together with the money wages. " In other words, the prices of domestic goods are not necessarily higher in a country of higher money wages. They will be higher only if the effectiveness of labour is *not* higher in the purely domestic field." [2] Given the relative effectiveness of labour, however, there are definite relations, on the one hand, between wages and prices within a country and, on the other hand, between wages and prices of one country and those of others. The connecting link of the latter is the wages and prices of the exporting industries. " The determining cause of the general rate of money incomes and wages in a country is to be found in the exporting industries. These set the pace ; not for real wages, but for money wages. Whatever is yielded by them tends to become, under the influence of competition, the ruling rate in the country at large—in other industries, as well as in those exporting." [3] The causal sequence runs as follows :—

If anything should occur which served to raise money wages—for example, altered and more favourable terms of international trade—a corresponding change would take place in domestic prices : they would rise to the same extent. . . . Money wages would rise first in the exporting industries ; the rise would then spread ; eventually prices of goods and money wages in the purely domestic industries would be such as to render them as attractive as the export industries. This assumes, of course, that other things remain the same ; that, for example, the technical methods of production remain unchanged—that no inventions or improvements are made which serve to increase the effectiveness of

[1] *International Trade*, pp. 37 f.
[2] Ibid., p. 36.
[3] *Principles*, vol. i, p. 503.

labour in the domestic industries. Such changes may operate to lower the price of a domestic article or series of articles at the same time in which international conditions are tending to lower them.[1]

That is, in effect, a modern version of the Seniorian doctrine, as modified by Mill.

Professor Taussig's restatement of Hume's law is also interesting. Here he makes three refinements. Firstly, he points out that although the whole trend of the reasoning of Hume's law rests on the assumption of the quantity theory of money, " the thing important for the mechanism of international payments, in relation to the theory of international trade, is not the validity of the complex and guarded " version of the quantity theory. " What signifies is a more special and limited proposition, namely that the specie constituent has a peculiar and determinative effect on the range of prices."[2] Although the effect of specie flow on price movements is different in different countries, doubtless the latter will ultimately be dominated by the former. In countries using deposits and cheques freely, with the pre-War British monetary system as the typical example, the correlation between specie flow and prices is very high.

> The links of connection were close : gold inflow and outflow, bank discount rates, the loosening or restriction of loans and deposits, the temper and spirit of the business community, the trend toward rising or falling prices.[3]

On the Continent of Europe, with France as the typical example, where the use of deposits and cheques is relatively small, and where the banknotes are not restricted in amount or regulated as regards the conditions of issue, the international flow of specie does not have an immediate and direct effect on prices. Yet "no doubt, gold was the dominant factor in the French monetary system. A steadily continuing increase or decrease of the country's gold could not fail to have its effect on prices ".[4] Secondly he declares that Hume's law is true only in the long run.[5] In connection with his discussion of the French monetary system and price structure, he says :—

---

[1] *International Trade*, p. 40. For his attempt to verify the Seniorian doctrine, see pp. 153–177, 178–196.
[2] Ibid., p. 199.　　　　　　　　[3] Ibid., pp. 203 ff., 205 f.
[4] Ibid., pp. 210 f.　　　　　　　[5] Ibid., p. 161 ; *Principles*, vol. i, p. 456.

The situation serves to bring into sharp relief a factor which Ricardo and his followers habitually neglected—the element of time. Given time, a country whose circulating medium consists solely or mainly of gold must find its prices vary with changes in the gold supply. But the time required for any measurable effect on prices may be long ; and while the long-drawn-out process is in course of operation, any number of other factors may also come into operation, strengthening or mitigating this one influence and always veiling it.[1]

The third refinement is connected with the order of events. He says: " In all countries using deposits and cheques freely, the looseness of the connection between bank reserves and bank deposits leads not infrequently to a chronological order different from that assumed in the classical reasoning. An inflow of specie may follow, not precede, an enlargement of the circulating medium and a rise in prices." [2]

8. The Theory of R. G. Hawtrey

One of the most detailed statements of the theory of international price relationships along classical lines is found in Mr. Hawtrey's treatise on currency and credit.[3] His chief contributions are a series of refinements of the theory presented with great vigour and an ingenious analysis of the dynamic aspects of the problem, especially upon the assumption of an elastic circulation.

He starts by differentiating between two kinds of products, viz. foreign trade products and home trade products. The behaviour of the prices of those two classes, according to him, are different :—

The prices of home trade products are free to vary in response to any change in effective demand, while the prices of foreign trade products have to preserve a certain relation to world prices. So long as markets work effectively, the wholesale price of any foreign trade product cannot differ from the price of the same product in a foreign country *expressed in the same currency* by more than the cost of transport to or

[1] *International Trade*, pp. 211 f.
[2] Ibid., pp. 207 f. ; see also p. 225. Other contributions of Professor Taussig will be dealt with in a later part of the essay.
[3] R. G. Hawtrey, *Currency and Credit*, London, 1919. We have used the 3rd ed., London, 1927.

from the foreign country. . . . The prices of home trade products will be determined by the market at such a level as to equalize demand and supply. Supply depends upon the productive resources of the community itself, and prices must be high enough to prevent demand outstripping the capacity of those resources. On the other hand, the demand for foreign trade products cannot be regulated in this manner. These are world markets to draw upon, and the demand from one country will be in general small in comparison with world supplies. Demand cannot be checked by the limited rise which might occur in world prices, but the equalizing factor is found in the rate of exchange. The rate of exchange is the link between prices at home and world prices. An unfavourable movement of the exchanges is equivalent to a general rise in the prices of foreign trade commodities, a favourable movement to a general fall.[1]

The key to the understanding of international price relationships is, therefore, found in the connection between those two classes of products, on the one hand, and the foreign exchanges on the other. With regard to the former he points out that the division of the consumers' outlay between two classes of products "depends upon the consumers' preferences",[2] and that the apportionment of a nation's productive power to them depends on the relative prosperity of industries producing each of them.[3] In regard to the foreign exchanges he adopts an eclectic view. He recognizes that there is an element of truth in the balance of payments theory. The exchange rate, like any other price, must, in equilibrium, equalize demand and supply. " In this, as in all other trades, a failure of equilibrium is corrected by an adjustment of price."[4] But that is far from a complete theory of foreign exchanges. " When we come to examine any particular market, this general law tells us very little about how the equilibrium price is determined. The excess or deficiency of the supply as compared with the demand is merely a *symptom* of a maladjustment of price ; it is no more than evidence that the price is too high or too low. And this is true of the foreign exchange market. If there is an excess of remittances in one direction over remittances in the other, that is a sign that the rate of exchange is not at the equilibrium point, but this does not throw any light on the conditions which determine where the equilibrium

---

[1] *Currency and Credit*, pp. 69–70.   [2] Ibid., p. 69.
[3] Ibid., p. 80.   [4] Ibid., p. 66.

point is."[1] Thus we must investigate what is behind the demand for, and the supply of, remittances. Mr. Hawtrey is of the opinion that it is the price relation which governs the state of international indebtedness, but the price relation which equalizes debits and credits in a nation's international account is not an international equality of general prices.[2] Nor is it a sufficient condition for the establishment of an equality between debit and credit items that prices of foreign trade products are internationally equalized. " The approximation of the rate of exchange to the ratio of purchasing power in terms of foreign trade products does not depend upon equilibrium being reached in the foreign exchange market. It is brought about by the free working of the markets in foreign trade products."[3] What then is the price relation which establishes an equilibrium for the foreign exchange market ? Mr. Hawtrey's answer is similar to that which was given by the classical economists, but is presented in different terminology :—

In every country the relation of the home trade price level and the foreign trade price level depends upon its exporting power. A country which is very rich in some exportable natural products may concentrate its productive resources upon them. Wages will tend to be high enough to make unremunerative the production of any commodities which can be imported at moderate cost. Prices of home trade products will be in proportion to wages, while prices of foreign trade products must, as always, correspond to world prices.[4]

Having described the conditions of equilibrium of the foreign exchanges and of international price relationships, Mr. Hawtrey turns to the causes and correctives of disturbance of equilibrium. The origin of disturbances might be due to the state of currency and credit or to international commodity or capital movements. In case the disturbance is due to an expansion of credit, the economic consequences under an international gold standard would be as follows :—

There ensues an increase in the consumers' income and in

[1] *Currency and Credit*, p. 67.
[2] Ibid., pp. 86 f.　　　　　　[3] Ibid., p. 72.
[4] Ibid., p. 85. See also p. 70. The following qualification is made by Mr. Hawtrey: " ' Exporting power ' is not the only factor. The same effect follows from the possession of foreign investments, the interest and dividends from which give command over imports without any corresponding exports. . . . Any condition which gives the country strength in external markets in these ways tends to raise the home trade price level and the wage level relatively to the foreign trade price level" (pp. 85–6).

R

the consumers' outlay. The increase in the consumers' outlay will be applied partly to home trade products, partly to foreign trade products. The increased outlay on home trade products will become increased income to the producers of those products, derived partly from increased output and partly from the higher prices they obtain. The increased outlay on foreign trade products may be met to some extent by increased output on the part of the home producers of such products, but mainly by increased imports and by the diversion of supplies from export to the home market. The pre-existing equilibrium is therefore disturbed. There is an excess of imports to be paid for, and a deficiency of exports to provide the means of paying. . . . The excess of imports causes a scarcity of foreign currencies in the foreign exchange market, and rates of exchange go up to the export gold point. Thereupon gold begins to be exported, and rates of exchange can go no further ; the excess of imports begins to be paid for by exports of gold. Equilibrium can be restored either by abandoning the gold standard . . . or by contracting credit till the consumers' outlay is so reduced as no longer to attract an excessive share of the world's supply of foreign trade products.[1]

The external drain of gold in a country, which is caused by an expansion of credit in which its neighbours do not participate, serves, therefore, as a warning to it and finally leads it to curb the expansion if it wants to remain on the gold standard.[2] At first sight it would seem that that factor would set a definite limit to the extension of credit. It does not, however, operate in the case of an expansion of credit which is common in the entire gold-using world. In such a case " however great the expansion of credit and the rise of prices may be in one country, there will be no loss of gold if there be an approximately equal expansion of credit and rise of prices everywhere else ". Thus he says :—

The general employment of the gold standard, combined with the systematic regulation of credit, does not prevent expansions and contractions of credit, but merely secures that they shall be approximately equal and simultaneous everywhere. A movement of gold from one country to another is simply a sign that they are not exactly keeping pace. One lets credit expand a little faster than the others and loses gold ; another lags behind and receives gold.[3]

He then shows how the credit expansion of a country might be spread abroad. That is effected mainly through the

[1] *Currency and Credit*, pp. 73–4.　　[2] Ibid., p. 108–9.　　[3] Ibid., pp. 110.

medium of the foreign exchanges and by specie movements. Shortly stated, the result is obtained through the export of gold that is caused by an inflation of credit, because the exported gold forms the basis of an expansion in other countries. The gold-using countries as a whole are, therefore, just as exposed to suffer from the inherent instability of credit as much as a closed community. The expansion of credit, once started, would continue until the gold stock of the world was insufficient to meet the demand for internal circulations of various countries.[1] Then the only means to restore equilibrium from an excessive credit would be a contraction of credit. The contraction of credit might lead to a financial crisis.[2] Where, however, will a crisis, if it does exist, occur ? What conditions predispose one country rather than another to be the scene of a crisis when a world credit contraction takes place ? Mr. Hawtrey's answer to that question is as follows :—

The conditions predisposing to a crisis . . . [include] those arising from the state of markets—the sensitiveness of commodity prices, the relations between the internal and the external price level, the state of the balance of payments, capital commitments, speculation. The actual outbreak of a crisis will depend at least as much on monetary conditions at the threatened point. Any country which has difficulty in keeping pace with the world credit contraction is threatened with a loss of gold. The intensity of the credit contraction which it must impose is then governed by the amount of gold it can afford to lose.[3]

Once a contraction of credit and its consequent crisis are started in any country it would spread to other countries.[4] That is effected through two channels, (a) forced liquidation of stocks and (b) contraction of consumers' demand. (a) The contraction of credit by raising the rate of interest[5] discourages borrowing and impels the merchant to redeem

---

[1] *Currency and Credit*, pp. 110, 117.

[2] " A crisis is not a necessary or universal accompaniment of a credit contraction. Nearly every world-wide credit contraction produces a crisis somewhere, but there are not usually more than two or three separate centres of crisis and sometimes not more than one. There is no reason in the nature of things why the process of contraction should not be completed without a crisis breaking out anywhere." (p. 191.)

[3] Ibid., p. 174.

[4] There is a difference between a contraction of credit in a country which is a financial centre and a contraction of credit in a country which is not. See pp. 136–7.

[5] For the role of the interest rate in this connection, see pp. 147, 152.

his indebtedness. He can do so in two ways. First he restricts orders for new supplies of goods. Such a reduction of orders generally takes a certain time to have any appreciable effect on production, because of the existence of latent demand.[1] But when it ultimately causes a restraint on production, the restraint will bring about a proportional contraction in the consumers' outlay. Secondly, the merchant will press forward to the sale of his existing stocks.[2] Now, so far as the home market is concerned, the possibility of selling goods is limited to the amount of the consumers' outlay. Therefore Mr. Hawtrey argues that the merchant will have a better opportunity in selling in foreign markets. The effects of forced sales are described by Mr. Hawtrey in the following passage :—

> Forced sales from a single country probably would not very greatly depress the world price level *as a whole*. But if, as is often the case, the country specializes in a particular product, forced sales of that product may cause a collapse of the price, and there may result serious embarrassment both among rival producers and among the merchants who hold stocks of it. The collapse and the panic would be thereby intensified, and sales in the world market would no longer afford relief, so far as that product is concerned. . . . Equally catastrophic is a crisis in a country which is a great financial centre. The merchants whom it finances are driven to effect forced sales all over the world, and precipitate falls of prices occur in many of the stable products.[3]

(b) The contraction of credit causes a diminution of the consumers' outlay, the country becomes a less favourable market to sell in, foreign trade products are kept out of it, and gold flows into it.[4] " As soon as gold begins to flow towards the crisis centre other countries, to safeguard their reserves, must resort to a contraction of credit almost as drastic as in the crisis centre itself." [5]

The preceding paragraph is based upon the supposition of an international gold standard. Let us turn now to the case of dissimilar currencies. In such a case, says Mr. Hawtrey, " contracting credit and falling prices in one might exist concurrently with expanding credit and rising prices in the other. The rate of exchange would move against the latter

[1] *Currency and Credit*, pp. 133 f.
[2] Ibid., pp. 135 f.   [3] Ibid., pp. 175 f.
[4] Ibid., p. 132.   [5] Ibid., p. 163 ; see also p. 188.

and would maintain equilibrium in the balance of payments."[1] In other words, equilibrium is restored not through changes in the consumers' income or consumers' outlay or the unspent margin, but through variations in the exchange rate.[2]

Besides disturbances of currency origin, there are disturbances which arise from changes in the national balance sheet itself. Suppose, for example, that there is a decline in the output of foreign trade products, such as might be due to a failure of the harvest in a grain-exporting country. Then its exporting power is impaired, its balance of payments turns unfavourable and the equilibrium is destroyed. Equilibrium may be restored either through changes in the consumers' outlay or through a contraction of credit. With regard to the former Mr. Hawtrey shows that equilibrium might be restored in two ways. First of all, " the immediate effect of the failure of the harvest is to diminish the income of the agricultural population, and therefore the consumers' income as a whole, to the extent of the deficiency. But this reduction in the consumers' income will be accompanied by a reduction in the consumers' outlay. . . . The shrinkage in the consumers' outlay as a whole will mean a shrinkage upon foreign trade products ; that will be a partial though not a complete relief to the foreign exchange market from the effects of the shrinkage in output and exports of such products."[3] Second, simultaneously with the shrinkage in the outlay on foreign trade products there is the shrinkage of outlay on home trade products. That decline in outlay on home products drags down the income derived from home trade products and thereby brings about a further decline in the outlay on foreign trade products.[4] There is, however, a short cut to equilibrium, i.e. by means of credit contraction. Credit contraction is the natural result of the unfavourable exchange and the loss of gold.[5]

[1] *Currency and Credit*, p. 140. " Nevertheless, there is some tendency for the contagion of a credit movement to be transmitted in spite of the use of mutually independent currencies." See pp. 140 f.
[2] Ibid., p. 82.
[3] Ibid., p. 76. That is, in essence, the Wicksellian doctrine that the balance of payments has in itself a self-adjusting power.
[4] Ibid., pp. 77 f,   [5] Ibid., p. 81.

9. SUMMARY

During the pre-War period, the development of the theory of international price relationships was stimulated mainly by two events, namely the gold discoveries of California and Australia and the gradual emergence of the international gold standard. The problem of the possible effects of the gold discoveries and the question whether gold or silver or both should be used as the monetary standard led the economists to go more deeply into the intermediate mechanisms which connect money, price, and trade. In the controversy over the gold discoveries of 1848–1851, the direct chain of effects which connect money and prices, on the one hand, and prices in the gold-producing countries and those in non-gold-producing countries on the other, were made clear by the efforts of many writers. Later, in the hands of Goschen, De Laveleye, Juglar, Giffen, Marshall, and Wicksell, the role of the money rate of interest in both intra-national and international price adjustments was examined. To Goschen, Bagehot, and Laughlin it was a regulator of the international movement of specie. To Giffen and Marshall it was a regulator of commodity prices. De Laveleye, Juglar, and Wicksell went a step further and combined those two bodies of thought into an organic whole. Therein lay one of the greatest contributions of the period under review, for the classical theory of international price adjustments, which had been formulated before 1848 only in a skeleton form, was elaborated with details of the intermediate mechanisms, direct or indirect.

Marshall, Wicksell, Mises, Taussig, and Hawtrey enriched the literature on other parts of the theory of international price relationships as well. Marshall and Mises re-stated the classical doctrine of the comparative values of money and the purchasing power parity theory. Wicksell answered many vexed questions on the subject. Most important of all were his modification of the classical doctrine of the differences on the levels of prices in various countries and his theory of transfer. Taussig gave an excellent restatement of the classical theory of international trade and international price relationships and, finally, Hawtrey explained the working of the international gold standard, especially upon the assumption of an elastic credit system.

CHAPTER VI

DEVELOPMENTS SINCE 1918 : THEORIES OF THE EXCHANGES UNDER DEPRECIATED CURRENCIES

1. PRELIMINARY REMARKS

The development of the theory of international price relationships since the Great War has been associated mainly with two important controversies : that in regard to the exchanges of depreciated currencies and that in regard to the transfer problem. The controversy concerning the rates of exchange of depreciated currencies has thrown light on the question of the adjustment of a violent disturbance due to a monetary cause, while the controversy concerning the transfer problem has clarified thought on the question of the correction of a disturbance due to an unfavourable balance of payments. We shall describe the former controversy in the present chapter and devote the following chapter to the latter controversy.

With the commencement of the Great War in 1914, the inflation of currencies became general in Europe, and the effects that it would produce on the foreign exchanges engaged the minds of the economists of the time. During the War the exchanges of the principal European currencies were artificially maintained at parity, but in the Spring of 1919, the " pegging " of the exchange values of the pound, the franc, and the lira to the American dollar was abandoned, and to the depreciation of the currencies of Central Europe was added the depreciation of the British, French, and Italian currencies. The exchanges of the depreciated currencies became one of the gravest problems of the time.

The various theories which were advanced to explain the exchanges of depreciated currencies have sometimes been classified in three groups : the balance of payments theory, according to which the state of foreign trade, international capital movements or other items of foreign indebtedness are the sources of exchange dislocation ; the purchasing power parity theory, according to which the initiating cause of exchange depreciation is inflation ; and the doctrine that disequilibrium in the finances of the governments is the source of all monetary and exchange troubles. Strictly speaking, however, the third doctrine is not an independent explanation of the subject. Disequilibrium in governmental finances by itself does not cause exchange troubles. It is only when an unbalanced budget effects a real, or an anticipated, change in the volume of the circulation that the exchanges are affected.

We may begin with a brief review of the balance of payments theory. According to the theory, the balance of payments was the source of the exchange troubles and the causal sequence runs from the balance of payments through the exchanges to prices and the volume of money. The theory has been widely held by the spokesmen of governments, by representatives of the business world, and by Knapp and his school. Since the views of the former two groups contain no recognition of any relation between currency inflation and exchange depreciation, they are clearly erroneous. Similarly, Knapp and his school are wrong when they refuse to recognize the existence of any relationship in the prices of trading countries. A more correct view would be that the balance of payments is the immediate cause governing the exchanges, and that other factors act on the exchanges only through the balance of payments. Even in that view there is a serious difficulty, namely the difficulty of defining the term, *the balance of payments*.

The international accounts of a country may be divided into two groups. The first group of items would include all imports and exports of goods and all imports and exports of services. The second group would consist of the payments of interest, profits, dividends and so on, on the one hand, and of international capital movements on the other hand. Under the latter, " one should distinguish between long term and short term investments. Long term capital exports consist in the purchase of shares in foreign undertakings, the repurchase of home securities or repayment of loans contracted abroad, the purchase of foreign holdings in property located at home, etc., etc. Short term capital exports include any increase in the volume of bank balances held abroad, or in the holdings of foreign bills, and any decrease in the volume of commercial indebtedness to foreign countries ".[1]

[1] See Haberler, *International Trade*, p. 16.

Now the question arises as to whether in drawing up the balance of payments we are to include the item of short-term capital movements. As Professor Aftalion very ably points out, if we exclude that item we neglect a very important factor ; if we include that item, then accounts are always balanced and that gives us no theory of foreign exchanges.[1]

The only way out of the difficulty is to discard the idea that the balance of payments is a fixed quantity and to interpret the term, the balance of payments, in the sense of demand and supply of foreign currencies in the foreign exchange markets.[2] We shall consider both the quantity demanded of foreign currencies (or the total debt the country owes to foreign countries) and the quantity supplied of foreign currencies (or the total debt the foreign countries owe to the country) as functions of the rates of the exchanges. Those functional relations give us the demand and supply curves of the exchanges, and they will give us the equilibrium rate of the exchanges.[3] The balance of payments theory would thus be that in equilibrium the rates of the exchanges equalize the quantity of the currencies demanded and the quantity of the currencies supplied in the foreign exchange markets.

The balance of payments theory in that form, though correct, is not a complete theory of foreign exchanges. We must go behind the demand and supply and see how they are determined.[4] The purchasing power parity theory, which we are going to examine in the following pages, will show

[1] Albert Aftalion, *Monnaie, prix et change*, Paris, 1927, pp. 257-260. " Un facteur constanment en equilibre ne pourrait avoir que des effets toujours identiques et ne saurait expliquer les fluctuations continuelles d'un phénomène aussi instable que le change " (p. 256). See also Gregory, *Foreign Exchange before, during, and after the War* (4th imp. 1927), pp. 37-39.

[2] Haberler, op. cit., pp. 19 ff.

[3] We cannot agree with Professor Haberler when he says that " the balance of payments is partially dependent on the exchanges ; it cannot, therefore, be used to explain them " (ibid., p. 31). If his argument be granted, then it follows that demand and supply cannot be used to explain prices.

[4] See Costantino Bresciani-Turroni, *Le Vicende del Marco Tedesco*, first published in Italian, 1931, English translation as *The Economics of Inflation : A Study of Currency Depreciation in Post-War Germany*, tr. by M. E. Sayers, edited with a foreword by Professor Lionel Robbins, London, 1937, pp. 90 f., 98 f., 399 f., and *passim*. According to Professor Bresciani-Turroni, even when the balance of payments is abnormally unfavourable, " if the quantity of money in the country with depreciating exchange, and therefore the money incomes of its people, *is not increased*, the rise

how monetary factors may influence the demand and supply of the exchanges. The general theory of international trade will help us to see some of the factors determining the imports and the exports of goods and services. The theory of transfer, which forms the subject of the following chapter, deals with the question how international capital movements or reparation payments may lead to changes in the foreign exchanges.

2. THE PURCHASING POWER PARITY THEORY AND CASSEL'S VERSION OF IT

Before we examine the purchasing power parity theory it is necessary briefly to state the meaning of the term, purchasing power parity theory. As pointed out by Professor Pigou,[1] the theory of the foreign exchanges consists of two parts, namely first, the *positive* part to which the problem of exchange equilibrium belongs; and second, the *comparative* part which deals with the causes of disturbance of the norm of the exchanges and its restoration. Likewise, the purchasing power parity theory had two forms. In its positive form the purchasing power parity theory is that the rate of exchange would be in equilibrium when the " purchasing power of the moneys " is equal in all trading countries. If the term *purchasing power* refers to the power of purchasing commodities, which are not only similar in technological composition, but also in the *same* geographical situation, the theory becomes the classical doctrine of comparative values of moneys in different countries and is a sound doctrine. But unfortunately the term purchasing power in connection with the theory sometimes implies the reciprocal of the general price level in a country. While so interpreted the theory becomes that the equilibrium point for the foreign exchanges is to be found at the quotient between the price levels of the different countries. That is, as we shall see, an erroneous version of the purchasing power parity theory. It seems better to retain the term, " the positive form of the purchasing power parity theory "

in the value of foreign currencies will not go beyond a certain limit. In fact, the people of that country cannot spend more than a certain sum on foreign goods and on the purchase of foreign currencies " (p. 91).
[1] A. C. Pigou, " The Foreign Exchanges," *Q.J.E.*, 1922, reprinted in his *Essays in Applied Economics*, pp. 156–173.

for the former or correct interpretation. In its comparative form, the purchasing power parity theory is that when we start with the condition of equilibrium in the foreign exchanges, an increase or decrease in the prices of one country will cause, other things being equal, a proportionate fall or rise in the rate of exchange. As a doctrine of comparative statics the theory is a correct one. Let us turn now to the evolution of the theory since the Great War.

Professor Cassel is generally recognized as the leading exponent of the purchasing power parity theory, and for that reason we shall begin with his particular version of the theory. Cassel starts from the quantity theory and makes it the basis of his theory of the foreign exchanges. He recognizes that the quantity of money not only determines the level of domestic prices but also, through prices, the rate of exchange :—

The rate of exchange is primary an expression for the value in the money of one country put upon the money of another country. If we consider two countries, A and B, with independent paper currencies, the money of A can have value in B only on the ground that it represents buying-power, or more generally paying-power, in A. The price in B of the money of A will, therefore, be broadly proportional to the buying power of the money of A and will consequently stay in inverse proportion to the general level of prices in A. Further, the price in B will, of course, tend to be proportional to the general level of prices in B. Thus the rate of exchange between the two countries will be determined by the quotient between the general levels of prices in the two countries. Now, according to the quantitative theory of money the general level of price varies, other things being equal, in direct proportion to the quantity of the circulating medium in a country. If this be true, the rate of exchange between the two countries must vary as the quotient between the quantities of their respective circulating media.[1]

[1] Cassel, " The Present Situation on the Foreign Exchanges " (*Economic Journal*, 1936), p. 62. " Even when both countries under consideration possess a gold standard, the rate of exchange between them must correspond to the purchasing power parity of their currencies. The purchasing power of each currency has to be regulated so as to correspond to that of gold ; and when this is the case, the purchasing power parity will stand in the neighbourhood of the gold parity of the two currencies. Only when the purchasing power of a country is regulated in this way will it be possible to keep the exchanges of this currency in their parities with other gold currencies " (*Post-war Monetary Stabilization*, New York, 1928, p. 31).

That is the purchasing power parity theory as stated by Professor Cassel during the War. It is what we describe as the erroneous version of the positive form of the theory. Three points may be noted in connection with the theory as expounded in the statement of Professor Cassel which we have quoted above. First by " buying power of money " in a country is meant the general purchasing power of money against all goods, but not the purchasing power merely in terms of internationally traded goods. The point is clearly stated in one of his later writings. In opposing the second interpretation he says :—

> If we assume that prices of all the export commodities of country B are doubled, whilst all other prices in B remain unchanged, it would not be possible for the rate of exchange to be reduced by a half, as a much smaller fall in the rate would bring out the latent export possibilities of a mass of other commodities in B, and would prevent a further fall in the exchange.[1]

Secondly, the purchasing power parity is simply a commodity price parity, because Cassel does not, as pointed out by Mr. Keilham, " take into account that there is not only an international market for wholesale articles, but for capital also." [2] Finally, the effect of Professor Cassel's doctrine thus interpreted is, as Mr. Keynes says, " that, even with the hindrances to free movements of goods which prevail in war time, *real* price levels in different countries tend to equality. That is to say, the index numbers of local prices corrected by the world-value of the local money, as measured by the exchanges, tend to equality." [3]

In that absolute form the purchasing power parity doctrine is certainly wrong. It neglects transport costs and other hindrances to trade, which were of special importance during the period in which Cassel wrote. It fails to take into consideration the element of truth which is contained in the classical doctrine of international price relationships.

In his later writings, i.e. writings of the post-war period, Professor Cassel makes many important revisions of the original, dogmatic version of his doctrine. Thus in 1918

---

[1] Cassel, *The Theory of Social Economy*, (Barron's ed.), p. 662.
[2] Wilhelm Keilham, " The Valuation Theory of Exchange," *Economic Journal*, 1925.
[3] See Keynes's editorial note in *Economic Journal*, 1916, p. 65.

he recognzied that the actual rate of exchange may permanently deviate from the purchasing power parity, because of obstacles to trade. " If the trade between the two countries is hampered more severely in one direction than in the other, the rate of exchange will be deviated from its purchasing-power parity. If the imports of a country are more severely restricted than its exports, the consequence will be that foreign money will sink in value, as claims on such money will be comparatively easy to procure, but difficult to make use of." [1] In 1919 he accounted for the abnormal deviations of the German mark from the parity by reference to the magnitude of her exports of capital and the sale of mark notes at substantial concessions of price, in addition to her limitation on the exportation of goods.[2] Finally, in 1922, he made a further modification, that is he admitted that changes in the conditions of foreign trade may occasion changes in the purchasing power parity.[3] Moreover, he pointed out :—

In judging the value of a country's money, a foreign country will naturally not only go by trade prices, but also by the height of wages. For the foreign country can buy labour for the money in question, as, for example, by having raw materials worked up in that country. But even if the country utilizes home-acquired raw material to make its export products nevertheless, the latter's value represents, to a considerable extent, labour expended on them. The level of wages in the country, therefore, is always a very important factor—in the long run may be the predominating one—in determining the international value of the country's currency.[4]

So much for his absolute version of the purchasing power parity theory. Let us turn now to his comparative version and see how he has used the doctrine to explain the variations of exchange rates. It was not until 1920 that he abandoned the concept of " purchasing power parity " as the quotient of price levels and began to consider it as equal to " the old rate multiplied by the quotient between the degrees of

[1] Cassel, " Abnormal Deviations in International Exchange " (*Economic Journal*, 1918), p. 413.
[2] Cassel, " The Depreciation of the German Mark " (*Economic Journal*, 1919), pp. 492–6.
[3] Cassel, *Money and Foreign Exchange after 1914*, London, 1922, pp. 154–162.
[4] Ibid., p. 144.

inflation of both countries ".[1] In 1922 he even went so far as to remark that " there is no need whatever to pre-suppose that the parity rate of exchange corresponds to the quotient of absolute price levels ".[2] In other words, starting from an equilibrium rate, the exchanges would tend to equal the original rate multiplied by the quotient between the degree of internal inflation in one trading country and that of another, if other things remained unchanged and if the prices of home-trade products moved together with the prices of foreign trade products.

Let us turn now to the causal sequence of events as assumed by the purchasing power parity theory. In general, we may say that it assumes the following sequence.[3]

Quantity of currency—rise of prices—the depreciation of the exchanges.

3. The Importance of Cost of Conveyance and the Role of International Demands : Pigou, Viner, and Heckscher

Although Professor Cassel must be remembered as one who has called attention to the danger of inflation, his version of the purchasing power parity theory is on the whole an incorrect one. We shall see in the present section how his version of the positive form of the theory should be modified or corrected and in the following section how his dynamic theory should be improved. It should be noted, however, that as a part of a doctrine of comparative statics his version of the comparative form of the theory is a correct one. But Professor Cassel never limits his version to the case of comparative statics.

The best way to show how Cassel's positive version of the theory should be corrected is perhaps to present the important criticisms raised by Professors Pigou, Viner, and Heckscher.

Professor Pigou begins by distinguishing the positive form and the comparative form of Cassel's doctrine of foreign exchange. He rightly points out that Cassel's

---

[1] Cassel, *The World's Monetary Problem*, London, 1921, p. 37.
[2] *Money and Foreign Exchanges*, p. 162.
[3] He recognizes that events may run from prices to quantity of money. See ibid., p. 28.

positive doctrine is false, for Cassel neglects the importance of the cost of transmitting goods from one country to another :—

If it were the fact that all commodities produced in either of the two countries flowed without cost between them, Professor Cassel's positive doctrine would follow immediately. But a large number of commodities not only fail to flow without cost but do not flow at all. There is no necessity, in order that exchange equilibrium may be established, for the internal purchasing power of sterling in respect of these commodities to be the same as its external purchasing power. . . . There is no reason to expect that the prices of various sorts of non-traded and partially-traded goods will bear the same ratio to the prices of traded goods in different countries. Consequently, there is no ground for assuming that, even in the absence of one-sided obstacles to trade, the rate of exchange which confirms to purchasing power parity, as defined by Professor Cassel, will be identical with, or even in the close neighbourhood of, the equilibrium rate. The positive doctrine of purchasing power parities cannot, therefore, be maintained without reservations and qualifications so extensive as practically to destroy it.[1]

According to Professor Pigou, if there do not exist monopolistic discriminations or import quota systems, exchange equilibrium simply means " that nobody can gain by diverting a unit of any kind of product that might have been sold in the English market, to the American market, or vice versa "—England and America being two trading countries.[2] Or, to put the same thing in other words, exchange equilibrium requires in general that a unit of international goods " in the country of export shall buy a claim in the country of import to a unit *minus* the cost in transport, taxes, loss of interest, and so forth involved in sending a unit there ". " For any commodity that does not flow between the two countries exchange equilibrium requires that a unit in one country shall exchange for a claim on a number of units in the other, not less than one unit *minus* the cost of transportation (including taxes) onwards, and not more than one unit *plus* the cost of transportation inwards." [3] If no article flowed between the two

---

[1] A. C. Pigou, " The Foreign Exchanges," *Q.J.E.*, 1922, reprinted in *Essays in Applied Economics*, pp. 156–173. The reference is to *Essays*, p. 166.
[2] Ibid., p. 161.   [3] Ibid., p. 157.

countries, then any rate of exchange would be an equilibrium rate and there would be no connection between the prices in one country and those in the other. As soon, however, as one or more articles enters into international trade, the prices of domestic goods in one country are connected with the prices of domestic goods in the other country through the channel of international goods.[1]

While recognizing the importance of the cost of conveyance in the determination of the norm of the exchanges,[2] Professor Pigou[3] does not, in this connection, analyse the role of reciprocal demands. The importance of the factor of reciprocal demands has been fully dealt with by Professor Viner and Professor Heckscher.   In January, 1928, Professor Viner had a debate with Professor Cassel at Chicago, in which Professor Viner showed that changes in the conditions of demands for imports and exports must lead to changes in the barter terms of trade and consequently to changes in the rate of exchange (even though the volumes of currencies remain unchanged in the trading countries).   In reply Professor Cassel admitted that the rate of exchange was determined partly by the conditions of reciprocal demands.[4] Similar criticism is raised by Professor Heckscher in his study of Swedish economic history during the Great War.

According to Professor Heckscher, Cassel's version of the positive form of the purchasing power parity theory " is correct only upon the never existing assumption that all goods and services can be transferred from one country to another without cost ".[5] Upon that assumption, Heckscher

---

[1] Ibid., p. 159.

[2] Similar criticism is raised by Mr. Keynes in his *Tract on Monetary Reform*, pp. 90 ff.

[3] In a footnote, Professor Pigou says : " Before the war it was sometimes believed that equilibrium, as between two countries with effective gold standards, required, not merely a rate of exchange somewhere within the specie points, but a rate definitely corresponding to Mint par. . . . That is . . . a delusion." The error has also been corrected by other writers. See, for example, H. D. White, *The French International Accounts 1880–1913*, 1933, p. 156. The correct statement is that in equilibrium, the exchange rate between the currencies of two gold standard countries must be somewhere within the gold points.

[4] See Haberler, *The Theory of International Trade*, English ed., p. 37. Professor Viner also pointed out that prices could rise in one country and fall in the other if the cost of conveyance in one direction went up and in the other direction went down.

[5] Eli F. Heckscher, *Sweden . . . in the World War*, published first in Swedish, 1928, English ed., New Haven, 1930. The reference is to the English ed., p. 151.

says, " not only the general level of prices, but also the prices for each particular commodity, will be the same in both countries, when all prices are computed on the basis of the exchanges,"[1] and consequently the proposition that " the rate of exchange between the two countries will be determined by the quotient between the general levels of prices in the two countries " becomes correct.[2] Even in that case, however, the part played by reciprocal demands is not unimportant. " An increased demand for the export goods of a country, as compared with its import goods, will influence the monetary system of the country in the direction of increasing the amount of its circulating medium. The reason is, (a) from the point of view of general economic life that the national income has increased ; and

[1] Ibid., p. 161.

[2] Cassel, as indicated above, rejects the view that the term " purchasing power " in his doctrine should be interpreted as the purchasing power of money in terms of international commodities only, because the range of international commodities is *variable*. Viner thinks that " Cassel is right in maintaining that the doctrine (as advanced by Heckscher) need not hold if applied to the price levels of a *variable* range of international commodities. But it need not hold even if applied to a fixed assortment of international commodities. Suppose that there are only two countries, that no new commodities enter into international trade, that no commodities already in international trade change the direction of their flow or disappear from trade, and that there are no tariffs or freight costs, so that all international commodities command identical prices in all markets, in terms of the standard currency when this is uniform and exchange is at par, or in terms of the currency of either of the countries converted from the other, when necessary, at the prevailing rate of exchange. Even in this case, the doctrine that the exchange rates will vary in exact inverse proportion with the relative variations in the index number of prices of international commodities would not only not be a truism, but would not necessarily or ordinarily be true if, as would be most appropriate, *weighted* index numbers were used and the basis for the weighting were, not the relative importance of the commodities in international trade (which, with only two countries, would mean identical weights for both countries), but their relative importance in the consumption of the total trade, external and internal, of the respective countries. In fact, it would be possible for the exchange rate under these conditions to change even if no change occurred in any price, provided there were changes in the weights in the two countries, or even if no change occurred in any weight, provided there were any changes in prices, notwithstanding the necessity under the conditions assumed that any price changes should be identical in both countries " (*Studies in the Theory of International Trade*, pp. 383–4).

In fact, Viner's criticism is applicable only to the doctrine " that the exchange rates will vary in exact inverse proportion with the relative variations in the index number of prices of international commodities in the two countries ", but not to the doctrine of Heckscher. The former doctrine is one concerning change and the measurement of change, while Heckscher's doctrine is one of economic statics. Heckscher's proposition as summarized in the text remains unscathed in spite of Viner's criticism.

s

(b) from the point of view of the machinery of the exchanges that exports would otherwise become incessantly greater than imports and an equilibrium consequently become impossible."[1] If the amount of its medium of circulation remains unchanged, it should be added, the rate of exchange must change so that at the new rate of exchange the international account of the country will again be balanced.[2]

In reality there always is a cost of carrying goods from one country to another. As soon as we take into consideration the cost of transferring goods two important consequences will follow. First, the identity in the price both of the particular goods and of goods in general in different countries will disappear. The identity in the price of the particular goods disappears, because " goods stand higher in the importing than in the exporting country, by just so much as is represented by the cost of carriage ".[3] The general price levels, compared on the basis of the exchanges, will not be the same in two trading countries, because the cost of transmission is never absolutely symmetrical, i.e. never influences import and export prices in the same way. There is consequently " a higher level of prices in a country the import goods of which have to pay a higher cost of carriage than the export goods, and vice versa ".[4] Otherwise the international exchange of goods will not be in equilibrium. The second consequence is this—

> that not all sorts of goods and services can be exchanged between countries. . . . Consequently the prices of a great number of goods and services are independent of international markets ; and these prices will stand in no direct connection with the rate of exchange. Even if the cost of carriage were the same for imports and exports, and the prices of the goods which were being interchanged were, on an average, at the same level in both countries (when computed on the basis of the rate of exchange), it would consequently by no means follow that general price levels would be the same (computed on the same basis).[5]

[1] Heckscher, op. cit., p. 161.
[2] " This situation is fundamentally the same, whether the Gold Standard or paper money prevails. The only difference is as follows. Under the Gold Standard, the foreign exchanges are practically immobile, and equilibrium must consequently be created through changes in the relative price levels ; under paper money, on the other hand, the exchanges are as moveable as the price levels, and equilibrium may consequently be brought about by changes in either, or in both." (*Sweden . . . in the World War*, p. 162).   [3] Ibid., pp. 152–3.
[4] Ibid., pp. 152–3, 162.   [5] Ibid., p. 154.

Although there is no direct connection between the price of wholly domestic goods in one country and that in other countries, yet indirectly he recognizes they are connected. "There is always a connection between all different prices within the same community, on the ground that the same means (or factors) of production are used for different products and must influence their prices, because they must themselves in the long run command the same price for all their different uses."[1] Consequently, through the price relations of the international goods between different countries, the prices of wholly domestic goods in different countries are also related.

Heckscher then shows how in this case changes in international demands may lead to changes in the rate of exchange and in international price relationships. He says :—

> Such goods, which for their production use much of some factor whose cost has been increased through a change in international demand, will rise in price relatively to other goods ; on the other hand goods produced by factors which have been cheapened, will move in the opposite direction. . . . If Swedish export goods, taken as a whole, have found an increased foreign demand, prices will rise for all such Swedish goods as are produced by factors of production which are used for export goods, as compared with the prices of other goods. . . . The final result of this, quite necessarily, will be a rise in price, as compared with foreign prices, for Swedish goods which are not exchanged, taken as a whole. For they are wholly produced by Swedish means of production. . . . Consequently, a country which is subject to an increased foreign demand for its goods and (at an unchanged rate of exchange) a rise in prices for its export goods will, almost certainly, also experience an average rise in prices in the case of those domestic goods which are not exchanged internationally ; while the opposite development takes place in a country which finds less demand for its export goods.[2]
>
> The value of Swedish, as compared with foreign, factors of production has permanently risen, which is the same thing as an increase in the national income of Sweden, created by a Swedish right to more foreign goods, in return for Swedish, than before.[3]

---

[1] *Sweden . . . in the World War*, p. 154.
[2] Ibid., p. 155. [3] Ibid., p. 158.

The Swedish authority may either maintain a fixed rate of exchange and increase the amount of its circulation, or maintain the amount of its circulation and let the rate of exchange vary. There is, of course, a third alternative, namely that Sweden lends to foreign countries so that the excess of debts due to her is wiped out.[1]

From the arguments described in the preceding paragraphs, Heckscher has succeeded in refuting Cassel's proposition that the point of equilibrium for the foreign exchanges is to be found at the quotient between the price levels of different countries.[2] It does not follow, however, that Cassel's version of the comparative form of the purchasing power parity theory should be entirely rejected. As a part of a doctrine of comparative statics, that version is, we think, unassailable. But as a dynamic doctrine it needs much modification. In the following section, we shall show some of the factors which we must take into account when we enter the domain of the dynamics of the theory of foreign exchanges of depreciated currencies.

4. THE DYNAMIC FACTORS

As a dynamic theory Cassel's version of the purchasing power parity theory is defective, because he fails to give due consideration to the problem whether a change in the volume of money would lead to secondary changes in the fundamental data of the price system and to the place of inertia and anticipation in the determination of the rate of exchange. It is incorrect to say, as Cassel did, that an increase in the volume of paper money in a country will lead to a proportionate fall in both its internal and external values. The increase in money may lead to the following four changes in the data. First of all it may, to a certain extent, increase the employment of labour and the volume of production and consequently bring about a change in the supply conditions of the exports of the country. Its supply conditions being changed, there will be a change also in the barter terms of trade and the rates of foreign exchange.

[1] " Equilibrium is, thereby, instantly restored to the exchange market, without any alterations, either in the rate of exchange or in relative price levels " (*Sweden . . . in the World War*, p. 159).
[2] The criticism made by Viner and Heckscher is accepted by Keynes (*Treatise on Money*, chap. 21) and Haberler (*Theory of International Trade*, English ed., pp. 35–8).

Secondly, an increase in the volume of the circulating medium usually means a redistribution of incomes. As the conditions of ownership are not the same, the demand conditions of the country cannot remain unchanged, and consequently the barter terms of trade and the rate of foreign exchange will be affected. Thirdly, when a country depreciates its currency the other countries may find it desirable to adopt a policy of protection for the purpose of preventing what has sometimes been vaguely called the evil effects of " exchange dumping ". The result will be a change in the cost of conveyance of goods from one country to another. Consequently the rate of exchange will be affected. Finally, during the process of inflation, the velocity of circulation of the currency is likely to change. The problem of the velocity of circulation is closely connected with the problem of confidence and loss of confidence and hence may be better discussed together with the latter problem, to which we shall now turn.

The problem of confidence and loss of confidence is essentially a psychological problem. Earlier writers on paper currencies had not failed to notice the importance of the psychological elements. Thus both Professor Mitchell and Professor Subercaseaux, in their studies of the paper currencies of the pre-War period, called attention to the importance of the psychological factor in the working of a paper standard.[1] They found that if confidence in the stability of the exchanges was established, it would suffice to maintain the stability of the exchanges. If, on the contrary, people lost all their confidence in a paper money, the paper money must necessarily cease to work as an independent standard of value. Usually, however, the confidence of the people in a paper currency is between the two extremes.[2] It becomes necessary, therefore, to investigate what are the elements which are likely to influence the confidence of the people. Both Mitchell and Subercaseaux found that the political and financial situations of the government were the major factors entering into the

---

[1] W. C. Mitchell, *A History of the Greenbacks*, Chicago, 1903, p. 198 ; Guillermo Subercaseaux, *Le papier-monnaie* (first published in Spanish, Santiago, 1912), the first French ed. (i.e. the edition used), Paris, 1920, pp. 133, 128, and *passim*.

[2] Under normal conditions, Subercaseaux said, " le facteur psychologique de méfiance est sans influence ou agit plus rarement ou avec moins d'intensité." op. cit., pp. 132 f.

psychological estimates of the people. If the government was participating in a war, then the course of military events, or news concerning it, would have much effect on confidence in the paper money.[1]

In the post-War period, the idea that the financial situation of the government of a paper-standard country may affect the rate of exchange through the degree of confidence of the people in the paper standard has appeared in the form of the doctrine that disequilibrium in the finances of the government is the source of all monetary and exchange troubles. Professor Young and Professor Rist are among the ablest who hold that view. According to Professor Young, the characteristic sequence of events in the post-War period of inflation was: unbalanced budget—disordered exchanges—inflation.[2] The connecting link between budgetary disequilibrium and the dislocations in external and internal values of money was found to be " speculation " or " anticipation ". By " speculation " he meant " something much more far-reaching than the technical processes of organized speculation or the transactions of professional speculators. Just as the housewife who buys sugar in advance of her needs because she thinks that if she waits she will have to pay a higher price is a speculator in sugar, so every person who spends or accumulates money or who borrows or lends with a view to securing gains or avoiding losses attaching to changes in its purchasing power is a speculator in money. The most striking instances of speculation in money occur when a sudden loss of confidence in the stability of its value, arising from the disclosure of a disappointing budgetary situation or from other developments which are likely to affect the national finances adversely leads to a ' flight ' from a country's money in the form of the precipitate buying of foreign exchange ".[3] Similarly, Professor Rist, in his study of inflation in the first half decade of the post-War period in England, the United States, France, and Czechoslovakia,[4] finds that budgetary equilibrium is both a necessary and precedent condition for deflation and stabilization of currency. He is of the opinion that, given a balanced budget, speculation

[1] Mitchell, op. cit., pp. 199 ff.
[2] A. A. Young, " War Debts, External and Internal " (*Foreign Affairs*, 1924), pp. 402–5.
[3] Young, Introduction to Dulles's *The French Franc*, p. xiii.
[4] Charles Rist, *La déflation en pratique*, Paris, 1924.

will turn favourable, foreign capital will flow in, the exchange will naturally improve, internal prices will fall, because of the increase in the supply of gold, which is a result of the improvement of the exchanges, and finally the quantity of money will contract as a natural consequence.[1]

Two comments may be made in connection with that doctrine of foreign exchange. First, while we should give budgetary disequilibrium its right place in the theory of the exchanges, we must recognize that budgetary equilibrium may exist together with a dislocation in the exchanges and that an unbalanced budget is not a necessary condition, nor is it always the initial cause, of exchange disturbance.[2] Secondly, that doctrine is not, as it is often said to be, a " synthesis " of the purchasing power parity theory and the balance of payments theory. It is true that the acceptance of that doctrine makes the former two theories appear closer together, because it admits of the sequence of events running either from exchange to prices or from prices to exchange. But instead of an independent or a synthetical doctrine, it may best be considered as an addendum to the purchasing power parity theory. We are in agreement with de Bordes when he says that

this would suggest an amendment to the purchasing power parity theory in the sense that during periods of depreciation the rates of exchange tend to coincide, not with the actual, but with the *expected purchasing power parity*. In other words, the foreign exchanges market may be so completely dominated by speculation and movements of capital that the rates of exchange move independently from the purchasing power parity, i.e. from the price levels.[3]

[1] *La déflation en pratique*, pp. 4, 10, 113, 128–130. He concludes the book with the following sentence, " Remettez d'abord votre budget en équilibre et tout le reste vous sera donne par-dessus," p. 130.

[2] " It is perfectly easy to keep the currency down *provided there is a real desire to do it*. The existence of ' budgetary equilibrium ' is not necessary. Before the War there were plenty of cases of sound currencies in countries which did not raise revenues sufficient to cover their expenditure. An absolutely bankrupt State can have a perfectly good currency without a trace of inflation " (Edwin Cannan, *An Economist's Protest*, p. 393).

[3] J. Van Walré de Bordes, *The Austrian Crown*, London, 1924, pp. 198–9. For an attempt to verify the doctrine that budgetary disequilibrium is the source of exchange and monetary troubles, see Eleanor L. Dulles, *The French Franc, 1914–28*, New York, 1929, especially pp. 326, 349, 2, 351, 370 ff. ; pp. 16–26, 255 ff., 451 ; pp. 27 ff., 32 ff., 37–42 ; pp. 42–8 ; pp. 265–321 ; pp. 322–368. See also C. Bresciani-Turroni, *The Economics of Inflation*, English translation, pp. 23, 48, 50–6, 62 ff., 97, 100 ff., 402 and *passim*.

In accordance with the degree of confidence or distrust, we may divide currency inflation into three stages, namely :—

(a) the stage of mild inflation or moderate depreciation ;
(b) the stage of extreme inflation or severe depreciation ; and
(c) the stage of collapse.

When the depreciation is a mild one, there is normally no distrust of the currency and the degree of confidence is high. We should expect the rate of exchange to lag behind the prices of commodities and the latter behind the volume of the circulating medium. The existence of those lags is due partly to inertia or, in other words, adjustments in the price system are a time-taking process. But there are more fundamental reasons why the internal and external values of the currency do not fall proportionately to the increase in the volume of money. They are the secondary changes in data that are the results of the very increase of money. One of the most important secondary changes is that of the velocity of circulation of money. Practically all writers on the subject agree that at the first stage of depreciation, the liquidity preference becomes greater and the velocity of circulation becomes smaller. One quotation may be sufficient to present that view :—

> The public is so much accustomed of thinking of money as the ultimate standard that, when prices begin to rise, believing that the rise must be temporary, they tend to hoard their money and to postpone purchases, with the result that they hold in monetary form a *larger* aggregate real value than before.[1]

Inertia is also a reason why the exchange rate lags behind the movement of internal prices. At the stage of mild inflation, an increase in the volume of money cannot affect the rate of foreign exchange until it directly or indirectly affects the balance of payments. If the increased money is used to buy domestic goods, then the balance of payments will be affected only after the prices of goods produced at home and/or the incomes of the owners of factors of production have been increased. In that case, the exchanges will lag behind both the increase of money and the movement of internal prices.[2]

---

[1] J. M. Keynes, *A Tract on Monetary Reforms* (1923), p. 45. See any other works on currency depreciation of the War and post-War period or of other periods.

[2] Subercaseaux, op. cit., pp. 155, 158, 165. See also Bresciani-Turroni, op. cit., pp. 121, 143.

As soon, however, as confidence in the paper money is declining, we have the stage of severe inflation. Severe depreciation, as pointed out by de Bordes, differs from mild depreciation both quantitatively and qualitatively.[1] The following are some of the conclusions reached by the various studies of the severe inflation in Austria and Germany in the period from the War to the years 1922 and 1923. First, when currency depreciation is great and rapid, people must sooner or later discover that the currency is declining in value, that is to say that to hold money would mean a loss to the holders. As soon as they discover that fact they become less willing to hold money and try to get rid of it quickly. In other words the velocity of the circulation of money is increasing. The rate of the increase in the velocity of circulation depends upon the speed and the scale of the depreciation.[2] Since the velocity of circulation is increasing, the rise in prices must be at a quicker rate than the increase in the volume of money. Second, in the foreign exchange market, speculation or anticipation is in full play. People watch closely the situations of all factors (including the situation of the budget), which may affect the future rate of increase of the paper money or the demand and supply of foreign currencies. Whenever there is a tendency for the volume of money to increase or people think that there is such a tendency, the rate of exchange immediately falls. The foreign exchange market becomes so sensitive that the external value of the money falls at a quicker rate than its internal value. Moreover, the very fall in the rate of exchange may lead to a further fall in the rate. Thus Professor Graham says of the demand and supply of the bills of exchange during the severe inflation of Germany in the years 1920 to 1923 :—

[1] de Bordes, op. cit., p. 2.
[2] See League of Nations, *Memorandum on Currency and Central Banks, 1913–1923,* p. 19 ; J. M. Keynes, *A Tract on Monetary Reforms,* p. 45 ; de Bordes, op. cit., p. 162 ; Frank D. Graham, *Exchange, Prices, and Production in Hyper-Inflation* : *Germany, 1920–1923* ; and the works of German writers. Graham says that while " there is no doubt that great and rapid currency depreciation gives a tremendous shock to such long-established habits as are of significance in determining the rate of monetary turnover and that *inertia* is probably banished at an increasing rate according to the speed and scale of the depreciation ", it is not right to suppose that there were no limits to the increase in the velocity of circulation of money, and that there is a certain physical check to its increase, (pp. 104 ff., 100, 113 and *passim*). See also Bresciani-Turroni, op. cit., pp. 80 ff., 132 ff., 141, 402 ff. and *passim*.

Reciprocal demand schedules for an inconvertible paper currency are by no means smoothly sloping curves. It is possible that a rising exchange value of a depreciated paper currency, instead of reducing the amount of that currency demanded by holders of foreign moneys, may increase it and, instead of increasing the amount of the cheapening foreign currencies demanded by holders of the said currency, may reduce it. . . . This phenomenon, which is common on all speculative markets, very much increases the range of paper currency exchange rate fluctuations.[1]

Therefore, during a great part of the stage of severe inflation, we should expect the exchanges to fall at a quicker rate than the increase of both the internal prices and the volume of money. Third, causes and effects here are often reciprocal. Various factors react upon one another. The rate of foreign exchange, for instance, is affected by the prices of commodities in different countries, while the latter is also affected by the rate of exchange. Similarly, the condition of the budget affects the rate of exchange through the anticipation of the future volume of paper money, while the rate of exchange may affect the budgetary condition if the government concerned has unconditional obligations in foreign currency and, consequently, affect the actual volume of money.[2]

A severe inflation cannot last very long without leading to a collapse of the currency. In the stage of collapse, the paper money no longer remains an independent standard of value. All business is directly transacted in a stable foreign currency. All prices are actually calculated in terms of that stable foreign currency and are simply expressed nominally in terms of the local paper money. Prices are therefore nothing but the product of prices in terms of the stable foreign currency multiplied by the rate of exchange between that currency and the local currency. It follows, therefore, that prices must rise in proportion to the fall in the rate of exchange.[3] Experience also shows that in the

---

[1] Graham, *Hyper-Inflation*: *Germany, 1920–3*, p. 128. See also de Bordes, op. cit., pp. 180 ff., 194 ff. Speculation, it may be noted, has been used throughout the present section in the broadest sense. It includes those acts as the flight from the currency, i.e. the sale of the currency for a more stable currency of a foreign country.
[2] Ibid, op. cit., pp. 47, 124, 146 ff., and *passim*; de Bordes, op. cit., 178 ff.; Bresciani-Turroni, op. cit., pp. 64–9.
[3] Bresciani-Turroni, op. cit., p. 136.

stage of collapse, the lags either way between the volume of currency and the prices of commodities " became either completely or largely eliminated ".[1]

We may now turn to the question of causal relationship and sequence of events. The question of causal relationship has often been misunderstood, especially by those who attempt at an inductive study of the problem. Firstly, causal relationship must be distinguished from chronological sequence. When the purchasing power parity theorists say that an increase in the volume of the circulating medium of a country (*cause*) will lead both to an increase in its internal price level and to a fall in the rate of exchange (*effect*), or when they say that the causal sequence would run from money through prices to the exchanges, they do not mean that the chronological sequence will also follow the causal sequence. People may anticipate an increase in the volume of money and that anticipation is usually sufficient to cause a rise in prices and a fall in the exchanges. Secondly, causes and effects are, as already indicated, often confused and reciprocal. What the purchasing power parity theory says is simply that currency inflation is practically the most important *initial* cause of disturbance. It does not deny that the effects of the initial currency inflation may, in turn, become causes for further currency inflation. Thirdly, causal sequence should be further distinguished from actual sequence. In the real world the actual course is governed by various causes. The actual course of events may not be the same as that expected by the theory, because new disturbances may enter in during the process of adjustment. In other words, other things may not be equal.[2] Professor Cassel is wrong when he expects the actual course of events to turn out in accordance with a doctrine of comparative statics. As a doctrine of dynamics, his doctrine must be corrected by the doctrines summarized in the present section. As an application to an actual case, his version of the purchasing power parity theory is again

---

[1] The best account of how a stable foreign currency may be gradually chosen to take the place of the depreciated currency as the standard of value is that of de Bordes (op. cit., pp. 161, 175 ff.). For the relations of the rate of exchange, prices, and the volume of the paper money, see Graham, op. cit., 116 ff. ; de Bordes, op. cit., p. 177 ; and James Harvey Rogers, *The Process of Inflation in France : 1914–1927*, New York, 1929, pp. 155 and *passim*.

[2] Cf. Graham, op. cit., p. 153.

incorrect, because he fails to pay sufficient attention to other changes in the price system.

. . . . .

The rate of exchange, as already indicated, may sometimes take the lead and leave the prices of commodities to follow. We may now see how a change in the rate of exchange, which is not the result of changes in prices of commodities, may lead to changes in the latter. Professor Mitchell is perhaps the first economist who subjects that question to an elaborate analysis. According to Professor Mitchell, when the rate of exchange falls the wholesale prices of imports are immediately raised [1] and the wholesale prices of goods exported in large quantities are also directly affected.[2] Those upward movements in the prices of international goods will cause similar movements in the prices of domestic goods :—

In a modern community the prices of different goods constitute a complexly organized system, in which the various parts are continually being adjusted to each other by intricate business processes. Any marked change in the prices of imported goods disturbs the equilibrium of this system, and business processes at once set going a series of readjustments in the prices of other goods to restore it. Thus a course which directly affects the price of one good only may indirectly affect the prices of many other goods.

[When the prices of imported and exported goods are raised by the fall of the exchanges] prices of commodities made from materials exported or imported were adjusted to compensate for the change in the expense of producing them. Prices of domestic commodities produced in competition with foreign goods had an opportunity to rise as the cost of the latter increased, and were forced down as the cost of the latter declined. Prices of goods capable of being substituted for wares imported or exported were kept more or less in harmony with the prices of the latter by shifting demand. And in general, men of all classes found that their business and living expenses were increased when they bought imports or exports, goods made from them, goods made in competition with them, or substitutes for them. These increasing expenses they sought to recoup by charging higher prices for whatever they had to sell.[3]

---

[1]. W. C. Mitchell, *Gold, Prices, and Wages under the Greenback Standard*, Berkeley, 1908, pp. 251 ff.
[2] Ibid., p. 258.   [3] Ibid., p. 258.

Ultimately, the influence of the depreciation in the exchanges will spread over the whole field of wholesale prices, " though with varying degrees of celerity and completeness." The average of retail prices moves more sluggishly than the average of wholesale prices, while the average wage moves more slowly than the retail prices.[1]

Similar conclusions have been reached by Professor Subercaseaux. According to him, a fall in the exchanges immediately raises the wholesale prices of those imported goods which are produced only in foreign countries. If the imported goods are also produced at home, the depreciation of the exchanges acts as a sort of protection to the manufacturers of those goods at home, because normally domestic costs of production lag behind the movement of the exchanges. The average price of the latter kind of imported goods will be affected by the fall of the exchanges in a degree somewhat less than that of the price of imports which are only produced abroad.[2] Wholesale prices of exports are also directly influenced by the fall of the exchanges. They will rise in proportion to the fall in the latter.[3] There Professor Subercaseaux tacitly assumes that the country with the depreciated currency is relatively unimportant in the world market so that the quantities of its exports offered could not affect the world prices of those exports. If that condition is not fulfilled, then the rise in the prices of those exports will not be proportionate to the fall of the exchanges. Finally, like Mitchell, Subercaseaux points out that the wholesale price of domestic goods lags behind that of international goods,[4] the retail prices behind the former [5] and the average wage behind the retail prices.[6]

In the post-war discussions, a similar doctrine was advanced. Professor Graham, for instance, has expressed similar views. But he, unlike Subercaseaux, is of the opinion that one should expect the export prices to lag behind the import prices. Graham says :—

When the value of a currency is relatively depressed on the exchange markets . . . all domestic commodities, both those exported and those consumed at home, become low in price

---

[1] *Gold, Prices, and Wages under the Greenback Standard, passim.*
[2] Subercaseaux, op. cit., pp. 208 f.
[3] Ibid., pp. 209 f.　　　　[4] Ibid., pp. 210 ff.
[5] Ibid., pp. 214–5.　　　　[6] Ibid., pp. 216–223.

in comparison with the price of imports, but the prices of exportable goods become high relative to those of commodities which find their market solely within the country. . . . The price of imports is normally established in foreign exchange markets and increased *pari passu* with a rise in the cost of foreign exchange. The prices of commodities produced and consumed at home are directly affected by neither the prices prevailing in foreign markets nor by the exchange rate. The prices of exports are affected, on the demand side, by foreign monetary conditions and by exchange rate while, on the supply side, the domestic situation is determinative. They therefore tend to assume an intermediate position *below* those of commodities produced abroad but *above* those of commodities produced and consumed at home.[1]

Graham is assuming that the prices of the exported goods in the world market change as the quantities supplied by the country change. Upon that assumption his conclusion naturally follows. It is clear, therefore, that there is no real contradiction between the view of Subercaseaux and that of Graham. They differ from each other because the underlying assumption concerning the relative importance of the country under consideration is not the same to them. Which is the more correct assumption depends upon the nature of each case.

The movements in the sectional price levels consequent upon a fall in the exchanges of a country, as described in the preceding three paragraphs, normally lead to an expansion of its exports. If the exports of the country are stimulated, it is reasonable to presume that, " by the parity of reasoning," the imports are checked. It is also possible, however, that the imports are not checked or are not checked to a similar extent as the exports are stimulated. Firstly the exports of the country may be elastic and its imports inelastic. In that case the rise in the prices of the imported goods will not lead to a decrease in the total value of the goods imported. Secondly, when the exports of the country are manufactures, which require for their production raw materials imported from other countries, an increase in its exports would necessarily cause an increase in the imports of the raw materials. Thirdly, if the exchange depreciation is quick in raising the incomes of the people of the country and if the exchange depreciation is slow in

[1] Graham, op. cit., pp. 186–193.

influencing the economic conditions of other countries, the income of the country would increase so that the same quantity or even a greater quantity of the imported goods are purchased in spite of the fact that their prices are higher in terms of local currency. What would be the actual effects of an exchange depreciation upon international trade depends upon the conditions of demand and supply, the nature of the monetary and financial structure of the trading countries, etc., and no definite rule can be laid down.[1]

Finally, it should be noted that the increase or decrease in the rate of exchange apart, the very possibility of changes or fluctuations in the exchanges means an additional element of uncertainty, and consequently would have injurious effects upon international trade.

[1] We are referring to that phase of inflation in which the depreciation of the exchange precedes for some time the depreciation of the internal value of the currency. In the stage of mild inflation and in those phases in which the depreciation of the exchange lags behind the rise of internal prices, the disparity between home and foreign prices stimulates imports instead of exports. See Bresciani-Turroni, op. cit., pp. 224-252.

CHAPTER VII

DEVELOPMENTS SINCE 1918 : THE TRANSFER PROBLEM

I. THEORIES OF TRANSFER AND THEIR DEVELOPMENTS BEFORE THE GREAT WAR

Another problem which had been much discussed during the post-War period was the transfer problem. By the " transfer problem " is meant the problem of the mechanism through which an international payment is actually transferred from one country to another or, in other words, the mechanism through which a disturbance in the balance of payments of a country that is caused by the making of a payment to a foreign country is corrected and equilibrium is restored. That international payment may be a reparation payment, an international loan, an interest payment, or a payment of debt arising from a great purchase of foreign goods or services. Allowance should, of course, be made for differences in details, but the main problem is the same for all cases, viz. how does a payment in monetary form ultimately lead to a payment in commodities and services. There are, as indicated above, two different theories of transfer, viz. the classical theory and the Wicksellian theory. According to the classical theory, when a payment has to be made to foreigners but is not accompanied by an equivalent receipt from them, the volume of buying power of the country (relative to other countries) would, *ceteris paribus*, become excessive. The currency being excessive, gold, in the case of an international gold standard, will flow out of the country. Prices will fall in that country and rise in the countries receiving gold. Those shifts in the prices of the trading countries will encourage exports of the paying country and discourage its imports. Thus the balance of trade turns favourable to the paying country and the payment is ultimately transferred in the form of commodities and services. The essence of the transfer mechanism, as described in the classical theory, is to be found in the contraction or expansion of the volume of circulation and in the fall or rise of prices. The transfer of a payment, therefore, leads to a shift of the barter terms of trade in favour of the receiving country.

The Wicksellian theory of transfer, on the contrary, denies the shift of the barter terms of trade in favour of the receiving country as a necessary consequence of transfer. According to the Wicksellian doctrine, when a payment to foreigners is not accompanied by an equivalent receipt, the aggregate expenditures or outlays of the country are greater than its aggregate receipts or incomes. The necessary consequence is for those citizens whose incomes are less than their expenditures to contract their expenditures so that the income of every citizen again equals his expenditure. Equilibrium in the balance of payments is thus restored without any shift in the barter term of trade.

The difference between those two theories of transfer may be explained also by the difference in the assumptions regarding the demand conditions in the countries between which the transfer is made. The classical economists seem to have made the assumption, at least implicitly, that the demand curves are given and remain unchanged when the transfer is made. Upon that assumption, as pointed out by Dr. Iversen, " an increase or decrease in the imports and exports of either country must be accompanied by *movements in their prices along these given demand curves*. And as an international capital movement means a change in the relation between exports and imports (or other current credit and debit items) in both countries, the conclusion . . . that it must also be accompanied by a shift in their relative price levels, seems inevitable ; to create the necessary export surplus the new lending country is forced to offer its goods at cheaper terms."[1] The advocates of the Wicksellian theory of transfer, on the contrary, question the legitimacy of making that assumption. Their argument may be given in the words of Professor Robbins :—

The fact that a loan is raised for abroad, or that reparation taxes are paid, deprives domestic payers of spending power. Some of this spending power would be spent on imports. The situation is, therefore, to that extent automatically eased. . . . It is a fundamental error to assume that the conditions of demand for export are unaffected by the fact that transfer is to be made. It is not merely a matter of the shape of the

[1] Iversen, *International Capital Movements*, p. 207.

T

demand curve. It is a question of the movement of the demand curve as a whole. If I lend a man £100 out of a fixed income that means that immediately my demand curves are moved to the left—at any price I demand less—while his demand curves are pushed to the right—at any price, he demands more.[1]

That shift in the demand curves is sometimes sufficient to increase the exports and to decrease the imports of the paying country to an extent that the payments to be made are actually transferred in the form of commodities, without any shift in the price levels.

Both doctrines of transfer have, as shown above, a long development. It was in the hands of Thornton that the transfer problem was first subject to elaborate analysis. Thornton, as pointed out above, subscribed both to the Wicksellian and the classical theories. He considered, however, the former to be true only in the long run. He was attacked by Wheatley and Ricardo, who insisted that even in the short run there was no reason to expect a transfer to cause an outflow of gold from the paying country, a fall in its prices and a shift of the term of trade against it. Thereby they came near to the Wicksellian theory of transfer. Ricardo was attacked by Malthus, who stood firmly for the classical theory.

In the first half of the nineteenth century the problem of Irish absenteeism received much discussion in Ireland and England. It had been said that " as much as one-third of the entire produce of Ireland was sent out of the country in payment of rents to absentee proprietors ". Naturally people were very much concerned about the question whether the large payments made to the absentee proprietors would be economically disadvantageous to Ireland or not. The vulgar writers thought that the income of the absentees was entirely drawn in specie and that the payment meant the outflow of money or " the Measure of all Commerce, a certain Quantity thereof is necessary, for the carrying in the Trade of each country, in Proportion to the Business thereof ".[2] Thus the outflow of gold that ensued would

---

[1] L. Robbins, "Notes on Some Arguments for Protection" (*Economica*, 1931,) p. 61 ; cf. Harry D. White, *The French International Accounts* (1933), pp. 17–18.

[2] See Thomas Prior, *A List of the Absentees of Ireland*, Dublin, 1729, 3rd ed., 1745, *passim* ; Jonathan Swift, *Drapier's Letters*, 7th letter.

discourage commerce and lead to unemployment or to a fall in wages in Ireland. That view was attacked by M'Culloch. In his evidence before the Committee on the state of Ireland, M'Culloch, in answering the question whether the population of Ireland would be benefited by the expenditure among them of a certain portion of the rent which would have been remitted to England if the proprietor had been absent, said :—

No, I do not see how it would be benefited in the least. If you have a certain value laid out against Irish commodities in the one case, you will have a certain value laid out against them in the other. The cattle are either exported to England, or they stay at home. If they are exported, the landlord will obtain an equivalent for them in English commodities ; if they are not, he will obtain an equivalent for them in Irish commodities ; so that in both cases the landlord lives on the cattle, or on the value of the cattle : and whether he lives in Ireland or in England, there is obviously just the same amount of commodities for the people of Ireland to subsist upon.[1]

It followed that wages in Ireland would not be affected,[2] or, in other words, the factorial term of trade would not be altered as a result of the payment of rent to the absentee proprietors. M'Culloch's reasoning is based upon the assumption that when the payment is made there will be be such a shift in the demand curves of the countries, between which the transfer is made, that the payment is actually transferred in the form of commodities without any movement of gold. For he considered as undoubtedly true that " in every instance, in which a demand arises for a bill of exchange to remit rents, it is, in point of fact, a demand for exportation of Irish produce, that would not otherwise have existed ". If the demand for the exchanges was one million pounds, the increased demand for exports would also be one million pounds.[3] Since the exports of Ireland were increased, there would be the same quantity of labourers employed on the whole, as if the landlord resided upon his own estate and spent his income upon it. A similar theory was advanced by Senior. Senior's reasoning

---

[1] *Report from the Select Committee of the State of Ireland*, London, 1825, p. 814.
[2] He recognized, however, that there might be a few menial servants thrown out of employment when landlords left the country. " But to what extent menials may be thrown out of employment, if they have the effect to reduce the rate of wages, they will increase the rate of profit" (ibid., p. 815).
[3] Ibid., p. 815. See also McCulloch's essay in *Edinburgh Review*, 1825.

also started with the assumption that the payment would not lead to any outflow of gold.[1] He found that M'Culloch's theory was correct in case a country did not export raw material or, to put the same thing in other words, in case the country did not export anything other than the products of labour. In that case the number of labourers employed would remain unaltered and the wages of labour would not be affected.[2] But M'Culloch's theory would not be correct if Ireland was exporting raw produce, i.e. produce of land and not produce of labour. In that case, wages in Ireland and consequently the factorial term of trade would be affected :—

In a country which exports raw produce, wages may be lowered by such non-residence. If an Irish landlord resides on his estate, he requires the services of certain persons who must also be resident there to minister his daily wants. He must have servants, gardeners, and perhaps gamekeepers. . . . A portion of his land or, what comes to the same thing, a portion of his rent, must be employed in producing food, clothing, and shelter for all these persons, and for those who produce that food, clothing, and shelter. If he were to remove to England, all these wants would be supplied by Englishmen. The land and capital which was formerly employed in producing corn and cattle to be exported to England to provide the subsistence of English labourers. The whole quantity of commodities appropriated to the use of Irish labourers would be diminished, and that appropriated to the use of English labourers increased, and wages would, consequently, rise in England and fall in Ireland.[3]

The theory advanced by M'Culloch and Senior, which is very near to the Wicksellian theory of transfer, was criticized by Longfield and Stuart Mill. Both Longfield and Mill showed that the making of a payment would have the same effect as an increase in the demand for foreign goods and consequently would lead to a shift in the barter terms of trade in favour of the receiving country and against the

---

[1] N. W. Senior, *Three Lectures on the Rate of Wages*, London, 1830, pp. 28 f. " It is impossible that he the [absentee owner] could receive his rent in money unless he chose to suffer a gratuitous loss. The rate of exchange between London and Paris is generally rather in favour of London, and scarcely even so deviates from par between any two countries, as to cover the expense of transferring the precious metals from the one to the other, excepting between the countries which do and those which do not possess mines."

[2] Ibid., p. 29.

[3] Ibid., pp. 22 f.

paying country. In other words they advanced the classical theory of transfer.[1]

Mill restated the classical theory in his *Principles*. The theory was then refined by the authors, whom we have described in Chapter V above. In 1854, as already indicated, the classical theory was criticized by Cairnes, who presented his version of the Wicksellian theory. In 1889, Mill's restatement was once more criticized, this time by Bastable.[2] Bastable doubted " whether Mill is correct in asserting that the quantity of money will be increased in the creditor [i.e. the receiving] and reduced in the debtor [i.e. the paying] country. . . . Nor does it follow that the scale of prices will be higher in the creditor than in the debtor country ". The argument was as follows :—

Suppose that A owes £1,000,000 annually. This debt is a claim in the hands of B, which increases her purchasing

[1] See S. M. Longfield, *Three Lectures on Commerce and One on Absenteeism*, Dublin, 1835, p. 81 ; and J. S. Mill, *Essays on Some Unsettled Questions of Political Economy*, London, 1844, p. 43. It is incorrect to say that either Longfield or Mill entirely neglected the relative shift in demands or buying powers as a factor contributing to the adjustment of international balances. Longfield noticed it but was of the opinion that it was insufficient to restore the equilibrium. He said : " A certain equilibrium exists between our average exports and imports. This is disturbed by the importation of corn. England suddenly demands a large quantity, perhaps six millions worth of corn. She may be ready to pay for them by her manufactures, but will those who sell it be willing to take those manufactures in exchange ? Will the Prussian or Russian landowner, whose wealth has been suddenly increased, be content to expend his increased wealth in the purchase of an increased amount of English manufactures ? We say that the contrary will take place, and that his habits will remain unchanged, and his increase of wealth will be spent in nearly the same manner as his former income, that is to say, not one fiftieth part in the purchase of English goods. His countrymen will, in the first instance, have the advantage of his increased expenditure. It will not be felt in England until after a long time, and passing through many channels. . . . Thus the English have six millions less than usual to expend in the purchase of the commodities which they are accustomed to consume, while the inhabitants of the corn exporting countries have six millions more. . . . The commodities, therefore, which the Russians and Prussians consume, will rise in price, while those which the English use will undergo a reduction. But a very great proportion, much more than nineteen-twentieths of the commodities consumed in any country, are the productions of that country. English manufactures will therefore fall, while Russian and Prussian goods will rise in price. The evil, after some time, works its own cure." Mill had also, in one occasion at least, recognized the relative shift in the buying power as a factor operating in the restoration of equilibrium. See Longfield, " Banking and Currency, Part I," *Dublin University Magazine*, 1840, p. 10 ; Mill, *Principles of Political Economy*, Ashley's ed., pp. 623–4. We owe those two references to Professor Viner. See his *Studies*, pp. 297–301.

[2] C. F. Bastable, " On Some Application of the Theory of International Trade," *Q.J.E.*, 1889, pp. 12–17.

power, being added to the amount of that power otherwise derived. To the extent that B's demand for foreign products *through the use of her exports* is reduced by this application of her claim and the terms of exchange are thereby rendered more favourable to her—so far, and so far only, does A lose. It is plain that, under the actual conditions of trade, any effect of the kind must be insignificant. The fluctuations of the terms of international exchange are confined within comparatively narrow limits, owing to the competition of different countries and the enormous number of commodities dealt in ; while, within those limits, the special force under consideration can have but little power. . . . The sum of money incomes will no doubt be higher in the former [B] ; but that increased amount may be expended in purchasing imported articles obtained by means of the obligations held against the debtor nation. . . . The inhabitants of the former, having larger money incomes, will purchase more *at the same price*, and thus bring about the necessary excess of imports over exports.[1]

Furthermore, B might wish to take from A new goods *beyond* the excess of A's exports over imports represented by the payment. In so far as that happened the terms of trade would be in A's favour.

Another criticism of the classical theory of transfer was raised by Nicholson.[2] Nicholson was of the opinion that the solution given by the classical economists, even upon the simplifying assumptions was merely a possible one, but " not the only one or the most probable ". Nicholson offered an alternative explanation that was similar to the explanation given by Bastable. He first examined the case " that owing to great natural discoveries—e.g. of mineral oil—England is able to add a considerable amount to its exports to other gold-standard countries, e.g. to France ". The mechanism of adjustment described by Nicholson was as follows :—

The new oil may at once take the place of one or more particular old exports and the balance may remain as before. Suppose, however, that the foreign consumer purchases the oil with money entirely saved from things produced at home, e.g. French candles. This money being transferred to the English oil providers, they may demand particular French goods and so far an additional import is secured to balance

[1] Bastable, ibid., p. 16.
[2] J. Shield Nicholson, *Principles of Political Economy*, vol. ii (London, 1897), pp. 287–291.

the new export. Or they may demand more English goods, in which case they consume the English goods (or their substitutes) formerly sent abroad, and there is a sufficient displacement of exports.[1]

He next examined the case of a tribute. The mechanism of adjustment was given in the following passage :—

The government of the paying country must levy taxes to the amount of the annual tribute, and thereby will diminish the consuming power of the people by so much. Assume that . . . actual money is taken from the pockets of the people. We may suppose that in consequence there will be partly a lessened demand for imports and partly an excess of home commodities available for export. At the same time the receiving country— when the money is sent to it—will have so much more to spend and can take more imports and also consume things formerly exported. In this way an excess of exports from the paying country equivalent to the tribute can be brought about without any change in general prices.[2]

The doctrine of adjustment of the balance of payments through changes in the demand schedules, as suggested by Cairnes, Bastable, Nicholson, and other economists, found one of its best presentations in Wicksell's *Lectures*, which was published at the beginning of the present century. Wicksell's statement is so excellent that we have associated the doctrine with his name.

Before the Great War, the most famous indemnity was that imposed upon France by the Treaty of Frankfort, in 1871. The discussions connecting with that indemnity[3] are also very interesting. Then came the Great War, the economic conditions of which induced a renewal of theoretical speculations upon the problem of transfer.

2. THE EARLIER CONTROVERSY : TAUSSIG, WICKSELL, AND VINER

The new discussion was opened by Professor Taussig. In a paper published in 1917,[4] Professor Taussig analysed

[1] Nicholson, ibid., pp. 288–9.   [2] Nicholson, op. cit., p. 290.
[3] For the literature concerning the Franco-German War indemnity, see the bibliography appended to Bernard Serrigny, *Les conséquences économiques et sociales de la prochaine guerre*, Paris, 1909. See also Norman Angell, *The Great Illusion*, London, 1910 ; and Horace Handley O'Farrell, *The Franco-German War Indemnity and its Economic Results*, London, 1913.
[4] F. W. Taussig, " International Trade under Depreciated Paper : A Contribution to Theory," *Quarterly Journal of Economics*, 1917, vol. xxxi, pp. 380–403.

the transfer mechanism both under an international gold standard and under a paper standard. His analysis was substantially the same as that of Mill. Taussig recognized, however, that a loan might increase the demand of the borrowing country for foreign goods. Should the borrowers use the money or credit put at their disposal in buying once for all the goods produced by the lending country, there would be " no remittance at all "; and foreign exchanges, prices of the two countries or the barter terms of trade would not be affected.[1] But that was, to Taussig, a highly improbable and extremely rare case. Normally, a great part of the funds borrowed would be spent at home on domestic goods and services. In the latter case Hume's law would work to restore equilibrium in the balance of payments.

Professor Taussig went a step further in investigating the case of depreciated paper.[2] The conclusions he reached in that original essay were restated with great lucidity in his book on international trade.[3] In that book, he started with a case of two countries each of which had a *fixed* quantity of inconvertible paper currency. He first inquired what would be the equilibrium rate of exchange under such a case. He found that :—

In the absence of a common monetary standard, the rate of foreign exchange depends on the mere impact of the two quantities on hand at the moment [i.e. the impact of the monetary supply on the monetary demand].

The price of foreign exchange . . . depends at any given time on the respective volumes of remittances. It results from the *impact* of two forces that meet. The outcome is simply such as to equalize the remittances; such that the money value of the two, expressed in the currency of either country, is the same.[4]

He next inquired how changes in the conditions of the balance of payment were brought about under that case and compared it with the mechanism under an international gold standard. He took for illustration a sudden burst of loans from Great Britain to the United States. The payments which the former had to make were increased. The amounts of the new payments were exactly the same as the amount

---

[1] Taussig, ibid., pp. 392 f.   [2] Taussig, ibid., pp. 381–391, 397–9.
[3] For Taussig's statement of the transfer mechanism under gold standard in his book, *International Trade*, see pp. 108–140 of that book.
[4] Ibid., pp. 345, 367; p. 344.

of the loan. " There is no more demand for sterling exchange than before ; no more purchases of British goods are made than before, and no larger remittances have to be made to London."[1] In other words, Professor Taussig made the assumption underlying the whole classical doctrine of transfer, viz. that the transfer does not of itself create, for the receiving country, a greater demand for the goods and services of the paying cou try. Upon that assumption, there was clearly an enlarged emand for bills of exchange to be met by an unchanged su ply. The price of the bills naturally rose sharply, since no money of one country could enter into the circulation of the other and the only means of remitting was by bills of exchange. Therein lies the first difference between the case of a dislocated exchange and that of a gold standard : " Under specie it is the foreign exchanges that never vary, barring the minor fluctuations within the gold points. Under paper, however, a new and different normal quotation for foreign exchange will be established."[2] Closely connected with that is another difference between the two cases : " Under specie the level of domestic prices in each country will be changed. . . . But with dislocated exchange, the level of domestic prices in each will remain as it was before."[3] Thus under specie the money income in both countries would change, while under paper it would not.[4] It followed that under paper the prices of exported goods—though during the stage of readjustment (during the lag) somewhat lower than before in the borrowing country and higher in the lending country—would ultimately return to their former level, because they followed in the long run the course of domestic prices. Under specie, on the other hand, exported prices, like the domestic prices, would fall in the lending country and rise in the borrowing country.[5] Only in regard to the prices of imported goods would there be the same result under paper as under specie, i.e. they would be permanently cheaper in the lending country than before.[6] It was necessarily so because only through that change in the relative prices of imported articles could more goods move from the lending to the borrowing countries, and lending was paid in commodities. Taken as a whole, the position of the borrowing

[1] Taussig, *International Trade*, p. 344.
[2] Ibid., p. 348. [3] Ibid., p. 348. [4] Ibid., pp. 352 f.
[5] Ibid., p. 349. [6] Ibid., pp. 348 f.

nation would, in the case of inconvertible paper, be as follows :—

The index number will register during the period of readjustment a fall in prices. Imported goods will be cheaper as the immediate consequence of the new rate of foreign exchange. Exported goods also will be cheaper. Domestic goods will be unchanged. The general price level will thus be shown by the index to be lower. As time goes on the exported goods will no longer show a fall in price, i.e. the initial fall will be succeeded by a rebound to the original figures. Their producers will be led to lessen supplies in such a way that the returns to them will be as great as to other domestic producers. But imported goods will have fallen in price definitively. When all has settled down the general price level . . . will be lower than it was before the disturbing influence set in, domestic prices (including those of exported goods) being the same as before but the prices of imported goods lower.[1]

The opposite was true of the lending nation. To sum up, the mechanism described by him has the following sequential order of events :—

The remittances [due to a sudden burst of loans] first set in ; then the exchanges are affected ; then prices shift ; at last the imports and exports of goods are modified.[2]

A similar result would be obtained if the initiating cause of disturbance was an altered state of demand for trading commodities,[3] or a change of their supply.[4]

In spite of all those differences between a case under gold and a case under paper, there was one fundamental similarity in the outcome, viz. that the barter terms of trade turned against the lending country and its consumers were worse off. The barter terms of trade were unfavourable to the lending country because, while its export prices remained unchanged, its import prices became higher. Its consumers were worse off because they bought dearer imported goods with the same money incomes.

---

[1] *International Trade*, p. 349.
[2] Ibid., pp. 363. For attempts to verify Taussig's doctrine of the mechanism of international capital movement under a paper currency, see J. H. Williams, *Argentine International Trade under Inconvertible Paper Money*, 1880–1900 (Cambridge, Mass., 1920), and F. D. Graham, "International Trade under Depreciated Paper : The United States, 1862–1879," 1922 (*Q.J.E.*).
[3] Ibid., pp. 363 ff.   [4] Ibid., pp. 366 ff.

Taussig's original article was criticized by both Wicksell[1] and Hollander.[2] The main argument put forward by them is similar to that of Bastable and Nicholson. Wicksell's view has been given in an earlier chapter above and need not detain us. Nor is anything to be gained from a detailed consideration of Hollander's view, because he presented nothing which was really new.

To the criticism of Wicksell and Hollander we may add another criticism. Professor Taussig started with the assumption that the quantity of paper money was fixed in both countries. He also tacitly assumed that the banks in the borrowing country did not expand their credit as a result of an increase in their foreign assets. The more reasonable assumption seems to be that of an increase in the quantity of the circulating medium in the borrowing country, which may or may not be accompanied by a contraction of currency in the lending country. Upon the latter assumption the difficulty in the making of a transfer becomes much smaller, and the exchange rate of the American dollar becomes lower than that expected by Professor Taussig.

The Taussig-Wicksell controversy was reviewed by Professor Jacob Viner. Viner agreed with Wicksell in that the use of the proceeds by the borrowing country in the purchase of its domestic goods would also operate to adjust the international balance since that purchase would reduce the amount of commodities in the borrowing country available for export. " Nevertheless," he said, " even with this correction, Taussig's argument still holds that without gold movements and changes in price levels there is no visible mechanism whereby increased purchases by the borrowers of foreign commodities, and of those domestic commodities which otherwise would be exported, will exactly equal the amount of the borrowings.'[3] The mechanism as described by the classical economists remained an indispensable means of adjustment in the balancing of international accounts. He then attempted to verify the classical doctrine by a study of the pre-War Canadian balance

[1] K. Wicksell, " International Freights and Prices," Q.J.E., 1918, pp. 404–410.
[2] Jacob H. Hollander, " International Trade under Depreciated Paper," Q.J.E., 1918, pp. 674–690.
[3] Jacob Viner, Canada's Balance of International Indebtedness, 1900–1913, Cambridge, Mass., 1924, p. 205.

of international indebtedness. He came to the conclusion that the evidence supplied by the pertinent statistical data of Canada's borrowing, trade, and price movements did give an inductive proof of the explanation given by the classical economists.

He was of the opinion, however, that the analysis must be extended beyond a general and unqualified discussion of changes in "general price levels". He followed the examples of Cairnes and particularly of Taussig in analysing the trends of what he called "the sectional price levels". Like Taussig, Viner began by distinguishing "domestic", "import," and "export" price levels. He then investigated what would be the effects of international capital inflow on those price levels. He found from Canadian experience that prices in general rose so much "that the rise in the prices of domestic commodities was most marked, that the prices of import commodities, which was least subject to the influence of domestic conditions, rose least, and that the rise in the prices of export commodities, which are subject to both internal and external influence, was intermediate between the rise in import prices and the rise in domestic prices".[1] As domestic prices rose relative to import prices, imports were stimulated. At the same time, exports were checked by two factors : First, labour would be withdrawn from industries producing for export to the development of the enterprises for which the foreign capital was borrowed. Secondly, exports being governed by the conditions of the world market the rise of their prices in any one country would decrease the volume of its exports considerably.[2]

3. THE REPARATION DISCUSSIONS : THE CONTROVERSY BETWEEN KEYNES AND OHLIN

The transfer problem was also much discussed during the period of post-War adjustment in connection with the Reparations Payments. Opinions may again be divided into two groups, viz. the classical doctrine and the Wicksellian doctrine. Mr. Keynes[3] and Professor Taussig[4] were the

[1] Viner, op. cit., pp. 229 f. ; see also pp. 209 ff.
[2] Viner, op. cit., p. 228.
[3] J. M. Keynes, *The Economic Consequences of the Peace*, London, 1919; *A Revision of the Treaty*, London, 1922.
[4] F. W. Taussig, "Germany's Reparation Payments," *A.E.R. Supplement*, 1920.

most important champions of the former view. Unlike them, Dr. Anderson [1] explained the transfer of reparations along the lines of Wicksellian doctrine. Assuming sound currency and acting industry in Germany (which was the essential pre-condition), the process of payment was as follows : " The first financial step . . . would be taxation of the German people, with the accumulation of bank balances in Germany to the credit of the German Government as a result of the tax receipts. The second step would be the transfer by the German Government of the right to draw against these bank balances to the French Government, to the Belgian Government, and to other countries to whom she owes indemnities. The third step would be the sale by these creditor countries of these German balances in the foreign exchange markets to whatever buyers appeared. The buyers of these balances in German banks would be those who had remittances to make to Germany, and these buyers would be primarily purchasers of German goods in every part of the world." The problem, however, is why and how there would be enough buyers to absorb those German balances to the amounts that the indemnity involved. To that Dr. Anderson gave the following answer :—

In the first place, the taxation in Germany would reduce the buying power of the German people to such an extent that they could not consume at home the whole of the products of their industry. As the Government reduced their incomes by taxation their ability to consume would be reduced. Secondly, the offering of large quantities of mark exchange in the foreign exchange markets of the world would tend to lower its value, and so make German goods a little cheaper than they otherwise would be when priced in dollars, francs, pesos, or yen. On the other hand, the buying power of the outside world would be increased by this same process.[2]

That is probably the first application of the Wicksellian doctrine to the German reparation problem.

There were many other writings on the reparation problem. It is, however, impossible for us in this general survey to examine all of them.[3] We propose to go directly to the

---

[1] B. M. Anderson, " Procedure in Paying the German Indemnity," *The Chase Economic Bulletin*, 1921.

[2] Anderson, ibid., p. 7.

[3] See, for a summary of the German contributions, Iversen, *International Capital Movements*, pp. 264–278.

controversy between Mr. Keynes and Professor Ohlin regarding the payment of German reparations.

In an article on the German transfer problem,[1] Mr. Keynes presents once more the classical doctrine of transfer. His statement is substantially the same as that which Taussig presented in an article in 1917.

It is untrue to say that Mr. Keynes ignored the fact that the demand schedules might shift as a result of a payment of reparation. He clearly says :—

> Let us suppose that the German factors of production produce nothing but exports and consume nothing but imports, in this case it is evident that there is . . . no Transfer Problem . . . If £1 is taken from you and given to me and I choose to increase my consumption of precisely the same goods as those of which you are compelled to diminish yours, there is no Transfer Problem.[2]

He recognizes that the balance of trade would adjust itself to the making of a reparation payment " to the extent that high taxation causes German consumers to buy less foreign goods ". What he insists on is that " only a proportion of their abstention from consuming will be in respect of foreign goods " and that is not, especially in the case under examination, a very large proportion. For that reason he turns to the classical doctrine of transfer.

Since the solution of the Transfer Problem does not come about, in the main, by the release to foreign consumers of part of the exportable goods now consumed by Germans and their abstention from buying part of the imported goods, the solution must come about " by the diversion of German factors of production from other employments into the export industries."[3] That diversion is possible only when the export industries can sell an increased output. " They cannot sell an increased output at a profit unless they can first reduce their costs of production." There are three ways of bringing that about :—

> Either German industrialists must increase their efficiency faster than industrialists elsewhere ; or the rate of interest in Germany must be lower than elsewhere ; or the gold-rates of efficiency-wages must be reduced compared with elsewhere.[4]

To him, only the last way, i.e. the reduction of money wages,

---

[1] J. M. Keynes, " The German Transfer Problem," *E.J.*, 1929.
[2] Ibid., p. 2.
[3] Ibid., p. 3.
[4] Ibid., p. 4.

is important in the case under consideration. It follows that the Transfer Problem requires a fall of German money-wages relative to other countries, a reduction of German export prices and a shift of the barter terms of trade against her.

A reduction in the money wages, however, does not always help her and sometimes may even injure her. That is true of the following cases :—

(i) When the output, e.g. personal services or buildings, cannot be exported anyhow ;

(ii) Where the world's demand for Germany's goods has an elasticity of less than unity, i.e. where a reduction in price stimulates demand less than in proportion, so that the greater quantity sells for a less aggregate sum ;

(iii) Where Germany's foreign competitors fight to retain their present trade connections by reducing their own rates of wages *pari passu* ;

(iv) Where Germany's foreign customers, reluctant to allow this more intensive competition with their home products, meet it by raising their tariff.[1]

" Moreover," he says, " if a reduction in price of 10 per cent stimulates the volume of trade by 20 per cent, this does not increase the value of the exports by 20 per cent, but only 8 per cent (1.20 × 90 = 108)."

There are, however, three points in which Mr. Keynes departs from the classical approach to the problem of transfer. First he assumes the economic structures of the commercial world to be inflexible. He says :—

My own view is that at a given time the economic structure of a country, in relation to the economic structures of its neighbours, permits of a certain " natural " level of exports, and that arbitrarily to effect a material alteration of this level by deliberate devices is extremely difficult.[2]

That is obviously not " classical ", because the classical economists assumed the cost and price structures to be flexible and the elasticity of demand to be greater than unity. Second, he asserts that some items in the international accounts other than the commodity items are more important in the adjustment of disturbance :—

Historically, the volume of foreign investment has tended, I think, to adjust itself—at least to a certain extent—to the balance of trade, rather than the other way round, the former being the sensitive and the latter the insensitive factor.[3]

[1] J. M. Keynes, " The German Transfer Problem," *E.J.*, 1929, p. 5.
[2] Ibid., p. 6. [3] Ibid., p. 6.

The classical economists, on the contrary, assumed the balance of trade to adjust itself to the volume of foreign investment. Third, in one of his rejoinders, he calls attention to a new problem, which was perhaps tacitly raised in his original paper. That problem is, how is the payment first transferred in *monetary* form ? It is only when payment can first be transferred in the form of money and credit that the transfer can have any effect on the demand conditions. " If Germany was in a position to export large quantities of gold or if foreign balances in Germany were acceptable to foreign Central Banks as a substitute for gold in their reserves, then it would . . . help the situation by changing demand conditions." [1] But what Germany could do along those lines would be, according to Mr. Keynes, quite negligible. For that reason Germany could only make the monetary transfer " if she has already sold the necessary exports " ; so that the monetary transfer itself " cannot be part of the mechanism which is to establish the situation which will permit her to sell the exports ".[2] Thus it is possible, at least in the case under consideration, that transfer in the form of commodities should precede monetary transfer. The traditional approach to the problem, on the contrary, always assumes an approach the other way round and takes the problem of monetary transfer for granted.

When Mr. Keynes comes back to the problem of adjustment of disturbances in the balance of payments in his general treatise on money,[3] he is contributing to the general theory and no longer confines himself to the particular case of German Reparation payments. There he takes his position on the classical doctrine.

Before going into his theory it is desirable for us to explain some of the symbols employed by him : In his book $B =$ the Foreign Balance $=$ " the balance of trade on *income* account, resulting from the excess of the value of home-owned output of goods and services (other than gold), whether produced at home or abroad, placed at the use and disposal of foreigners, over the value of the corresponding foreign-owned output placed at our use and disposal," $L =$ the values of foreign Lending $=$ " the

[1] " Mr. Keynes's view on the Transfer Problem : III. A Reply by Mr. Keynes," *E.J.,* Sept., 1929, p. 407. Cf. Harry D. White, *The French International Accounts* (Cambridge, Mass., 1933), pp. 30–32.

[2] Keynes, ibid., p. 408.

[3] J. M. Keynes, *A Treatise on Money* (in two volumes), London, 1933.

unfavourable balance of transactions on *capital* account, i.e. the excess of the amount of our own money put at the disposal of foreigners through the net purchase by our nationals of investments situated abroad, over the corresponding amount expended by foreigners on the purchase of our investments situated at home " ; $G =$ the exports of gold. By definition we have $L = B + G$. There cannot be, however, equilibrium in international trade so long as there is a continuous movement of gold into or out of the country. " The condition of external equilibrium is, therefore, that $G = O$, i.e. that $L = B$." [1] Thus the existence of external equilibrium depends upon the factors governing L and those governing B. He finds that the former are the relative interest rates at home and abroad, while the latter are the relative price-levels at home and abroad of the goods and services which enter into international trade. But " there is no direct or automatic connection between these two things ; nor has a Central Bank any direct means of altering relative price-levels. The weapon of a Central Bank consists in the power to alter interest rates and the terms of lending generally." [2] Thus, he still denies the doctrine that B is directly a function of L.

The direct weapon that the Central Bank can use in regulating external disequilibrium is the bank rate. But to employ the bank rate as a weapon to meet external disequilibrium would, for a time, mean a divergence of the terms of credit from their domestic equilibrium level, if they are originally in equilibrium. Hence the first effect of using bank rate to preserve external equilibrium will be to produce internal disequilibrium. [3] That, however, is true only of a transitional period. When the change in bank rate has worked out its effect via prices on B so as to bring about a stable equilibrium between L and B, the internal equilibrium will once again be restored. Thus he says :—

Bank-rate is both an expedient and a solution. It supplies both the temporary pick-me-up and the permanent cure— provided we ignore the *malaise* which may intervene between the pick-me-up and the cure. . . . The essence of the matter can be set out briefly. Raising the bank-rate obviously has the effect of diminishing L, the net amount of lending to

---

[1] J. M. Keynes, *A Treatise on Money*, vol. i, p. 163.
[2] *Treatise*, vol. i, p. 163 ; see also pp. 326 f.
[3] Ibid., vol. i, pp. 164, 184, 214.

foreigners. But it has no direct influence in the direction of increasing B. On the other hand, just as the dearer money discourages foreign borrowers, so also it discourages borrowers for the purposes of home investment—with the result that the higher bank-rate diminishes . . . the volume of home investment. Consequently total investment falls below current savings (assuming that there was previously equilibrium), so that prices and profits, and ultimately earnings, fall, which has the effect of increasing B, because it reduces the costs of production in terms of money relatively to the corresponding costs abroad. On both accounts, therefore, B and L are brought nearer together, until in the new position of equilibrium they are again equal. . . . At the new level of equilibrium we shall once again have . . . $I = S$. But we shall also have $B = L$. For since B moves in the opposite direction to P and P in the opposite direction to $L — B$, whilst L moves in the opposite direction to the bank rate, for every value of bank-rate there is a value of P at which $B = L$; and since S moves in the same direction as bank-rate and I moves in , the opposite direction, there is always a value of bank-rate for which $I = S$. Consequently there is always a pair of values of bank-rates and of P at which both $I = S$ and $B = L$.[1]

Mr. Keynes calls attention to the growing importance of the role of the international movement of liquid capital :—

> In modern times, when large reserves are held by capitalists in a liquid form, comparatively small changes in the rate of interest in one centre relatively to the rate in others may swing a large volume of lending from one to the other. That is to say, the amount of foreign lending is highly sensitive to small changes. The amount of the foreign balance, on the other hand, is by no means so sensitive. . . . This high degree of short-period mobility of international lending, combined with a low degree of short-period mobility of international trade, means—failing steps to deal with the former—that even a small and temporary divergence in the local rate of interest from the international rate may be dangerous.[2]

When the bank rate is put up against an unfavourable balance of payments, the existence of capital in liquid form in the international market would cause the gap between L and B to be filled by the flow of short-term capital. That will quickly restore apparent equilibrium at a stage quite insufficient to work out its effect on B and to re-establish

---

[1] *Treatise*, vol. i, pp. 214–5. $I =$ the value of increment of new investment goods. $S =$ the amount of saving.
[2] Ibid., vol. ii, p. 309. See also vol. i, p. 165.

underlying equilibrium. The result is to delay the credit measures, while the progressive accumulation of short-term indebtedness becomes itself an independent threat to equilibrium.

As indicated above, the fulfilment of the condition of external equilibrium depends on two things : first, relative price-levels which affect B ; and, second, relative interest-rates which affect L. External disequilibrium may thus arise either from disequilibrium in relative price-levels or from disequilibrium in relative interest rates. He finds that there is a radical difference between those two cases. " In the first case, the disequilibrium can be cured by a change in price-levels (or, rather, of income-levels) without any permanent change in interest rates, though a temporary change in interest-rates will be necessary as a means of bringing about the change in income-levels. In the second case, on the other hand, the restoration of equilibrium may require not only a change in interest-rates, but also a lasting change in income-levels (and probably in price-levels). That is to say, a country's price level and income-level are affected not only by changes in the price-level abroad, *but also by changes in the interest rate, due to a change in the demand for investment abroad relatively to the demand at home.*"[1]

Mr. Keynes's original article are criticized by Professor Ohlin.[2] Professor Ohlin finds Mr. Keynes's main thesis to be erroneous. " This erroneous conclusion is reached because of the fact that the shift in buying power is ignored, except in so far as it *directly* affects demand for international goods." [3] Professor Ohlin is of the opinion that the shift in buying power consequent on a payment of reparation or an international loan affects both directly and indirectly the demand for international goods. Its direct effect in increasing the borrowers' demand for foreign goods and reducing the lenders' may not be important. But it has an indirect effect : It increases the demand for home market goods in the borrowing country. That increased demand for home markets goods " will lead to an increased output of these goods. In a progressive country this means that

[1] *Treatise*, vol. i, pp. 326–7 ; see also pp. 327–9.
[2] B. Ohlin, " Transfer Difficulties, Real and Imagined," *E.J.*, June, 1929. " Mr. Keynes's Views on the Transfer Problem, a Rejoinder," *E.J.*, Sept., 1929.
[3] " Transfer Difficulties," p. 175.

labour and capital, that would otherwise have passed to export industries and industries producing goods which compete directly with import goods, now go to the home market industries instead. Output of these import-competing goods and of export goods increases less than it would otherwise have done. Thus, there is a relative decline in exports and an increase of imports and an excess of imports is created ". A corresponding adjustment takes place in the lending country and an excess of its exports is created.[1] As the shift in purchasing power indirectly affects the demands for foreign goods, it also occasions changes in the sectional price levels. Home market prices tend to rise in the borrowing country and fall in the lending country, relative to prices of export and import goods and prices of the goods which compete with import goods. But it is not necessary, according to Professor Ohlin, that the borrowing country's *export* prices should rise and the lending country's fall.[2] In other words, there is no reason to suppose, as Mr. Keynes did, that the barter terms of trade must turn against the paying country.[3]

Professor Ohlin restates his theory of transfer in his book on international trade.[4] He starts with the case of demand variation and investigates the possible effects of an increase of B's demand for some of A's goods. A and B being two trading regions. The first effect which he finds is on the distribution of buying power, which is equal to " total gross income, increased by borrowings and reduced by loans, and expressed in terms of money with reference to a *period* of time ". The total buying power of the two regions being constant, A will have, as a result of the change in demand, a greater buying power and B a smaller one than before. That alteration in buying power means a corresponding shift in the demand curves. A demands more of B's goods so that " the balance of trade is automatically kept in equilibrium ". The second effect is that on the scarcity of A's factors in relation to the scarcity of B's factors. As the demand for A's export goods increases, the relative scarcity of the factors required for the production

[1] " Transfer Difficulties," p. 174.
[2] Ibid., p. 175.
[3] Cf. also Jacques Rueff's criticism of Keynes's views in E.J., Sept., 1929.
[4] B. Ohlin, *Inter-regional and International Trade*, Cambridge, Mass., 1935. The reader is advised to read first the section on Ohlin's general theory of international trade given in Ch. VIII, Sec. 2 below.

of those goods, and consequently the relative scarcity of all
A's factors regarded as a group is increased. That leads us
immediately to the third effect, viz. " if the total money
value of the product of both regions is kept constant, A
will get a higher, B a lower money income than before ",
and the fourth effect, viz. " if the price level for factors in
general in A and B taken together is kept constant, the
level of A factors rises and that of B factors drops ". Since
prices of factors entering into the export industries in A
rise relative to B one should expect—the fifth effect—that
prices of A's export goods and goods using factors of the
same sort as the export goods will also rise relative to B.
That means the movement of the terms of trade in
favour of A.[1] That shift in the terms of trade is, however, not the same as the shift postulated by the classical
economists. The former is purely the result of the *original*
change in the demand data, while the latter is a part of the
process of adjustment.

He next examines the case of international capital
movements from B to A. The first effect is that the buying
power in A is increased and that in B reduced. " *There is
thus a market in A for more of B's goods than formerly.* On
the other hand, the market in B for A's goods is not as big
as it was before. The local *distribution* of the total demand
has changed. A has become a better and B a worse market
for goods of all kinds." Consequently A buys more and B
less of their combined production than before. A will
acquire " an import surplus corresponding to the size of
the loans ", if the additional demand of A is directed to
those goods which B abstained from buying as a result of
lending. " If the borrowing individuals in A demand other
goods than those demanded by the lenders in B, the *direction*
of the total demand will obviously have undergone a change.
This results in a change also in the relative scarcity of the
factors of production and in the relative prices of goods.
The goods for which there is a greater demand than before
becomes somewhat dearer and the others somewhat
cheaper." In other words, there may be a change in the
terms of trade. But that change may be as well in favour as
against the lending country. It all depends upon the
direction of demand.[2]

[1] *Inter-regional and International Trade*, pp. 59–62. For a more elaborate
analysis of the problem, see ibid., chap. xxiv.   [2] Ibid., pp. 406–8.

Costs of transfer are so far left out of account. As soon as we take into consideration costs of transfer, we are introducing " domestic " or " home market " goods, which may be competing or non-competing with " international " goods. In that case Professor Ohlin's treatment is the same as that given in his original paper. There will be an increase in the manufacture of non-competing home market goods in A, and of international goods and competing home-market goods in B.[1] " The result of the change in the direction of production will be a changed relative scarcity of the corresponding factors."[2] " The productive factors used in large proportions in expanding industries become more scarce and the others less scarce than before."[3] The change in the relative scarcity of factors naturally involves a change in the price of factors. Such a readjustment also leads to changes in sectional price levels. In A home market prices and, to a lesser extent, also semi-international prices rise in comparison with export prices. In B the former fall in comparison with the latter.[4] There is, however, " no justification for assuming that a noticeable change of the terms of exchange in favour of A is the normal or probable outcome, either in the beginning of the borrowing period or later." " The shift in demand from B factors, regarded as a whole, to A factors, which the borrowing implies, need not enhance the scarcity of the various productive factors used in A's export industries compared with those used in B's." Hence it is conceivable that, in spite of the changes in the sectional price levels, the relative position between A's export prices and B's (and therefore the terms of trade) may remain unchanged.[5]

Professor Ohlin also goes into the question of monetary transfer. He recognizes now that a monetary transfer comes *before* the real transfer of goods and services.[6] That monetary transfer involves an increase in the foreign currency reserves in A, which leads to an inflation of credit " probably by lowering the discount rate ".[7] " Such an increase in credit and buying power must tend to affect the prices of various sorts of commodities and industrial agents. Directly or indirectly it also tends to increase

---

[1] *Inter-regional and International Trade*, p. 410.   [2] Ibid., p. 421.
[3] Ibid., p. 424.   [4] Ibid., pp. 421–9.
[5] Ibid., pp. 425, 426.   [6] Ibid., p. 411.
[7] Ibid., pp. 410–417.

imports, while keeping back exports."[1] Therein Professor Ohlin comes, consciously or unconsciously, very near to the classical theory of transfer.

The Keynes-Ohlin controversy occasioned some very interesting reflections on the part of Mr. Robertson, Professor Pigou, and other economists.[2] According to Mr. Robertson, there is no real contradiction between the two views.[3] It is, however, reasonable to expect the terms of trade to move against the reparation paying country (say Germany) and in favour of the receiving country (say America). The reason is as follows :—

In all probability German goods have more nearly the character of money—which can be surrendered or gained without leading to a change in its marginal utility—to Germans than they have to Englishmen, and English goods have more nearly the character of money to Englishmen than they have to Germans. Hence there is a considerable balance of probability that the willingness of Englishmen to trade will be reduced more than the willingness of Germans, and so that the ratio of interchange will be turned against Germany.[4]

[1] *Inter-regional and International Trade*, p. 412.
[2] We may call special attention to the works of Dr. Roland Wilson and Professor C. Bresciani-Turroni. In the fourth chapter (pp. 47–81) of his *Capital Imports and the Terms of Trade* (Melbourne, 1931), Dr. Wilson gave a penetrating analysis of the problem of possible effects of international capital movements on the barter terms of trade and on the sectional price levels. The result of his analysis " show little more than the possibility that the net terms of trade, as usually measured, might move in either direction, according to the particular circumstances of time and place ; and the probability that domestic prices will in general rise relatively to import and export prices in the borrowing countries". Professor Bresciani-Turroni, in his *Inductive Verification of the Theory of International Payments* (Cairo, 1932), points out that while the classical doctrine of transfer is not unreal, " it does not tell the whole story." We must also take into consideration of the influence of the shift of the demand curves (to the right in the borrowing country, to the left in the lending country) which brings about a much quicker adjustment of the balance of international payments than the mechanism described in the clasical doctrine. The shift in the demand curves in the borrowing country may result in an increase in the demand for foreign goods, not only because more import goods or goods competing with the import goods are demanded, but also because " consumers in the borrowing country demand more domestic goods which are manufactured wholly or in part with foreign materials ". See also Otte Yntema, *A Mathematical Reformation of the General Theory of International Trade* (1932), chap. v.
[3] D. H. Robertson, " The Transfer Problem," printed in Pigou and Robertson, *Economic Essays and Addresses*, London, 1931, pp. 170–181.
[4] Ibid., p. 180.

Similar conclusions have been reached by Professor Pegou.[1]

4. THE RESTATEMENTS BY HABERLER, IVERSEN, AND NURKSE

Professor Haberler's view, especially that given in his book on international trade, is an eclectic one.[2] He begins by presenting Wicksell's proposition that because of the endeavour of people to maintain a balance of their incomes and expenditures, the debit items and the credit items in the national balance sheet tend to be equal. If each individual's balance of payments is in equilibrium,

his receipts exactly equal his expenditure over the appropriate period of time. This implies that the balance of payments between any economic group and the rest of the economy must also be in equilibrium ; for the external balance of payments of a group is merely an aggregate of the balance of payments between members of the group and persons outside it. . . . When an individual *A* in the dollar country pays 100 to the crown country, there must be an individual *B* in the dollar country, whether he is identical with *A* or not, who is in receipt of 100 from the crown country. This is an obvious corollary of the postulate that every individual balance of payments is in equilibrium.[3]

He next reviews the Keynes-Ohlin controversy and comes to the conclusion that " the truth lies in this case midway between the two conflicting theories, both of which are one-sided and give an over-simplified picture of the facts ".[4] Keynes is one-sided because he " ignores the shifts on the demand side produced by the payments themselves ". The doctrine that the terms of trade are unaffected by an act of transfer is also one-sided because it is true only of a frictionless market, in which the adjustment would be instantaneous. During the period of transition, Keynes is right to expect the barter term of trade to turn in the normal case in favour of the receiving country. That shift " is to be

---

[1] A. C. Pigou, " The Effect of Reparations on the Ratio of International Exchange," *E.J.*, 1932, pp. 532–543. For a very interesting analysis of Pigou's view see Viner, *Studies in the Theory of International Trade*, 336–352.
[2] Gottfried Haberler, *The Theory of International Trade*, first published in German, 1933, English tr. by Alfred Stonier and Frederic Benham, London, 1936. For Haberler's view as given in his earlier writing, see Iversen, *International Capital Movements*, pp. 282–7.
[3] Haberler, *The Theory* (Eng. ed.), p. 14.   [4] Haberler, ibid., pp. 72 f.

expected in the normal case where the direct influence of changes in demand on the balance of trade is insufficient to create the necessary export surplus, because foreign countries spend only a small part of their receipts for reparations on the purchase of German exports ". The extent of the fall in the price of German exports depends on two factors : first on the elasticity of demand " after the payment had been made and the curve has therefore shifted " ; and, second, on the conditions of supply in Germany and also, *mutatis mutandis*, in the competing industries abroad.[1]

Finally Professor Haberler calls attention to the possibility which " has not been considered by either party ", viz. that the terms of trade may move in favour of the paying country. It would arise " if the increase of foreign demand were for German exports, and the fall in Germany's demand related to imports ".[2] That, however, is only a theoretically possible, but not a very probable, case.

The theory of transfer is carried a step forward, in 1935, by both Mr. Iversen and Dr. Nurkse. The most important contributions they made is their analysis of the effects of transfer on the terms of trade. As pointed out above, critics of the classical doctrines have come to the conclusion that as a result of transfer " the terms of trade may remain unaffected, they may move against the country paying reparations or, on the other hand, they may move in favour of it ". Although Professor Pigou and Mr. Robertson have shown that normally we should expect the barter terms of trade to turn against the paying country, yet neither of them has given an answer as satisfactory as that of Iversen or Nurkse.[3]

Dr. Iversen [4] presents a doctrine of transfer which amounts to a combination of the doctrines of Ohlin, Robertson, Pigou, Keynes, and Haberler. Like Keynes and White, Iversen makes a distinction between the problem of monetary transfer and that of real transfer. Iversen considers gold and short-term credit as the two important media of international payment through which monetary transfer is effected.[5] His treatment of the problem of real transfer [6]

---

[1] Haberler, *The Theory*, p. 75. In contrast to Keynes, Haberler is of the opinion that " demand is as a rule very elastic ".
[2] Ibid., p. 76. [3] Cf. however, Haberler, op. cit., Eng. ed., p. 74 n.
[4] Carl Iversen, *International Capital Movements*, Copenhagen, 1935.
[5] Ibid., pp. 513–525. There Iversen's analysis follows closely that of White. [6] Ibid., pp. 456–510.

is, on the whole, similar to that of Ohlin. Upon the assumption that all goods were " international ", the trade balances of the borrowing and the lending countries are easily adjusted to changes in their " balances of payments " through a shift in the buying power—a reduction by the amount of the loan in the lending country and a corresponding increase in the borrowing country. If that leads the borrower to buy exactly the same goods which the lender refrains from buying, then the adjustment is complete and there is no change in the barter terms of trade. But that is highly improbable. " In all likelihood, a transfer of capital will be accompanied by *a change in the direction of demand :* for some goods (now wanted by the borrower) the demand will be greater than before, for others (previously used by the lender) it will be less." The changed conditions of demand may alter the relative scarcity of the factors of production, thus influence all prices and quantities within the price structure, and cause a change in the barter terms of trade. When costs of transporting commodities and hence the existence of home-market goods are introduced, the changed demand conditions will mean changed localization of demand and will lead to changes in the relative positions of sectional price levels. " The most important aspect of the change in demand conditions caused by the transfer of buying power is that the demand for domestic commodities is increased in the borrowing country and decreased in the lending." That shift in demand will cause the home-market prices to go up in the borrowing and to fall in the lending country. In that case, as in the case of zero cost of transport, it is impossible to lay down a definite rule regarding the change and the direction of the barter terms of trade. " There is a certain probability, however, that the terms of trade will move against the lending country." The reason is twofold. On the one hand, the direct effect of the change in the direction of demand for international goods is likely to turn the terms of trade against the lending country because of the reason given by Mr. Robertson and Professor Pigou.[1] On the other hand, the indirect effects of the shifts in the demand for home-market goods are also likely to turn the terms of trade against the lending country. One of those effects, as already indicated, is that the home-market prices go up in the

[1] *International Capital Movements*, p. 511.

borrowing and fall in the lending country. That shift in prices will also alter the factor prices. Upon the assumption underlying most of the classical expositions of international trade theory—that all goods produced in a country require for their production identical " units of productive power " (i.e. a combination of the factors of production in fixed proportion)—or upon the assumption that the factor combinations used in a country's home-market industries are similar to those in its export industries, the prices of export goods will also go up in the borrowing and fall in the lending country. Hence the terms of trade are in favour of the former.[1]

The conclusion that it is reasonable to expect the terms of trade to turn against the lending country has also been reached independently by Dr. Nurkse.[2] He begins by assuming that the costs of transfer were equal to zero and consequently there were no " domestic " goods. Upon that simplifying assumption, the effects of transfer might be either to turn the terms of trade in favour of the borrowing country or against it, according to the conditions of income elasticity of demand. As soon as costs of transport are introduced, he continues to show, there are reasons to expect, as the classical economists did, the terms of trade to turn against the lending country. For the introduction of transport costs gives rise to a new class of goods, viz. " domestic goods " as distinguished from " international goods ". In the actual world, the volume of " domestic goods ", is, in almost all countries, large in comparison with that of international goods. If one assumes, as it is reasonable to do, that the borrowing or receiving country divides the extra income between domestic goods and international goods in about the some proportion as the old income, then the terms of trade will move against the lending and in favour of the borrowing country.[3]

---

[1] *International Capital Movements*, pp. 479–480, 511.
[2] R. Nurkse, *Internationale Kapitalbewegungen*, Vienna, 1935.
[3] Similar conclusion has recently been reached by Professor Viner. He recognizes now that his earlier analysis is at least partially wrong and conceded at the outset " that, in the case, for instance, of the initiation of continuing unilateral remittances, the aggregate demand for commodities, in the sense of the amounts buyers are willing to purchase at the prevailing prices, will, in the absence of price changes, fall in the paying country and rise in the lending country, and that unless there is an extreme and unusual distortion of the relative demands for different classes of commodities from their previous proportions this shift in demands

In the restatements of Haberler, Iversen, and Nurkse, we find the solution of the problem of transfer. While we must recognize the importance of the shift in demand as a mechanism of transfer, normally, for the reasons given by Nurkse and Iversen, we should expect the barter terms of trade to change as a result of the making of a transfer and, furthermore, to change in the direction indicated by the classical doctrine.

will of itself contribute to an adjustment of the balance of payments to the remittances " (*Studies*, pp. 293-4). Like Nurkse, and with a reason substantially the same as that given by Nurkse, Professor Viner comes to the conclusion " that a unilateral transfer of means of payment may shift the . . . terms of trade in either direction, but is much more likely to shift them against than in favour of the paying country " (*Studies*, pp. 353-360). " The tendency of the terms of trade to move against the paying country will be more marked, *cæteris paribus*, the greater the excess in each country, prior to the transfer, of consumption of native products to consumption of imported products, to the extent that such excess if not due to trade barriers or to higher international than internal transportation costs " (p. 360). See also Viner's interesting chapter on the international mechanism in relation to modern banking process (ibid., pp. 387-436).

CHAPTER VIII

DEVELOPMENTS SINCE 1918: ATTEMPTS TO EXTEND THE MUTUAL INTERDEPENDENCE THEORY OF PRICING TO THE DOMAIN OF INTERNATIONAL ECONOMICS

1. The Case of Joint Production and the Problem of General Equilibrium

Most of the doctrines that we have described in the preceding chapters are based upon a hypothesis of simple production, i.e. production with only one scarce factor, viz. homogeneous labour. This study would be incomplete if we do not take into consideration also the case of joint production, i.e. production with two or more scarce factors of production. Later exponents of the classical theory— Bastable, Edgeworth, and the Cambridge economists, for example—tried to treat the case of joint production by substituting " a unit of productive power " for " a unit of labour " as the unit of measurement of real cost. That treatment is correct in so far as the combination of factors is in a fixed proportion for all commodities. In that case the problem is the same as that of simple production. Therefore the term, " a typical combination of labour and capital," is sometimes explicitly employed to take the place of " a unit of productive power ".

More important, however, is the case when the combination of factors is not in the same proportion for different commodities. As early as 1803 Sismondi noticed the importance of that case.[1] He called attention to the fact that those manufactures which required for their production little capital but considerable labour were produced in countries where wages were low, while countries like England produced those commodities which required much capital.[2] In the eighteen-thirties, Longfield studied

---

[1] We owe the reference to Sismondi to Professor Jacob Viner. See his " Angell's Theory of International Prices ", *J.P.E.*, 1926, vol. xxxiv, p. 622 n.

[2] J. C. L. Simonde de Sismondi, *De la richesse commerciale*, Geneva, 1803, in two volumes. " Il y a certaines manufactures q'un très petit

the case of the existence of different kinds of labour. He found firstly that, other things being equal, each country would export those goods which required for their production those kinds of labour which were abundant in the country and would import those goods which required those kinds of labour which were scarce in it. He said :—

> Suppose two countries between which existed a perfect freedom of intercourse, let them be similarly circumstanced as to soil and climate, but in one the inhabitants are all free, while in the other the labouring part of the population is in a state of slavery. The commerce between those countries will necessarily consist of exchange of the products of harsh disagreeable labour from the country of slave, for the results of skilled and educated labour from the land of freemen. The master will not employ his slave in a more agreeable kind of labour when he can gain a little more by a different sort, whatever be the hardship and disagreeableness. But the freeman will not sell so cheap this additional sacrifice of ease and comfort ; but as his own interests, not those of his master, are concerned, he will learn every kind of skilled labour with greater facility and less expense than the slave.[1]
>
> Hence, independent of every difference of soil and climate, the exchange between two countries such as I have described will consist principally of articles produced by that species of labour which in each country is relatively cheapest.[2]

Secondly, Longfield showed that the wage of each kind of labour was high in the country in which it was scarce and low in the country in which it was abundant.[3] Finally, he

capital suffit pour mettre en mouvement, parce que la matiere prèmière est de peu de valeur, et qu'elle en acquiert une très considerable par le travail d'un seul artisan. Le point de la France et d'Alençon, la dentelle de la Flandre et celle de Mirecourt sont des examples de cette espèce de manufactures. Les femmes qui les travaillent ne gagnoient que 25 à 40 centimes par jour suivant leur habileté. . . . Le bas prix de la main d'oeuvre permet donc toujours aux pays pauvres de vendre certaines productions à meilleur marché que les pays riches ; aussi l'Angleterre, la nation la plus riche de l'Europe, a-t-elle toujours besoin de celles qui ont moin de capitaux qu'elle, non-seulement pour les production qui ne sont pas propres à son climat, mais encore pour celles dont le prix est surtout composé de main d'oeuvre ; tandis qu'elle peut vendre meilleur marché que toute autre nation celles dont le prix est surtout composé de profit ; elle tire des dentelles et des toiles de la France et de l'Allemagne, de la bonnèterie de l'Ecosse, et elle distribue des étoffes, de la quincaillerie, et des marchandises qu'elle a importées des Indes, et non ouvré elle-même, à tout l'occident." (Ibid., i, pp. 256–269.)

[1] M. Longfield, *Lectures on Political Economy*, Dublin, 1834 (*L.S.E.*, reprint, London, 1931), pp. 70–71.

[2] Ibid., p. 240.

[3] M. Longfield, *Three Lectures on Commerce*, Dublin, 1834. " The relative wages of labour in one country may vary by a different law. . . . In one

demonstrated that in a country where slavery existed, capital was scarce and it would export goods which required little " skill and honesty ", while in a country of freemen, the rate of interest was low and it would export goods which required much capital.[1]

Before following that line of thought, we may turn to another line of thought, which has now become associated with the former. The line of thought that we are going to follow is that of the extension of the mutual-interdependence theory of pricing or, in other words, the general equilibrium theory of value, to the domain of international trade. With the possible exception of Cournot,[2] Pareto was the first economist to extend his system of equations for a closed community to the case of two or more trading communities or countries. His way of extension is this : Write, according to the theory of value within a closed community, the system of equations for each of the two trading countries as separate entities. Now the opening of trade between the two countries introduces new unknowns. There are the n quantities of the n commodities exchanged between the two countries, and there is also the rate of exchange between the two currencies. There are $n + 1$ new unknowns. It requires, therefore, $n + 1$ additional equations to determine the economic equilibrium. Since there is a definite relation between the price of a trading commodity in the exporting country and the price in the importing country, we can write an equation for each of the trading commodities according to that relation. For n commodities there are n

country, honesty and skill may be rare and high-priced qualities, and add much to the relative wages of the labourer who is required to possess them. In another country, the general comfortable condition of the people may render the labourer most unwilling to encounter severe toil, and a great increase of price may be necessary to induce him to engage in a disagreeable or unhealthy occupation. In this latter country, honesty, and that attentive disposition which quickly produced skill, may be the general qualifications of the people. On this supposition, if no disturbing causes exist, manufactures which require honesty and skill will exist in the latter country, as the labourers possessing these qualities will sell their labour cheaper in proportion to its productiveness. In these two circumstances all commerce may be said to originate—namely, a difference in the proportion of the productiveness of labour of different kinds, in different countries ; and the different scales by which the relative wages of labour vary in different countries." (Ibid., pp. 56–7.)

[1] Longfield, *Lectures on Political Economy*, p. 241.

[2] See A. A. Cournot, *Researches into the Mathematical Principles of the Theory of Wealth*, first published in French, 1838, English tr. by N. T. Bacons, New York, 1897 ; *Principes se la theorie des richesses*, Paris, 1863 ; *Revue sommaire des doctrines economiques*, Paris, 1877.

equations. We still require one more equation, which is supplied by the condition that in equilibrium the value of imports must be equal to that of exports. The system of equations thus becomes complete.[1]

The disciples of Pareto, such as Barone and Amoroso, have copied Pareto's method of dealing with the problem without any important alteration.

2. OHLIN'S THEORY OF INTERNATIONAL TRADE

In the last decade,[2] there have been many important attempts made to extend the mutual interdependence theory or the general equilibrium theory to the domain of international economics. Among them the most important are those of Professors Ohlin and Haberler.[3] Professor Haberler's theory is essentially an extension of the classical theory and

---

[1] Vilfredo Pareto, *Cours d'économie politique*, Lausanne, vol. i, 1896, sec. 294, esp. pp. 180–2 n.

[2] A word may be said of Professor Angell's *Theory of International Prices*. In that work he tries to criticize the classical theory and to work out an alternative doctrine. In fact, however, most of his criticisms are unsound, and he is not successful in producing an independent analysis. (a) He criticizes the doctrine of comparative costs mainly on the ground " that comparative costs do not, *in themselves alone*, provide a sufficient *a priori* explanation of the course and terms of trade " (p. 373). We wonder who was the classical economist that Angell had in mind when he made that statement, because we fail to find any important economist who has committed the error. The " alternative doctrine " worked out by him is only the Marshallian doctrine with the modification that inertia, imperfect competition, etc., often prevent the actual rate reaching the point *P*. That is, however, not an alternative doctrine to the classical doctrine, for no classical economist would deny the modification suggested by Angell. (b) On the classical theory of international price relationships Angell does not make any important attack. But he rightly calls attention to the possibility of the existence of wide differences in prices in different countries greater than costs of transport, arising out of a lack of accurate information, a lack of sufficient initiative and enterprise, a lack of trade connections, or to the fact that production has already reached the point of maximum utilization of the existing available plant (pp. 379 ff.). (c) He next discusses the transfer problem. He finds that Hume's law " is sound in its underlying principles, but has practical value when the specie-flow analysis is replaced " by an explanation resting on the effects that changes in the demand and supply of the bills of exchange produce in the volume of bank credits and deposits and in the levels of general prices (pp. 400 ff.). His theory of transfer, therefore, is only the classical theory, but he emphasizes the importance of bank credits and discounts the importance of the movement of gold.

[3] For other attempts towards the same end, see Yntema's *A Mathematical Reformation of the General Theory of International Trade* and Whale's *International Trade*.

has been reviewed in Chapter IV above. Professor Ohlin's Work,[1] on the other hand, deals with the case of joint production at the very outset and is really an attempt at an alternative approach to the problem of international trade. Although we cannot approve of his hostile attitude towards the classical theory and cannot see, as he does, how the latter is not reconcilable with his theory, we think that his great work opens a new chapter in the history of thought on the economics of international trade. It is in his hands that the two trends of thought described in the preceding section are, for the first time, combined to form a comprehensive theory of international trade.

We may now examine his extension of the mutual inter-dependence theory of pricing to the domain of inter-regional and international trade.[2] He begins with the consideration of a case of full mobility and divisibility within each market and assumes the supply of the various factors of production to be constant and known. On those assumptions the price system of each market, if *isolated*, contains five sets of functional relations : (i) The quantity—" the technical coefficient "—of any one of the factors of production needed for the production of one unit of any one of the commodities produced is a function of the prices of factors of production. The form of that function is determined by the physical conditions of production. In other words, the technical coefficients depend partly on the physical conditions of production and partly on the prices of factors of production. (ii) The price of any one commodity is equal to its cost of production, which is obtained by multiplying the quantity of each factor required (i.e. the technical coefficient) by its price. (iii) Demand for each commodity is a function, on the one hand, of the prices of all commodities and, on the other hand, of the various individual incomes of the inhabitants. The form of the demand function is determined by the wants and desires of the consumers. (iv) Each individual income in turn depends partly on the number of units of the various factors the individual owns and partly on their prices. (v) The demand for each factor of

[1] Bertil Ohlin, *Inter-regional and International Trade*, Cambridge, Mass., 1935.
[2] Since Professor Ohlin sees only quantitative differences between inter-regional and international trade, his treatment of the one is applicable to the other. In this chapter read " inter-regional " or " inter-market " as " international ".

production—which is the sum of the products of the demand for each commodity, into the production of which that factor enters, multiplied by the quantity that factor needed for producing one unit of that commodity—is equal to the supply of that factor which is assumed to be given. From those five sets of relations it is obvious that all prices of goods and of factors are ultimately, in each region at any given moment, determined by (a) the wants and desires of consumers, (b) the conditions of ownership of the factors of production which affect individual incomes and thus demand (c) the supply of productive factors and (d) the physical conditions of production. Those four basic data being given, one can deduce from the five sets of relations given above both factor prices and commodity prices.

He next investigates the conditions, which make the opening of trade between different markets possible. It is obvious that " the immediate cause of trade is always that goods can be bought cheaper from outside in terms of money than they can be produced at home, and vice versa. . . . In other words inequality as to the relative commodity prices in the isolated state is a necessary condition for the establishment of trade ".[1] That does not, however, answer the question. One has to go further and to investigate what lies behind such inequality in prices. From the one market theory described in the preceding paragraph, it is clear that equality or inequality in prices depends on the factors (a), (b), (c), and (d). Factor (d), however, is "everywhere the same", and may hence be left out of account.[2] Consequently, differences in commodity prices depend upon the state of the supply of the industrial agents, i.e. factor (c), and upon demand conditions—factors (a) and (b) taken together. The supply of factors of production *in relation* to demand creates what he calls " the relative scarcities of factors ". " If differences in supply between the regions are balanced by differences in demand, the relative scarcity of all factors and relative commodity prices will be the same," and hence trade becomes impossible. In reality, however, the relative scarcity of productive factors is not the same in different isolated regions. It is that difference in the relative scarcities of productive factors that is a necessary condition

---

[1] *Inter-regional and International Trade*, pp. 12 ff.
[2] Ibid., pp. 14, 15.

to the opening of trade.[1] That condition is fulfilled when the equipment of productive factors is distinctly different in various regions, for it is practically inconceivable that a corresponding consumers' demand, being indirectly a demand for factors, should exactly offset the difference in factor supply.[2] Then he comes to the following conclusion :—

> Roughly speaking, abundant industrial agents are relatively cheap, scanty agents relatively dear, in each region. Commodities requiring for their production much of the former and little of the latter are exported in exchange for goods that call for factors in the opposite proportions. Thus, indirectly, factors in abundant supply are exported and factors in scanty supply are imported.[3]

Although "inequality in the prices of factors in the isolated state is sufficient to cause different commodity prices and thus to cause trade ", that condition alone is not sufficient to determine entirely the nature of international trade. Even given the relative scarcity of factors, we cannot know definitely " which and how many factors will be cheaper in one region than in the other ". The difference in relative factor prices can reveal itself in the form of absolute difference in commodity prices (which is the immediate cause of trade) only through the rates of the foreign exchanges. The latter depend upon the condition of the balance of trade (i.e. the equilibrium between imports and exports), and thus upon the *intensity of reciprocal demand*.[4]

What would be the price systems in the trading regions after trade is opened between them ? The first of the five sets of relations given above would remain the same in each of the trading regions.[5] The only difference would be that one would have only to deal in each region with those commodities which are still produced after the opening of trade. Since it is assumed that each commodity is to be produced only in one region, the commodities to be dealt

---

[1] *Inter-regional and International Trade*, p. 15. For " relative scarcity of factors ", see pp. 10–12, 16, 19, 20, 22, and *passim*.
  [2] Ibid., pp. 16 f.   [3] Ibid., p. 92.   [4] Ibid., pp. 21, 22.
  [5] Not only it remains the same in its region, but the form of the function would also be the same in all trading regions, since the physical conditions of production are everywhere the same.

with in each region are simply its exported commodities. A similar change would be made of the second set of relations. The more important changes are found in the third and the fifth set of relations. The demand function which depends, before trade, partly on the prices of all home products, now depends not only on prices of home products but also on prices of imported goods. Similarly, on the supply side, each trading country has now to produce a quantity of those commodities on the production of which it specializes sufficient not only for its own consumption but also for the total consumption of them at home and abroad.[1] Furthermore, prices of foreign products can be converted into prices in terms of local currency only through the medium of the foreign exchanges. Hence demand is also a function of the exchange rate. Similarly the fifth set of relations which involves demand is also affected by the variation in the rate of exchange. Thus, the exchange rate must be simultaneously solved with the price systems of the trading regions as a whole and "a solution of the fundamental problem of foreign exchange . . . is tantamount to constructing a theory of international trade ".[2] According to Professor Ohlin, the rate of exchange which gives equilibrium would be such that the imports from and the exports to each of the trading regions balance. So is the price system of the trading regions.

Professor Ohlin's theory of international trade as described in the preceding paragraphs is, we think, reconcilable with the classical theory, as restated by Professor Haberler. Professor Haberler, as indicated above, pointed out that each trading country exports those goods which it produces at lower opportunity costs and imports those goods which it produces at higher opportunity costs than other countries. Now commodities requiring for their production much of the abundant factors and little of the scarce factors are commodities that the country can produce at lower opportunity costs ; and commodities requiring much of the scarce factors and little of the abundant factors are commodities produced at higher opportunity costs. In that way Professor Ohlin's theory may be combined with Professor Haberler's theory.

[1] *Inter-regional and International Trade*, pp. 18 f.
[2] Ibid., p. viii.

3. THE THEORY OF INTERNATIONAL PRICE RELATIONSHIPS IN THE CASE OF JOINT PRODUCTION

Professor Ohlin also examines the problems of international price relationships in the case of joint production. He starts with the case of zero cost of production. Upon that assumption, prices of commodities would be equal in the trading countries. The tendency of commodity prices towards equality among trading countries, together with the new conditions of the fifth set of relations, exercises an influence on the prices and employment of factors, after trade is opened between different countries. The first effect of trade on factor prices is given by Ohlin in the following passage :—

The amounts paid for the use of all the productive factors during a year is always equal to the total value of the goods produced. As trade and inter-regional division of labour means a more efficient production and a larger volume of commodities, the prices of the factors must obviously rise in terms of commodities. Assuming that the commodity price level in each region has been kept constant, factor prices expressed in terms of money must rise. . . . What determines the extent of that rise ? Evidently this is to ask if all regions reap any gain from trade and what determines the amount of the gain that goes to each of them.[1]

In other words, the factor prices in each region taken as a whole will, as a result of trade, tend to rise relative to commodity prices ; and the amount of gain of trade or the barter terms of trade determine the degree of such a rise. That is, in effect, the Seniorian doctrine resuscitated. The relative prices of factors in a trading region also change when trade is opened. " The factor which is relatively abundant becomes more in demand and fetches a higher price, whereas the factor that is scantily supplied becomes less in demand and gets a relatively lower reward than before. *The relative scarcity of the productive factors is made less different in the two regions.*"[2] That generalization of a tendency towards international equalization of factor prices

[1] *Inter-regional and International Trade*, p. 42.
[2] Ibid., p. 35. " Thus, the mobility of goods to some extent compensates the lack of inter-regional mobility of the factors : or . . . trade mitigates the disadvantages of the unsuitable geographical distribution of the productive facilities. That is the cause of gain from inter-regional trade " (p. 42). See also pp. 96 f.

needs some qualifications. First the proposition presupposes the comparability and similarity of factors in different countries, but in fact " the qualities of the productive factors and of the various commodities differ, even when they are treated as being the same factor or sub-factor or as the same commodity ".[1] Although the existence of those differences in the quality of the factors makes the proposition less precise, that does not, according to Professor Ohlin, invalidate the main argument of the proposition. Second, even upon the assumption of similarity of factors in different regions, there will be no complete equalization of factor prices. The reason is :—

The localization of industry and thereby the demand for production factors cannot completely adapt themselves to the equipment with them in each region, chiefly because the industrial demand is always the " joint demand " for several factors. Their combination cannot be varied at will ; on the contrary the most economical combination is determined by the prices of the factors and the physical conditions. Consequently, the best adaptation of production to the geographical distribution of industrial agents . . . cannot lead to a complete inter-regional price equalization ; some factors will still command higher prices in one region and lower in the others and vice versa.[2]

Third, " trade does not tend to equalize factor prices when *quite different factors are closely competitive,* being used in one industry to produce the same or a similar commodity while rendering otherwise quite different services." [3] He recognizes that " the factors may be so highly competitive that the result for relative prices is the opposite of what the general rule would lead one to expect ".[4]

Professor Ohlin next discusses the problem of international price relationships with the space factor and transport costs taken into full account. The general effect of the existence of costs of transport is as follows :—

If there were no such costs trade would take place in all or practically all commodities, whereas large groups of commodities are now excluded. In a word, costs of transfer reduce trade and weaken its effects upon prices. These effects were . . . a tendency towards an equalization of commodity

[1] *Inter-regional and International Trade,* p. 97 ; see also pp. 98–100.
[2] Ibid., p. 38.   [3] Ibid., p. 100.
[4] Ibid., p. 103. The problem of factors which exist only in one country is similar ; see pp. 105 f.

and factor prices. That tendency is vitiated by the costs of transfer, although the trade which goes on in spite of them must exercise a price-equalizing influence so far as it goes. Trade means that the outside demand is brought to play on the inside supply and the inside demand on the outside supply. Costs of transfer interfere with this process, and lessen its influence upon prices in different markets.[1]

As between various regions, commodity prices tend to differ by the costs of transfer. But this is true only of goods subject to inter-regional trade ; if the costs of transfer are greater than the differences in the costs of production in the various regions, then naturally each region will produce such goods itself and they will not enter into inter-regional trade.[2]

Following Cairnes and Taussig, he calls the latter " home-market goods " as opposed to imported and exported commodities, which together are called " international goods ". Home-market goods are subdivided by him into " competing home-market goods ", which are in more or less competition with international goods ; and " non-competing home-market goods " which have no direct connection with other goods.[3]

Professor Ohlin shows that the connection between prices of international goods of one country and those of another is less direct than might be assumed at first sight, while the connection between prices of home-market goods in one country and those in another is more direct. The general statement that prices of international goods tend to differ by the costs of transfer needs qualification. It is true only of the relationship between a certain exporting region and the regions which import a particular commodity from it. It is not true of a comparison of prices of the commodity in the various importing regions. " Consider four regions of which A imports certain goods from B, while C obtains the same goods from D. Costs of production in B and D may differ considerably, perhaps as much as the costs of transfer between these regions. Furthermore, the costs of transfer from B to A and from D to C may be quite unequal. It follows that the import prices of A and C may also differ, although not more than the costs of transfer between them.

---

[1] *Inter-regional and International Trade*, p. 145.
[2] Ibid., p. 142.
[3] Ibid., p. 247. " It goes without saying that there are no fixed border lines between these groups. . . . This fact does not impair the usefulness of such distinctions " (p. 248).

The difference will in most cases be smaller, but no general rule can be given as to its dimensions. Inter-regional price relations are fixed by the costs of transfer only with regard to the regions which trade with one another in the goods concerned. Prices of inter-regional goods in two groups of regions which do not trade in them are not directly related." [1] Even when different exporting regions have common markets which connect their prices, the relation between prices in various producing regions is still " far from fixed ", because " the position of the common market may vary ".[2]

The inter-relation of prices of home-market goods (which are of similar technological composition) in different regions is more close than appears at first sight. Professor Ohlin emphasizes that international discrepancies in home-market prices are kept within narrow limits not only through the potentiality of home-market goods to enter into trade, which would come into existence if international price differences came to exceed the costs of transfer, but also through the actual trade in *other* goods. In the case of joint production, the production of a finished product passes through many stages of production. Goods in any one of the different stages of production—raw materials, semi-finished goods, auxiliary materials (tools, machines, etc.), and finished consumers' goods—may enter into international trade when goods in other stages remain as domestic goods. When a raw material is an international good and the goods, which are products of that material, are not international goods, the tendency towards an international equalization in the price of the former leads to a similar equalization of the prices of the latter. The latter tendency follows the former, because the price of a product must in equilibrium equal its cost of production. The tendency of the price of the products of that material, however, is not towards a complete equalization, even upon the assumption that the technical conditions of production are everywhere the same. For that material may not be the only factor of production and accounts should be taken of other factors which also enter into the production of those products. In general, we may say that international trade in goods in the earlier stages (materials, machinery, etc.) tends to make the cost of

---

[1] *Inter-regional and International Trade*, p. 156.
[2] Ibid., p. 157.

production and hence the prices of domestic goods of later stages more closely related in different countries than they would otherwise be. Similarly, if goods in the earlier stages do not enter into international trade but goods in the later stages are international goods, the trade in the latter affects the prices of the former by making their prices more closely related in different countries. The price relation of domestic goods of identical technological composition among nations also becomes closer when the substitutes of those goods enter into trade. International trade in the latter prevents great differences in the prices of the former among countries. " The case is similar when two or more commodities are subject to joint supply, i.e. are manufactured in one process of production out of a common raw material ; their prices are naturally intimately related. If in certain countries only one of them enters international trade, the prices of the other belonging to the home-market group are affected by their trade. Increased demand for the former commodity and its higher price in these countries will tend to depress the prices of the other goods. In other words, home-market prices tend to vary in the same way in all these countries." [1]

There is another influence of a similar, though still more indirect, character, i.e. the influence through factor prices. Factor prices, upon the assumption of immobility of factors, are a kind of home-market prices. " But the trade in commodities of whatever sort tends to bring factor prices in various countries closer to each other; thereby costs of production of goods that do not enter international trade—home market goods—are brought more into harmony. The price at which a flat can be hired depends largely upon the height of the rate of interest. If the inter-regional differences in interest levels are reduced through trade, a tendency towards equalization of the price of flats is clearly brought about." [2]

There is another equalizing influence which is peculiar to " competing home-market goods ". By its nature that kind of goods offers intense competition with international goods and hence its demand will react so as " to counteract any tendency towards price variations in one region exclusively " :—

Although a certain commodity is an export commodity in

[1] *Inter-regional and International Trade*, pp. 153 f.
[2] Ibid., p. 154.

A (exported to C) and a home-market commodity in B, the prices will not vary arbitrarily ; a special case of this sort is " rival demand ", which exists when one commodity can be substituted for another. International trade in margarine tends to prevent great differences in butter prices between countries where the latter is a home-market commodity. Furthermore, prices of competing home-market goods in B and C, which are both importing similar products from A, will move more or less in harmony. If competition between imported and domestic goods is very close, then home-market prices in B and C tend to be equal, and to exceed A's export prices by the costs of transfer.[1]

Finally, he endorses Professor Angell's doctrine that in spite of all influences which tend to equalize prices, the existence of " friction " makes possible wide differences in prices in different countries greater than costs of transfer.[2]

So far we have dealt with Professor Ohlin's doctrine concerning price relations of a particular commodity or a particular group of commodities. There remains his doctrine of factor-price relationships and of relationships of general commodity price-levels among trading countries. He again emphasizes the importance of costs of transfer. He lays down the following general rule : Productive factors situated close to the demand for their products (or so situated that those products can be easily moved there) obtain higher value than distant factors, and a country with its productive factors so situated will have higher levels both of factor prices and of commodity prices.[3] That can be illustrated thus :—

Suppose . . . three regions A, B, and C . . . B and C have a similar equipment of productive factors (farm-land, etc). C is either situated further away from A than is B, or its means of communication with this region are for other reasons not so good as those of B. Costs of transport for import and export goods are assumed to be about equal. It follows . . . that B's productive factors will be in relatively greater demand than C's, in other words that their prices will be higher. The general level of commodity prices, as measured by a whole-sale price index of the ordinary type, is therefore also higher in B than in C. It is true that import prices are higher in C, but export goods common to these two regions command higher prices in the ports of B than in C, since they are closer

---

[1] *Inter-regional and International Trade*, p. 155.
[2] Ibid., pp. 163–6.   [3] Ibid., p. 162.

to the market in A. The consequent relative cheapness of C factors tends to make home market goods in C also cheaper than in B. Observe, however, that some home market goods in C are *import* goods in B. They may well cost more in the former regions. On the other hand, certain goods which B is able to export are home market goods in C, and will probably cost less than in B. These two qualifications do not impair the conclusion that the general price, as commonly computed, is lower in a region far from its markets than in another with similar equipment of productive factors but situated closer to the main markets.[1]

In the case of two or more trading nations, commodity price-levels would also be different, if costs of transport for imported and exported goods were not equal. Suppose two countries A and B. If A imports goods that are easier to transport than the imported goods of B, then the level of international prices must " evidently be lower in A than in B ".[2] The differences in the costs of transport and those in the grades of labour being taken care of, " high level for wages goes hand in hand with a high commodity price level." [3] Thus a country with relative scarcity of common labour will have both high wages and high commodity price-levels.[4] There is still another factor influencing price relations. " Other things being equal, home market prices will be low in regions where the factors of production important to home market industries are cheap."[5] Finally, the size of the market also affects price relations. " Home market goods, *ceteris paribus*, tend to be cheaper in regions where the home market is large, i.e. the number of people great, their standard of living high, and their demand for the commodity in question lively."[6] Taking his position as a whole, it is obvious that his doctrine is a continuation of the doctrines of Ricardo, Senior, Mill, and Taussig.[7]

The next contribution of Professor Ohlin is his analysis of international movements of factors of production and their relations to commodity movements and to international price relationships. In general, natural resources are immobile. The problem of factor movements concerns those of labour and capital only. To both labour and capital movements the obstacles consist not so much in

---

[1] *Inter-regional and International Trade*, p. 161.
[2] Ibid., p. 152. [3] Ibid., p. 279.
[4] Ibid., pp. 277 f. [5] Ibid., pp. 162 f.
[6] Ibid., p. 163. [7] Ibid., pp. 280 f., 282 f.

actual costs of transport as in a psychological aversion to changes. " However, the stimulus which makes labourers and capitalists overcome the obstacles is chiefly a desire to receive a higher price, i.e. higher wages or interest rates." [1] What is the effect of those movements, if they do exist ? " In general, factor movements—like commodity movements—tend to equalize factor prices in different districts," and hence bring the price systems of trading regions closer together.[2]

What are the relations between factor movements and commodity movements ? In general those two movements act as substitutes for one another. Through the exchange of commodities, not only commodity prices but also the prices of the productive factors are to some extent equalized among trading regions. Therefore international discrepancies in factor prices are reduced and international factor movements are rendered unnecessary. Factor movements make the differences of relative factor prices less and hence reduce the need for international trade. Thus he says :—

> Variations would increase price discrepancies will be counteracted both by a change in trade, which directly affects commodity prices and indirectly factor prices, and by a change in factor movements, which affects the latter prices directly and the former indirectly. The tendency towards price equalization thus operates in two ways.[3]

> Everything depends upon the intensity of the reaction of factor prices and therefore factor movements when trade varies ; and upon the intensity of the reaction of commodity prices and therefore trade when factor movements vary.[4]

There end recent developments of the theory of international price relationships upon the assumption of joint production. We may now try to sum up the contributions of the authors, whose doctrines we have explained in the preceding chapters, by stating briefly the present position of the theory of international price relationships.

---

[1] *Inter-regional and International Trade*, p. 168.
[2] Ibid., p. 227.   [3] Ibid., p. 170.
[4] Ibid., p. 169. See also pp. 168 ff., 224 ff., 178 ff., 339 ff., 359 ff.

CHAPTER IX

CONCLUSION

1. The Present Position of the Theory of International Price Relationships

The subject of international price relationships, as pointed out in the first chapter, comprehends four distinct problems, viz. (1) the relation between the value of money in one country and the value of money in other countries ; (2) the relation of the price level of one country to the price level in other countries ; (3) the price relations of goods of identical technological composition among trading countries ; and (4) the comparison of prices of factors of production, especially labour, in different countries. Let V_a denote the value of money in country A ; V_b that in country B ; P_a the general price level in A ; P_b the price level in B ; p_a the price of an article in A ; p_b the price of a technologically similar article in B ; W_a the average wage of labour in A ; W_b the average wage in B ; and R the rate of exchange, i.e. the number of units of A's currency that a unit of B's currency is exchanged for. Then problem (1) becomes the problem of the relation between V_a and $V_b R$; problem (2) that between P_a and $P_b R$; problem (3) that between p_a and $p_b R$; and problem (4) that between W_a and $W_b R$.

Upon the assumptions of simple production, of free mobility of both factors of production and products, and of *zero* cost of transport, international price relationships would, in equilibrium, be as follows :—

$$R = \frac{V_a}{V_b} = \frac{P_a}{P_b} = \frac{p_a}{p_b} = \frac{W_a}{W_b} \qquad (1)$$

The relation $R V_b = V_a$ represents the classical doctrine of the international comparison of the values of moneys. The relations $R P_b = P_a$, $R p_b = p_a$, and $R W_b = W_a$ follow from the assumption that both factors and products could freely move from one country to another without any cost of transport.

If we discard the assumption that factors of production are perfectly mobile between countries and introduce the assumption underlying the classical analysis, viz. that labour and capital are immobile between nations, equation (1) becomes :—

$$R = \frac{V_a}{V_b} = \frac{P_a}{P_b} = \frac{p_a}{p_b} = \frac{W_a P_m m_b}{W_b P_n n_a} \qquad (2)$$

in which P_n is the average export price of country A ; P_m the average import price of A, or the average export price of B ; n_a denotes the efficiency of A's labour in the production of its exports (i.e. the quantity of goods that an average unit of labour will produce in A) ; m_b denotes the efficiency of B's labour in the production of B's exports. The relation

$$RW_b P_n n_a = W_a P_m m_b$$

is only another way of writing an equation given in Chapter IV, Section 7 above, $(P_n \div P_m)$ representing the barter term of trade.

We may also abandon the unrealistic assumption that the cost of carrying products from one country to another is zero. As soon as we introduce transport cost, however, we are introducing four important changes. Firstly the price of goods of identical technological composition is not the same for all trading countries. The price in the importing country is normally higher than that in the exporting country by the cost of carriage. Let us assume that the cost of carrying an article from A to B is the same as that from B to A and is equal to t. If p_a is the price of any article in A, then the price (p_b) of an article of identical technological composition in B, when expressed in terms of A's currency, cannot be greater than $(p_a + t)$ and cannot be less than $(p_a - t)$. In the former case it is an article exported from A and in the latter case it is an article imported to A. Thus for every article which enters into international trade we have :—

$$R = \frac{(p_a \pm t)}{p_b}$$

Secondly there appears a new class of goods, viz. domestic goods, which do not enter into international trade. Although it remains true that the price of a domestic good in A cannot be greater than the price of a similar good in B plus the cost of carrying it from B to A and cannot be smaller than its price in B less the cost of carrying it from A to B, the prices of domestic goods are more or less independent of international markets and will stand in no direct connection with the rate of exchange. Thirdly, the general price levels become different in different countries. The degree of the difference between the general price level of A and that of B depends partly on the costs of transport and partly on the price levels of domestic goods of the two countries. Finally, the relation between the wage level of A and that of B is also somewhat different. We have now the following relation—

$$W_a P_m m'_b = R W_b P_n n_a$$

in which P_m (i.e. the average import price of A) is no longer the same as the average export price of B. The term m'_b is equal to $m_b \times$ (the average export price of B ÷ the average import price of A). Thus the equation of foreign exchanges now has the following form :—

$$R = \frac{V_a}{V_b} = \frac{P_a}{h \times P_b} = \frac{p_a \pm t}{p_b} = \frac{W_a P_m m'_b}{W_b P_n n_a} \qquad (3)$$

in which h represents the difference in the price levels of the two countries.

If we discard the assumption of simple production and introduce the case of joint production, the price relations between countries become closer in many ways. The nature of the price relations is that described in Chapter VIII, Section 3 above.

2. THE SAME SUBJECT—*Continued*

The next important question in the theory is that of the possible causes of disturbances.[1] Broadly speaking, we may classify causes of disturbances into two groups : first, monetary disturbances and, second, disturbances connected with the state of the balance of international payments.

[1] " By a ' disturbance ' to international equilibrium will be meant a change in *one* of the elements in a pre-existing equilibrium such as to require a new equilibrium, and that this change, whether it takes the form of a series of crop failure, of international tributes or loans, of new import duties, or of a relative change in the demands of the two countries for each other's products, is presumed to continue indefinitely, and its cessation is treated as a new change in the reverse direction " (Viner, *Studies in the Theory of International Trade*, p. 290).

The latter include changes in any of the following factors : (1) the desires and wants of the consumers, (2) the conditions of ownerships of factors of production, (3) the supply of factors, (4) the efficiency and productivity of factors, (5) the technical conditions of production, (6) the non-commodity or invisible items, and (7) the costs of carriage. Changes in any one of the above factors will lead to changes either in prices or in the rate of exchange or in both.

The last but the most important part of the theory is that dealing with the mechanism which corrects the disturbances.

In discussing the problem of monetary disturbances, one should distinguish between the case of a fixed rate of exchange and that of a varying rate of exchange. The international gold standard is a typical example of the former, while paper currencies are typical examples of the latter. International price adjustments under an international gold standard have been dealt with by the authors described in Chapter V above. International price adjustments under paper currencies form the subject matter of Chapter VI, in which we have already given the present position of the theory concerning the correction of monetary disturbances in paper currencies.

To the disturbances arising from the state of international balance of payments, we have also devoted a separate chapter, i.e. Chapter VII.

One interesting problem connected with the dynamics of the theory has not yet been explicitly dealt with in the present essay. That is the question whether movements of prices in different countries are in the same direction. Upon the assumption of an international gold standard, we may lay down the following general rule : When disturbances are caused by monetary factors, the movement of prices of factors of production and of their products in one country tends to be in the *same* direction as the movement of factor prices and product prices in another country ; but when disturbances originate from the state of the balance of payments, the movement of prices in one country and that in the other are in *opposite* directions. In the case of dissimilar currencies, although it remains true that disturbances originating from the balance of payments would lead to opposite movements of prices, it is not certain whether monetary disturbance would lead to similar movements of prices.

There is, of course, much room for improvement, especially in the dynamics of the theory. Professor Robbins has recently pointed out

that it does not contain sufficient analysis either of imperfect competition or of the international aspects of short-run oscillations . . . are criticisms . . . of the present state of the theory. It is not clear how much we really do not know as regards imperfect competition in international markets. My impression is that most of the knowledge does exist, scattered about in works on particular problems, and that the main business here is to give it coherent shape. But as regards short-run oscillations there is no doubt much more to do.[1]

In that passage Professor Robbins indicates the directions in which progress may be made in the theory of international trade and the theory of international price relationships.

[1] *Economica*, Feb., 1937, pp. 104–5.

Y

BIBLIOGRAPHY

Abbreviations used

A.E.R.	*American Economic Review.*
A.E.S.S.	*American Encyclopedia of Social Sciences.*
An.	*Annuals of American Academy of Political and Social Sciences.*
E.J.	*Economic Journal.*
Econ.	*Economica.*
Economet.	*Econometrica.*
J.A.S.A.	*Journal of American Statistical Association.*
J.d.E.	*Journal des économists.*
J.P.E.	*Journal of Political Economy.*
J.R.S.S.	*Journal of Royal Statistical Society.*
J.S.S.P.	*Journal de la société de statistique de Paris.*
L.S.E.	London School of Economics.
Q.J.E.	*Quarterly Journal of Economics.*
R.d.E.P.	*Revue d'économie politique.*
R.d.H.D.E.	*Revue d'histoire des doctrines économiques et sociales,* 1908–1912 ; or, since 1913, *Revue d'histoire économique et sociale.*
R.E.I.	*Revue économique internationale.*
R.E.S.	*Review of Economic Statistics* (Cambridge, Mass.).
W.A.	*Weltwirtschaftliches Archiv.*

1. Mercantilistic Theories

ARIAS, G. " Les idées économiques d'Antonio Serra," *J.d.E.*, 1922.

ASGILL, J. *Several Assertions Proved.* London, 1696.

—— *Remarks on the. . . . Establishing of a Land-Bank.* London, 1696.

ASHLEY, W. J. " The Tory Origin of Free Trade Policy," *Q.J.E.*, 1897.

—— *An Introduction to English Economic History and Theory.* London, 1906.

BARBON, N. *A Discourse of Trade.* London, 1690.

—— *A Discourse concerning Coining the New Money Lighter, in answer to Mr. Locke's Consideration.* London, 1696.

BEER, M. *Early British Economics.* London, 1938.

BELLONI, G. *A Dissertation on Commerce.* First published in Italian, English ed., London, 1752.

BODIN, J. *La réponse de Jean Bodin à M. de Malestroit.* Paris, 1568. New edition issued with an introduction by H. Hauser, Paris, 1932.

—— *Discovrs sur le rehavssement et diminvtion des monnoyes tant d'or que d'argent, et le moyen d'y remedier.* Paris, 1578.

—— *Les six livres de la République,* 1576, done into English by R. Knolles, London, 1606.

BOISQUILBERT, PIERRE DE. *Détail de la France.* 1697.

—— *Factum de la France.* 1707. (Both reprinted in *Collection des principaux économists,* edited by E. Daire, Paris, 1843–7.)

BREWSTER, FRANCIS. *Essays on Trade and Navigation.* London, 1695.
—— *New Essays on Trade.* London, 1702.
BRISCOE, JOHN. *A Discourse on the Late Fund.* London, 1694.
—— *A Discourse of Money, etc.* London, 1696.
—— *To the Knights, etc.: A Short Scheme . . . for a National Land Bank.* MS. 1695.
—— *Reasons humbly offered for the Establishment of the National Land Bank.* MS. 1695.
—— *Defence of Dr. H. Chamberlain's Bank of Land Credit.* MS. 1696.
BROWNE, JOHN. *An Essay on Trade in General ; and, that of Ireland in Particular.* Dublin, 1728.
BURGHILL, F. *A Proposal for the Speedy Enrichment both of the Bank and the People.* London, 1662.
BURGON, J. W. *Life and Time of Sir Thomas Greshams.* London, 1839.
BUTCHART, M. *Money : Selected passages presenting the concepts of money in the English tradition, 1640–1935.* London, 1935.
CANTILLON, PHILIP. *The Analysis of Trade.* London, 1759.
CANTILLON, RICHARD. *Essai sur la nature du commerce en général.* Probably written in 1730–34, first printed in 1755. New edition with an English translation and other materials, ed. by H. Higg, London, 1931.
CARY, JOHN. *A Discourse concerning the East India Trade.* London, 1695.
—— *An Essay on the Coyn and Credit of England.* Bristol, 1696.
CHAMBERLAIN, H. *Papers relating to a Bank of Credit upon Land Security.* Edinburgh, 1693.
—— *A Proposal for a Bank of Secure Current Credit.* London, 1695.
—— *A Few Proposals humbly recommending . . . the Establishing a Land-Credit.* Edinburgh, 1700.
—— *Several Matters relating to . . . Establishment of a Land Credit.* Edinburgh, 1700.
CHILD, JOSIAH. *Brief Observation concerning Trade and Interest of Money.* London, 1668.
—— *A New Discourse of Trade.* London, 1693.
—— *The Great Honour and Advantages of the East-India Trade.* London, 1697.
CLEMENT, SIMON. *The General Notions of Money, Trade, and Exchanges.* London, 1695.
—— *A Dialogue . . . concerning the Falling of Guineas.* London, 1696.
COKE, ROGER. *A Discourse of Trade.* London, 1670.
—— *England's Improvements.* London, 1675.
—— *A Treatise concerning the Regulation of the Coyn of England.* London, 1696.
COSSA, LUIGI. *Introduction to the Study of Political Economy,* translated by L. Dyer. London, 1893.
CUNNINGHAM, WILLIAM. *Growth of English Industry and Commerce in Modern Times.* Cambridge, 1882. 1927.
—— " The Progress of Economic Doctrine in England in the Eighteenth Century," *E.J.,* 1891.

DAVANZATI-BOSTICHI, BERNARDO. *Lezione delle moneta*, 1588, translated as *A discourse upon Coin* by J. Toland. London,1696.
DAVENANT, CHARLES. *The Political and Commercial Works of Charles Davenant*, ed. by C. Whitworth. London, 1771.
DECKER, MATHEW. *An Essay on the Causes of the Decline of the Foreign Trade*. Edinburgh, 1744 ; 1756.
DEFOE, DANIEL. *An Enquiry into the Disposition of the Equivalent*, 1706.
—— *A Tour through Great Britain*. London, 1724–7. New ed. by G. D. H. Cole London, 1928.
—— *A Plan of the English Commerce*. London, 1728.
—— *The Works of Daniel Defoe*, ed. by W. Hazlitt. London, 1840.
DEMPSEY, B. W. " The Historical Emergence of Quantity Theory," *Q.J.E.*, November, 1935.
DUBOIS, A. *Précis de l'histoire des doctrines economiques*. Paris, 1903.
FETTER, F. W. " The term Favourable Balance of Trade," *Q.J.E.*, 1935.
FORBONNAIS, FRANÇOIS VÉRON DE. *Élémens du commerce*. 2nd. ed. Leyden, 1754 ; 3rd. ed., Paris, 1766.
—— *Principes économiques*. Amsterdam, 1767. (Reprinted in Daire's *Collection*, 1847.)
FORTREY, SAMUEL. *England's Interest and Improvement*. London, 1663.
FURNISS, E. S. *The Position of Labourer in a System of Nationalism*. New York, 1920.
GALIANI, FERDINANDO. *Della moneta*. Naples, 1750. An abridged English translation is found in A. E. Monroe's *Early Economic Thought*, Cambridge, Mass., 1927.
GEE, J. *The Trade and Navigation of Great Britain Considered*. London, 1729 ; 1767.
GERVAISE, I. *The System or Theory of Trade of the World*. London, 1720.
GONNARD, RENÉ. " Les doctrines mercantilistes au xviie siècle en Portugal," *R.d.H.D.E.*, 1935.
GREGORY, T. E. " The Economics of Employment in England, 1660–1713," *Economica*, 1921.
HALES, JOHN. *A Discourse of the Common Weal of this Realm of England*. Written about 1549, first published in 1581 by W. S. New ed. by Elizabeth Lamond, Cambridge, 1893.
HAMILTON, EARL J. *American Treasure and the Price Revolution in Spain, 1501–1650*. Cambridge, Mass., 1934.
—— *Money, Prices, and Wages in Valencia, Aragon, and Navarre, 1351–1500*. Cambridge, Mass., 1936.
HARRIS, JOSEPH. *Essays upon Money and Coins*. London, 1757–8.
HARSIN, PAUL. " L'afflux des métaux précieux au xvie siècle et la théorie de la monnaie chez les auteurs français," *R.d.H.D.E.*, 1927.
—— *Les doctrines monétaires et financiers de la France du xvie au xviiie siècle*. Paris, 1928.
HECKSCHER, ELI F. *Mercantilism*, translated by Mendel Shapiro. London, 1935.

HIGGS, HENRY. " Cantillon's Place in Economics," *Q.J.E.*, 1892.

HOLLANDER, J. H. (ed.). Reprint of Economic Tracts. Baltimore, 1903.

HOLTROP, M. W. " Theories of the Velocity of Circulation of Money in Early Economic Literature," *E.J.*, *Economic History Supplement*, 1929.

HOUGHTON, JOHN. *A Collection of Letters for the Improvement of Husbandry and Trade*, vol. ii. London, 1683.

HOUGHTON, THOMAS. *A Plain and Easy Method for Supplying the Scarcity of Money and Promoting Trade*. London, 1696.

—— *The Alteration of the Coyn*. London, 1695.

JOHNSON, E. A. J. " British Mercantilist Doctrines concerning the ' Export of Work ' and ' Foreign Paid Incomes '," *J.P.E.*, 1932.

—— " Unemployment and Consumption : the Mercantile View," *Q.J.E.*, 1932.

—— " Gerard de Malynes and the Theory of Foreign Exchanges," *A.E.R.*, 1933.

—— *Predecessors of Adam Smith*. New York, 1937.

JUSTICE, A. *A General Treatise of Monies and Exchanges*. London, 1707.

KNIGHT, MELVIN M., and others. *Economic History of Europe*. Boston, 1928.

LAW, JOHN. *Money and Credit Considered*. Glasgow, 1705.

—— *Œuvres complètes*, ed. by Paul Harsin. Paris, 1934.

LE BRANDRU. " La théorie quantitative de la monnaie au xvie siècle," *R.E.P.*, 1934.

LEWIŃSKI, JAN ST. *The Founders of Political Economy*. London, 1922.

LIPSON, E. *The Economic History of England*, vol. iii. London, 1931.

LOCKE, JOHN. *Some Considerations of the Consequences of the Lowering of Interest and Raising the Value of Money*. London, 1691, 1692.

—— *Several Papers relating to Money, Interest, and Trade*. London, 1696.

—— *The Works of John Locke*, edited by Desmaizeaux. London, 1751.

LOWNDES, WILLIAM. *An Essay for the Amendment of the Silver Coins*. London, 1695.

McCULLOCH, J. R. (ed.). *A Select Collection of Early English Tracts on Commerce*. London, 1856.

—— *A Select Collection of Scarce and Valuable Tracts on Money* London, 1856.

—— *Tracts on Commerce*. London, 1859.

MALESTROICT, DE. *Les paradoxes sur le faict des monnyes*. Paris, 1566, 1578.

MALYNES, GERRARD DE. *A Treatise of the Caker of Englands Common Wealth*. London, 1601.

—— *Saint George for England*. London, 1601.

—— *England's View, in the Vnmasking of Two Paradoxes (of de Malestroict) with the Replication vnto the Answer of Maister Iohn Bodine*. London, 1603.

—— *Lex Mercatoria*. London, 1622.

—— *The Maintenance of Free Trade*. London, 1622.

—— *The Center of the Circle of Commerce*. London, 1623.

MELON, J. F. *Essai politique sur le commerce*, 1734 ; English translation as *A Political Essay upon Commerce*, tr. by David Bindon, Dublin, 1738 ; new French edition with new chapters, Paris, 1761.

MILLES, THOMAS. *The Replie, or Second Apologie*. London, 1604.

—— *The Customers Apologie*. London, 1609.

—— *An Out-port-customers Accompt*. London, 1609.

MISSELDEN, EDW. *Free Trade*. London, 1622.

—— *The Circle of Commerce*. London, 1623.

MONROE, A. E. *Monetary Theory before Adam Smith*. Cambridge, Mass., 1923.

—— *Early Economic Thought*. Cambridge, Mass., 1927.

MONTANARI, GERMINIANO. (*Breve Trattato del valore delle monete in tutti gli stati*, 1680.) (*La zecca in consulto di stato* (Della moneta), 1683–7.) Both reprinted in Custodi collection of reprints.

MONTCHRÉTIEN, ANTOYNE DE. *Traicté de l'économie politique*. 1615. New edition ed. by Th. Funck-Brentano, Paris, 1889.

MORINI-COMBY, J. *Mercantilisme et protectionisme*. Paris, 1930.

MUN, THOMAS. *A Discourse of Trade from England vuto the East Indies*. London, ca. 1609 ; 2nd ed., London, 1621.

—— *England's Treasure by Foreign Trade*, written about 1635–40, first published in London, 1664. (Both reprinted in MacCulloch's *Early English Tracts*, 1856.)

NORTH, DUDLEY. *Discourses upon Trade*. London, 1691.

—— *Considerations upon East India Trade*. London, 1701.

—— *The Advantages of the East India Trade, etc.* London, 1720.

PACKARD, LAWRENCE B. " International Rivalry and Free-Trade Origins, 1661–1678," *Q.J.E.*, 1923.

PASQUIER, MAURICE. *Sir William Petty : ses idées économiques*. Paris, 1903.

PETTY, WILLIAM. *The Economic Writings of Sir William Petty*, ed. by C. H. Hull. Cambridge, 1899.

PHILIPS, E. *An Appeal to Common Sense : or, Some Considerations offer'd to restore Public Credit*. London, 1720.

—— *The State of the Nation, in respect to her Commerce, Debts, and Money*. London, 1725.

POLLEXFEN, JOHN. *England and East-India Inconsistent in their Manufactures*. London, 1697.

—— *A Discourse of Trade and Coyn*. London, 1697.

—— *A Vindication of some Assertions relating to Coin and Trade*. London, 1699.

POSE, ALFRED. " Les théories monétaires de Jean Law," *R.d.H.D.E.*, 1928.

POTTER, WILLIAM. *The Key of Wealth*. London, 1650.

—— *The Trades-man's Jewel*. London, 1650.

—— *Humble Proposals, etc.* London, 1651.

PRATT, S. *The Regulating Silver Coin*. London, 1696.

PRICE, W. H. " The Origin of the Phase ' Balance of Trade '," *Q.J.E.*, 1905.

PRIOR, THOMAS. *Observations on Coins in General*. Dublin, 1729.

—— *A list of the Absentees of Ireland*, Dublin, 1729; 3rd ed., Dublin, 1745.

RAVEAU, PAUL. *Précédé d'un étude sur le pouvoir d'achat de la livre.* Paris, 1926.

ROBERTS, LEWIS. *The Treasure of Trafficke, or a Discourse of Forraign Trade.* London, 1641.

ROBERTS, HAZEL VAN DYKE. *Boisguilbert.* New York, 1935.

ROBINSON, HENRY. *England's Safety in Trades Encrease.* London, 1641.

—— *Briefe Considerations concerning Advancement of Trade and Navigation.* London, 1649.

—— *Certain Proposals, etc.* London, 1652.

SCHMOLLER, GUSTAV. *The Mercantile System.* New York, 1902.

SERRA, ANTANIO. *A Brief Treatise on the Causes which can make Gold and Silver Plentiful,* published in Italian, Naples, 1613. English translation in Monroe's *Early Economic Thought,* 1927.

SEWALL, H. R. *The Theory of Value before Adam Smith.* New York, 1901.

SOMMER, LOUISE. "Mercantilisme et théorie de la valeur," *R.d.H.D.E.,* 1927.

SPANN, OTHMAR. *Types of Economic Theory.* English translation tr. by Eden and Paul, London, 1930.

STEUART, JAMES D. *Principles of Political Economy.* London, 1767.

SUVIRANTA, BR. *The Theory of the Balance of Trade in England.* Helsingfors, 1923.

SWIFT, JONATHAN. *Drapier's Letters.* 1725.

TAWNEY, R. H., and others, editors. *Tudor Economic Documents,* in 3 vols. London, 1924.

TERSEN, ANDRÉ-C. *John Hales, économiste anglais du milieu de xvie siècle.* Avallon, 1901.

THOMAS, P. J. *Mercantilism and the East India Trade.* London, 1926.

TUCKER, J. *A Brief Essay on the Advantages and Disadvantages . . . with regard to Trade.* London, 1749.

—— *The Elements of Commerce and Theory of Taxes.* Bristol, 1755.

UNWIN, G. *Studies in Economic History,* ed. with an introductory memoir by R. H. Tawney. London, 1927.

VANDERLINT, JACOB. *Money Answers All Things.* London, 1734.

VAUGHAN, RICE. *A Discourse of Coin and Coinage.* London, 1675.

VINER, JACOB. "The English Theories of Foreign Trade before Adam Smith," *J.P.E.,* 1930.

WILSON, THOMAS. *A Discourse upon Usury,* 1572. New edition ed. with an introduction by R. H. Tawney, London, 1925.

WOOD, WILLIAM. *A Survey of Trade.* London, 1718.?

—— *Considerations on the East-India Trade,* 1701, reprinted in *MacCulloch's Early English Tracts on Commerce* (London, 1856).

2. FROM DAVID HUME TO J. S. MILL.

ACWORTH, A. W. *Financial Reconstruction in England, 1815–1822.* London, 1925.

ANDRÉADÈS, A. *History of the Bank of England, 1640 to 1903,* first published in French, tr. into English by C. Meredith, with preface by H. S. Foxwell. London, 1909, 1924.

ATTWOOD, THOMAS. *A Letter . . . on the Creation of Money, etc.* Birmingham, 1817.

—— *Prosperity Restored, etc.* London, 1817.

—— *Observations on Currency, etc.* Birmingham, 1818.

—— *A Letter to the Earl of Liverpool, on the Report . . . on the Question of the Bank Restriction Act.* Birmingham, 1819.

—— *A Second Letter to the Earl of Liverpool, on the Bank Reports, as Occasioning the National Dangers and Distresses.* Birmingham, 1819.

BACALAN, ISAAC DE. See Sauvaire-Jourdan.

BARING, FRANCIS. *Observations on the Establishment of the Bank of England, and on the Paper Circulation of the Country.* London, 1797.

—— *Further Observations on the Establishment of the Bank of England.* London, 1797.

—— *Brief Observations on a late Letter by W. Boyd.* London, 1801.

—— *Observations on the Publication of Walter Boyd.* London, 1801.

—— *A Twelve-penny Answer, etc.* London, 1801.

—— *A Second Twelve-penny Answer, etc.* London, 1801.

BENTHAM, JEREMY. *The Works of J. Bentham,* ed. by John Bowring. Edinburgh, 1843.

BLAKE, W. *Observations on the Principles which regulate the Course of Exchanges.* London, 1801.

—— *Observations on the Effects produced by the Expenditure of Government during the Restriction of Cash Payments.* London, 1823.

BOASE, HENRY. *A Letter to . . . Lord King, in Defence of the Conduct of the Directors of the Banks of England and Ireland.* London, 1804.

BOOTH, GEORGE. *Observations on Paper Currency, etc.* Liverpool, 1815.

BOSANQUET, CHARLES. *Practical Observations on the Report of the Bullion Committee.* London, 1810 ; 2nd ed., 1810.

BOSANQUET, J. W. *Metallic, Paper, and Credit Currency.* London, 1842.

BOWLEY, MARIAN. *Nassau Senior and Classical Economics.* London, 1937.

BOYD, WALTER. *A Letter to the Right Honourable William Pitt, on the Influence of the Stoppage of Issues in Specie at the Bank of England ; on the Prices of Provisions and other Commodities.* London, 1801.

BURGESS, HENRY. *A Letter to the Right Honourable George Canning, etc.* London, 1826.

BURTON, JOHN HILL. *Life and Correspondence of David Hume.* Edinburgh, 1846.

CANNAN, EDWARD. *The Paper Pound of 1797–1821.* London, 1919.

CARGILL, W. *The Currency, showing how a Fixed Gold Standard places England in Permanent Disadvantage in respect to other Countries.* London, 1845.

CONDILLAC, ETIENNE B. DE. *Le commerce et le gouvernement.* 1776.

COURNOT, AUGUSTIN. *Recherches sur les principes mathématiques de la théorie des richesses.* Paris, 1838. English translation as *Researches into the Mathematical Principles of the Theory of*

Wealth, tr. by N. T. Bacon, with an introduction and mathematical notes by I. Fisher, New York, 1927.

COURNOT, AUGUSTIN. *Principes de la théorie des richesses.* Paris, 1863.

—— *Revue sommaire des doctrines économique.* Paris, 1877.

CROMBIE, A. *Letter to D. Ricardo, Esq., etc.* London, 1817.

DAIRE, EUGÉNE. *Collection des principaux économists.* Paris, 1843–8.

DUBOIS, A. " An rapport d'Isaac de Bacalan," *R.d.H.D.E.*, 1908.

EINAUDI, LUIGI. " James Pennington or James Mill : an Early Correction of Ricardo," *Q.J.E.*, 1929.

ELIOT, FRANCIS PERCEVAL. *Observations on the Fallacy of the Supposed Depreciation of the Paper Currency.* London, 1811.

—— *A Supplement to Observations, etc.* London, 1811.

FEAVEARYEAR, A. E. *The Pound Sterling, A History of English Money.* Oxford, 1931.

FISHER, IRVING. " Cournot and Mathematical Economics," *Q.J.E.*, 1898.

FOSTER, J. L. *An Essay on the Principles of Commercial Exchanges.* London, 1804.

FOX, E. L. *Cursory Reflections on the Causes and . . . Consequences of the Stoppage of the Bank of England.* Bristol, 1797.

FULLARTON, JOHN. *On the Regulation of Currencies.* London, 1844.

GIDE, CHARLES, and C. RIST. *A History of Economic Doctrines.* Published in French, tr. into English by R. Richard. London, 1915, 1928.

GREGORY, T. E. *An Introduction to Tooke and Newmarch's "A History of Prices".* London, 1928.

HALL, W. *A View of Our Late and of Our Future Currency.* London, 1819.

HAWTREY, R. G. " The Bank Restriction of 1797," *E.J.*, 1918.

HAYEK, F. A. VON. " A Note on the Development of the Doctrine of Forced Saving," *Q.J.E.*, 1932.

HERRIES, J. C. *A Review of the Controversy respecting the High Price of Bullion, and the State of our Currency.* London, 1811.

HIGGS, HENRY. *The Physiocrats.* London, 1897.

—— *Bibliography of Economics, 1751–1775.* Cambridge, 1935.

HILL, JOHN. *An Inquiry into the Causes of the Present High Price of Gold Bullion in England.* London, 1810.

HOLLANDER, JACOB H. " The Development of the Theory of Money from Adam Smith to David Ricardo," *Q.J.E.*, 1911.

—— *Ricardo : a Centenary Estimate.* Baltimore, 1910.

HOPKINS, THOMAS. *Bank-notes, the Cause of the Disappearance of the Guineas, etc.* London, 1811.

—— *Economical Enquiries relative to the Laws which regulate Rent, Profit, Wages, and the Value of Money.* London, 1822.

HORNER, FRANCIS. " An Inquiry into the Nature and Effects of the Paper Credit of Great Britain, by Henry Thornton," *Edinburgh Review*, 1802.

—— " Lord King's Thoughts, etc.," *Edinburgh Review*, 1803.

—— " John Wheatley's Remarks, etc." *Edinburgh Review*, 1803.

—— *Resolution proposed to the . . . Commons on the Report of the Committee appointed to inquire into the High Price of Bullion.* London, 1811.

BIBLIOGRAPHY 331

HUME, DAVID. *Essays and Treatises on Several Subjects.* London, 1758, 1770.

HUSKISSON, WILLIAM. *The Question concerning the Depreciation of our Currency.* London, 1810.

JAMES, HENRY. *Considerations on the Policy or Impolicy of the Further Continuance of the Bank Restriction Act.* London, 1818.

—— *Essays on Money, Exchanges and Political Economy.* London, 1820.

—— *State of the Nation.* London, 1835.

JOHNSON, E. A. J. " L'économie synthétique de Hume," *R.d.H.D.E.*, 1931.

JOPLIN, THOMAS. *Outlines of a System of Political Economy.* London, 1823.

—— *Views on the Subject of Corn and Currency.* London, 1826.

—— *Views on the Currency.* London, 1828.

—— *An Analysis and History of the Currency Question, etc.* London, 1832.

—— *The Cause and Cure of our Commercial Embarrassments.* London, 1841.

—— *Currency Reform : Improvement not Depreciation.* London, 1844.

—— *An Examination of Sir Robert Peel's Currency Bill of 1844.* London, 1844.

KING, PETER. *Thoughts on the Restriction of Payments in Specie.* London, 1803.

LONGFIELD, MOUNTIFORT. *Lectures on Political Economy.* Dublin, 1834. L.S.E. reprint, London, 1931.

—— *Three Lectures on Commerce and One on Absenteeism.* Dublin, 1835.

—— " Banking and Currency," *Dublin University Magazine,* 1840.

LOYD, SAMUEL JONES (LORD OVERSTONE). *Tracts on Metallic and Paper Money,* 1837–1857. London, 1858.

McCULLOCH, J. R. *On Fluctuations in the Supply and Value of Money, and the Banking System of England.* Edinburgh, 1826.

—— *Historical Sketch of the Bank of England.* London, 1831.

—— " An Essay showing the Erroneousness of the Prevailing Opinions in regard to Absenteeism," *Edinburgh Review,* 1825.

—— (ed.) *A Select Collection of Scarce and Valuable Tracts . . . on Paper Currency and Banking.* London, 1857.

—— *The Literature of Political Economy.* London, 1845.

MACLEOD, HENRY DUNNING. *Theory and Practice of Banking,* in 2 vols. London, 1855 ; 5th ed., 1892–3.

—— *Theory of Credit.* London, 1893–7 ; 2nd ed., 1894–7.

MAITLAND, JAMES (8TH EARL OF LAUDERDALE). *An Inquiry into the Nature and Origin of Public Wealth.* London, 1804.

—— *Thoughts on the Alarming State of the Circulation and on the Means of Redressing the Pecuniary Grievances in Ireland.* London, 1805.

—— *The Depreciation of the Paper Currency of Great Britain Proved.* London, 1812.

MALTHUS, T. R. " Depreciation of Paper Currency," *Edinburgh Review,* 1811.

—— *The Measure of Value.* London, 1823.

332   BIBLIOGRAPHY

MAYOR, W. *Theory of Money and Exchanges.* London, 1812.
MILL, JAMES. *Elements of Political Economy.* London, 1821; 3rd edition (revised), London, 1826.
MILL, J. S. *Essays on some Unsettled Questions of Political Economy.* London, 1844, 1874.
—— *Principles of Political Economy.* London, 1848. Ashley's edition, London, 1909, 1923.
—— *Autobiography,* H. J. Luski's edition. London, 1924.
—— *The Letters of J. S. Mill,* ed. by H. S. R. Elliot. London, 1910.
MUSHET, ROBERT. *An Inquiry into the Effects produced on National Currency and Rates of Exchange by the Bank Restriction Bill.* London, 1810.
NORMAN, G. W. *Remarks on Currency and Banking.* London, 1833.
—— *Letter to Charles Wood on Money, etc.* London, 1841.
—— *Papers on Various Subjects.* London, 1869.
OPIE, REDVERS. " A Neglected English Economist : George Poulett Scrope," *Q.J.E.,* 1929.
PALMER, J. HORSLEY. *The Causes and Consequences of the Pressure upon the Money-Market.* London, 1837.
—— *Reply to the Reflections of Mr. S. J. Loyd.* London, 1837.
PARNELL, HENRY BROOKE. *Observations upon the State of Currency in Ireland.* London and Dublin, 1804.
PARSONS, L. *Observations on the Present State of the Currency of England.* London, 1811.
PENNINGTON, JAMES. *A Letter to Kirkman Finlay, Esq., on the Importation of Foreign Corn.* . . . London, 1840.
QUESNAY, F. *Œuvres économiques et philosophiques,* ed. by Oncken. Frankfort and Paris, 1888.
RICARDO, DAVID. *Three Letters on the Price of Gold,* 1809. Reprinted with an introduction by J. H. Hollander, Baltimore, 1903.
—— *Economic Essays by David Ricardo,* ed. by E. C. K. Gonner. London, 1923.
—— *Letters to T. R. Malthus, 1810–1823,* ed. by James Bonar. Oxford, 1887.
—— *Letters to Hutches Trower and others, 1811–1823,* ed. by J. Bonar and J. H. Hollander. Oxford, 1899.
—— *Letters to J. R. McCulloch, 1816–1823,* ed. J. H. Hollander. New York, 1896.
—— *Principles of Political Economy and Taxation.* London, 1817. Gonner's ed., London, 1891, 1932.
RIVIÈRE, LE MERCIER DE LA. *L'ordre naturel et essential des sociétés politiques.* London and Paris, 1767.
ROSE, GEORGE. *Substance of the Speech delivered in the House of Commons* . . . *on the Report of the Bullion Committee.* London, 1811.
ROSENSTEIN-RODAN, P. N. *History of Economic Theory from Aristotle to Adam Smith.* London, 1920.
SAUVAIRE-JOURDAN, F. *Isaac de Bacalan et les idées libre-échangistes en France.* Paris, 1903.
SAY, JEAN BAPTISTE. *Traité d'économie politique.* Paris, 1803. 4th ed., Paris, 1819 ; English tr. from the 4th ed. by C. R. Prinsep, Boston, 1821. 7th ed. ed. by A. Clement, Paris, 1861.
—— *Cours complet d'économie politique pratique.* Paris, 1828–9.

SAYERS, R. S. " The Question of the Standard, 1815–1844," *E.J.*, *Economic History Supplement*, 1935.

SCROPE, GEORGE POULETT. *On Credit-Currency and its Superiority to Coin*. London, 1830.

—— *The Currency Question freed from Mystery*. London, 1830.

—— *A Plain Statement of . . . the Prevailing Distress*. London, 1832.

—— *An Examination of the Bank Charter Question*. London, 1833.

—— *Principles of Political Economy*. London, 1833.

SELIGMAN, E. R. A. *Essays in Economics*. New York, 1925.

SENIOR, NAUSSAU WILLIAM. *Three Lectures on the Transmission of the Precious Metals*. London, 1828. L.S.E. reprint, London, 1931.

—— *Three Lectures on the Value of Money, delivered before the Oxford University*, 1829, privately printed, 1840, L.S.E. reprint, London, 1931.

—— *Three Lectures on the Cost of Obtaining Money*. London, 1830 ; L.S.E. reprint, London, 1931.

—— *Lectures on the Rate of Wages*. London, 1830.

—— " Free Trade and Retaliation," *Edinburgh Review*, 1843.

—— *Political Economy*. London, 1848.

—— *Industrial Efficiency and Social Economy*, published posthumously from original MSS. by S. Leon Levy. New York, 1928.

SILBERLING, NORMAN J. " Financial and Monetary Policy of Great Britain during the Napoleonic War," *Q.J.E.*, 1924.

SIMONDI DE SISMONDI, J. C. L. *De la richesse commerciale*. Genève, 1803.

SINCLAIR, J. *Observations on the Report of the Bullion Committee*. London, 1810.

SMITH, ADAM. *Lectures on Justice, Police, Revenue, and Arms, delivered in the University of Glasgow*, ed. and printed by E. Cannan. Oxford, 1896.

—— *An Inquiry into the Nature and Causes of the Wealth of Nations*. London, 1776. Cannan's ed., London, 1904, 1920.

SMITH, THOMAS. *The Theory of Money and Exchange*. London, 1807.

—— *The Bullion Question*. London, 1812.

SMITH, VERA C. *The Rationale of Central Banking*. London, 1936.

SRAFFA, PIERO. " An Alleged Correction of Ricardo," *Q.J.E.*, 1930.

STEWART, DUGALD. *Lectures on Political Economy*, printed posthumously in William Hamilton's *The Collected Works of Dugald Stewart*, vols. viii and ix. London, 1855.

THORNTON, HENRY. *An Inquiry into the Nature and Effects of the Paper Credit of Great Britain*. London, 1802.

TOOKE, THOMAS. *Thoughts and Details on the High and Low Prices of the Last Thirty Years*. London, 1823.

—— *Considerations on the State of the Currency*. London, 1826.

—— *Letter to Lord Grenville*. London, 1829.

—— *On the Currency in connection with the Corn Trade*. London, 1829.

—— *A History of Prices . . . from 1792 to 1856*. London, 1835–1857.

—— *An Inquiry into the Currency Principle*. London, 1844 ; 2nd. ed., 1844.

—— *On the Bank Charter Act of 1844*. London, 1856.

334   BIBLIOGRAPHY

Torrens, Robert. *The Economists Refuted.* London, 1808.
—— *An Essay on Money and Paper Currency.* London, 1812.
—— *An Essay on the External Corn Trade.* London, 1815 ; 4th ed., 1829.
—— *A Comparative Estimate of the Effects of Removing the Restriction on Cash Payments.* London, 1819.
—— *An Essay on the Production of Wealth.* London, 1821.
—— *On Wages and Combination.* London, 1834.
—— *Letters on Commercial Policy.* London, 1833.
—— *The Budget : a Series of Letters on Financial, Commercial, and Colonial Policy.* London, 1841–4.
—— *A Letter to Sir Robert Peel.* . . . London, 1843.
—— *Postscript to a Letter to Sir Robert Peel.* . . . London, 1843 ; 2nd ed. 1843.
—— *A Letter to N. W. Senior, Esq.* London, 1843.
—— *A Letter to Thomas Tooke.* . . . London, 1840.
—— *An Inquiry into the.* . . . *Renewal of the Charter of the Bank of England.* London, 1844.
—— *The Principles and Practical Operation of Sir Robert Peel's Bill of 1844.* London, 1848 ; 4th ed., 1858.
Tozer, J. " On the Effect of the Non-Residence of Landlords, etc., on the Wealth of a Community," *Transactions of the Cambridge Philosophical Society,* 1842.
Trotter, Coutts. *The Principles of Currency and Exchange.* London, 1810.
Turgot, Anne Robert Jacques. *Œuvres,* in Daire's *Collection.*
United Kingdom (Parliament). *Report, Minutes of Evidence, and Appendix from the Committee on the Circulating Paper, the Specie, and the Current Coin of Ireland ; and also, on the Exchange between that Part of the United Kingdom and Great Britain.* First printed in three separate volumes, May and June, 1804 ; reprinted and paged continuously. London, 1826.
—— *Report, together with Minutes of Evidence and Accounts, from the Select Committee on the High Price of Gold Bullion.* London, 1810.
—— *Report from the Select Committee of the State of Ireland.* London, 1825.
—— *Report of the Committee of Secrecy on the Bank of England Charter.* London, 1833.
Vansittart, N. *Substance of Two Speeches.* London, 1811.
Vigreux, Benjamin. " Le fondement de la valeur de la monnaie d'après Turgot," *R.d.H.D.E.,* 1935.
Weulersse, M. *Le mouvement physiocratique en France de 1756 à 1770.* Paris, 1910.
Wheatley, John. *Remarks on Currency and Commerce.* London, 1803.
—— *An Essay on the Theory of Money and Principles of Commerce.* Vol. i, London, 1807 ; vol. ii, London, 1822.
—— *A Letter to Lord Grenville, on the Distress of the Country.* London, 1816.
Wilson, J. *Capital, Currency, and Banking.* London, 1847.
Wilson, R. *Observations on the Depreciation of Money.* Edinburgh, 1811.
—— *Further Observations, etc.* Edinburgh, 1811.

.WOODS, G. *Observations on the Present Price of Bullion and Rates of Exchange.* London, 1811.
? *A Letter on the True Principles of Advantageous Exportation.* London, 1818. Reprinted with an introduction by Arnold Plant in *Economica*, 1933, pp. 40–50.

3. THE POST-CLASSICAL WRITINGS : 1848–1918.

ANGELL, NORMAN. *The Great Illusion.* London, 1910.
ARNAUNÉ, F. A. *La monnaie, le crédit et le change.* Paris, 1894; 1922.
—— *Le commerce extérieur et les tarifs de douane.* Paris, 1911.
AUSPITZ, RUDOLF, and RICHARD LIEBEN. *Recherches sur la théorie du prix.* First published in German, Leipzig, 1889 ; French tr. by L. Suret, Paris, 1914.
AUSTIN, WILLIAM. *On the Imminent Depreciation of Gold and how to Avoid Loss.* London, 1853.
BAGEHOT, W. *Lombard Street.* London, 1873 ; 4th ed., with an introduction by Hartley Wither, London, 1915.
—— *Some Articles on the Depreciation of Silver.* London, 1887.
—— *The Works and Life of W. Bagehot*, ed. by Mrs. Russell Barrington. London, 1915.
BARBOUR, DAVID. *The Theory of Bimetallism.* London, 1886.
—— *The Standard of Value.* London, 1912.
—— *The Influence of Gold Supply on Prices and Profits.* London, 1913.
BARRAULT, H. E. " Le sens et le portée des théories anti-quantitatives de la monnaie," *R.d.H.D.E.*, 1910.
—— " Les doctrines de Cournot sur le commerce international," *R.d.H.D.E.*, 1912.
BASTABLE, C. F. *Commerce of Nations.* London, 1892.
—— *The Theory of International Trade.* London, 1893 ; 4th ed., 1903.
—— " On Some Applications of the Theory of International Trade," *Q.J.E.*, 1889.
—— " On Some Disputed Points in the Theory of International Trade," *E.J.*, 1901.
BELL, S. " A Statistical Point in Ricardian Theory of Gold Movements," *J.P.E.*, 1907.
BONAR, J. " Knapp's Theory of Money," *E.J.*, 1922.
BOWEN, FRANCIS. *Principles of Political Economy.* London, 1856.
BROWN, HARRY GUNISON. *Principles of Commerce.* New York, 1914.
BROWNING, R. *Reflection on the Currency.* London, 1869.
CAIRNES, J. E. *Essays in Political Economy, theoretical and applied.* London, 1873.
—— *An Examination into the Principles of Currency involved in the Bank Charter Act of* 1844. Dublin, 1854.
—— *Some Leading Principles of Political Economy newly Expounded.* London, 1874 ; 1884.
CARLILE, W. W. *Monetary Economics.* London, 1912.
CHERBULIEZ, A. E. *Précis de la science économie.* Paris, 1862.
CHEVALIER, MICHEL. *Cours d'économie politique*, vol. iii, " La monnaie." Paris, 1850.

CHEVALIER, MICHEL. *Remarks on the Production . . . . and dep. of Gold*, tr. from the French by D. F. Campbell. London, 1853.
—— *De la baisse probable de l'or, des consequences commerciales et sociales*. Paris, 1859. English tr. by Richard Cobden, Manchester, 1859.
CLARE, GEORGE. *A Money-Market Premier, and Key to the Exchanges*. London, 1891.
CLOW, F. R. "The Quantity Theory and its Critics," *J.P.E.*, 1903.
COBB, A. S. *Banks' Cash Reserves : Threadneedle Street*. London, 1891.
CONANT, CHARLES A. *A History of Modern Banks of Issue*. New York, 1896 ; 1915 ; 1927.
—— "The Development of Credit," *J.P.E.*, 1899.
—— "The Distribution of Money," *J.P.E.*, 1901.
—— "Securities as a Means of Payment," *An.*, vol. xiv.
—— "What determines the Value of Money," *Q.J.E.*, 1904.
CUNNYNGHAM, H. H. *A Geometrical Political Economy*. Oxford, 1904.
DEL MAR, ALEXANDER. *A History of the Precious Metals*. New York, 2nd ed. (revised), 1902.
—— *The Science of Money*. London, 2nd ed., 1896.
—— *Money and Civilization*. London, 1886.
EDGEWORTH, F. Y. *Papers relating to Political Economy*. London, 1925.
—— "On a Point in the Theory of International Trade," *E.J.*, 1899.
—— "Disputed Points in the Theory of International Trade," *E.J.*, 1901.
FARRER, THOMAS HENRY. *What do We Pay With ?* London, 1889.
—— *Studies in Currency*. London, 1898.
FAUCHER, L. *Recherches sur l'or et sur l'argent considérés comme étalon de la valeur*. Paris, 1843.
—— *Remarks on the Production of the Precious Metals and on the Demonetization of Gold in Several Countries in Europe*, tr. from the French by T. Hankey. London, 1852.
—— *Mélanges d'économie politique et de finances*. Paris, 1856.
FAURE, F. "Le mouvement international des capitaux," *R.E.I.*, 1911.
FAVRE, JEAN. *Les changes dépréciés*. Paris, 1906.
FAWCETT, HENRY. "On the Social and Economic Influence of the New Gold," *British Association Transaction*, 1859.
—— *Manual of Political Economy*. London, 1863 ; 8th ed., 1907.
FISHER, IRVING. *Appreciation and Interest*. New York, 1896.
—— *The Purchasing Power of Money*. Assisted by H. G. Brown. New York, 1911 ; 2nd ed., 1922.
FLAMINGO, G. M. "Prevailing Theories in Europe as to the Influence of Money on International Trade," *Yale Review*, 1898.
FOVILLE, A. DE. *La monnaie*. Paris, 1907.
GIFFEN, ROBERT. *Stock Exchange Securities : an Essay on the General Causes of Fluctuation of their Prices*. London, 1817.

GIFFEN, ROBERT. *Essays in Finance*, in two series. London, 2nd ed., 1880–1886 ; 5th ed., 1890.
—— *Economic Enquiries and Studies*. London, 1904.
—— *The Case against Bimetallism*. London, 1892.
GOSCHEN, G. J. *The Theory of Foreign Exchanges*. London, 1861 ; 9th ed., 1876.
—— *Essays and Addresses on Economic Questions*, 1865–1893. London, 1905.
HADLEY, A. T. *Economics*. New York, 1896.
HARDY, S. MACLEAN. " Quantity of Money and Prices, 1861–1892," *J.P.E.*, 1895.
HAWTREY, R. G. *Currency and Credit*. London, 1913.
—— *Good and Bad Trade*. London, 1913.
HELFERICH, CARL THEODOR. *Money*, tr. from the German by Louis Infield. First German ed., Leipzig, 1903 ; English tr. ed. with an introduction by T. E. Gregory, London, 1927.
HOBSON, C. K. *The Export of Capital*. London, 1912.
HOBSON, J. A. *International Trade*. London, 1904.
—— *Gold, Prices, and Wages with an Examination of the Quantity Theory*. London, 1913 ; 3rd ed., 1924.
HUMBOLDT, F. H. A. VON. *The Fluctuation of Gold*, tr. by W. Mande. New York, 1900.
JACOB, WILLIAM. *An Historical Inquiry into the Production and Consumption of the Precious Metals*. London, 1881.
JEVONS, W. S. *A Serious fall in the Value of Gold Ascertained*. London, 1836.
—— *Investigations in Currency and Finance*, ed. with an introduction by H. S. Foxwell. London, 1884.
—— *Money and the Mechanism of Exchange*. London, 1875.
JUGLAR, CLÉMENT. *Des crises commerciales et de leur retour périodique en France, en Angleterre, et aux États-unis*. Paris, 1862.
—— *Du change et de la liberté d'emission*. Paris, 1868.
—— *A Brief History of Panics*, tr. by De Courey W. Thom. New York, 1916.
KEMMERER, EDWIN WALTER. *Money and Credit Instruments in their Relation to General Prices*, written 1903 ; published, 1903 ; 2nd ed., 1909.
—— *Modern Monetary Reforms*. New York, 1916.
—— " The Theory of Foreign Investments," *An.*, 1916.
KINLEY, DAVID. *Money*. New York, 1904.
—— " The Relation of the Credit System to the Value of Money," *Publications of the American Economic Association*, 1905.
KNAPP, G. F. *The State Theory of Money*. First published in German, Munich, 1905 ; tr. into English by H. M. Lucas and J. Bonar, London, 1924.
LANDRY, A. " La rapidité de la circulation monétaire," *R.d.E.P.*, 1905.
LAUGHLIN, J. LAURENCE. *Principles of Money*. New York, 1903.
—— " The Quantity Theory and its Critics," *J.P.E.*, 1903.
LAVELEYE, ÉMILE DE. *Le marché monétaire et ses crises depuis cinquante ans*. Paris, 1865.

LAVELEYE, ÉMILE DE. *La monnaie et le bimetallism international.*
    Paris, 2nd ed., 1891.
—— *Éléments d'économie politique.* Paris, 1882. English tr.
    by A. W. Polland. New York, 1884.
LESLIE, T. E. C. *Essays in Political Economy.* Dublin, 1878 ;
    2nd ed., ed. by J. K. Ingram and C. F. Bastable. Dublin,
    1878.
LEVASSEUR, ÉMILE. *La question de l'or : les mines de Californie.* . . .
    Paris, 1858.
—— *Précis d'économie politique,* quatrième éd., Paris, 1883.
LEXIS, W. "The Agio on Gold and International Trade." *E.J.,*
    1895.
LORIA, A. "Notes on the Theory of International Trade," *E.J.,*
    1901.
McCULLOCH, J. R. "Precious Metals," in the 8th ed. of
    Encyclopædia Britannica (1858).
MACLEOD, H. D. *The Theory and Practice of Banking.* London,
    1855–6 ; 5th ed., 1892.
—— *The Principles of Economic Philosophy,* 2nd ed., vol. i, London,
    1872.
MANGOLDT, HANS CARL EMIL VON. *Grundiss der Volkswirtschaftslehre.*
    Stuttgart, 1863 ; 2nd ed., 1871. (A summary of it is found
    in Edgeworth's *Papers relating to Political Economy,* ii, pp.53 ff.)
MARGET, ARTHUR W. "Léon Walras and the Cash-Balance Approach
    to the Problem of the Value of Money," *J.P.E.,* 1932.
MARSHALL, ALFRED. *The Pure Theory of Foreign Trade,* privately
    printed in 1879 ; L.S.E. reprint, London, 1930, 1935.
—— *Official Papers by A. Marshall,* ed. by J. M. Keynes. London,
    1926.
—— and MARY PALEY MARSHALL : *The Economics of Industry.*
    London, 1879.
MARX, KARL. *Capital.* First published in German, 1859 ; tr.
    into English by Moore and Aveling, London, 1887.
MILLER, H. E. "Earlier Theories of Crises and Cycles in United
    States," *Q.J.E.,* 1924.
MILNER, T. H. *On the Regulation of Floating Capital, and Freedom
    of Currency.* London, 1848.
MISES, LUDWIG VON. "The Foreign Exchange Policy of the Austro-
    Hungary Bank," *E.J.,* 1909.
—— *The Theory of Money and Credit.* First German ed., 1912 ;
    2nd German ed., 1924 ; English ed. tr. by H. E. Batson,
    ed. with an introduction by Professor L. Robbins, London,
    1934.
MITCHELL, W. C. "Quantity Theory of the Value of Money,"
    J.P.E., 1896.
—— "The Real Issues in the Quantity Theory Controversy,"
    J.P.E., 1904.
—— *The History of Greenbacks.* Chicago, 1903.
—— *Gold, Prices, and Wages under the Greenback Standard.* Berkeley,
    1908.
MONGIN, M. "La monnaie et la mesure des valeurs," *R.d.E.P.,*
    1897.

MULHALL, M. G. *History of Prices since the Year* 1850. London, 1885.

MUSGRAVE, ANTHONY. *Studies in Political Economy.* London, 1875.

NEWCOMB, SIMON. *Principles of Political Economy.* New York, 1885.

NEWMARCH, WILLIAM. *A History of Prices and of the State of the Circulation, during the Nine Years* 1848–1856. In 2 volumes. London, 1857. (Being vols. v and vi of Tooke and Newmarch's *History of Prices from* 1792.)

NICHOLSON, J. S. *A Treatise on Money and Essays on Monetary Problems.* London, 1888 ; 5th ed., 1901.

—— *Principles of Political Economy.* London, 1893.

—— *Elements of Political Economy.* London, 1903 ; 2nd, 1906.

—— " The Effects of the Depreciation of Silver," *E.J.*, 1894.

NOGARO, BERTRAND. *Le rôle de la monnaie dans le commerce international et la théorie quantitative.* Paris, 1904.

—— " Contribution à une théorie réaliste de la monnaie," *R.d.E.P.*, 1906.

—— " L'expérience bimétalliste du xixe siècle et la théorie générale de la monnaie," *R.d.E.P.*, 1908.

NORMAN, J. H. *A Colloquy upon the Science of Money.* London, 1889.

—— *The Quantity Theory and the Value Theory of Money.* London, 1890.

—— *The Science of Money.* London, 1895.

—— *Lecture upon Locke's School of Money.* London, 1900.

O'FARRELL, H. H. *The Franco-German War Indemnity.* London, 1913.

PALGRAVE, R. H. I. *An Analysis of the Transactions of the Bank of England* . . . *1844–1872.* London, 1874.

—— *On the Influence of a Note Circulation in the Conduct of Banking Business.* Salford, 1877.

—— *The Bank Act of* 1844–5 *and the Bank Rate.* London, 1892.

—— *Bank Rate and the Money Market in England, France, Germany, Holland and Belgium, 1844–1900.* London, 1903.

—— (Editor) : *Dictionary of Political Economy.* London, 1910.

PANTALEONI, MAFFEO. *Pure Economics*, first published in Italian, Florence, 1889 ; English tr. by T. B. Bruce, London, 1898.

PARETO, V. " Économie mathématique," in *Encyclopédie des sciences mathématiques.* Paris, 1911.

—— *Cours d'économie politique.* Lausanne, 1896.

—— *Manuel d'économie politique*, first published in Italian. Milan, 1906 ; tr. into French from the 2nd Italian ed. by A. Bonnet, Paris, 1909, 1927.

PARKER, U. S. " An Increase in Gold and the Price-making Process," *J.P.E.*, 1903.

PATTEN, S. N. *The Economic Basis of Protection.* Philadelphia, 1890.

PATTERSON, R. H. " On the Rate of Interest . . . and the Effects of a High Bank-rate during Commercial and Monetary Crisis," *J.R.S.S.*, 1871.

PERSONS, W. M. " The Quantity Theory as Tested by Kemmerer," *Q.J.E.*, 1908.

PRICE, L. L. *Money and its Relations to Prices.* London, 1896.

340 BIBLIOGRAPHY

ROLL, E. " Menger on Money," *Economica*, 1936.

ROSCHER, WILLIAM. *Principles of Political Economy*, first published in German ; English tr. by J. J. Lalor, 1882.

SAUERBECK, A. *Course of Average Prices of General Commodities in England*. London, 1894.

—— " Prices of Commodities and the Precious Metals," *J.R.S.S.*, vol. xlix, 1886.

SAY, LÉON. *Rapport fait du nom de la Commission du Budget de 1875 sur le payment de l'indemnité de guerre*, appended to the 4th ed. of his tr. of Goschen's *Théorie des changes étrangers*, Paris, 1896.

SAYERS, R. S. *Bank of England Operations*, 1890–1914. London, 1936.

SCHOENHOF, J. *A History of Money and Prices*. New York, 1896.

SCHÜLLER, RICHARD. *Schutzzoll und Freihandel*. Vienna, 1905. A summary tr. in Taussig's *Selected Readings*. . . . 1921.

SCOTT, W. A. *The Quantity Theory*. Philadelphia, 1897.

—— *Money and Banking*. New York, 1903.

SERRIGNY, BERNARD. *Les conséquencés économiques et sociales de la prochaine guerre*. Paris, 1909.

SHADWELL, J. L. *A System of Political Economy*. London, 1877.

SIDGWICK, H. *Principles of Political Economy*. London, 1883 ; 3rd ed., ed. by J. N. Keynes, 1901.

SPALDING, W. F. *Eastern Exchange, Currency, and Finance*. London, 1917.

SPRAGUE. O. M. W. " The Distribution of Money between the Banks and the People since 1893," *Q.J.E.*, 1914.

STIRLING, PATRICK JAMES. *The Australian and Californian Gold Discoveries and Their Probable Consequences*. Edinburgh, 1853.

,SUBERCASEAUX, G. *Le papier-monnaie*. First published in Spanish, Santiago, 1912 ; French ed., Paris, 1920.

TAUSSIG, F. W. *The Silver Situation in the United States*. New York, 2nd ed., 1896.

—— " Wages and Prices in Relation to International Trade," *Q.J.E.*, 1906.

—— *Principles of Economics*. New York, 1911 ; 3rd ed., 1921.

—— *Some Aspects of the Tariff Question*. Cambridge, Mass., 1915.

—— (ed.) *Selected Readings in International Trade and Tariff Problems*. Boston, 1921.

TAYLOR, F. M. *Chapters on Money*. 1906.

UNITED KINGDOM. *Report of the Select Committee on Depreciation of Silver*. London, 1876.

—— *Papers received from the Government of India, etc., having Reference to the Silver Question*. London, 1877.

—— *Reports of the Royal Commission appointed to inquire into the Recent Changes in the Relative Values of the Precious Metals*. London, 1887–8. New ed. of the Final Report by Robey, New York, 1936.

—— *Report of the Indian Currency Committee of 1893*. London, 1893.

—— *Reports of the Indian Currency Committee of 1898*. London, 1898–9.

—— *Reports of the Indian Currency Commission*. London, 1914.

WALKER, FRANCIS A. *Money.* New York, 1878 ; 1888.
—— *Political Economy.* New York, 1888.
—— *Money and its Relation to Industry and Trade.* New York, 1889.
—— " Value of Money," *Q.J.E.*, 1893.
—— " The Quantity Theory," *Q.J.E.*, 1895.
—— *International Bimetallism.* New York, 1897.
—— " Increasing and Diminishing Costs in International Trade," *Yale Review*, 1903.
WALRAS LÉON. *Elements d'économie politique pure.* Lausanne. 1874 ; 2nd ed., Lausanne, 1889 ; 3rd ed., 1896 ; 4th ed., 1926.
—— *Théorie mathématique du billet de banque*, 1879 (reprinted in *Études d'économie politique appliqué*, Lausanne, 1898 ; new ed., Paris, 1936).
—— *D'une méthode de régulation de la variation de valeur de la monnaie.* Lausanne, 1885.
—— *Théorie de la monnaie.* Lausanne, 1886.
WHEWELL, W. " Mathematical Exposition of Some Doctrines of Political Economy," in three memoirs, *Transactions of the Cambridge Philosophical Society*, 1853-6.
WHITAKER, A. C. " The Ricardian Theory of Gold Movements and Professor Laughlin's Views on Money," *Q.J.E.*, 1904.
WICKSELL, KNUT. *Interest and Prices*, first published in German, Jena, 1898 ; English tr. tr. from the German by R. F. Kahn (with an introduction by B. Ohlin), London, 1936.
—— " The Influence of the Rate of Interest on Prices," *E.J.*, 1907.
—— *Lectures on Political Economy*, first published in Sweden, 1901-1906 ; tr. into English by E. Classen, ed. with an introduction by Professor L. Robbins, London, 1934-5.
—— " The Scandinavian Gold Policy," *E.J.*, 1916.
WIESER, FRIEDRICH. *Natural Value*, first published in German, 1883 ; translated into English by Christian A. Malloch, London, 1893.
—— *Social Economics*, first published in German ; English tr. by A. F. Hinrichs, with a preface by W. C. Mitchell, New York, 1927.
WILLIS, H. P. " Credit Devices and the Quantity Theory," *J.P.E.*, 1896.
—— " History and Present Application of the Quantity Theory," *J.P.E.*, 1896.
—— *A History of the Latin Monetary Union.* Chicago, 1901.
WOLOWISKI, LUDWIK F. M. R. *De la monnaie.* St.-Germain, 1866.
—— *Le change et la circulation.* Paris, 1869.
—— *L'or et l'argent.* Paris, 1870.

4. THE DEVELOPMENTS SINCE THE WAR

ADARKAR, B. P. *The Theory of International Prices.* Benares, 1934.
—— *The Theory of Monetary Policy.* London, 1935.
AFTALION, ALBERT. *Les crises périodiques de surproduction.* Paris, 1914.
—— " Les variations du change tiennent-elles aux cycles économiques ? " *R.E.I.*, 1925.
—— *Monnaie, prix et change.* Paris, 1927 ; 1933.

AFTALION, ALBERT. *Monnaie et industrie.* Paris, 1929.
—— " L'histoire du change en France de 1915 à 1926 et la Théorie Psychologique du Change," *R.d.E.P.*, 1930.
—— *L'or et sa distribution mondiale.* Paris, 1932.
—— " Les variations cycliques irrégulières dans les relations internationales," *R.d.E.P.*, 1933.
—— " La théorie du troc et l'equilibre de la balance des comptes," *R.d.E.P.*, 1936.
—— *L'équilibre dans les relations économiques internationales.* Paris, 1937.
AMBEDKAR, B. R. *The Problem of the Rupee.* London, 1923.
AMERICAN ACADEMY OF POLITICAL AND SOCIAL SCIENCES. *Annuals,* vol. lxxv, " Financing the War " (Philadelphia, 1918) ; vol. lxxxiii, " International Economics " (1919) ; and vol. lxxxiv, " Prices " (1920).
ANDERSON, B. M. *Effects of the War on Money, Credit, and Banking.* New York, 1916.
—— " Procedure in paying the German Indemnity," *Chase Economic Bulletin,* New York, 1921.
—— " The inter-allied debts as a banking problem," *Chase Economic Bulletin,* 1922.
—— " The Report of the Dawes Committee," *Chase Economic Bulletin,* 1924.
—— " The Gold Standard vs. a Managed Currency," *Chase Economic Bulletin,* 1925.
—— *The Value of Money.* New York, 1926.
ANGAS, L. L. B. *Reparations, Trade, and Foreign Exchanges.* London, 1922.
—— *Germany and her Debts.* London, 1923.
—— *Investment.* London, 1930.
—— *Inflate or Perish.* London, 1932.
—— *The Problems of the Foreign Exchanges.* London, 1935.
ANGELL, JAMES W. " International Trade under Inconvertible Paper," *Q.J.E.*, 1922.
—— " Monetary Theory and Monetary Policy," *Q.J.E.*, 1925.
—— *The Theory of International Prices.* Cambridge, Mass., 1926.
—— " Reparations and the Cash Transfer Problem," *Political Science Quarterly,* 1926.
—— " Equilibrium in International Trade : the United States, 1919-1926," *Q.J.E.*, 1928.
—— *The Recovery of Germany.* New Haven, 1929.
—— " The Reparation Settlement and the International Flow of Capital," *A.E.R.*, supplement, 1930.
—— " Foreign Exchange," *A.E.S.S.*, 1931.
—— " Reparation," *A.E.S.S.*
—— *The Behaviour of Money.* New York, 1936.
BAKER, AUGUSTUS. *Money and Prices.* London, 1931.
BALOGH, THOMAS. " Devaluation," *A.E.S.S.*
—— " The Import of Gold into France," *E.J.*, 1930.
—— " Some Theoretical Aspects of the Central Europe Credit and Transfer Crisis," *International Affairs,* 1932.

BARBEY, E. *Les principaux aspects du problème de la balances des comptes dans l'économie général.* Paris, 1936.

BARONE, ENRICO. *Grundzüge der theoretischen Nationalökonomie,* German translation by Hans Staehle, Bonn, 1927; 2nd ed., 1935. (A summary of it is found in Haberler's *Theory of International Trade,* 1933.)

BASS, J. F., and H. G. MOULTON. *America and the Balance Sheet of Europe.* New York, 1922.

BAUDIN, LOUIS. "La vitesse de la circulation de la monnaie," *R.E.I.,* 1933.

BEACH, W. E. *British International Gold Movements and Banking Policy,* 1881–1913. Cambridge, Mass., 1935.

BELLERBY, J. R. *Monetary Stability.* London, 1925.

BENHAM, F. C. C. *Go Back to Gold.* London, 1931.

—— *British Monetary Policy.* London, 1932.

BEVERIDGE, W. H. *Tariffs, the Case Examined.* London, 1931.

BICKERDIKE, C. F. "The Instability of Foreign Exchange," *E.J.,* 1920.

—— "Internal and External Purchasing Power of Paper Currencies," *E.J.,* 1922.

—— "Saving and the Monetary System," *E.J.,* 1925.

BOGGS, THEODORE H. *The International Trade Balance in Theory and Practice.* New York, 1922.

BONGRAS, E. *Les théories monétaires allemandes contemporains.* Paris, 1930.

BONN, MORITZ JULIUS. "The Fall in German Exchange," *Q.J.E.,* 1916.

—— *Stabilization of the Mark.* First published in German (Berlin, 1922), English ed., Chicago, 1922.

—— "Les leçons de l'inflation allemande," *Europe nouvelles,* 1926.

BONNET, GEORGES-EDGARD. *Les expériences monétaires contemporaines.* Paris, 1926.

BORDES, J. VAN WALRÉ DE. *The Austrian Crown.* London, 1924.

BRADFORD, FREDERICK A. *Money.* New York, 1928; 2nd ed. 1933; new ed., 1935.

BRESCIANI-TURRONI, COSTANTINO. *Inductive Verification of the Theory of International Payments.* Cairo, 1932.

—— *Le Vicende del Marco Tedesco,* 1932, English ed. (thoroughly revised) translated from the Italian by Millicent Sayers under the title, *The Economics of Inflation, a Study of Currency Depreciation in post-War Germany,* with a foreword by Professor Lionel Robbins. London, 1937.

—— *Some Considerations on Egypt's Monetary System.* (1934.)

BRUSSELS INTERNATIONAL FINANCIAL CONFERENCE, 1919: *Proceedings, Reports, etc.* London, 1920.

BULLOCK, C. J. *The American Money Market.* Cambridge, Mass., 1930.

BURNS, A. F. "A Note on Comparative Costs," *Q.J.E.,* 1928.

CANNAN, EDWIN. *The Influence of the War on Commercial Policy.* London, 1917.

—— *Money: its Connection with . . . Prices.* London, 1918; 8th ed., 1935.

CANNAN, EDWIN. *An Economist's Protest.* London, 1927.
—— *Modern Currency and the Regulation of its Value.* London, 1931.
—— " The Future of Gold," *E.J.*, 1934.
CARNEGIE ENDOWMENT FOR INTERNATIONAL PEACE and INTER-
    NATIONAL CHAMBER OF COMMERCE, JOINT COMMITTEE :
    International Economic Reconstruction, report by B. Ohlin and
    T. E. Gregory. Paris, 1936.
CARR, R. M. " The rôle of price in International Trade Mechanism,"
    Q.J.E., 1931.
CARSOW, MICHEL. " L'étalion or, les prix et la spéculation," *J.d.E.*,
    1932.
—— " La malaise économique mondial," *J.d.E.*, 1932.
—— " Les emprunts internationaux et la crise," *J.d.E.*, 1933.
CASSEL, GUSTAV. *Germany's Economic Power of Resistance.*
    Stockholm, 1916.
—— " The Present Situation of the Foreign Exchanges," *E.J.*,
    1916.
—— " Depreciation of Gold," *E.J.*, 1917.
—— " Abnormal Deviations in International Exchanges," *E.J.*,
    1918.
—— *The Theory of Social Economy.* First German ed., Leipzig,
    1918 ; 2nd German ed., 1921 ; 1st English tr. tr. from
    the 2nd German ed. by Joseph McCabe, London, 1923 ; New
    English ed. tr. from the 4th German ed. by S. L. Barron,
    London, 1932.
—— " The Depreciation of the Mark," *E.J.*, 1919.
—— " Observations on the World's Monetary Problem," *E.J.*,
    1920.
—— *The World's Monetary Problems.* London, 1921.
—— *Money and Foreign Exchange after 1914.* London, 1922.
—— " The Foreign Exchanges," *Encyclopædia Britannica,* 13th
    ed., 1926.
—— " International Trade, Capital Movements, and Exchanges,"
    Harris Foundation Lectures : Foreign Investments, Chicago, 1928.
—— " The Rate of Interest, the Bank Rate, and the Stabilization
    of Prices," *Q.J.E.*, 1928.
—— *Post-War Monetary Stabilization.* New York, 1928.
—— *The Crisis in the World's Monetary System.* London, 1932.
—— *The Destruction in the World's Monetary System.* Sidcup, 1932.
—— *The Downfall of the Gold Standard.* Oxford, 1936.
—— *Economic Essays in honour of Gustav Cassel.* London, 1933.
CAUBAUE, PIERRE. " Le marché des changes depuis la baisse de la
    livre sterling," *J.d.E.*, 1932.
CHINA, MINISTRY OF INDUSTRY. *Silver and Prices in China,* being
    the report of the Committee for the Study of Silver Values and
    Commodity Prices, Shanghai, 1935.
COLE, G. D. H. *Studies in World Economics.* London, 1934.
COPLAND, D. B. " Currency Inflation and Price Movements in
    Australia," *E.J.*, 1920.
COPLAND, M. A. " Money, Trade, and Prices—a Test of Causal
    Primacy," *Q.J.E.*, 1929.
—— *Australia in the World Crisis, 1929–1933.* Cambridge, 1934.

CRUMP, N. B. "A Review of Recent Foreign Exchange Fluctuations," *J.R.S.S.*, 1921.

CURRIE, LAUCHLIN. "Money, Gold, and Income in the United States, 1921—1932," *Q.J.E.*, 1934.

D'ABERNON, VISCOUNT. "German Currency: its Collapse and Recovery, 1920–1926," *J.R.S.S.*, 1927.

DALTON, HUGH (and others). *London Essays in Economics: in Honour of Edwin Cannan.* London, 1927.

DAVIES, A. E. *Investment Abroad.* Chicago, 1927.

DAVIES, J. R. "The Quantity Theory and Recent Statistical Studies," *J.P.E.*, 1921.

DECAMPS, J. *Les changes étrangers.* Paris, 1922.

DESPAUX, ALBERT. *L'inflation dans l'histoire.* Paris, 1922.
—— *Principes de dynamique monétaire.* Paris, 1925.

DONALDSON, JOHN. *International Economic Relations.* New York, 1928.
—— "The World Monetary Problem," *W.A.*, 1933.
—— "Ohlin's Theory of Inter-regional and International Trade," *W.A.*, 1934.

DROP, E. C. VAN. "The Deviation of Exchanges," *E.J.*, 1919.
—— "Abnormal Deviations in International Exchanges," *E.J.*, 1920.

DUBLIN, JACQUES. *La stabilization du franc.* Paris, 1927.

DULLES, ELEANOR LAUSING. *The French Franc, 1914–1928.* New York, 1929.
—— *The Bank of International Settlements at Work.* New York, 1932.

DURBIN, E. F. M. *Purchasing Power and Trade Depression.* London, 1933.
—— *The Problem of Credit Policy.* London, 1935.

EDIE, L. D. *Gold Production and Prices before and after the War.* Bloomington, 1928.

EINZIG, PAUL. *Le mouvement des prix en France depuis 1914.* Paris, 1923.
—— *International Gold Movements.* London, 1929.
—— *The Bank for International Settlement.* London, 1930.
—— *Behind the Scene of International Finance.* London, 1931.
—— *The World Economic Crisis 1929–1931.* London, 1931.
—— *The Fight for Financial Supremacy.* London, 1931.
—— *The Tragedy of the Pound.* London, 1932.
—— *The Sterling-Dollar-Franc Tangle.* London, 1933.
—— *France's Crisis.* London, 1934.
—— *The Future of Gold.* London, 1934.
—— *Exchange Control.* London, 1934.
—— *The Exchange Clearing System.* London, 1935.
—— *World Finance since 1914.* London, 1935.
—— *Monetary Reform in Theory and Practice.* London, 1936.
—— "Some Theoretical Aspects of Forward Exchanges," *E.J.*, 1936.
—— *The Theory of Forward Exchanges.* London, 1937.

ELLIOTT, G. A. "Transfer of Means-of-Payment and the Terms of International Trade," *The Canadian Journal of Economics and Political Science*, Toronto, 1936.

ELLIS, HOWARD S. *German Monetary Theory* 1905–1933. Cambridge, Mass., 1934.

ELSAS, M. " The Internal Purchasing Power of the German Mark," *E.J.*, 1921–2.

FANNO, MARCO. " Credit Expansion, Savings, and Gold Export," *E.J.*, 1928.

FEILER, ARTHUR. " International Movements of Capital," *A.E.R.*, supplement, 1935.

FEIS, HERBERT. " What determines the Volume of a Country's International Trade," *A.E.R.*, 1922.

—— " The Mechanism of Adjustment of International Balances," *A.E.R.*, 1926.

—— *Europe, the World's Banker* 1870–1914. New Haven, 1930.

FLUX, A. W. *The Foreign Exchanges*. London, 1924.

FOSTER, WILLIAM T., and W. CATCHING. *Money*. Boston, 1923.

—— *Profit*. Boston, 1925.

FOX, BERTRAND. " Gold Prices and Exchange Rates," *R.E.S.*, 1935.

FRAYSSINET, PIERRE. *La politique monétaire de la France* (1924–8). Paris, 1928.

FURNISS, E. S. *Foreign Exchange*. Boston, 1922.

FURUYA, S. F. *Japan's Foreign Exchange and her Balance of International Payments with Special Reference to Recent Theories of Foreign Exchange*. New York, 1928.

GAYER, A. D. *Monetary Policy and Economic Stablization*. London, 1935.

GIDE, CHARLES. " L'or et le change," *R.d.E.P.*, 1915.

—— " De l'influence de la guerre sur les prix," *R.d.E.P.*, 1916.

GILBERT, DONALD W. " Foreign Trade and Exchange Stabilization," *A.E.R.*, 1936.

GILBERT, J. C. " The present Position of the Theory of International Trade," *The Review of Economic Studies*, London, 1935.

GILBERT, WALKER. " The Payment of Reparation," *Econ.*, 1931.

GRAHAM, F. D. " International Trade under Depreciated Paper : the United States, 1862–1879," *Q.J.E.*, 1922.

—— " The Theory of International Trade Re-examined," *Q.J.E.*, 1923.

—— " Some Aspects of Protection further Considered," *Q.J.E.*, 1923.

—— " Germany's Capacity to Pay and the Reparation Plan," *A.E.R.*, 1925.

—— " Self-limiting and Self-inflammatory Movements in Exchange Rates : Germany," *Q.J.E.*, 1929.

—— *Exchange, Prices, and Production in Hyper-Inflation : Germany, 1920–1923*. Princeton, 1930.

—— " The Fall in the Value of Silver and its Consequences," *J.P.E.*, 1931.

—— " The Theory of International Values," *Q.J.E.*, 1932.

—— " Monetary Stabilization," *A.E.S.S.*

GREGORY, T. E. *Foreign Exchange before, during, and after the War*. London, 1921.

—— *Tariff : A Study of Method*. London, 1921.

—— " Recent Theories of Currency Reform," *Econ.*, 1924.

GREGORY, T. E. *The Return to Gold.* London, 1925.
—— *The First Year of the Gold Standard.* London, 1926.
—— *Central Bank Policy.* Manchester, 1926.
—— *The Gold Standard and its Future.* London, 1932.
—— *The Silver Situation.* London, 1932.
—— *Gold, Unemployment, and Capitalism.* London, 1933.
—— *Currency Stabilization and Business Recovery.* Paris, 1935.
—— *Memorandum on Japanese Competition.* London, 1935.
—— " Expansionist Theories of Currency and Banking policy,"
Journal of the Institute of Bankers (London), 1935.
GREIDANUS, TJARDUS. *The value of Money.* London, 1932.
GUYOT, YVES. *Les problèmes de la déflation.* Paris, 1923.
—— " Le professeur Cassel et la dépréciation systématique de la
monnaie," *R.E.I.*, 1923.
—— and A. RAFFALORICH. *Inflation et deflation.* Paris, 1921.
HABERLER, GOTTFRIED. " The Meaning and Use of a General
Index Number," *Q.J.E.*, 1928.
—— " Money and the Business Cycle," *Harris Foundation Lectures :
Gold and Monetary Stabilization,* Chicago, 1932.
—— *The Theory of International Trade,* first published in German,
1933, tr. into English by A. Stonier and F. Benham,
London, 1936.
—— *Systematic Analysis of the Theories of the Business Cycles.*
L.o.N., Geneva, 1935.
HAIGHT, F. A. *French Import Quotas.* London, 1935.
HALL, N. F. *The Exchange Equalization Fund.* London, 1935.
HANSEN, A. H. *Business Cycle Theory : its Development and
Present Status.* Boston, 1927.
—— *Stabilization in an Unbalanced World.* New York, 1932.
—— and H. TONT. " Annual Survey of Business Cycle Theory :
Investment and Saving in Business Cycle Theory," *Economet.*,
1933.
HARRIS, CHARLES R. S. *Germany's Foreign Indebtedness.* London,
1935.
HARRIS, S. E. *The Assignats.* Cambridge, Mass., 1930.
—— *Monetary Problems of the British Empire.* New York, 1931.
—— *Twenty Years of Federal Reserve Policy.* Cambridge, Mass., 1933.
—— *Exchange Depreciation : Its Theory and Its History : 1931–5.*
Cambridge, Mass., 1936.
HARROD, R. F. *International Economics.* London, 1933.
—— " The Expansion of Credit in an Advanced Community,"
Econ., 1934.
—— *The Trade Cycle.* Oxford, 1936.
—— " Mr. Keynes and Traditional Theory," *Economet.*, 1937.
HASTINGS, H. B. " The Circuit Velocity of Money," *A.E.R.*, 1923.
HAWTREY, R. G. *Currency and Credit.* 2nd ed., 1923 ; 3rd ed. 1927.
—— *Monetary Reconstruction.* London, 1923.
—— " The Gold Standard and the Balance of Payments," *E.J.*, 1926.
—— " The Monetary Theory of the Trade Cycle and its Statistical
Test," *Q.J.E.*, 1927.
—— *The Gold Standard in Theory and Practice.* London, 1927.
—— *Trade and Credit.* London, 1928.

HAWTREY, R. G. " The Monetary Theory of the Trade Cycle," *E.J.*, 1929.
—— " Taussig's International Trade," *W.A.*, 1929.
—— *Trade Depression and the Way out.* London, 1931.
—— *The Art of Central Banking.* London, 1932.
—— " Monetary Analysis and the Investment Market," *E.J.*, 1934.
—— *Capital and Employment.* London, 1937.
HAYEK, F. A. VON. *Monetary Theory and the Trade Cycles,* published first in German, Vienna, 1929 ; tr. into English by N. Kaldor and H. M. Croome, London, 1933.
—— *Prices and Production.* London, 1931 ; 2nd ed., 1935.
—— " Reflections on the Pure Theory of Money of Mr. J. M. Keynes," *Econ.* 1931–2.
HECKSCHER, ELI F. *Sweden . . . in the World War,* first published in Swedish, 1928 ; English ed., New Haven, 1930.
HENNEBICQ, L. " Le commerce international et l'organisation des échanges," *R.E.I.*, 1934.
HICKS, J. R. " A Suggestion for Simplifying the Theory of Money," *Econ.*, 1935.
—— " Mr. Keynes' Theory of Employment," *E.J.*, 1936.
HILGERDT, FLOKE. " Foreign Trade and the Short Business Cycle," in *Economic Essays in Honour of Gustav Cassel,* 1933.
HOBSON, C. K. " The Measurement of the Balance of Trade," *Econ.*, 1921.
—— " Export of Capital," *Encyclopædia Britannica,* 14th ed., 1929.
HOLLANDER, J. H. " International Trade under Depreciated Currency," *Q.J.E.*, 1918.
INTERNATIONAL LABOUR OFFICE. *The Workers' Standard of Living in Countries with Depreciated Currency.* Geneva, 1925.
—— *Wage Changes in Various Countries, 1914–1925.* Geneva, 1926.
—— *A Contribution to the Study of International Comparisons of Costs of Living.* Geneva, 1932.
IVERSON, CARL. *Aspects of the Theory of International Capital Movements.* Copenhagen, 1935.
JACK, D. T. *The Economics of the Gold Standard.* London, 1925.
—— *The Restoration of European Currencies.* London, 1927.
—— *International Trade.* London, 1931.
—— *The Crisis of 1931.* London, 1931.
—— *Currency and Banking.* London, 1932.
JAEGER, RUTH MULLER. *Stabilization of the Foreign Exchanges.* New York, 1922.
JEANNENEY, J. M. *Essai sur les mouvements des prix en France depuis la stabilisation monétaire, 1927–1935.* Paris, 1936.
JENKS, L. H. *The Migration of British Capital to 1875.* New York, 1927.
JONES, J. H. " Exchange Stability *versus* Internal Price Stability," *J.R.S.S.*, 1934.
KATZENELLENBAUM, S. S. *Russian Currency and Banking, 1914–1921.* London, 1925.
KEILHAM, W. " The Valuation Theory of Exchange," *E.J.*, 1925.
KEMMERER, E. W. " Inflation," *A.E.R.*, 1918.
—— *High Prices and Deflation.* Princeton, 1920.

KEMMERER, E. W. *Money*. Philadelphia, 1934.
KEYNES. J. M. *Indian Currency and Finance*. London, 1913.
—— *The Economic Consequences of the Peace*. London, 1919.
—— *A Tract on Monetary Reform*. London, 1923.
—— " A Comment on Professor Cannan's Article, Limitation of Currency or Limitation of Credit," *E.J.*, 1924.
—— " The German Transfer Problem," *E.J.*, 1929.
—— " The German Transfer Problem : Discussions," *E.J.*, 1929.
—— *Essays in Persuasion*. London, 1931.
—— *A Treatise on Money*. London, 1930.
—— *The Means to Prosperity*. London, 1933.
—— " The Future of the Foreign Exchanges," *Lloyds Bank Monthly Review*, 1935.
—— *The General Theory of Employment, Interest, and Money*, London, 1936.
KINDLEBERGER, CHARLES P. " Flexibility of Demand in International Trade Theory," *Q.J.E.*, 1937.
—— *International Short-Term Capital Movements*. New York, 1938.
KING, W. I. " Recent Monetary Experiments and their Effect upon the Theory of Money and Prices," *J.A.S.A.*, 1935.
KING, W. T. C. *History of London Discount Market*. London, 1935.
KNIGHT, F. H. *Risk, Uncertainty, and Profit*. Boston, 1921 ; L.S.E. reprint, London, 1935.
—— *The Ethics of Competition, and other Essays*. London, 1935.
KOH, TSUNG-FEI. *Silver at Work*. Shanghai, 1935.
KREP, T. J. " Import and Export Prices in the United States and the Terms of International Trade, 1880–1914," *Q.J.E.*, 1926.
—— " Export, Import, and Domestic Prices in the United States, 1926–1930," *Q.J.E.*, 1932.
—— " The Price of Silver and Chinese Purchasing Power," *Q.J.E.*, 1934.
LACHAPELLE, G. " Les théories du professeur Cassel sur la monnaie et le change," *R.d.E.P.*, 1923.
—— *Les batailles du franc*. Paris, 1928.
LAUGHLIN, J. LAURENCE. *Money and Prices*. New York, 1919.
—— " The Quantity Theory of Money," *J.P.E.*, 1924.
—— *A New Exposition of Money, Credit, and Prices*. Chicago, 1931.
LAVINGTON, FREDERICK. *The Trade Cycle*. London, 1922.
—— *The English Capital Market*. London, 1921 ; 3rd ed., 1934.
LAWRENCE, J. S. *Stabilization of Prices*. New York, 1928.
LAYTON, W. T. *An Introduction to the Study of Prices*. London, 1922 ; 2nd ed., 1935.
LEAGUE OF NATIONS. Proceedings, Reports, and Publications, especially the annual memoranda, such as those on international trade and balance of payments, on production and trade, on currency, on central banks, on commercial banks, on world production 'and prices, and finally the annual World Economic Survey.
—— *Interim Report of the Gold Delegation of the Financial Committee*, Geneva, 1930 ; *Second Report*, 1931.
—— *Selected Documents on the Distribution of Gold submitted to the Gold Delegation of the Financial Committee*. Geneva, 1931.

LEAGUE OF NATIONS. *Enquiry into Clearing Agreement.* Geneva, 1935.

LEHFELHT, R. A. *Gold, Prices, and the Witwatersrand.* London, 1919.

—— " Statistics of Extremely Depreciated Currency," *E.J.*, 1922.

—— *Restoration of the World's Currencies.* London, 1923.

—— " Currency and Bank Credit," *E.J.*, 1924.

—— *Money.* London, 1926.

—— *Controlling the Output of Gold.* London, 1926.

—— " Credit Issues and Price Level," *E.J.*, 1926.

LEONTIEF, W. W. " The Use of Indifference Curves in the Analysis of Foreign Trade," *Q.J.E.*, 1933.

LERNER, A. P. " The Diagrammetical Representation of Cost Conditions in International Trade," *Econ.*, 1932.

—— " The Diagrammetical Representation of Demand Conditions in International Trade," *Econ.*, 1934.

—— " The Symmetry between Import and Export Duties,"*Econ.*,1936.

LEURENCE, FERNAUD. *La Stabilisation du franc.* Paris, 1926.

LEWIŃSKI, JAN ST. *Money, Credit, and Prices.* London, 1929.

LEWIS, A. B., and L. L. CHANG. *Silver and the Chinese Price Level.* Nanking, 1934.

LEWIS, C. *The International Account.* New York, 1927.

LIN, WEI-YING. *China under Depreciated Silver, 1926–1931.* Shanghai, 1935.

—— *The New Monetary System of China.* Shanghai, 1936.

LORIA, ACHILLE. " On a Passage in Professor Taussig's International Trade," *Q.J.E.*, 1931.

LOTZ, W. " Les crédits étrangers," *R.E.I.*, 1929.

MACFIE, A. L. *Theories of the Trade Cycle.* London, 1934.

MADDEN, J. T., and M. NADLER. *The International Money Markets.* London, 1935.

MAGNUSSON, L. " An International Inquiry into Costs of Living," *J.A.S.A.*, 1933.

MALPAS, JEAN. *Les mouvements internationaux de capitaux.* Paris, 1934.

MANOILESCO, M. *Théorie du protectionnisme et de l'échange international,* Paris, 1929 ; English ed. under the title, *The Theory of Protection and International Trade,* London, 1931.

MARCHEL, JEAN. *Les grands marchés financiers . . . leur solidarité internationale.* Paris, 1932.

MARGET, ARTHUR W. *The Velocity of Circulation of Goods.* (Collected papers, Minnesota, 1932–1933.)

—— *The Theory of Prices.* New York, 1938.

MARSHALL, ALFRED. *Money, Credit, and Commerce.* London, 1923.

MASON, E. S. " The Doctrine of Comparative Costs," *Q.J.E.*, 1926.

MASSA, E. H. " La théorie quantitative et la crise économique," *J.d.E.*, 1933.

MAWAS, A. *Le système monétaire et le change anglais depuis la guerre.* Paris, 1921.

MILLS, F. C. *The Behaviour of Prices.* New York, 1927.

—— *Prices in Recession and Recovery : A Survey of Recent Changes.* New York, 1936.

MILLS, R. C., and F. C. C. BENHAM. *The Principles of Money, Banking, and Foreign Exchange.* Sydney, 2nd ed., 1925.

MITCHELL, W. C. *Business Cycles.* Berkeley, 1913.
—— *Business Cycles.* New York, 1927.
—— (ed.) *History of Prices during the War.* Washington, 1919.
—— (ed.) *International Price Comparisons, 1913–8.* Washington, 1919.
MOÏSSEEV, M. " Théories Monétaires des crises économiques," *R.d.H.D.E.,* 1930.
MONROE, A. E. " The French Indemnity of 1871 and its Effects," *R.E.S.,* 1919.
MOULTON, HAROLD G. *The Reparation Plan.* New York, 1923.
—— " War Debts and International Trade Theory," *A.E.R.,* 1925.
—— and C. E. McGUIRE. *Germany's Capacity to Pay.* New York, 1923.
—— and C. LEWIS. *The French Debt Problems.* New York, 1925.
—— and L. PASVOLSKY. *World War Debt Settlement.* New York, 1926.
—— and L. PASVOLSKY. *War Debt and World Prosperity.* Washington, 1932.
NEISSER, H. *Some International Aspects of the Business Cycles.* Philadelphia, 1936.
NICHOLSON, J. S. *Inflation.* London, 1919.
—— *War Finance.* London 1917 ; 2nd ed., 1918.
NOGARO, B. *Réparations, dettes inter-alliées, restauration monétaire.* Paris, 1922.
—— *La monnaie et les phenomènes monétaires contemporains,* Paris, 1924 ; 2nd ed., 1935. English ed. tr. from the first French ed. under the title, *Modern Monetary System,* London, 1927.
—— " Le problème de la dévaluation en France," *R.E.I.,* 1935.
—— *La crise économique dans le monde et en France.* Paris, 1936.
NOYES, C. R. "Stable Prices vs. Stable Exchanges," *Economet.,* 1935.
NURKSE, RAYNAR. *Internationale Kapitalbewegungen.* Vienna, 1935.
OHLIN, BERTIL. " The Future of the World Price Level," *Index,* Stockholm, 1927.
—— " The Reparation Problem," *Index,* 1928.
—— " Equilibrium in International Trade," *Q.J.E.,* 1928.
—— " Mr. Keynes' View on the Transfer Problem," *E.J.,* 1929.
—— " The Reparation Problem : A Discussion," *E.J.,* 1929.
—— " Protection and Non-competing Groups," *W.A.,* 1930.
—— *The Course and Phases of World Economic Depression.* L.o.N., Geneva, 1931.
—— *Inter-regional and International Trade.* Cambridge, Mass., 1933.
OLIVIER, M. " Le change et les prix," *R.d.E.P.,* 1922.
OULÈS, FIRMIN. *Le problème du commerce international.* Paris, 1934.
PAISH, F. W. " Banking Policy and the Balance of International Payments," *Econ.,* 1936.
PARSHAD, I. D. *Some Aspects of Indian Foreign Trade.* London, 1932.
PATTERSON, E. M. *The World's Economic Dilemma.* New York, 1930.
—— " A Rigid Economy in a Dynamic World," *W.A.,* 1935.
PEAKE, E. G. *An Academic Study of some Money Market and other Statistics.* London, 1923 ; 2nd ed., 1926.
PENSON, J. H. " The Polish Mark in 1921," *E.J.,* 1922.

PHILLIPS, C. A. *Bank Credit.* New York, 1920 ; 1926.
PIGOU, ARTHUR CECIL. *Protective and Preferential Import Duties.* London, 1906 ; L.S.E. reprint, 1935.
—— " Interest after the War and the Export of Capital," *E.J.*, 1916.
—— " Economics of War Loan," *E.J.*, 1917.
—— " Inflation," *E.J.*, 1917.
—— *The Political Economy of War.* London, 1921.
—— *Essays on Applied Economics.* London, 1923.
—— " A Contribution to the Theory of Credit," *E.J.*, 1926.
—— *Industrial Fluctuations.* London, 1927 ; 1929.
—— *A Study in Public Finance.* London, 1928.
—— " Disturbance of Equilibrium in International Trade," *E.J.*, 1929.
—— " The Monetary Theory of the Trade Cycle," *E.J.*, 1929.
—— " Reparations and the Ratio of International Interchange," *E.J.*, 1932.
—— *Economics in Practice.* London, 1935.
—— and D. H. ROBERTSON. *Economic Essays and Addresses.* London, 1931.
POUJADE, MARCEL. *Étude sur les variations du taux de l'escompte en France et leurs conséquences aux xixe et xxe siècles.* Paris, 1923.
PUPIN R. " L'or, les prix, la guerre," *J.d.E.*, 1917.
PUXLEY, H. L. *A Critique of the Gold Standard.* London, 1933.
RAY, PARIMAL. *India's Foreign Trade since 1870.* London, 1934.
REED, H. L. " International Control of Price Levels," *Q.J.E.*, 1931.
REMER, C. F. *The Foreign Trade of China.* Shanghai, 1926.
—— " International Trade between Gold and Silver Countries : China, 1885–1913," *Q.J.E.*, 1926.
—— *Foreign Investments in China.* New York, 1933.
RICHARDSON, J. H. " International Comparisons of Real Wages," *J.R.S.S.*, 1930.
RIST, CHARLES. *Les finances de guerre de l'Allemagne.* Paris, 1921.
—— *La déflation en pratique.* Paris, 1924 ; 1927.
—— *Essais sur quelques problèmes économiques et monétaires.* Paris, 1933.
—— " Monnaie et commerce," *R.E.I.*, 1936.
ROBBINS, LIONEL. " The Present Position of Economic Science," *Econ.*, 1930.
—— " Economic Notes on some Arguments for Protection," *Econ.*, 1931.
—— *The Great Depression.* London, 1934.
—— " Certain Aspects of the Theory of Costs," *E.J.*, 1934.
—— *International Trade and Economic Planning.* London, 1937.
ROBERT, J. M. *Depreciation de la monnaie et équilibre budgétaire : étude sur les finances allemandes, 1922–3.* Paris, 1926.
ROBERTSON, D. H. *Money.* London, 1926 ; 7th ed., 1932.
—— *Banking Policy and the Price Level.* London, 1926 ; 1932.
—— " The Monetary Doctrines of Messrs. Foster and Cathching," *Q.J.E.*, 1929.

ROBERTSON, D. H. " Mr. Keynes' Theory of Money," *E.J.*, 1931.
—— " A note on the Theory of Money," *Econ.*, 1933.
ROBERTSON, J. S. *The Income Theory of Money*. London, 1935.
ROBIN, PIERRE. *La réforme monétaire en Poloque*. Paris, 1932.
ROBINSON, JOAN. *Essays in the Theory of Employment*. London, 1937
ROGERS, JAMES H. *Stock Speculation and the Money Market*. Missouri, 1927.
—— *The Process of Inflation in France, 1914–1927*. New York, 1929.
—— " Gold, International Credits, and Depression," *J.A.S.A.*, 1932.
ROSENSTEIN-RODAN, P. N. " The Co-ordination of the General Theories of Money and Prices," *Econ.*, 1936.
ROYAL INSTITUTE OF INTERNATIONAL AFFAIRS. *The International Gold Problem*. London, 1931.
—— *Monetary Policy and the Depression*. London, 1933.
—— *The Future of Monetary Policy*. London, 1935.
ROYOT, G. " Les mouvements internationaux de capitaux," *J.S.S.P.*, 1933.
RUEFF, JACQUE. *Théorie des phénomènes monétaires*. Paris, 1927.
—— " Mr. Keynes' View on the Transfer Problem," *E.J.*, 1929 ; see also *R.d.E.P.*, 1929.
SALTER, JAMES ARTHER. *Recovery*. London, 1932.
—— *China and the Depression*, supplement to the *Economist*, 19th May, 1934.
—— *World Trade and its Future*. London, 1936.
SAMUEL, A. M. " Has Foreign Investment Paid ? " *E.J.*, 1930
SANCERY, J. *Le retour à l'or dans les régimes monétaires après la guerre*. Paris, 1925.
SCHACHT, HJALMAR. *The Stabilization of the Mark*, first published in German, 1926 ; English ed., London, 1927.
SCHMIDT, CARL T. *German Business Cycles :* 1924–1933. New York, 1934.
SELIGMAN, E. R. A. *Currency Inflation and Public Debts*. New York, 1921.
SHAW, W. A. *Currency, Credit, and the Exchanges during the Great War and Since, 1914–1926*. London, 1927.
—— *The Theory and Principles of Central Banking*. London, 1930.
—— and A. WIGGLESWORTH. *The Principles of Currency, Credit, and Exchange*. London, 1934.
SIMPSON, KEMPER. " A Re-examination of the Doctrine of Comparative Costs," *J.P.E.*, 1927.
SINCLAIR, H. M. *The Principles of International Trade*. New York, 1932.
SMITH, N. S. " Japanese Competition and International Trade," *E.J.*, 1936.
SNOW, E. C. " The Relative Importance of Export Trade," *J.R.S.S.*, 1931.
SNYDER, C. " New Measures in the Equation of Exchange," *A.E.R.*, 1924.
—— *Business Cycles*. New York, 1927.
STAMP, J. *Reparation Payments and future International Trade*. Paris, 1925.
—— *Papers on Gold and the Price Level*. London, 1931.

STERN, S. *Fourteen Years of European Investment, 1914–1928.* New York, 1929.

STUART, G. M. V. " The Gold Question," *E.J.*, 1919.
—— " Metallic and Non-metallic Standard of Money," *E.J.*, 1923.

SUBERCASEAUX, GUILLERMO. *Monetary and Banking Policy of Chile.* Oxford, 1922.

TAUSSIG, F. W. " International Trade under Depreciated Paper," *Q.J.E.*, 1917.
—— " International Trade under Depreciated Paper, Discussions," *Q.J.E.*, 1918.
—— *Free Trade, the Tariff, and Reciprocity.* New York, 1920.
—— " German Reparation Payments," *A.E.R.*, supplement, 1920.
—— *International Trade.* New York, 1927.

TERBORGH, G. W. " The Purchasing-Power Parity Theory," *J.P.E.*, 1926.

THOMAS, BRINLEY. *Monetary Policy and Crises : a Study of Swedish Experience.* London, 1936.

UNITED KINGDOM. COMMITTEE ON CURRENCY AND FOREIGN EXCHANGES AFTER THE WAR. *First Interim Report,* London, 1918 ; *Final Report,* 1919.
—— COMMITTEE ON FINANCE AND INDUSTRY. *Report.* London, 1931.

UNITED STATES. FEDERAL RESERVE BOARD. *Prices in the United States and Abroad, 1919–1923.* Washington, 1923.
—— TARIFF COMMISSION. *Depreciated Exchange and International Trade.* Washington, 1922.

UPGREN, A. R. " Devaluation of the Dollar in relation to Exports and Imports," *J.P.E.*, 1936.
—— and R. CASSADY, JR. " International Trade and Devaluation of the Dollar, 1932–4," *Q.J.E.*, 1936.

UYEHARA, S. *The Industry and Trade of Japan.* London, 1926.

VINEBERG, P. F. *The French Franc and the Gold Standard, 1926–1936.* Montreal, 1936.

VINER, JACOB. *Dumping : a Problem in International Trade.* Chicago, 1923 ; 2nd ed., 1931.
—— *Canada's Balance of International Trade, 1900–1913.* Cambridge, Mass., 1924.
—— " Angell's Theory of International Prices," *J.P.E.*, 1926.
—— " Comparative Costs," *Q.J.E.*, 1928.
—— " Balance of Trade," *A.E.S.S.*, 1931.
—— " International Trade : Theory." *A.E.S.S.*, 1932.
—— " The Doctrine of Comparative Costs," *W.A.*, 1932.
—— *Studies in the Theory of International Trade.* London, 1937.

WAGEMANN, E. *Economic Rhythm,* tr. from the German by D. H. Blelloch. New York, 1930.

WALKER, GILBERT. " The Payment of reparations," *Econ.*, 1931.

WALTER, H. C. *Modern Foreign Exchange.* London, 1923.
—— *Foreign Exchange and Foreign Debts.* London, 1926.

WEILLER, J. *L'influence du change sur le commerce extérieur . . . 1919–1928.* Paris, 1929.

WHALE, P. B. " Notes on International Bank and the Creation of Credit," *Econ.*, 1930.

WHALE, P. B. *International Trade*. London, 1932.
—— " International Trade in the Absence of an International Gold Standard," *Econ.*, 1936.
—— " The Working of the pre-War Gold Standard," *Econ.*, 1937.
WHEELER-BENNETT, J. W. *The Wreck of Reparations*. London, 1933.
WHITAKER, A. C. *Foreign Exchange*. New York, 1919 ; 2nd. ed., 1933.
WHITE, H. D. *The French International Accounts, 1880–1913*. Cambridge, Mass., 1933.
WHITTLESEY, C. R. " Foreign Investment and the Terms of Trade," *Q.J.E.*, 1932.
WICKSELL, K. " International Freights and Prices," *Q.J.E.*, 1918.
—— " Gold, Inflation, and the Exchange," *E.J.*, 1918.
WILLIAMS, J. H. " Latin American Foreign Exchange and International Balances during the War," *Q.J.E.*, 1919.
—— *Argentine International Trade*. Cambridge, Mass., 1920.
—— " Foreign Exchange, Prices, and the Course of International Trade," *An.*, 1920.
—— " The Foreign Trade Balance of the United States since the Armistice," *A.E.R.*, supplement, 1921.
—— " Balance of International Payments of the United States for the Year 1921," *R.E.S.*, 1922.
—— " German Foreign Trade and the Reparation Payments," *Q.J.E.*, 1922.
—— " Foreign Trade under Depreciated Paper," *Journal of the American Bankers' Association*, 1922.
—— " The Theory of International Trade Reconsidered," *E.J.*, 1929.
—— " The Monetary Doctrines of J. M. Keynes," *Q.J.E.*, 1931.
—— " Reparation and the Flow of Capital," *A.E.R.*, supplement, 1930.
—— " Monetary Stabilization from an International Point of View," *A.E.R.*, supplement, 1935.
WILLIS, H. P., and J. M. CLAPMAN. *The Economics of Inflation*. New York, 1935.
WILSON, ROLAND. *Capital Imports and the Terms of Trade*. Melbourne, 1931.
WORKING, H. " Prices and the Quantity of Circulating Medium, 1890–1921," *Q.J.E.*, 1923.
YNTEMA, THEODORE OTTE. *A Mathematical Reformulation of the General Theory of International Trade*. Chicago, 1932.
YOUNG, ALLYN A. " War Debts, External and Internal," *Foreign Affairs*, 1924.
—— " Marshall on Consumers' Surplus in International Trade," *Q.J.E.*, 1924.
ZAPOLEON, L. B. " International and Domestic Commodities and the Theory of Prices," *Q.J.E.*, 1931.

INDEX OF SUBJECTS

INDEX OF NAMES

The Ludwig von Mises Institute

The Ludwig von Mises Institute, founded in 1982, is the research and educational center of classical liberalism, libertarian political theory, and the Austrian School of economics. Working in the intellectual tradition of Ludwig von Mises (1881-1973) and Murray N. Rothbard (1926-1995), with a vast array of publications, programs, and fellowships, the Mises Institute, with offices in Auburn, Alabama, seeks a radical shift in the intellectual climate as the foundation for a renewal of the free and prosperous commonwealth. This print-on-demand series is one division of a larger publishing program that offers new and classic works in high-quality editions. For more information and ordering, see mises.org

Ludwig von Mises Institute
518 West Magnolia Avenue
Auburn, Alabama 36832-4528
334.321.2100 · Phone
34.321.2119 · Fax
contact@mises.org